★ ANTHONY QUINN

★ ANDY WILLIAMS

W9-BUU-235

★ ANDY GRIFFITH

★ EVA GABOR

★ DESI ARNAZ

★ JULIE ANDREWS

★ KIRK DOUGLAS

★ STEVE ALLEN

★ GEORGE BURNS

★ JAMES WHITMORE

★ STEVE LAWRENCE

★ JOHN TRAVOLTA

★ JANET LEIGH

★ ZSA ZSA GABOR

★ GREGORY PECK

★ HENRY WINKLER

★ DICK CLARK

★ CHARLTON HESTON

★ LUCILLE BALL

★ PHYLLIS DILLER

★ PAUL WILLIAMS

★ DICK VAN PATTEN

★ ROY ROGERS

★ MERV GRIFFIN

★ LARRY HAGMAN

★ DANNY THOMAS

★ JOHNNY MATHIS

★ RED SKELTON

★ GEORGE GOBEL

★ JACK LEMON

★ LEE MAJORS

★ HELEN REDDY

★ SHIRLEY JONES

★ CESAR ROMERO

★ BETTY WHITE

★ RODDY McDOWALL

★ GEORGE PEPPARD

★ ART LINKLETTER

# THE HOLLYWOOD™ WALK OF FAME

The only guide to the world's most
famous stars in the world's most famous
sidewalk! More than 1400 listings,
with more than 200 photographs.

## Marianne Morino

introduction by Burt Reynolds

Ten Speed Press

An officially licensed product of the Hollywood Chamber of Commerce

*Dedicated to my mother, Annette,*
*the brightest star in my life.*

*And to my family:*
*Beth, Cherilyn, Anna, Dr. John, and Angel*
*And in loving memory of my sister,*
*Cynthia.*

1🟤 **Ten Speed Press**
Post Office Box 7123
Berkeley, California 94707

Book, cover design, and typography by
Fifth Street Design, Berkeley, California.

**Library of Congress Cataloging-in-Publication Data**

Morino, Marianne.
   The Hollywood Walk of Fame.

   Includes index.
   1. Hollywood Boulevard (Los Angeles, Calif.)
2. Moving-picture actors and actresses — Biography.
3. Hollywood (Los Angeles, Calif.) — Biography).
I. Title.
PN1993.5.U65M66   1987   791.43'092'2   [B]      86-30202

Printed in the United States of America
1   2   3   4   5   6   7   8   9   10   —   91   90   89   88   87

BILL WELSH
President and
Chief Operating Officer

Welcome to Hollywood and to the world's most famous sidewalk, the Hollywood Walk of Fame. As you read about the stars in the Walk, you will realize just how many people earned international recognition as a part of the entertainment industry.

The Hollywood Walk of Fame was developed by the Hollywood Chamber of Commerce to accomplish two things. First, it is to give those of you who visit the Entertainment Capitol of the World an opportunity to be reminded of the great performers and technicians who have brought you many hours of entertainment. Second, this is our way of saying to the people honored with stars on the Walk that we have great affection for them and great appreciation for their talents.

This book gives you the opportunity to enjoy the Hollywood Walk of Fame whether or not you can visit in person. Our thanks go to Marianne Morino for bringing together so much wonderful information in such a convenient form. The listings are organized in the order in which they appear in the Walk, so as you read, you will experience the world's most famous sidewalk just as if you were really there.

Enjoy your stroll along the Hollywood Walk of Fame. Enjoy the memories these stars bring back for you, and realize that you and the rest of the world are joining together to salute great talents.

Bill Welsh
President

6255 Sunset Boulevard ▪ #911 ▪ Hollywood, California 90028 ▪ (213) 469-8311

# ⋆ CONTENTS ⋆

*Douglas Fairbanks prepares for a battle scene in* Robin Hood *(1922).*

# * ACKNOWLEDGEMENTS *

*The author wishes to thank the many people who have made this book possible through their advice, assistance, and encouragement:*

Joe Hooper & Associates

Bill Welsh, president
  Hollywood Chamber of Commerce

Ed Lewis, executive vice-president
  Hollywood Chamber of Commerce

Marian Gibbons, founder
  Hollywood Heritage

George Deukemejian, Governor
  State of California

Earl Lestz, president, studio group,
  Paramount Pictures Corp.

William Hertz, director
  Mann Theaters

Robert and Wynn Develle
  Walt Disney Imagineering

Carol Walters, Bob Salvatore, Fran
  Tygell
  Max Factor

John McDonough and Donald Adams
  Eastman Kodak

Pete Noyes, managing editor
  KNBC news

Richard and Stanton Groman

Helen Gruning, actress and screenwriter

Lian Wang

Larry Burks, Deputy City Engineer

Dr. Michael J. Kwiker, Sacramento

Timothy J. Burke, director
  The Hollywood Studio Museum

Mark Locher, Harry Medved and Tony
  Phipps, Screen Actors Guild

Jim Buell

Krista Allen

Eileen Pawlowski

Susan Zilber
  Paramount

Michael Neustadt

Burt Reynolds

Johnny Grant,
  honorary mayor of Hollywood;
  chairman Walk of Fame Committee

Sir Michael Teilmann, president
  International Celebrity Promotions;
  producer, Hollywood Centennial

Mayor Tom Bradley, Los Angeles

Councilman Michael Woo

Bart Andrews and Sherry Robb

Patti Breitman, the best editor
  Hollywood ever had

Brenton Beck & Clifton Meek,
  Judy Hicks & Lenore Philips,
  Fifth Street Design, Berkeley, CA

Dr. Irving Posalski, Los Angeles

Phil Wood and George Young

William Kohn

Edward Van Artsdalen Wetzork

Veronica Newell

David S. Gershenson

Patricia Ode-Viala

Patty Duke, Academy Award winning
  actress, president Screen Actors Guild

Ed Asner, Emmy Award winning actor

John J. Ginelli, Hollywood Reporter

Tony Assenza

Sanford Wall

Martin Goodman

Richard Adkins, president
  Hollywood Heritage

Leo Buscaglia, author

Perry Botkin, Grammy winning musician

Mark Lindsay, singer

Mary Lyday

*Tony Swan*
*Ralph Buddemeyer*
*Marc Meshekow*
*Kathy and Gary Conrad*
*Eric Zimmerman*
*Susanne and Steve Horne*
*Bill Mays*
*Mike Clifford*
*Joe D'Amore*
*John Costello*
*Jo Ann Deck*
*Tommy Hawkins, sports, radio and TV
  personality*

*Michael Wright*
*Jeff Faymen*
*All of my friends at the Hollywood
  Chamber of Commerce*
*Academy of Motion Pictures Arts and
  Sciences*
*Universal Studio*
*Warner Bros.*
*20th Century-Fox*
*Goldie and Harmony Kwiker*
*Ira Lassman*

# ⋆ Introduction ⋆

The stars on the Walk of Fame — as so wonderfully described in this book — make actors happy because an award set in stone seems so permanent. This is especially attractive in a town where so much is based on illusion. The business of Hollywood is to give people the option to be entertained, relaxed, stimulated, inspired, terrified, horrified, or agitated. Dreamy or crisp images of the world (or from out of this world) are evoked by the actors who — when a film works — whisk you away to their make-believe lives. Sometimes my whole career seems like a dream. I still can't believe it all happened.

When I was younger I thought I was indestructible. I did a lot of crazy TV and movie stunts, like jumping out of a second story window for $110, which I thought was pretty good money at the time.

I was fortunate during those lean "paying your dues" years because I played the role of the "heavy," and in those days Hollywood was cranking out plenty of westerns. I could ride a horse, and since my grandmother was a full-blooded Cherokee, I was just as likely to turn up as an Indian as a cowboy. Hollywood was exciting then, and I was in it for the fun.

But there was a tough side to Hollywood, too. The worst time I ever had was in 1959 when I was fired from Universal. I had to go hungry occasionally, but I left Hollywood for New York, found work on Broadway, and survived.

Despite the setbacks, the challenges, the toughest competition in the world, what keeps the actors in Hollywood, and what keeps us acting, is the joy we get from the fans. If there's one consistent thing about Hollywood, it's that it exists because of the fans.

One of the strangest fans I ever heard about actually mailed herself to me! It could have been a disaster, because I was gone for the weekend. It must have been horrendous being stuck inside that box. I don't know how long it took her to realize no one was going to open. She finally clawed her way out!

I know what it's like to be a fan, too. My favorite actor is Spencer Tracy. He was the greatest film actor, and I had always wanted to meet him. Tracy's favorite was Laurence Olivier. He called him "the greatest of them all." So you see, even most movie stars are fans of other stars.

Aspiring actors often ask me about making good in Hollywood. My advice to them is to realize you can't learn to act by reading about it, or even by being close to it. If that were the case, there would be a million people walking close behind Laurence Olivier hoping some of it would trail off on them. The only way to learn to act is to act. So, do it any way you can. Do community theater, low budget or student films. Get on stage or behind the camera any way you can. Activity breeds activity. And since Hollywood always wants what it can't have, keep busy! Acting anywhere is still acting. New York is tough, but it is possible to begin there. Begin anywhere, but do begin.

Every Hollywood success story has talent, luck, and courage behind it. I'm not sure what the proportions are, but everyone who's made it has had all three.

The Hollywood Walk of Fame honors those success stories.

I feel privileged to be among them. And I thank Marianne Morino for making this tribute to the stars available in book form! As you read these pages and enjoy your walk among the stars, remember that none of us could have done it without you!

*Burt Reynolds*

Burt Reynolds

# · Layout of My Book ·

I've designed this book so that the stars on the Walk of Fame are laid out geographically, starting at one of the most well-known spots in the world.

The book begins in front of the famous Chinese Theater box office. The walk continues eastward to Vine Street*, and wraps around the entire 2.3 miles of the Walk of Fame. You will end your tour at Barbra Streisand's star, back in front of the Chinese Theater. The Walk of Fame lines both sides of Hollywood Boulevard, from Gower to Sycamore, and both sides of Vine Street, from Yucca to Sunset. (See map, page xiv).

Even if you are reading this book from outside Hollywood, you can still enjoy the excitement of actually walking down the Walk, and identifying these celebrities.

I have taken every precaution to insure the accuracy of the data contained in each biography. However, in a town based on illusion, birth dates tend to vary slightly in both male and female statistics. I have made every effort to select the most likely date.

Occasionally, you will note a star whose light dimmed into obscurity. My best private investigative work turned up little on these few people. (Magnum, where were you when I needed you?) There were no birth, or death dates available. Also, every now and then a celebrity asked me personally to leave the date off, and I obliged.

In the golden years of Hollywood, a movie was frequently remade under the exact same title, but with new scripts. An example of this is *George White's Scandals* (made in both 1934 and 1945). The former was about backstage romance, and the latter about an ex-Scandals get together. Only the dates distinguish the plots. Therefore, you can rest assured that movie dates are correct for the particular musical, dramatic, or comic greats who starred in them. (Today we rarely have this problem because *Rocky II, III* and *IV* follow *Rocky I* and we know right off the bat these pictures are sequels to America's favorite fighter.)

Since new faces are constantly appearing on the scene, this book will reappear from time to time in new editions reflecting the current state of the entertainment world.

And yes, I'm interested in hearing from you, too! If you have any questions, comments, true stories, etc. about Hollywood, please write to: Dear Marianne — Hollywood Scoop, c/o Ten Speed Press, P.O. Box 7123, Berkeley, CA 94707. (If you would like a response, please enclose a self-addressed, stamped envelope. I'll try to answer each letter.)

To those of you fond of art, and interested in obtaining a complete catalog of the works of the very talented celebrity illustrator, Cherilyn Ann, please send a self-addressed, stamped envelope to: Cherilyn Ann, P.O. Box 938, Buellton, CA 93427.

Happy 100th Birthday Hollywood, and thank you readers!

* *Everyone knows about the famous intersection of Hollywood and Vine, yet many of the prominent businesses on Vine Street are not aware that "North" Vine does not exist. Do not be confused with any building address that lists "North" Vine.*

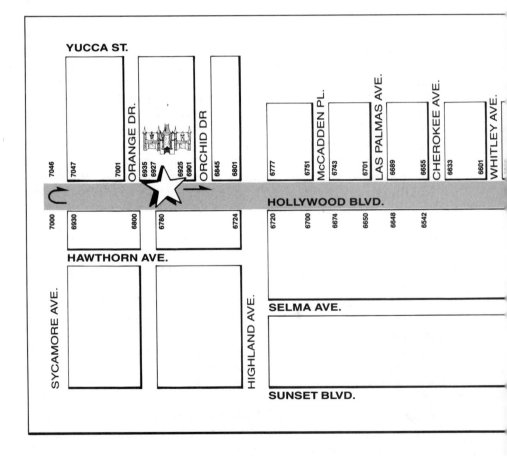

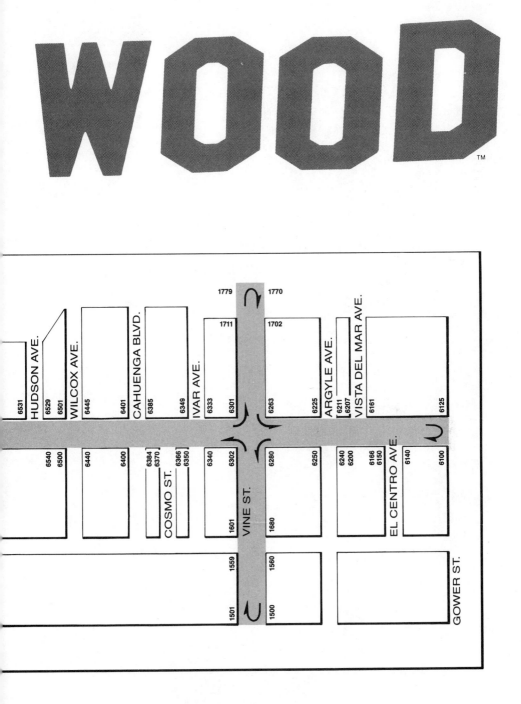

# ⋆ The First Star ⋆

For more than thirty years Hollywood has recognized the talented group of artists that has embodied the word *entertainment*.

Thomas Edison's invention of the Kinetoscope, a peep show viewing machine, in 1889 was the beginning of the motion picture business. These "moving picture" machines were installed in Kinetoscope parlors (not unlike the 1980s video arcade), and each one was used by an individual viewer to watch a film that ran approximately for thirteen seconds. Within a few years the Vitascope projector, which projected the images of film onto the screen, made group screenings in a theater possible. The notion of a "moving" action picture showing a detailed story gradually developed and then took hold in Edwin S. Porter's twelve-minute, one-reeler, *The Great Train Robbery* (1903).

Nickelodeons, and then picture palaces, quickly became the newest fad in America. Films at the turn of the century were produced at studios such as Edison's Black Maria, in Orange, New Jersey; Biograph on East 14th Street in New York City; and Vitagraph in New York City. Hollywood, as we know it, did not yet exist.

In 1886 Kansas Prohibitionist, Harvey Henderson Wilcox and his wife, Daeida, purchased a 120-acre citrus ranch in sleepy Cahuenga Valley, a Los Angeles suburb, for $150 an acre.

As construction on their new Victorian house got underway, Daeida Wilcox traveled back East to visit relatives. On the train, we made the acquaintance of an interesting woman, who unwittingly, inspired the naming of the Wilcox citrus ranch, a piece of land destined to become internationally famous. The woman was Mary A. T. Peck, of Chicago, Illinois, and with enthusiasm she described her elegant and delightful summer home, called Hollywood. It was located right outside the Windy City on the Burlington route, which is now the Burlington Northern railroad line.

Mrs. Wilcox embraced the English-sounding name, Hollywood, and on February 1, 1887, Mr. Wilcox registered their ranch name as Hollywood with the Los Angeles recorder.

Subdivision ensued, but with strict Victorian standards in mind. The Wilcoxes sought well-educated, worldly, decent buyers for the area, and were surprised to discover that a saloon keeper had been able to buy a parcel of land. Eventually an eight-member board of trustees enacted an ordinance to prohibit the sale of alcohol, except at a pharmacy with a doctor's prescription. This was not good news to the

Cahuenga House saloon. The owner happily leased his near-bankrupt property to the Nestor Film Company in 1910. Thus Hollywood's first studio was located at Sunset and Gower streets (today CBS studios are located at this site).

The Nestor Film Company had originally been based in New Jersey. The harsh New Jersey winters had been a deciding factor in the owners relocating to Southern California. Another motivating factor, though, had been money. To keep any profits the owners made, they had had to get 3,000 miles out of the reach of the restrictive New York-based Motion Pictures Patent Company (MPPC). The MPPC was a trust instigated by Thomas Edison and nine other producers/patent holders to force independent producers to pay a hefty licensing fee, royalties, and other payments to use patented film equipment, as well as to prohibit distribution of films, except to licensed theaters.*

By 1911 the Nestor Film Company was making three one-reelers a week. These films were making profits, and the company was able to avoid the costly MPPC payments.

In 1913 Cecil B. DeMille, as director-general of the Jesse L. Lasky Feature Play Company, traveled westward from the East Coast to look for a sunny location to shoot *The Squaw Man*. He had intended to set down operations in Flagstaff, Arizona, but it was raining when he got there. He got back on the train and took it to its last stop in Southern California. (Had it not been raining in Arizona, might Flagstaff have become Tinseltown? Possibly, but DeMille later remarked that the terrain hadn't been right anyway).

* *Many people could not pay the high fee and were forced out of business; others were denied licenses. One tough businessman, William Fox, founder of Fox Film Corp., launched a court battle against the MPPC's restraint of trade, and won. The group was dissolved in 1917.*

*L to R: Richard Adkins, president, Hollywood Heritage; Marion Gibbons, founder, Hollywood Heritage; spokesman Gene Barry; DeMille star Signe Hasso; Timothy Burke, Museum Director.*

In Hollywood, DeMille rented half a barn from Jacob Stern for $75 a month to use as a motion picture studio. The other half sheltered Stern's horses. Only a partition divided the stable and the movie crew. A humble beginning for what was later to become Paramount Pictures.

DeMille began work on Hollywood's first feature-length film, *The Squaw Man*. It had been a successful Broadway play about an Englishman who married an Indian woman in the American Wild West. The movie cost $15,450.25 and took eighteen days to make. It was a phenomenal success, grossing more than $250,000.

In California, DeMille had discovered ideal conditions for shooting movies: three hundred days of sunshine glistening on white beaches, tree-topped mountains, lush valleys, colorful citrus orchards, and arid deserts. Directors, producers, screenwriters, and actors flocked to the quaint village of Hollywood. Although the town prospered, it was not exactly in the way that the founders had in mind. Signs were hung on restaurant doors: No Dogs, or Actors Allowed. Most thespians were probably more upset to get second billing than to be denied permission to enter. (It's not the only time this happened, as we'll see in Rin-Tin-Tin's biography).

Hollywood Boulevard and Vine Street, called Little Paris during this period, were bustling with activity. More money was being made than any one of Hollywood's inhabitants had ever seen before, and everyone thought it would never stop. Stars promenaded down the streets dressed like royalty. One screen tigress strolled down the street, showing off her genuine big cat with a jeweled leash and collar, while a red-headed spitfire star walked two chows, with their fur dyed red to match her hair, down the other side of the street.

Creative advances in film making came quickly, with D. W. Griffith's epic Civil War film, *The Birth of a Nation* (1915), which was the forerunner of elaborate productions such as David O. Selznick's masterpiece, *Gone with the Wind* (1939).

The first talkie, Warner Brothers' *Jazz Singer* (1927), introduced the world to glorious sound. When Al Jolson opened his mouth and said, "You ain't heard nothing yet," it was a historical moment. It was also "the end" for many silent screen actors, whose careers came to a halt because of high-pitched or otherwise irritating voices.

The 1930s brought us cinema gangsters James Cagney and Edward G. Robinson, monsters Dracula and Frankenstein, humorist Will Rogers, the Busby Berkeley musicals, dramas about war, such as *All Quiet on the Western Front* (1930), glimpses into theater life, in movies such as *Stage Door* (1937), and even peeks at Hollywood, in films such as *A Star is Born* (1937). Sophisticated comediennes also sparkled on the screen. Carole Lombard, Jean Harlow, Katharine Hepburn, and Claudette Colbert were gems of this comedic genre. The 1930s also gave us Marlene Dietrich, Bette Davis, Gary Cooper, Spencer Tracy, and Cary Grant.

The great directors, William A. Wellman, Mervyn LeRoy, Howard Hawks, "One-take" Woody Van Dyke, Frank Capra, and many others whose names are implanted on the Walk of Fame, made "movie stars" out of their actors.

Radio transmissions were clearer in the 1930s. Big band broadcasts from Harlem began swinging the U.S.A. Adventure serials became popular: "Who's that little chatterbox? The one with the auburn locks? Who can it be? It's Little Orphan Annie."

*The famous Capitol Records building, brilliantly restored by the top entertainment design firm, Joe Hooper and Associates.*

America practically came to a halt when "Amos 'n' Andy" aired. Almost everybody who had a radio tuned in five nights a week. Department stores, restaurants, and theaters piped it in from 7:00 to 7:15, so they wouldn't lose customers. Radio's most famous serial, "One Man's Family," created by Carlton E. Morse, launched the fictional lives of the Barbour family. Fans called it addicting for twenty seven-years.

Brothers Ken and Wendell Niles were pioneer announcers in broadcasting. From local stations to coast to coast, they collectively and individually worked with the top bananas at the mike, among them Bob Hope, Burns and Allen, Groucho Marx, and Eddie Cantor.

*Sunset and Vine: Originally the site of Universal Studios, NBC is seen here in the late 1940's.*

Radio's Golden Age delighted us with brilliant comedy writers and performers, including the king of satire, Fred Allen: "A vice president is a man who comes into his office at nine o'clock in the morning and finds a molehill on his desk. It's his job to make a mountain out of it by five o'clock."

The 1940s introduced the newfangled contraption called television and its number one selling attraction, Mr. Television himself, Milton Berle.

Musical talents Louis Armstrong, Bing Crosby, Lauritz Melchior, and Lily Pons fortified recording studios with their million-plus record sales.

Jukeboxes stacked great swing dance records: Glenn Miller's "In the Mood," Harry James's "Two O'Clock Jump," and Count Basie's "Bugle Blues."

Gossip columnists Hedda Hopper and Louella Parsons wielded such power that they could create stars, pictures, and deals, and just as easily destroy them.

The "queen clown of television," glamorous Lucille Ball, reigned during the 1950s. While Frank Sinatra, John Wayne, and Marilyn Monroe were busy dazzling crowds with their soulful, salty, and sumptuous performances, members of the Hollywood community were entertaining ideas about how to honor the greats who made their town glitter.

Things had changed since the pioneering and golden eras of the movies. After World War II television had previous moviegoers spending their money on sets

*The most famous gate in Hollywood. The Bronson Gate as seen in Paramount's* Sunset Boulevard (1950).

instead of tickets. Some studios experienced financial trouble, others converted empty sound stages to accommodate this "combination of radio and pictures" as Bob Hope described it. Walt Disney approached TV with an eager spirit and an eye on opening Disneyland, and was successful in both.

In 1955, the Hollywood Chamber of Commerce created a plan to bring back the buzz of showbiz activity to Hollywood Boulevard. Older members of the community recalled the excitement, glory, and glamour of great personalities appearing on the streets, at local events, at USO shows, at the Hollywood Canteen, and were devoted to bringing that ambience back to their city.

The Walk of Fame had been the brainchild of businessman/Chamber member Harry Sugarman. His family had been on the exhibiting side of cinema all his life, owning the oldest theater in California. But his greatest influence came from master impresario, Sid Grauman. Inspired by Grauman's Chinese Theater's sparkling premieres and famous handprints in cement, the beautiful terrazzo sidewalk began to take shape in Sugarman's mind.

The Hollywood Chamber of Commerce devised a three fold plan to accomplish their goals. First, they wanted to brighten up Hollywood Boulevard with new, powerful streetlights to make every night look like a special night. Second, they wanted to plant large ficus trees to enhance visitors' strolls through the area. Third, and most important, they wanted to preserve the memory of the multi-talented entertainers

*Russian born make-up artist whose name became synonymous with Hollywood's leading beauties.*

responsible for putting Hollywood on the map. This commemoration had to include historic figures as well as contemporary personalities to be a true chronological representation of the multifaceted business, and each figure had to have made an important show business contribution. Their idea was to implant star landmarks in the sidewalk.

These improvements were calculated to cost $1.25 million, to be paid by assessments of the adjacent property owners, according to their square front footage. Some shop owners fought the initiative, but they lost to the majority.

The city council approved the project in 1956, and plans were set forth by the city engineer.

John Milford, an assistant civil engineer and actor (everyone in Hollywood is in show biz), remembers the many considerations involved in laying out the sidewalk. Color was one of the hottest subjects debated. One affluent property owner, who was also one of Hollywood's biggest developers, C. E. Toberman, was concerned that the colors might clash with his brown marble building. Finally, it was decided that the stars would be made of coral terrazzo, with the celebrity names and the outlines of the

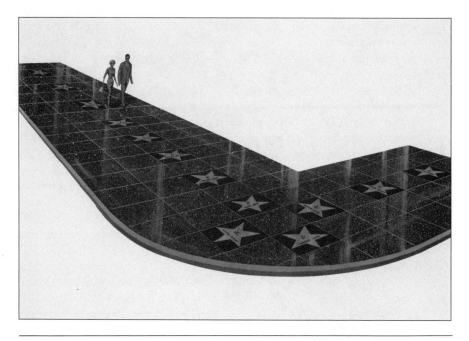

*The beautiful terrazzo and brass star-studded sidewalks have attracted millions of sightseers since the first dedication ceremony in 1958.*

stars in bronze, inset in three-foot square black terrazzo blocks.

A large New York-based record company with offices in Hollywood was upset because it believed the promotion of motion picture stars would be in direct competition with the promotion of its recording artists. In time, however, all concerned parties were able to agree.

Finally, all the construction details were worked out, including the placement of the stars; they were implanted in two directions for effect, fans glance every which way to catch all their favorite names.

2,518 stars were installed in five acres of terrazzo sidewalk. The first dedication ceremony held in 1958 featured eight screen actors: Joanne Woodward, Burt Lancaster, Ronald Colman, Olive Borden, Edward Sedgwick, Ernst Torrence, Preston Foster, and Louise Fazenda.

Within sixteen months, 1,539 luminaries had been forever immortalized in one sweeping, continuing installation. Shop owners were not too pleased about the sidewalks being torn up during this period, but the joy was unanimous at the official ground breaking ceremonies conducted on February 9, 1960.

Hundreds of the stars embedded in the sidewalk have been left blank for future dedication ceremonies. There are enough blank stars to last until approximately the year 2000. Performers and those behind the scenes keep their fingers crossed in the hope that one day they will see their own name honored and immortalized in the boulevard.

For many years, fans and celebrities alike strolled down the boulevard enjoying this salute to the industry. The community shared a sense of pride, and visitors from round the world saw that Lala Land preserved its history, in a thoroughly show biz way.

During the late 1960s and early 1970s, however, the country was in political and social tumult, and glamour was less appealing to moviegoers. Apathy overtook the movie industry; Woodstock-type rock concerts has eclipsed Hollywood's shining lights.

Then, in the mid 1970s, William F. Hertz, a Hollywood Chamber of Commerce board member, and Oscar-winning Jerry Fairbanks, then president of the Chamber of Commerce, combined forces to revitalize the Walk. Their goal was to dedicate one star a month. Their timing was right; the idea caught on in the entertainment sector. In 1978 the Walk of Fame was designated a cultural/historic landmark by the city of Los Angeles and since then has become a major component of the Hollywood Historic Trust.

Despite renewed interest in the Walk, the property in the area was neglected and did not live up to the glory of the Walk.

The title of Dean Martin and Jerry Lewis's last film together, *Hollywood or Bust* (1956), aptly describes the gutsy spirit of a few farsighted Hollywood real estate developers.

Like a producer who believes in a good script, Nicholas E. Olaerts (of Westmark Development Association), is one of the pioneers of the revitalization project. He has spent tens of millions of dollars buying properties (it's amazing that Hollywood in its entirety cost only $18,000 in 1886), on the Walk of Fame and restoring them to their original splendor, winning architectural awards along the way. Westmark was instrumental in striking the deal wherein Melvin Simon & Associates, with Greg Glass

*Joanne Woodward*

as West Coast representative, would build a $150 million entertainment center at Highland and Hollywood boulevards.

If you're reading this book while strolling the Walk, look up at the Security Pacific Bank building on the corner of Hollywood and Highland. It was designed in 1927 by Meyer and Holler, the architects of the Chinese Theater, and is an excellent example of the Classical Revival style popular during that period. The building is resplendent with flying buttresses, and the tower is an ornamental mix of Deco and Gothic. Does the building look familiar? If it does, I know you're a TV buff. That mythological-looking copper dome was used as the "Up, up, and away!" jumping-off point for TV's Superman.

Many of these magnificent older buildings on the Walk of Fame are the most architecturally beautiful structures to be found in Southern California. Most were built in the 1920s and 1930s, but a few date back to the turn of the century. The cornices of the Security Pacific National Bank building on Hollywood and Cahuenga glimmer with inset blue semiprecious stones.

In 1927, the Hollywood Roosevelt Hotel (named after President Theodore Roosevelt) made its debut. Several of its backers, film greats Mary Pickford, Douglas Fairbanks, Joseph Schenck, Louis B. Mayer, and Marcus Loew, toasted this palatial "home of the stars" with champagne and caviar. Its beauty, charm, and elegance encouraged motion picture personnel to locate the first headquarters of the Academy of Motion Picture Arts and Sciences there that same year.

Its grandeur, so comfortable for this country's rich and famous, also became home to the first Academy Awards presentation, held in the Blossom Room in 1928.

In 1934, a starry-eyed hopeful entered Hollywood to become a movie star. He wandered into the Blossom Room dreaming about winning his own Oscar one day. (He did win a Best Actor Oscar for *Separate Tables* in 1958). "When I first arrived in California, broke and twenty-two years old, I had no training as an actor. I met Al Weingard, the reception clerk at the Hollywood Roosevelt Hotel, and he gave me a room in the servants' quarters," David Niven later recalled in gratitude.

Bill "Bojangles" Robinson taught Shirley Temple the famous staircase dance at the Roosevelt's stairway leading from the lobby to the mezzanine.

Their stunning on-premises club, the Cinegrill, showcased a young Mary Martin (at $35 a week). Not wanting to leave her son, Larry Hagman, with a babysitter, she often brought him with her. The Cinegrill was also a favorite hangout of Marilyn Monroe.

In 1984, after many decades of serving dignitaries, celebrities, and Southern California tourists, the hotel, like an aging starlet, needed a "vacation" for a facelift. After two years of meticulous work, the Hollywood Roosevelt Hotel has now been restored to its original Spanish Colonial Revival magnificence, in time to celebrate Hollywood's centennial.

If you're planning a visit to Hollywood, this hotel, centrally located on the Walk of Fame, is highly recommended. The toll-free numbers are 1 (800) 358-2244 (outside California) or 1 (800) 423-8263 (in California). If you're calling from outside the U.S., dial the direct line, at (213) 466-7000. For the honeymooners or hopeless romantics,

Second Anniversary and Awards Banquet, Academy of Motion Picture Arts and Sciences.

Clark Gable and Carole Lombard rendezvoused in the two-story Celebrity Suite, still available with reservations.

Another crusader for Hollywood is Marian Gibbons, founder of Hollywood Heritage, a historical preservation society. Her tireless efforts have been instrumental in Hollywood's comeback. From saving the famous hat-shaped Brown Derby restaurant to saving "The Barn,*" Gibbons does whatever is necessary to revitalize the area: "from scraping the floors to fighting the battle of the budget with the state legislature." Her good will and sincere enthusiasm for the cause have had a domino effect in bringing pride to Hollywood and have helped get backing for the $1 billion community redevelopment project. Marian Gibbons put it well when she stated that all the world loves Hollywood: "It's our country's royalty."

Celebrities joke about seeing their names in bronze. At Dick Van Patten's dedication ceremony he asked everyone to "please curb your dog." Bette Midler commented, "now people can walk all over me!"

Although pets do not create a problem, the upkeep of the 2.3 miles of star-studded terrazzo sidewalk is a challenge. Millions of tourists annually "Walk the Walk," and, of course, residents and workers do likewise daily. Decades of wear and tear have had their effect on a number of stars.

But the magic of Hollywood springs from its creative, resourceful people. Such a

* Be sure to visit "The Barn," the Hollywood Studio Museum (look for the big yellow structure) when you're in town. It's located across the street from the Hollywood Bowl at 2100 N. Highland Avenue, (213) 874-2276.

Ed Lewis                                    Bill Welsh

person is Ed Lewis, current vice president of the Chamber of Commerce, and likewise is Bill Welsh, its current president. Together they have spearheaded a licensing program, not unlike that of the Statue of Liberty restoration and that of the 1984 Olympics, to raise funds for maintenance and expansion of the world-famous Walk of Fame, as well as maintenance of the fabled Hollywood sign overlooking the city lights.

Lewis sparkles like a celebrity when creating marketing plans to refurbish, continually clean (the Walk of fame sidewalk is the only one in the world cleaned seven days a week), and maintain these landmarks. Elizabeth Taylor, Audrey Hepburn, James Stewart, Gregory Peck, Ernest Borgnine, and two hundred other Walk of Famers have responded to Lewis's and Welsh's requests for permission to use their names in related fund-raising programs.

Because the Hollywood Chamber of Commerce is a nonprofit organization, the Walk of Fame, the Hollywood sign, and the surrounding community are especially grateful for these efforts.

As Bill Welsh, affectionately called Mr. Hollywood, puts it: "In the world there are only two words that never need to be translated. One is 'OK' and the other is 'Hollywood.' "

# ⋆ The Nomination Proceedings ⋆

To be honored with a star in Hollywood's Walk of Fame, the world's most famous sidewalk, is a tribute as coveted and sought after as any of the entertainment industry's equally prestigious awards—including the Oscar, Emmy, Grammy, Tony and Golden Mike. And because it recognizes a lifelong contribution and both public and peer appreciation, it is a unique honor, in a class by itself, a permanent monument of the past, as well as the present.

Countless aspiring performers hope to be recognized as great talents. Ultimately, if their skills and accomplishments are realized, they want to be remembered even after reaching the pinnacle of their careers. Will Rogers once said, "Popularity is the easiest thing in the world to gain and the hardest thing to hold."

The Hollywood Walk of Fame is, in part, a key to immortality. The gleaming bronze landmarks testify that silent screen star Clara Bow was the "It" girl, that the gigantic studios of today were born of the effects of enterprising, independent Americans (often immigrants), that the broadcasting, recording, stage, and film industries united this country through comedy, songs, sports, and news. The Walk of Fame embraces those gifted pioneers for those historic years of hard work and devotion. Stars were dedicated to them so they would not be forgotten. Yet contemporary contributors to showbiz cannot be overlooked either. Actor Tom Cruise and singer Michael Jackson are recognized as two of Hollywood's new superstar generation. They are gifted and accomplished at a young age. Both have

*Superstar Michael Jackson and Walk of Fame chairman Johnny Grant.*

*Tom Selleck surrounded by friends, fans and family.*

broken records in their respective professions, as well as meeting the other criteria established by the Walk's Selection Committee. Thus, both are recipients of stars. Yet the Hollywood Historic Trust does *not* nominate or solicit stars. But *you* can.

The president of the Tom Selleck fan club was successful in her bid for his placement on the boulevard. Family, friends, studios, managers, and agents are all able to nominate their favorite entertainer for this accolade. However, it would be inappropriate for the artist to nominate himself or herself. A few celebrities have personally asked for stars on the Walk of Fame and were rejected by the selection committee for that year's consideration because of it! (Sorry, I've been sworn to secrecy.)

### Who can be chosen for a star?

Motion pictures and television categories are made up of actors, writers, producers, directors, inventors (of the motion picture camera, sound, color, etc.), musicians, composers (film scores, theme songs, etc.), stuntmen and women, and make up artists.

Radio celebrates eloquent storytellers, newscasters, sportscasters, singers, musicians, comedians, announcers, even ventriloquists. Oddly enough, ventriloquists were enormously popular on the airwaves. Listeners got a kick out of

Edgar Bergen's dummy, Charlie McCarthy, chiding him about seeing his lips move during the act. Announcers were vital to the success of any show; often they were as famous as the lead players. For example, Don Wilson became a personality for his work on "The Jack Benny Show." Comedy announcers warmed studio audiences up with gags, "Okay folks, we have thirty seconds to go if anybody has to!" Elaborate pranks were devised to bring the audience to a crescendo of laughter just at the moment the show was going on the air. An announcer often played straight man to the comedian, read commercials, and introduced and closed the broadcasts: "Well, the little clock on the studio wall tells us it's time to go."

Recording stars comprise a range of America's finest music, from opera to country and western.

Live Theater is the newest category—added on November 8, 1984—and salutes stage, concert, rodeo, and other arenas of live performance.

Distinct emblems represent each of the five categories. It is rumored that someone from the greatest group of animation talent, the Walt Disney Company, drew the first four cartoon-like logos centered inside the stars. Those logos were designed in the early 1950s.

| Motion Pictures | Television | Recording | Radio | Live Theatre |
|---|---|---|---|---|

Great directors such as Cecil B. DeMille helped create the standards by which the stars were selected. Box office or vocal appeal/attraction, artistic skills, award achievements, versatility, range and endurance, and humanitarian efforts were all critical factors for determining eligibility for the reward. These important industry standards were actually formulated many years prior to the final installation of the Walk of Fame.

What criteria does the selection committee consider today when reviewing a potential nominee's application? First, professional accomplishments and achievements. This might include a string of hit records coupled with Grammy awards. Other awards may be taken into consideration also. For example, a Medal of Freedom award is one of the non-industry honors that is significant. Second, longevity in the business is a must. In Hollywood that's five years. (That illustrates how tough it is to break into show biz, as well as stay on top; audiences can be very fickle.) Third, contributions to society are counted and weighed. Walk of Famers, for the most part, are good Samaritans. They must donate their time, talent, and/or money to help those less fortunate then themselves. Fourth, the selected honoree must agree to be present at the dedication ceremony on a mutually satisfactory date. (This rule was enacted to answer one question—"Where can I see a star?—which was repeatedly asked by visitors to Hollywood.)

Only a handful of people understand the nomination and selection proceedings. Yet, unlike the privileged members of the Academy, whose professionalism helps decide the winner or loser, *anyone* can nominate a star! After all, the fans truly decide who is a star and who isn't.

You can sponsor your favorite star. Let's say you want to sponsor director Steven Spielberg. First, you complete the questions on the official Walk of Fame nomination application.* Besides the nominee's name, you must select which category — motion pictures, television, recording, radio, or live theater — the nominee is to be reviewed. Now this can be tricky. Frequently, an artist qualifies in more than one category. For example, Madonna is both a singer and actress. She could be nominated in either recording or motion picture. However, only one category per application is allowed. Separate applications must be submitted for each category. You must choose the most prominent one. Then you must describe the qualifications of the nominee. In Spielberg's case, you could describe his perfect direction in outstanding adventure films and the colossal box office appeal of his movies; *Jaws* (1975); *Close Encounters of the Third Kind* (1977); *Raiders of the Lost Ark* (1981); *E.T. the Extra-Terrestrial* (1982); more. He has earned many honors, including the Irving G. Thalberg Memorial Award. Contributions to society count too. For example, one of his many charitable donations was to the University of Southern California, which many years ago rejected him as a film student. Upon receipt of the money, the school admitted half in embarrassment and half-jokingly, "He didn't tell us who he was."

A photograph of the nominee must be submitted with the application. In Los Angeles there's access to a large number of photographs. (If you live in the Midwest, the East, or even in California, I don't want you to run up your phone bill, refer to Michael Levine's *The New Address Book: How to Reach Anyone Who's Anyone,*

---

* *An application may be obtained by sending a legal size, self-addressed, stamped envelope to: Walk of Fame Committee, c/o Hollywood Historic Trust, 6255 Sunset Boulevard, Suite 911, Hollywood, California 90028.*

*Earl Lestz — President of Studio Group, Paramount Pictures Corporation, was instrumental in preserving the "Barn" and furthering Hollywood causes.*

available from Perigee Books, Putnam Publishing Group. The book lists addresses of studios, stars' offices, etc. and will enable you to inquire about obtaining a photograph).

Next, you must return the application during the official nomination period, April 7 to May 31. The May 31 deadline must be met for consideration in the upcoming year's ceremonies.

The award process is now ready to begin. Johnny Grant, honorary mayor of Hollywood and chairman of the Selection Committee, calls the secret panel of experts to begin reviewing applications in June.

The identity of the panel is kept top secret; otherwise the members would be deluged by well-meaning calls from fans with rich testimonials for the star of their choice.

These entertainment specialists, one representing each of the five categories, judge and vote on hundreds of applications. The ones with the highest scores get set aside. The Selection Committee carefully scrutinizes the merits of each nominee. Discussions are held, shows may be watched, records listened to, etc. Finally, after a very difficult period with so many worthy personalities to consider, all votes are cast. Twelve to twenty-five lucky artists will have their stars implanted in the following 12-month period. Dedication ceremonies will occur at the rate of one or two and occasionally three a month. Anyone may attend these events free-of-charge.*

The accepted nominees are notified and congratulated. Appointments are juggled to arrange the ceremony dates. Often, finding available time slots in their hectic schedules can be complicated.

Next, a fee must be paid for primary costs of the bronze commemorative star since the trust is a nonprofit organization which relies solely on these payments to fund the award ceremonies.

At Tom Selleck's 1986 dedication ceremony, John Hillerman, that very fine and capable Texas-born actor who plays Jonathan Quale Higgens III on "Magnum P.I.," asked me how much a star ceremony costs. After I told him, he looked at me with a twinkle in his eyes and a mischievous grin and said: "Hmmm, $3,500 (pause) not a bad price to pay for a bit of immortality."

This $3,500 payment covers the actual cost of ripping up the blank star in there now, and replacing it with a newly made one, complete with name and emblem of recipient. The labor as well as the costs of the terrazzo and bronze are not cheap, as you might imagine. Security guards/officers must be hired, calls must be made, and hundreds of press releases distributed. The one-time fee does *not* cover cleaning, maintenance, or repair of damaged stars.

The sponsor is responsible for arranging the tax-deductible donation to the Hollywood Historic Trust. The sponsor can be a fan club, family members of the artist,

---

* *If you'd like to coordinate your visit to Hollywood with a Walk of Fame ceremony, send a legal size, self-addressed, stamped envelope to: Walk of Fame Upcoming Ceremonies, 6255 Sunset Blvd., Suite 911, Hollywood, CA 90028. Be sure to specify which month you are planning your visit. Remember, too, that the Upcoming Star Ceremonies List sent to you by the Chamber of Commerce is subject to change without notice (but usually doesn't).*

or a business such as a celebrity's agent, manager, or studio. Sometimes the sponsor is simply an adoring fan. Occasionally a concerned group will rally on an individual's behalf.

Singer Billie Holiday would have been very proud of the musicians, fans and restaurateurs who obtained a recording star for her. Because this dedication ceremony occurred posthumously, there wasn't a corporate interest to pick up the tab. Instead, the sponsors held a successful fund raiser in the Lady's memory.

A star on the Walk of Fame is a tribute bestowed upon a worthy artist. A star on the Walk of Fame cannot just be bought. If it could, believe me, you'd see the entire 464 square miles of Los Angeles sidewalks dominated by stars.

Every name on the boulevard has a good reason for being there. Each one has made an important contribution to Hollywood's entertainment industry. As you read the biographies in this book, you'll see that even seemingly unusual honorees accomplished a great deal during their career.

A good example of an unusual recipient is Rin-Tin-Tin. Most people remember him merely as a smart German Shepherd who knew a lot of tricks. But Rin-Tin-Tin was far greater than that; that dog saved Warner Brothers Studio from bankruptcy. He was their biggest box office attraction in a long series of silent hits that pulled the studio through some of its neediest hours. Their very close first runner-up, John Barrymore, was not thrilled to be less valuable than a dog, in those early years surely he tired of hearing friends jokingly remark, "It's a dog's life" and "It's a dog-eat-dog world" or ultimately regarding his status as romantic leading man, "It's puppy love." Well, Hollywood can be ruff-ruff.

If there's a significant personality missing from the Walk, you can bet it's because he or she (1) has never been nominated; (2) was nominated but was up against stiff competition and was asked to resubmit—it may take several consecutive nominations before a nominee is finally selected as a recipient of a star; (3) was unable to schedule a date to attend the dedication ceremony, which is a stipulation for acceptance, or (4) declines the award. For example, Paul Newman has certainly obtained an enduring level of excellence in filmmaking. He is also a compassionate, generous humanitarian. His wife, actress Joanne Woodward, was one of the first eight recipients of a star. The trust has approved a star for Newman, yet, at this date, he has declined the award. If he changes his mind, rest assured, he'd be granted one promptly.

"On That Long and Winding Road" you'll also note the absence of the Beatles. The Beatles certainly fulfill the qualification requirements. Their musical impact is legendary. Their countless humanitarian contributions have improved thousands of lives. And, in fact, the Fab Four were nominated in 1983. The Selection Committee approved them. If Ringo, Paul, or George would attend the ceremony honoring the Beatles, their bronze star would be installed. Although the rule about the celebrity's presence may sound rough, it was established decades ago by the pathfinders of the Walk. Only once in its recent history of individual dedication ceremonies has the honoree not shown up. That no-show person was Barbra Streisand.

Who picks the location on the sidewalk? The receiver is asked for his or her preference. A popular location, which is now limited to one or two blank spaces- -is in front of the famous Chinese Theater. Singer Tina Turner chose to have hers placed in front of the circular Capitol Records office building on Vine Street, which resembles a stack of records, appropriately enough.

Merchants vie for certain stars in front of their shops. Frederick's of Hollywood (housed in the art deco structure, built in 1935, and is called the "Purple Palace") has a variety of stars paving the entrance to its boutique: Fleetwood Mac, Jack Palance, Will Rogers, Dyan Cannon, and Margaret O'Brien.

Frank Mancuso        Patty Duke        Grant Tinker

There is an enormous demand from studios, producers, directors, other performers and fans to recognize deserving talents. There are enough blank stars—ready to be dedicated and occupied—on the Walk of Fame to last until about the year 2000. If the Walk of Fame is to continue to be a chronological history of the entertainment industry, and reflect the changing tastes of American audiences, it has to be expanded. This ties in beautifully with the 1986 Screen Actors Guild's return to Hollywood Boulevard with the assistance of designer Joe Hooper, SAG board member Dean Santoro, and the SAG executive committee. The SAG headquarters are housed in the former Hollywood Congregational Church, an historic landmark built in 1919, and transformed by Joe Hooper & Associates in the mid-1980s. The Walk of Fame will logically extend in front of this actors' union, and to their next door neighbor, Stephen Cannell Productions.

Which of these gifted "unknowns" of today will be the immortalized lum—inaries of tomorrow? Cylk Cozart? Elizabeth Pena? Paul Rodriguez? Helen Gruning?

Author's personal choice for this year's stars: Handsome, distinguished movie studio talent par excellence, Frank Mancuso, Chairman and Chief Executive Officer of Paramount Pictures Corporation; Lovely Patty Duke, Academy Award winning actress and president of the Screen Actors Guild; Grant A. Tinker, president of GTG Entertainment, Chairman of the Board, excels in high quality, creative programming.

# ⋆ 6925 HOLLYWOOD ⋆

## Harry Langdon 🎥 *Comedian*

**Born:** June 15, 1884, in Council Bluffs, Iowa.

**Spotlights:** Had the cutest little baby face during the silent era. Very funny, bewildered-looking in the two- and three-reelers, including *There He Goes* (1925) and *Fiddlesticks* (1926). Harry Edward's *Tramp, Tramp, Tramp* (1926; written by Frank Capra) was probably Langdon's best work. Certainly in the league with the big boys; Charlie Chaplin, Buster Keaton, and Harold Lloyd.

**Sidelights:** His career slipped somewhat in 1927 as a result of personal problems. Died 1944, of a cerebral hemorrhage.

## John Green 🎥 *Composer, conductor*

**Born:** Oct. 10, 1908, in New York.

**Spotlights:** Creative music force, collaborated in scoring some of Hollywood's finest: *Easter Parade* (1948), *An American in Paris* (1951), *West Side Story* (1961), *Bye Bye Birdie* (1963), *Oliver* (1968). Known as "Johnny."

**Achievements:** 1948, 1951, 1961, 1968, Academy awards.

## Basil Rathbone 📺 *See page 71.*

## Chill Wills 🎥 *Actor*

**Born:** July 18, 1903, in Seagoville, TX.

**Spotlights:** As a tot, he performed in tent shows across Texas, Oklahoma and Nevada. By 1935 the cowboy and his group, "Chill Wills and the Avalon Boys," sang in *Bar 20 Rides Again*. The friendly, scratchy-voiced character actor made close to 100 pictures, including *Boom Town* (1940) and *The Alamo* (1960). Also provided the voice for Francis the Talking Mule in a series starring Donald O'Connor (1951–55) and then Mickey Rooney (1956).

**Sidelights:** Born on a record-breaking hot day in Texas, so his parents christened him Chill. Died 1978.

## Marion Martin 🎥 *Actress*

**Born:** June 7, 1916, in Philadelphia, PA.

**Spotlights:** Pretty Follies of 1933 entertainer. Remained on stage in *George White's Scandals* (1945). Films include *Cinderella Jones* (1946); *Angel on My Shoulder* (1946).

## Elton John 💿 *Singer, composer*

**Born:** Reginald Dwight on March 25, 1947, in England.

**Spotlights:**   Composed music to Bernie Taupin's poignant lyrics (teamed 1967–75), e.g., and "Someone Saved My Life Tonight." Known for eccentric fashions and colorful eyeglasses. Stylish and chic, Elton John hobnobs with the best of them—the British Royal Family. Still going strong.

### Dick Powell   *Actor*                                                   6915 Hollywood

**Born:**   Nov. 14, 1904, in Mountain View, AR.

**Spotlights:**   Memorable wavy-haired, boyish-looking crooner of Busby Berkeley classic musicals, including *42nd Street* (1933) and *Gold Diggers of 1933*, opposite sweet-faced Ruby Keeler. Later played steely heroes in thrillers. Directed five films in the fifties. Radio: Host of "Campana Serenade" (1945); vocalist. TV: Host of "Dick Powell's Zane Gray Theater" (1956–61); actor in numerous productions. Also, head of Four Star T.V. Production Co.

**Highlights:**   Married to Joan Blondell (1935–45; second of three) and to June Allyson (1945 until his death). Died: 1963, of cancer.

### Richard D. Zanuck   *Executive*                                          6915 Hollywood

**Born:**   Dec. 13, 1934, in Los Angeles, CA.

**Spotlights:**   Stanford educated. Started in 20th Century-Fox's story dept., worked his way up to president in 1969. Became senior executive V.P. at Warner Bros. in 1972 to form Zanuck Brown Prod. Co., Universal. Son of executive- producer Darryl Zanuck.

**Achievements:**   1973, Oscar for *The Sting*.

*Elton John*                                   *Zsa Zsa Gabor*

## Zsa Zsa Gabor  📺  *Actress*                                   6915 Hollywood

**Born:** Sari Gabor ; Feb. 6, 1920, in Budapest, Hungary.
**Spotlights:** Former Miss Hungary, famous for her glamorous society headlines and affected "dahlink." TV guest spots.

## Johnny Grant  📺  *Executive producer, host, moderator,*           6915 Hollywood
*Honorary Mayor of Hollywood*

**Born:** May 9, 1923, in Goldsboro, NC.
**Spotlights:** An exuberant "Hi Tiger" is his catch-phrase. Energetic, positive spokesman for Hollywood. V.P. of Public Affairs Special Projects for KTLA (Los Angeles Television Station 5). Took over as the Hollywood Christmas Parade producer in 1973 when it was just a local event and created the nation's second largest parade televised live, distributed to over 95% of the United States, and in 88 foreign countries. Numerous humanitarian contributions; including the first telethon ever produced to raise funds to send our Olympic athletes to Helsinski in 1952. Creator-producer-co-host of the arthritis telethon for over 20 years. Over 37-year career in the entertainment industry. Enthusiastic supporter of men and women in the Armed Forces: 13 trips to Korea; 14 to Vietnam; in all, 44 USO junkets entertaining GIs overseas.
**Achievements:** 1982, Emmy; 1982, "Wrangler Award" in the Cowboy Hall of Fame for "outstanding contributions to western heritage through television programming"; Major General in the California State Military Reserve; USO's Distinguished American Award; dozens of other awards.

## Glenn Miller  🎵  *Bandleader, trombonist*                       6915 Hollywood

**Born:** Alton Glenn Miller; March 1, 1904, in Clarinda, IA.
**Spotlights:** Jazzy, hot trombonist during the late thirties and early forties whose music was easily identifiable as having that "Glenn Miller sound." Noted for precise playing of arrangements. His special device was doubling a melody on saxophone with a clarinet an octave higher. Became a celebrity with two gigantic hits "In the Mood" and "Tuxedo Junction." Big band leader during the Swing era, who gave the

| *Johnny Grant* | *Tom Selleck* | *William Shatner* |

world "Chattanooga Choo-Choo" and "Moonlight Serenade." Films: *Sun Valley Serenade* (1941) and *Orchestra Wives* (1942). Died: 1944, in a World War II plane crash between London and Paris.

### Leon Shamroy  *Cinematographer* 6915 Hollywood

**Born:**  July 16, 1901, in New York.
**Achievements:**  Oscars for photography: *The Black Swan* (1942), *Wilson* (1944), *Leave Her to Heaven* (1945), *Cleopatra* (1963). Died: 1974.

### Creighton Hale  *Actor* 6901 Hollywood

**Born:**  Patrick Fitzgerald May 13, 1883, in Ireland.
**Spotlights:**  Used his winning, worldly ways to seduce early film audiences in *Forbidden Love* (1921). *The Perils of Pauline* (1947) was one of his last films. Died: 1965.

### Tom Selleck  *Actor* 6901 Hollywood

**Born:**  Jan. 29, 1945 in Detroit, MI.
**Spotlights:**  *Lassiter* (1983) did not *Runaway* (1985) to the *High Road to China* (1982) because of a 1970 appearance in *Myra Breckenridge*. His *Magnum P.I.* TV series (1980–) made him a household name.
**Sidelights:**  Who's his ideal of a leading lady? The ultra-thin, ultra-elegant, Academy award-winning Audrey Hepburn.

### William Dieterle  *Director* 6901 Hollywood

**Born:**  July 15, 1893, in Germany.
**Spotlights:**  Dieterle directed Richard Barthelmess and Helen Chandler in the brilliant postwar study of battered human nature, *The Last Flight* (1931). He didn't sell his soul for *All That Money Can Buy* (1941), but the "farmer" in this wonderful picture did. Died: 1972.

### William Shatner  *Actor* 6901 Hollywood

**Born:**  Mar. 22, 1931, in Canada.
**Spotlights:**  Respected by millions of "Trekkies" as the intelligent, passionate Captain James T. Kirk of the Starship *U.S.S. Enterprise* on "Star Trek" (1966–69). Just as popular 20 years later in motion pictures. Sergeant T. J. Hooker on the police drama, "T. J. Hooker" (1982–).

### Danny Thomas  *Actor, singer* 6901 Hollywood

**Born:**  Amos Muzyad Jacobs; Jan. 6, 1914, in Deerfield, MI.
**Spotlights:**  "The Danny Thomas Show" (1953–64) was one of the longest-running family comedies, with Thomas exuding humor, warmth, and human frailty. (Rerun in syndication under the title "Make Room for Daddy" (1960–1965).
**Achievements:**  1954, Emmy.

### Charles Bronson  *Actor*   6901 Hollywood

**Born:** Charles Bunchinsky; Nov. 3, 1922, in Ehronfeld, PA.
**Spotlights:** His tough-looking face with a physique to match had him originally cast as villain. Later his ruggedness proved believable in the hero image. *The Magnificent Seven* (1960), *The Dirty Dozen* (1967), *Death Wish* (1974).
**Achievements:** 1968 top box office star in Europe; 1971, world's most popular actor (Golden Globe), 1973–81 one of the world's top box office stars.
**Highlights:** Married to British actress, co-star Jill Ireland (since 1968).

### Dinah Shore  *See page 346.*   6901 Hollywood

### Broderick Crawford  *See page 327.*   6901 Hollywood

### John Travolta  *Actor, singer*   6901 Hollywood

**Born:** Feb. 18, 1954, in Englewood, N.J.
**Spotlights:** Dark-haired, cleft-chinned actor whose Broadway performances led to TV work in Hollywood. He played the not-too-bright, but well meaning Vinnie Barbarino on "Welcome Back Kotter." He leaped into international fame with the movie *Saturday Night Fever* (1977); then *Grease* (1978).

### Buster Crabbe  *Actor*   6901 Hollywood

**Born:** Feb. 17, 1907, in Oakland, CA.
**Spotlights:** On-screen in *King of the Jungle* (1933). TV: His edited *Buck Rogers* movies, of which he was the star, were shown as a TV serial.
**Achievements:** 1928; Olympic bronze medal—swimming: 1932; gold medal—swimming. 1971, broke the world's record in 400 meter freestyle for people over sixty. Died: 1983.

### Wayne Newton  *Singer, actor*   6901 Hollywood

**Born:** April 3, 1942, in Roanoke, VA.
**Spotlights:** Las Vegas entertainer. In 1980 co-owner of the $85 million Aladdin Hotel on the Strip. Recordings include "Heart!" and "Danke Schoen."

### Beniamino Gigli  *Opera Singer*   6901 Hollywood

**Born:** March 20, 1890, in Recanati, Italy.
**Spotlights:** A great, bel canto lyric tenor in a class with Enrico Caruso and Tito Schipa. Powerful, superb, sweet tonal quality. Recordings: Puccini's *Tosca* on Victor label; Leoncavallo's *Pagliacci*. Died: 1957.

### Judy Holliday  *Actress*   6901 Hollywood

**Born:** Judith Tuvim on June 21, 1922, in New York.
**Spotlights:** Perky, "dumb" blonde who was a master of comedy. *Adam's Rib* (1949),

opposite Katharine Hepburn and Spencer Tracy; *The Marrying Kind* (1952).
**Achievements:**   1950, Best Actress Oscar for *Born Yesterday.*
**Sidelights:**   Hardly stupid in real life, her IQ was 172! Died: 1965 of throat cancer.

## Julie Andrews   *Actress, singer*                    6901 Hollywood
**Born:**   Julia Wells; Oct. 1, 1935, in England.
**Spotlights:**   This pretty actress with a golden throat triumphantly made her film debut in *Mary Poppins* (1964) and became an instant celebrity. In 1965 she starred in *The Sound of Music*, portraying a lively, singing novice; later starred as a woman impersonating a man impersonating a woman in *Victor Victoria* (1983).
**Achievements:**   1964, Best Actress Oscar for *Mary Poppins* (her first movie).

## Edgar Kennedy   *Actor*                    6901 Hollywood
**Born:**   April 26, 1890, in Monterey, CA.
**Spotlights:**   Comedian who clowned with the best, including Charlie Chaplin and Laurel and Hardy. He did a talkie with the Marx Brothers, *Duck Soup* (1933). Died: 1948, of throat cancer.

## Olivia Newton-John   *Singer, actress*                    6901 Hollywood
**Born:**   Sept. 26, 1948, in England.
**Spotlights:**   Vivacious, blonde, blue-eyed singer from Australia, who arrived in the U.S. in 1965. Had a string of popular songs in and appeared in films, including *Grease* (1978). Albums: *Come on Over; Have You Never Been Mellow.*

*Julie Andrews in* Mary Poppins          *Greta Garbo*

**Achievements:** 1973, Grammy, country, "Let Me Be There". 1974, Grammy, pop vocalist and record of the year, "I Honestly Love You".

### Greta Garbo 🎥 *Actress*                6901 Hollywood

**Born:** Greta Gustafsson on Sept. 18, 1905, in Sweden.
**Spotlights:** Mysterious. Divine. Haunting. Beautiful. Glamorous. A few of her classic films: *Flesh and the Devil* (1926), *Anna Christie* (1930), *Camille* (1937), *Ninotchka* (1939). Retired in 1942. "I just vant to be left alone."
**Achievements:** 1954, special Oscar.
**Sidelights:** Discovered by another Walk of Famer, Mauritz Stiller. Upon seeing her, Louis B. Mayer of MGM remarked, "American men don't like fat women." Oh yeah?

### Earl Holliman 📺 *Actor*                6901 Hollywood

**Born:** Sept. 11, 1928, in Tennesas Swamp, LA.
**Spotlights:** Lieutenant Bill Crowley in the drama series "Police Woman" (1974–78). Felt comfortable in a cowboy hat in the series "The Wide Country" (1962–63), as bronco rider Mitch Guthrie.

### Joel McCrea 🎥 *Actor*                6901 Hollywood

**Born:** Nov. 5, 1905, in Los Angeles, CA.
**Spotlights:** Cowboy. Started as a stuntman in silents (1923) and made over 100 pictures (until 1976). Leading man in *Foreign Correspondent* (1940) and *Reaching for the Sun* (1941). Guest radio spots.

*Joan Collins*                *Leonard Goldberg*

### Joan Collins  *Actress*                    6901 Hollywood

**Born:** May 23, 1933, in England.

**Spotlights:** Sultry, dark-haired, determined beauty, who eventually beat the system by becoming a superstar on TV's "Dynasty" (1981–) as sexy, rich, powerful Alexis Carrington Colby. On the big screen since 1951, *Lady Godiva Rides Again*. Stunning in MGM's *The Opposite Sex* (1956)

**Sidelights:** Her sister is author Jackie Collins.

### Ellen Drew  *Actress*                    6901 Hollywood

**Born:** Terry Ray; Nov. 23, 1915, in Kansas City, MO.

**Spotlights:** A former Kansas City beauty queen, with large hazel eyes, full lips, and thick dark hair. At Paramount, her home studio for close to a decade, she became a leading lady and showed a comic flair in *Christmas in July* (1940). Retired to Palm Springs, CA.

### Leonard Goldberg  *Producer, executive*                    6901 Hollywood

**Born:** Jan. 24, 1934, in New York, NY.

**Spotlights:** Goldberg has had a significant impact on the entertainment industry. His creative contributions include developing and introducing the concept of movies made for TV. This type of programming quickly became an American viewing institution. One of his many accomplishments is the critically acclaimed production of *Brian's Song*. In 1972 Goldberg formed his partnership with Aaron Spelling, resulting in a number of hit series including "Charlie's Angels" and "Fantasy Island". Bursting with energy and talent, an independent now, he formed the Leonard Goldberg Co. and Mandy Films. With a keen eye for new talent, he gave "breaks" to John Travolta, Farrah Fawcett, Matthew Broderick (*War Games*). Also president and C.O.O. of 20th Century-Fox Film Corp.

**Highlights:** Married to the lovely Wendy Howard.

# ⋆ 6800 HOLLYWOOD ⋆

**Penny Singleton**   *See page 71.*   6800 Hollywood

**Bee Gees**  *Musicians, singers*   6845 Hollywood
**Born:**  Barry, Sept. 1, 1946; Maurice and Robin (twins); Dec. 22, 1949; on the Isle of Man, England.
**The Group:**  The Gibb Brothers — includes Andy, Barry, Robin, and Maurice. The family emigrated to Australia in 1958. Albums: *Saturday Night Fever* and *Too Much Heaven*.
**Highlights:**  Baby brother Andy was born March 5, 1958 in Australia. Big song: "I Just Want To Be Your Everything".
**Achievements:**  1977, six Grammys.

**Sammy Kaye**   *See page 86.*   6845 Hollywood

**James Mason**  *Actor*   6845 Hollywood
**Born:**  May 15, 1909, in England.
**Spotlights:**  Earned a degree in architecture from Cambridge before deciding on a career in drama. Narrated "The Search for the Nile" (1972) and has appeared in many plays and specials, usually as cruel characters. Has made over 100 motion pictures in England, America, France, Germany, Italy and Spain. Brilliant in *Odd Man Out* (1947 — filmed in England). Died: 1984

**Robert Rossen**  *Director*   6845 Hollywood
**Born:**  Robert Rosen; March 16, 1908, in New York.
**Spotlights:**  *Body and Soul* (1947), starred John Garfield and Lilli Palmer. It dealt with boxing, a subject the former fighter Rossen could identify with. Received critical acclaim for writing and directing *All the King's Men* (1949), "absolute power corrupts absolutely."
**Sidelights:**  The House Un-American Activities Committee identified Rossen as a Communist party member, and he was blacklisted. Died: 1966.

**Gig Young**  *Actor*   6845 Hollywood
**Born:**  Byron Barr on Nov. 4, 1913, in St. Cloud, MN.
**Spotlights:**  1969 Academy award-winning performance in *They Shoot Horses, Don't They?* led to numerous dramatic TV specials. He was very good in light comedies too. Starring oppposite David Niven and Charles Boyer in the television series *The Rogues*, his character was scoundrel, Tony Fleming, "honor before

honesty" (1964–65). First stage name: Bryant Fleming.
**Highlights:** Third wife (of five) was Elizabeth Montgomery. Died: 1978

### Ida Lupino  *Actress, director, screenwriter*  6845 Hollywood
**Born:** Feb. 4, 1918, in England.
**Spotlights:** Very pretty, brunette leading lady: *Her First Affair* (1932) and *The Adventures of Sherlock Holmes* (1939). Directed *The Trouble with Angels* (1966). TV: played Eve Drake on "Mr. Adams and Eve," situation comedy (1957–58).
**Sidelights:** Actors in her family can be traced back hundreds of years.

### Al Lichtman *Executive*  6841 Hollywood
**Born:** April 9, 1888, in Hungary.
**Spotlights:** Began career in theater as an usher. Vaudeville, exhibitor and distribution followed. Key position with Famous Players, Lasky Paramount; co-founded Preferred Pictures; later president of United Artists. Changed desks (and parking spaces) at MGM in 1935. Finally joined 20th Century-Fox as vice president, before being repositioned as director of distribution. Member of the Motion Picture Pioneers.
**Sidelights:** To my readers: above is typical of the revolving doors at Hollywood studios.

### Celeste Holm *See page 227.*  6841 Hollywood

### Dick Haymes *See page 180.*  6841 Hollywood

### Paul Lukas *Actor*  6841 Hollywood
**Born:** May 26, 1894, in Hungary.
**Spotlights:** Handsome leading and supporting actor with Paramount: *To Each His Own* (1946) and *Miss Tatlock's Millions* (1948). Died: 1971.

### Stuart Hamblen *Singer, bandleader, songwriter*  6841 Hollywood
**Born:** Carl S. Hamblen; Oct. 20, 1908, in Kellyville, TX.
**Spotlights:** Moved to Hollywood in 1929. Landed a job at local radio station, KFI, where he became known as "Cowboy Joe." In 1930 he was known as Dave Donner with the Beverly Hillbillies on neighboring station, KMPC. Started "Cowboy Church of the Air." Recordings include: "My Mary-My Brown Eyed Texas Rose," "Old Pappy's New Banjo," "It's No Secret (What God Can Do)," and "This Ole House-When My Lord Picks Up the Phone."

### Paul Douglas *See page 208.*  6841 Hollywood

### Sons of the Pioneers *Vocal and instrumental group*  6821 Hollywood
Members of the group during 40 + years of its existence include: Roy Rogers, Bob

Nolan, Tim Spencer, Hugh and Karl Farr (brothers), Lloyd Perryman, Pat Brady, Doye O'Dell, Ken Carson, Deuce Spriggins, Tommy Doss, Ken Curtis, Rusty Richards, Dale Warren, and Roy Landham.

**Spotlights:** Roy Rogers formed the Sons of the Pioneers trio in 1930. The band increased to six members, but fluctuated in numbers and members over the years. Popular hit recordings include: "Cool Water," "There's a New Moon Over My Shoulder," "Lie Low, Little Dogies," "Room Full of Roses," and "Cowboy Hymns and Spirituals." Dozens of hit songs.

### Taylor Holmes  *Actor* 6821 Hollywood

**Born:** May 18, 1872, in Newark, NJ.
**Spotlights:** 5' 8", 154 lb., grey-haired, brown-eyed. Career spanned six decades (1899–1959). Started in vaudeville, but turned to legitimate theater in 1901. Played Hamlet at the Garden Theater in New York. Became matinee idol of the early 1900s. Films include: *Dinner at Eight* (1933), *Gentlemen Prefer Blondes* (1953).
**Sidelights:** Family sent young Holmes to a diction teacher because of his high-pitched voice; it led to acting. Died: 1959.

### Rex Allen *Actor* 6821 Hollywood

**Born:** Dec. 31, 1922, in Wilcox, AZ.
**Spotlights:** Singing cowboy in "B" westerns. *Old Overland Trail* (1953), teamed with pal, Slim Pickens. Voice-over work for Disney (1970s).

### Anthony Perkins *Actor* 6821 Hollywood

**Born:** April 4, 1932, in New York.
**Spotlights:** Intense, tall, dark-haired talent whose portrayal of Norman Bates, the creepy motel keeper in Hitchcock's *Psycho* (1960), made him an international celebrity: "Mother, uh, what is that phrase? She isn't quite herself today." Starred on "Kraft Television Theater" dramas during the fifties. TV movies: *How Awful About Allan* (1970) and *First You Cry* (1979).
**Sidelights:** *Psycho* property is seen daily on the Universal Studios tour. Guides inform sightseers that the blood in the shower scene was really America's favorite chocolate sauce!

### Frank Parker *Tenor, actor* 6821 Hollywood

**Born:** Nov. 8, 1900, in Fillmore, MO.
**Spotlights:** Early singer on the A & P (Atlantic and Pacific) "Gypsies" (1923); vocalist on "Arthur Godfrey Time" (CBS, 1945). Guest appearances on many shows. Died: 1962.

### Bill Stern *Sportscaster* 6821 Hollywood

**Born:** July 1, 1907, in Rochester, N.Y.

**Spotlights:** "The Colgate Sports Newsreel Starring Bill Stern" enthusiastically covered every sport imaginable from the Olympics to bowling and fishing (CBS, 1939–51). Died: 1971.

### Mario Lanza 🎥 *Singer, actor* 6821 Hollywood
**Born:** Alfred Cocozza; Jan. 31, 1921, in Philadelphia, PA.
**Spotlights:** As a youth Lanza was a piano mover; that should give you an idea about his size. Hollywood Bowl debut in opera *Madame Butterfly* in 1947 won him praise as the best male classical vocalist. His outstanding portrayal of *The Great Caruso* (1951) proved a tremendous success at the box office. Lanza's voice (not Edmund Purdom's) was used for the *The Student Prince* (1954) music soundtrack. Died: 1959, from a heart attack while undertaking a crash diet to lose weight.

### Henri Mancini 🎵 *Composer, conductor, arranger, songwriter* 6821 Hollywood
**Born:** April 16, 1924, in Cleveland, OH.
**Spotlights:** Brilliant individual. Albums include *The Hollywood Musicals, Brass on Ivory, Pink Panther Strikes Again*; more.
**Achievements:** 1962, Oscar, score and song, "Moon River"; 1963, Oscar, song, "Days of Wine and Roses." Master of 70 film scores. Twenty (and growing) Grammys. Many TV theme songs, including "Peter Gunn."

### Jules C. Stein 🎥 *Executive* 6821 Hollywood
**Born:** April 26, 1896, in South Bend, IN.
**Spotlights:** Extremely well-educated, Dr. Stein (opthalmologist) was Founder-President of Music Corporation of America (MCA).
**Achievements:** 1976 Jean Hersholt Humanitarian Award. Died: 1981.

### Y Frank Freeman 🎥 *Executive* 6821 Hollywood
**Born:** Dec. 14, 1890, In Greenville, GA.
**Spotlights:** The "Y" stands for Young. Vice President at Paramount Pictures, retiring in 1959. Chairman of the Board of the Association of Motion Picture Producers (1959–64). Died: 1969.

### Anita Louise 🎥 *Actress* 6821 Hollywood
**Born:** Anita Louis Fremault; Jan. 9, 1915, in New York.
**Spotlights:** Beautiful blond who decorated thirties period pictures including: *Madame DuBarry* (1934), Warner's *A Midsummer Night's Dream* (1935), which holds up superbly today, and Warner's *The Story of Louis Pasteur* (1935), which also was the first biography turned into a picture. Died: 1970.

### Peter Frampton 🎵 *Singer, musician* 6819 Hollywood
**Born:** April 22, 1950, in England.

**Spotlights:** Recordings include "Something's Happening" "Frampton Comes Alive," and "I'm In You." Formerly with group Humble Pie.

### Jerry Lewis 🎥 *Actor, director*      6819 Hollywood
**Born:** Joseph Levitch; March 16, 1926, in Newark, NJ.
**Spotlights:** Teamed with Dean Martin in Atlantic City in 1946. Skinny Lewis played the bumbling, childlike (often idiotic) characters, and handsome Martin played the suave, romantic, confident half of the duo. *The Stooge, Scared Stiff* (both 1953). TV: Martin-Lewis were the funniest hosts on TV's "The Colgate Comedy Hour" (1950–55). Split their partnership in 1956. Solo, Lewis wrote, directed, produced, and starred in *The Nutty Professor* (1963). TV: "The Jerry Lewis Show" (NBC, 1967–69).

### Billy Daniels 💿 *Singer, actor*      6819 Hollywood
**Born:** Sept. 12, 1915, in Jacksonville, FL.
**Spotlights:** A dynamic child vocalist who was a regular on the variety radio show, "The Horn and Hardart Children's Hour." The program, which aired during the 1930s and 1940s, was a training ground for youngsters such as Connie Francis, Eddie Fisher, and Joey Heatherton. Later, Daniel's hit recording was "That Old Black Magic." Also had his own show in 1952. Many fine performances on stage and TV during the 1960s, 1970s and 1980s.

### Mabel Normand 🎥 *Comedienne, actress*      6819 Hollywood
**Born:** Mabel Fortescue; Nov. 16, 1894, in Boston, MA.
**Spotlights:** Number-one silent comedienne. Vivacious brunette with an engaging smile. Often directed by Mack Sennett. *Mabel's Adventures* (1912 — first in a long-running series), *Tillie's Punctured Romance* (1914) with Charlie Chaplin, *Mabel's and Fatty's Wash Day* (1915) with co-star Roscoe "Fatty" Arbuckle. Died: 1930.

### Judy Canova 🎥 *See page 38.*      6819 Hollywood

### Frances Drake 🎥 *Actress*      6819 Hollywood
**Born:** Frances Dean; Oct. 22, 1908, in New York.
**Spotlights:** Supporting talent in *Les Miserables* (1935), a brilliant classic, and the comedy mystery *It's a Wonderful World* (1939).

### Harriet Nelson 📺 *Actress, singer*      6819 Hollywood
**Born:** Harriet Hilliard; July 18, 1914, in Des Moines, IA.
**Spotlights:** "The Adventures of Ozzie and Harriet," a family situation comedy, (1952–66), starred the pleasant, real-life family of Ozzie, Harriet, David, and Eric "Ricky" Nelson. Baby boomers fondly recall growing up with the series and sensing the real love and care that made "Ozzie and Harriet" fun to watch. Radio and film work too.

**Amelita Galli-Curci** 🔘 *Opera singer*                    6819 Hollywood
**Born:** Nov. 18, 1882, in Milan, Italy.
**Spotlights:** Golden-voiced singer; performed with tenor Tito Schipa on Victor recording of Bellini's *La Sonnambula*. Died: 1963.

**Groucho Marx** 🎙 *See page 120.*                    6819 Hollywood

**Ted Husing** 🎙 *Actor, announcer, sportswriter, screenwriter*  6819 Hollywood
**Born:** Nov. 27, 1901 in Bronx, N.Y.
**Spotlights:** Sportscaster, emcee Husing's sensational delivery often made sports events more exciting to listen to than to watch. Announcer on "The True Story Hour with Mary and Bob" (CBS, 1928), "The George Burns and Gracie Allen Show" (CBS, 1931); narrator on "The March of Time," documentary (CBS, 1931). Appeared in and narrated sports films, too. Died: 1962.

**Henry O'Neill** 🎥 *Actor*                    6819 Hollywood
**Born:** Aug. 10, 1891, in Orange, N.J.
**Spotlights:** Film buffs recognize this veteran character talent; over 150 films from 1930–57: Warner's *The Story of Louis Pasteur* (1935), MGM's *The Human Comedy* (1943). Died: 1961.

**Leon Errol** 🎥 *Actor*                    6819 Hollywood
**Born:** July 3, 1881, in Australia.
**Spotlights:** The revealing titles of two of his movies, *The Lunatic at Large* (1928) and *Pop Always Pays* (1940), glorify his best-loved characterization in comedy shorts, that of a henpecked, rubbery-legged drunk. Excellent with W. C. Fields in *Never Give a Sucker an Even Break* (1941). Died: 1951, of a heart attack.

**Alice Calhoun** 🎥 *Actress*                    6801 Hollywood
**Born:** Nov. 21, 1900, in Cleveland, OH.
**Spotlights:** Brunette beauty in 52 vitagraph and Warner Bros. films from 1916–32. Died: 1966.

**Edgar Bergen** 🎙 *Ventriloquist, actor*                    6801 Hollywood
**Born:** Feb. 16, 1903, in Chicago, IL.
**Spotlights:** No dummy when he spent $35 to make his wooden creation, Charlie McCarthy. Two other alter egos, Mortimer Snerd and Effie Klinker, joined radio's "The Edgar Bergen and Charlie McCarthy Show" (NBC first aired the long- running comedy variety program in 1936). Charlie McCarthy, always a swell dresser in top hat and tux, a real lady's man, also sported a monocle. A wise guy, he chided Bergen for moving his lips perceptively. Charlie, perpetually prepared for fisticuffs, would threaten: "I'll clip ya! So help me, I'll mow ya down!" TV: Quiz show "Do You Trust Your

Wife?" (1956–57); and more. Films include *Charlie McCarthy Detective* (1939) and *I Remember Mama* (1948).

**Achievements:** 1937, special Oscar.

**Sidelights:** Father of two gorgeous and wonderful people, Candice and Chris Bergen. You can visit the dummy, Charlie McCarthy, at the Smithsonian Institution in Washington, D.C. Died: 1978.

**J. Peverell Marley** 🎥 *Cinematographer*  6801 Hollywood

**Born:** Aug. 14, 1901, in San Jose, CA.

**Spotlights:** Marley's keen eye for aesthetics brought symmetry to pictures, and it's evident in *The Ten Commandments* (1923), his first work (he was the chief camera-man). *Charlie's Aunt* (1941); *The Greatest Show on Earth* (1952), with associate cinematographer, George Barnes. Died: 1964.

**William Primrose** 💿 *Musician*  6801 Hollywood

**Born:** Aug. 23 1904, in Scotland.

**Spotlights:** Distinguished violinist playing for American audiences since the late 1930s.

**Achievements:** 1956, co-founded the Festival Quartet.

**Bobbie Vernon** 🎥 *Comedian*  6801 Hollywood

**Born:** Silvion Jardins; March 9, 1897, in Chicago, IL.

**Spotlights:** 19-year-old Vernon paired with 19-year-old Mack Sennett and bathing beauty Gloria Swanson for comedy shorts; *Hearts and Sparks* (1916). "Teddy the Great Dane" was one of their regular cast "members" in the series. When slapstick became dated, he went behind the sceens. Died: 1939, of a heart attack.

**Milburn Stone** 📺 *Actor*  6801 Hollywood

**Born:** July 5, 1904, in Burton, KS.

**Spotlights:** Supporting actor: *Young Mr. Lincoln* (1939) and *Sherlock Holmes Faces Death* (1943).

**Achievements:** 1967–68, Emmy, outstanding performance in a drama: *Gunsmoke's* Dr. Galen (Doc) Adams, (1955–75). His horse's name? Popcorn. Died: 1980.

**Tony Curtis** 🎥 *Actor*  6801 Hollywood

**Born:** Bernard Schwartz; June 3, 1925, in Bronx, N.Y.

**Spotlights:** Handsome, beefcake actor whose action films led to better, more challenging roles: *The Sweet Smell of Success* (1957), *The Defiant Ones* (1958). At his comic best in *Some Like It Hot* (1959,) with Marilyn Monroe and Jack Lemmon.

**Louise Fazenda** 🎥 *Actress*  6801 Hollywood

**Born:** June 17, 1889, in Lafayette, IN.

**Spotlights:** On-screen in *The Cheese Special* (1913) and proved her comic talents in comedies, *A Hash House Fraud* and *Fatty's Tin Type Tangle* (both 1915). Last film was *The Old Maid* (1939). Died: 1962, of cerebral hemorrhage.

### Telly Savalas   Actor     6801 Hollywood
**Born:** Aristotle Savalas; Jan. 21, 1924, in Garden City, NY
**Spotlights:** Bald, tough-looking, former executive. Supporting role in *Birdman of Alcatraz* (1962); *The Dirty Dozen* (1967); more.
**Achievements:** 1974, Emmy for "Kojak."

### Burt Lancaster   Actor     6801 Hollywood
**Born:** Nov. 2, 1913, in New York.
**Spotlights:** If Lancaster's temper on the set is legendary, his good qualities of honesty and hard work help to balance out the notoriety. He has excelled in thrillers, action films, and dramas, including *Come Back, Little Sheba* (1952), *From Here to Eternity* (1953), *Gunfight at the OK Corral* (1957), *Airport* (1970); more.
**Achievements:** 1960, Best Actor Oscar for *Elmer Gantry.*

### Beverly Garland   Actress     6801 Hollywood
**Born:** Beverly Fessenden; Oct. 17, 1926, in Santa Cruz, CA.
**Spotlights:** After 9 years of resisting eligible bachelorettes, Steve Douglas (Fred MacMurray) finally succumbed to the irresistible charms of teacher, Barbara Harper, on "My Three Sons," (1969–72). She has played Dottie West, mother of Amanda King, on "Scarecrow and Mrs. King" (since 1983).

### Preston Foster   Actor     6801 Hollywood
**Born:** Oct. 24, 1902, in Ocean City, NJ.
**Spotlights:** A professional wrestler before an impressive resume of over 100 films, he was Captain John Herrick of the ship, the *Cheryl Ann* on the adventure series "Waterfront" (1953–56). He was Captain Zachary Wingate in the western "Gunslinger" series (1961). Died: 1970.

### Edward Sedgwick   Director     6801 Hollywood
**Born:** Nov. 7, 1892, in Galveston, TX.
**Spotlights:** Sedgwick made over 100 pictures in various capacities — acting, writing, and directing, from 1915–1951; *Parlor Bedroom and Bath* (1930) and *Ma and Pa Kettle Back on the Farm* (1951). Died: 1953.

### Cliff Robertson   , Actor     6801 Hollywood
**Born:** Sept. 9, 1925, in La Jolla, CA.
**Spotlights:** Very masculine, handsome, dark-haired leading man. Onscreen in *Picnic* (1956). Selected to play President John F. Kennedy in *PT–109* (1963) by JFK

himself. Directorial debut in *J. W. Coop* (1972.).

**Achievements:** 1968, Best Actor Oscar for *Charly*, 1966 Emmy for "The Game".

**Highlights:** Married to second wife, Dina Merrill since 1966. What did he do before becoming a movie star? Busboy, waiter, and taxi driver.

## Ronald Colman  *Actor* 6801 Hollywood

**Born:** Feb. 9, 1891, in England.

**Spotlights:** His first film job paid him a pound a day, a lowly scale by American standards. In the U.S., both Selznick and Goldwyn recognized that his bracing good looks would translate on the silent screen. Heartthrob Colman exuded a wide range of emotions while winning the title of the top male star in 1927 and 1928. He also accomplished what only two or three other actors had, the successful transition to the talkies. TV: His wife, pretty British actress Benita Hume, appeared with him on "The Jack Benny Show" and the series "The Halls of Ivy."

**Achievements:** 1947, Best Actor Oscar for *A Double Life*. Died: 1958, of pneumonia.

## Olive Borden  *Actress* 6801 Hollywood

**Born:** Sybil Tinkle, July 14, 1907, in Richmond, VA.

**Spotlights:** A former bathing beauty who was highly successful in the twenties; *Three Bad Men* (1926), *Sinners in Love* (1928). Her voice was no good in talkies, and her career abruptly ended. Died: 1941.

## Joanne Woodward  *Actress* 6801 Hollywood

**Born:** Feb. 27, 1930, in Thomasville, GA.

*Ernest Torrence* *Monty Hall*

**Spotlights:**   Never one to be pigeonholed, this selective actress intelligently chooses her roles: *Rachel, Rachel* (1968); *The Effects of Gamma Rays on Man- in-the-Moon Marigolds* (1972); *Summer Wishes, Winter Dreams* (1973).
**Achievements:**   1957, Best Actress Oscar for *The Three Faces of Eve.*
**Highlights:**   Happily married to Paul Newman since 1958.

## Ernest Torrence   ♀ *Actor*                        6801 Hollywood

**Born:**   June 26, 1878, in Scotland.
**Spotlights:**   *Mantrap* (1920), with the flirty, bouncy, bees' knees, Clara Bow. *Queen Christina* (1933), starred hauntingly beautiful Greta Garbo. His brother David also appeared in it. Died: 1933.

## Monty Hall   ◄ *Host*                        6801 Hollywood

**Born:**   Aug. 25, 1923, in Canada.
**Spotlights:**   Former stage actor in Canada. Pleasant game show personality/ producer of the wacky "Let's Make a Deal" (1963–76) where contestants' greed sometimes left them with turkey prizes.
**Sidelights:**   He has a reputation of being extremely reliable. He never called in sick during his series work.
**Achievements:**   Served as Honorary Mayor of Hollywood. Many accolades for his endless charitable contributions.

# ⋆ 6777 HOLLYWOOD ⋆

**Lanny Ross**  *Singer*                    6777 Hollywood

**Spotlights:** Tenor on "Show Boat" (NBC, 1932). Had a lovely singing voice, but had a "double" to talk for him: The network didn't like his speaking voice! Guest singer on countless shows.

**Judy Canova**  *Singer, comedienne*                    6777 Hollywood

**Born:** Nov. 20, 1916, in Jacksonville, FL.
**Spotlights:** Yodeling was her trademark on radio comedy: "The Judy Canova Show," (NBC, 1945). The lively backwoods country brunette with a gigantic mouth entertained motion picture audiences from 1935–1976: *Puddin' Head* (1941) and *Honeychile* (1951); more. Died: 1983.

**Jascha Heifetz**  *Musician*                    6777 Hollywood

**Born:** Feb. 2, 1901, in Russia.
**Spotlights:** Internationally renowned violinist, gave his first concert in 1911–at 10 years old. Numerous recordings.
**Achievements:** 1961, 1962, 1964, Grammys.

**Bessie Love** 🎥 *Actress*                    6777 Hollywood

**Born:** Juanita Horton; Sept. 10, 1898, in Midland, TX.
**Spotlights:** From silents — *Intolerance* (1916) — to the first MGM sound musical *The Broadway Melody* (1929). Love kept busy on stage, TV, and playwriting in America and England. Died: 1986.

**Andrew L. Stone** 🎥 *Director, screenwriter, producer*                    6777 Hollywood

**Born:** July 16, 1902, in Oakland, CA.
**Spotlights:** Worked as screenwriter, director, and producer of *The Bachelor's Daughters* (1946), the story of a group of struggling girls who pass themselves off as an upper-crust family to attract rich bachelors.
**Highlights:** His "thriller" films owe their tension-packed sequences to his editor wife, Virginia Stone: *Cry Terror!* (1958).

**Kirsten Flagstad**  *Opera singer*                    6777 Hollywood

**Born:** July 12, 1895, in Hamar, Norway.
**Spotlights:** A great operatic soprano who excelled in her renditions of works by fellow Norwegian, Edvard Grieg. Idolized in Wagnerian roles. The temperamental prima donna made many recordings including Purcell's *Dido and Aeneas*. Died: 1962.

## Bill Burrud  *Host, producer*    **6777 Hollywood**

**Born:** Jan. 12, 1925, in Hollywood, CA.

**Spotlights:** Specializing in wildlife documentaries, he introduced audiences to the earth's wondrous animals and its ecological chain in "Animal World" (1968–71) and "Safari to Adventure" (1969–75). These programs inadvertently demonstrated the need for conscious environmental action.

## Elvis Presley *Singer, actor*    **6777 Hollywood**

**Born:** Jan. 8, 1935, in Tupelo, MS.

**Spotlights:** "The King." Instant RCA recording star in 1955. TV debut on Jan. 28, 1956, on Tommy and Jimmy Dorsey's "Stage Show," singing "Heartbreak Hotel." "Elvis the Pelvis" thrilled studio audience members and TV viewers alike. In the fall of 1956, Ed Sullivan invited the good-looking, gyrating youth on his show, though most shots were from above the hips. Over 600 million albums and singles sold. A couple of his hit recordings include a rhythm-and-blues tune, "Hound Dog," and a love ballad, "Love Me Tender." Made 33 commercially successful motion pictures.

**Sidelights:** The survivor of identical twins, Presley wasn't always singing "My Way." As a young hopeful, he tried out for TV's "Arthur Godfrey's Talent Scout" and was rejected! Another loser? Buddy Holly. Died: 1977, from a heart attack.

## Ray Charles *Singer, pianist, composer*    **6775 Hollywood**

**Born:** R. Robinson; Sept. 23, 1930, in Albany, GA.

**Spotlights:** Blind since childhood. Blues voice. Roots in gospel music. Played jazz, alto sax and piano, also known for soulful R & B renditions. Recordings include:

*Jascha Heifetz*                    *Elvis Presley*

39

"Georgia on My Mind," "Let the Good Times Roll," "Al Di La," "Hallelujah, I Love Her So"; more.
**Achievements:**   Eight Grammys.

### Vivien Leigh   *Actress*                                6775 Hollywood

**Born:**   Vivian Hartley; Nov. 5, 1913, in India.
**Spotlights:**   She was immortalized as Scarlett O'Hara in *Gone With the Wind* (1939). That one role is considered *la creme de la creme* among all female leading roles. She was a ravishing brunette with blue eyes. Off-screen she was an ambitious "princess," who wanted what she wanted when she wanted it.
**Achievements:**   Best Actress Academy awards for *Gone With the Wind* (1939) and *A Streetcar Named Desire* (1951).
**Highlights:**   The Lady was married to Sir Laurence Olivier (1940–60). They were the most glamorous couple in the world in the early 1940s.
**Sidelights:**   Plagued by tuberculosis, frequently ill. Died: 1967, in her sleep.

### Milton Berle   *See page 149.*                           6771 Hollywood

### Al Christie   *Director, screenwriter, producer*            6769 Hollywood

**Born:**   Nov. 24, 1886, in Canada.
**Spotlights:**   Started in the infant days (1909) of movie making and lasted through the late thirties; specialized in comedies. *When the Mummy Cried for Help* (1915). Died: 1951.

### Lindsay Wagner   *Actress*                               6767 Hollywood

**Born:**   June 22, 1949, in Los Angeles, CA.
**Spotlights:**   Confident, "super hero," she was Jaime Sommers, "The Bionic Woman" (1976–78).
**Achievements:**   1976–77 Emmy.

### Bing Crosby   *See page 251.*                            6767 Hollywood

### Rafael Mendez    *Trumpet player*      6767 Hollywood

**Born:**   Mar. 26, 1906, in Mexico.
**Spotlights:**   His father was a composer-arranger who encouraged young Rafael to pursue his favorite instrument. By the early 1930s Mendez was playing with Rudy Vallee's orchestra. During the 1940s, he was with MGM's orchestra. A trumpet virtuoso, he recorded "Scherzo in D Minor," "Mendez Jota," and "The Virgin of the Macarena."
**Highlights:**   The third son of 19 children. Died: 1981.

### Edgar Bergen   *See page 33.*                            6767 Hollywood

**Sammy Kaye** 🔘 *See page 86.*  6767 Hollywood

**Chick Hearn** 🎙 *Sportscaster*  6765 Hollywood
**Born:** Francis Dayle Hearn; in Aurora, IL.
**Spotlights:** "From high above the western sideline of the L.A. Forum." Sportscaster nationally famous for his fast, accurate play-by-play action for the L.A. Lakers for over 26 years. Started with that team in 1961. Familiar phrases: "The mustard came off the hotdog," "Faked him into the popcorn machine," "No harm, no foul," "Air ball," and "Give and go." Also covers boxing and football.

**Marie Wilson** 📺 *See page 68.*  6765 Hollywood

**Eddie Cantor** 🎙 *See page 314.*  6763 Hollywood

**Robert Merrill** 🔘 *Opera singer*  6763 Hollywood
**Born:** Robert Miller; June 4, 1917, in Brooklyn, NY.
**Spotlights:** Eminent baritone. Broke records with his popular, beautiful voice by performing hundreds of times at the Metropolitan since 1945 — *La Traviata*.

**Red Skelton** 🎙 *See page 315.*  6763 Hollywood

**Katherine Macdonald** 🎥 *Actress, producer*  6761 Hollywood
**Born:** Dec. 14, 1891, in PA.

*Rafael Mendez*                    *Robert Merrill*

**Spotlights:** Gorgeous in *Headin' South* (1918) and *The Untamed Women* (1925). Died: 1956.

### Ingrid Bergman  *Actress*      6761 Hollywood

**Born:** Aug. 29, 1915, in Stockholm, Sweden.

**Spotlights:** *Intermezzo* (1939) won her international acclaim, but she was immortalized in a "B" movie, *Casablanca*, in 1942. She and Humphrey Bogart played in this romantic drama, one of Hollywood's true legends.

**Achievements:** Best Actress Oscars for *Gaslight* (1944), *Anastasia* (1956), and *Murder on the Orient Express* (1974). Died: 1982.

### Lee Strasberg *Acting teacher*      6757 Hollywood

**Born:** Nov. 17, 1901, in Austria.

**Spotlights:** Strasberg's talents embraced acting, stage directing, and teaching Stanislavski's method acting. He was 73 when he made his first screen appearance in *The Godfather, Part II*.

**Achievements:** 1930–37 co-founder and director of the Group Theater; 1948, director of Actor's Studio in New York. 1969, founder of the Lee Strasberg Institute of the Theater in New York and Los Angeles. Died: 1982.

### Fran Allison *Hostess*      6757 Hollywood

**Born:** 1925, in La Porte City, IA.

**Spotlights:** Popular in her well-loved children's puppet show, "Kukla, Fran, and Ollie" (1947–57). The only live member of the "cast," she was extremely witty. The entire show was improvised.

### Joseph Schenck *Film pioneer, producer*      6755 Hollywood

**Born:** Dec. 25, 1878, in Russia.

**Spotlights:** Associated with MGM before becoming an independent producer in 1917. Head of United Artists in 1924 before co-founding 20th Century in 1933; two years later top executive of 20th Century-Fox.

**Achievements:** 1952, special Oscar.

**Sidelights:** Lived the rags-to-riches American dream. Died: 1961.

### Richard Barthelmess *Actor*      6755 Hollywood

**Born:** May 9, 1895, in New York,

**Spotlights:** The handsome leading man in D. W. Griffith's *Broken Blossoms* (1919). In *Way Down East* (1920), he was one of the silent era's first romantic heros.

**Achievements:** Academy Award nominations for *The Patent Leather Kid* (1927) and *The Noose* (1928). Died: 1963, of cancer.

## Richard Arlen  *Actor*  6755 Hollywood

**Born:** Cornelius Mattimore; Sept. 1, 1899, in Charlottesville, VA.
**Spotlights:** Was an extra in 1920, then moved on to bit parts and supporting roles. In *Wings* (1927), his acting talent soared. Vacillated between leading and supporting roles into the 1970s. Died: 1976, from lung congestion.

## Joel Grey  *Actor*  6755 Hollywood

**Born:** Joel Katz; April 11, 1932, in Cleveland, OH.
**Spotlights:** Lithe, precise, energetic Grey began performing on stage when he was 9 (he starred as Pud in *On Borrowed Time* at the Cleveland Playhouse). By 19, he had entertained at New York's Copacabana and the London Palladium. Broadway plays include *George M!* and *The Grand Tour*; more. TV and films too.
**Achievements:** 1967, Tony Award, Best Supporting Actor, *Cabaret*. 1972, Oscar, Best Supporting Actor, *Cabaret*.

## Ilka Chase  *See page 93.*  6755 Hollywood

## Eddie Bracken  *Actor, comedian*  6751 Hollywood

**Born:** Feb. 7, 1920, in Astoria, Long Island, N.Y.
**Spotlights:** 5′ 10″, 165-lb., blue-eyed, wavy brown-haired stage and television screen talent. Won a "cute babies" contest at age 4 and has been "wowing 'em" ever since. Films include: *Too Many Girls* (1940), *Sweater Girl* (1942), *Bring on the Girls* (1945), *National Lampoon's Vacation* (1983). TV: "I've Got a Secret" panelist (1952); "Masquerade Party" moderator (1957).

## Hanna-Barbera  William Hanna and Joseph Barbera  6751 Hollywood
### *Cartoon animators, creators, producers*

**Born:** Hanna, July 14, 1911, in Melrose, NM; Barbera, March 24, 1911, in New York.
**Spotlights:** The Hanna-Barbera Company, founded in 1957, produced "The Flint-stones" and "Yogi Bear," among other popular cartoon series.
**Achievements:** Collected seven Academy Awards for cartoons, including *Tom and Jerry*; 1973 and 1974 Emmys.

## Ken Maynard  *Actor*  6751 Hollywood

**Born:** July 21, 1895, in Vevay, IN.
**Spotlights:** Big Saturday matinee cowboy idol in hundreds of westerns. A trick rider on his Palomino horse named Tarzan. Pleased fans during the 1920s and 1930s with *Senor Daredevil* (1926) and *Song of the Caballero* (1931). Died: 1973, of malnutrition.

Charles Chaplin          Betty White          Rod McKuen

## Charles Chaplin  *Pantomimist, actor, director,*    **6751 Hollywood**
*producer, screenwriter, composer*

**Born:** April 16, 1889, in England.

**Spotlights:** The greatest silent screen comedian. His endearing "Little Tramp" character, with mustache, bowler hat, baggy trousers, and cane, brought both laughter and tears to his films, which were ingeniously made. Comedy shorts, *The Rink* (1916) and *Easy Street* (1917), and feature-length films, *The Kid* 1921, and *The Gold Rush* (1925) and, with sound, *Modern Times* (1936) and *The Great Dictator* (1940).

**Achievements:** 1927–28, special Academy Award. 1973, special Academy Award. Knighted by the Queen of England in 1975 (Sir Charles Spencer Chaplin). Died: 1977.

## Bing Crosby  *See page 251.*    **6751 Hollywood**

# ⋆ 6743 HOLLYWOOD ⋆

**Tyrone Power**  🎥  *Actor*  6743 Hollywood

**Born:**  May 5, 1913, in Cincinnati, OH.

**Spotlights:**  One of Hollywood's most handsome stars in the late 1930s and early 1940s. Was a major box office asset, among the Top Ten, 1938–40. One of his best films, *Witness for the Prosecution* (1957), was also his last. Other noteworthy films include such widely different types as *The Razor's Edge* (1946) and *Nightmare Alley* (1947), where his acting capacity outshone his beauty. Died: 1958, of a heart attack on a movie set, as did his father.

**Betty White**  📺  *Actress*  6743 Hollywood

**Born:**  Jan. 17, 1924, in Oak Park, IL.

**Spotlights:**  Her perky radio personality led to starring roles on TV shows in the early 1950s. Pretty, friendly, funny wife on "Life with Elizabeth" and "Date with the Angels". Her own "Betty White Show" has been both a comedy- variety and a situation comedy. Absolutely delicious as Sue Ann Nivens (1973–77) on "The Mary Tyler Moore Show." Her sense of humor makes her one of "The Golden Girls."

**Achievements:**  Four-time Emmy winner.

**Sidelights:**  Her secret to happiness? Pick up a copy of her book, *Betty White's Pet Love* (1983), published by William Morrow.

**Gary Owens**  🎙  *Disc jockey, announcer, actor*  6743 Hollywood

**Born:**  May 10, 1936, in Mitchell, S.Dak.

**Spotlights:**  Gained national recognition on TV's "Laugh-In" (1968–73). Distinctive voice, humorous, pleasant style, star of Los Angeles radio show. Also writes and does voices for cartoons.

**Walt Disney**  📺  *See page 364.*  6743 Hollywood

**Rod McKuen**  💿  *Poet, pop and classical composer,*  6743 Hollywood
*songwriter, performer*

**Born:**  April 29, 1933, in Oakland, CA.

**Spotlights:**  Songs include "Jean," "Listen to the Warm," "Stanyan Street" (sung by Glen Yarbrough).

**Achievements:**  1968, Grammy, "Spoken Work."

**Dick Powell**  📺  *See page 21.*  6743 Hollywood

## Shari Lewis ![TV icon] *Ventriloquist, puppeteer*  6743 Hollywood

**Born:** Shari Hurwitz; Jan. 17, 1934, in Bronx, N.Y.

**Spotlights:** Like a multifaceted diamond, Lewis is famous for brilliant talents in diversified areas. Baby boomers recall growing up with her right hand lamb, Lamb Chop, Charlie Horse, and Hush Puppy. The puppets were back on "The Shari Show," 1976–77. An emancipated woman, she has conducted more than 200 symphony orchestras. Author of 29 books.

**Achievements:** Five Emmys.

**Highlights:** Married to L. A. book publisher, Jeremy Tarcher.

## King Vidor ![Camera icon] *Director*  6743 Hollywood

**Born:** Feb. 8, 1894, in Galveston, TX.

**Spotlights:** Long and distinguished directing career began in silent films. Early movies attempted to make social statements, but his later work was motivated by commercial demands. One of his best films, *Northwest Passage* (1940), demonstrates full maturity of craftsmanship. Other films include *The Champ* (1931), *The Citadel* (1938), *The Fountainhead* (1949).

**Achievements:** 1979, honorary Oscar. Died: 1982.

*Shari Lewis and Lamb Chop*

## Harold Robbins  *Author*                 6743 Hollywood

**Born:**  Francis Kane; May 21, 1916, in Hell's Kitchen, New York.

**Spotlights:**  An orphan. Began to write when he was 30 years old. Used his real name as a hero in his first novel, *Never Love a Stranger*, published in 1948. Writes "people" stories about riches, sex, fancy automobiles, life in the fast lane. Describes his books as "picturesque novels about doomed people." *The Carpetbaggers* (1967), *The Betsy* (1967), and *Lonely Lady* (1976) were a few of his novels turned into movies.

**Sidelights:**  Over 25 thousand people a day buy his books, which have been translated into almost every printed language and are sold in 57 foreign countries.

## Anne Baxter  *Actress*                 6743 Hollywood

**Born:**  May 7, 1923, in Michigan City, IN.

**Spotlights:**  Her 1936 debut on Broadway in *Seen but Not Heard* launched her brilliant film career: *The Razor's Edge* (1946) and *All About Eve* (1950). Star of TV's "Hotel" series until her death.

**Achievements:**  1946, Best Supporting Actress Oscar. Died: 1985, of a heart attack.

## Liberace  *See page 76.*                 6739 Hollywood

## Jane Darwell  *Actress*                 6737 Hollywood

**Born:**  Patti Woodward; Oct. 15, 1880, in Palmyra, MO.

**Spotlights:**  Stage, screen, and television star. Films include *Rose of the Rancho* (1914), *Jimmy the Gent* (1934); and *Mary Poppins* (1964); 150 other pictures.

**Achievements:**  1940, Best Supporting Actress Academy Award for *The Grapes of Wrath*. She portrayed Ma Joad. Died: 1967, of a heart attack.

## Doris Day  *See page 198*                 6735 Hollywood

## Carleton Young  *Actor*                 6733 Hollywood

**Born:**  May 26, 1907, in New York.

**Spotlights:**  Lead role in "The Adventures of Ellery Queen." First aired on CBS in 1939, on NBC in 1941. Starring role in "The Count of Monte Cristo" (1946). Died: 1971.

**Ann Blyth**  *Actress, singer*  6733 Hollywood

**Born:** Aug. 16, 1928, in Mt. Kisco, N.Y.

**Spotlights:** Her vengeful portrayal of Joan Crawford's daughter in *Mildred Pierce* (1945) was truly good and horrifying. Her well-trained singing voice was used in MGM musicals before she retired from films at age 29.

**Thomas Ince**  *Producer, director*  6727 Hollywood

**Born:** Nov. 6, 1882, in Newport, R.I.

**Spotlights:** "The Pioneer Producer-Director of Films." Began acting on stage, as soon as he could walk and talk. Film work paid more than stage so he worked in front of the camera until 1911, when he directed his first picture, *Across the Plains*. High quality, strong story, and realism his trademarks. Often wrote screenplays for his silent films — innovative in his detailed script writing. Brought honesty to American westerns (starring William S. Hart). *Civilization* (1916), one of his masterpieces. Died: 1924.

**Owen Moore** *Actor*  6725 Hollywood

**Born:** Dec. 12, 1886, in Ireland.

**Spotlights:** Romantic leading man during silent era, especially opposite "America's Sweetheart," Mary Pickford, in *The Call to Arms* (1910).

**Highlights:** Married to co-star Pickford (1909–15). Died: 1939.

**Arturo Toscanini** *See page 277.*  6723 Hollywood

**The Spinners** *Detroit-based soul harmony group*  6723 Hollywood

Original 1957 members were Bobby Smith and Billy Henderson (tenors), Henry Fambrough (baritone), Pervis Jackson (bass). G. C. Cameron became a member in the late 1960s, and departed in 1971. Lead vocalist Phillipe Wynne signed on in 1971, but left in 1977. John Edwards teamed with the group in 1980.

**Spotlights:** Rhythm and blues singing sensation inspired by the doo-wop style of groups such as the Clovers and Flamingos. Album: *Lovin' Feelings*. Singles: "Could It Be I'm Falling in Love," "I'll Be Around," "It's a Shame." Big hit with the remake of The Four Seasons' song, "I'm Working My Way Back To You."

**Sidelights:** The name of their band is Motown's slang word for hubcaps.

**Aileen Pringle** *Actress*  6723 Hollywood

**Born:** Aileen Bisbee; July 23, 1895, in San Francisco, CA.

**Spotlights:** Provocative, dark-haired, gray-green eyed, 5' 4", 119-lb. stage- trained starlet of the silent screen: *Redhead* (1919) and *A Kiss in the Dark* (1925).

**Ernest Truex** *Actor*  6721 Hollywood

**Born:** Sept. 19, 1890, in Kansas City, MO.

**Spotlights:** Was already into his sixties when he was cast in several situation comedies. Memorable in "Mr. Peepers" (1952–55) as Mr. Remington. Died: 1973.

### Oscar Micheaux 🎥 *Writer, director, producer* 6721 Hollywood
**Born:** 1889, in Metropolis, IL (most likely).
**Spotlights:** Not much known about his childhood, but he was the first black independent filmmaker to initiate and sustain a film company. In response to racist scenes in *The Birth of a Nation* (1915), his film *The Birth of a Race* (1918) portrayed a different view of black people. Micheaux's film, *The Homesteader* (1919), was an adaptation of his novel which was published in 1913. High quality, conscious *Symbol of the Unconquered* (1921) pictures were also entertaining; *Body and Soul* (1924). Died: 1951.

### Harry Belafonte 💿 *Singer, actor* 6721 Hollywood
**Born:** March 1, 1927, in Harlem, N.Y.
**Spotlights:** Gained recognition for his calypso (West Indian) music. His beautiful voice made memorable hits of "Day-O," "Matilda, Matilda," "When the Saints Go Marching In," and "Mama Look a Boo Boo." TV and films too.
**Achievements:** 1960, three Grammys; 1961 and 1965, Grammys; 1960 Emmy.
**Highlights:** His lovely actress daughter, Shari, can be seen on TV's "Hotel."

### Dorothy Dandridge 🎥 *Actress* 6719 Hollywood
**Born:** Nov. 9, 1923, in Cleveland, OH.

*Harry Belafonte*

**Spotlights:** A beautiful singer and dancer in *A Day at the Races* (1937), *Carmen Jones* (1954), *Porgy and Bess* (1959). Died: 1965.

**Barton Maclane**  *Actor*                    6719 Hollywood

**Born:** Dec. 25, 1902, in Columbia, SC.
**Spotlights:** Star of "The Outlaws" (1960–61), as U. S. Marshal Frank Caine. Played commanding officer, General Martin Peterson (1965–69), on "I Dream of Jeannie." Made over 200 motion pictures. Died: 1969.

**Dr. Frank C. Baxter** *Lecturer, host*                    6717 Hollywood

**Born:** 1897.
**Spotlights:** "Telephone Time" host (1957–58), he selected plays from original short stories and used relatively unknown talent in each show. The "Dr." stood for Ph.D. Died: 1982.

**Yvonne Decarlo** *See page 181.*                    6715 Hollywood

**Ken Niles** *Host, actor*                    6715 Hollywood

**Born:** Dec. 9, 1906, in Livingston, MT.

*Dorothy Dandridge*

**Spotlights:** "Crime detective" announcer on "Big Town," which starred Edward G. Robinson and Ona Munson (CBS, 1937); comic regular on "The Abbott and Costello Show" (NBC, 1942); more.

### Fred Allen   *Comedian, writer*                                6711 Hollywood

**Born:** John Sullivan; May 31, 1894, in Cambridge, MA.

**Spotlights:** Kicked off his career in vaudeville, then went to New York stage before becoming America's king of satire. He wrote much of his own acerbic radio material on "The Fred Allen Show" (1932–49). Skits included the "Mr. & Mrs. Show," "The Average Man's Round Table," and "People You Don't Expect to Meet." No subject was safe from Allen's parodies. Tallulah Bankhead, Alfred Hitchcock, and hundreds of other stars appeared on his show over the years. His catch phrase: "That's a joke, son!" A long-running comedy "feud" with Jack Benny (1936-49) started when Allen accused Benny of being incompetent as a violinist. The end of Allen's show marked the end of an era in radio's golden years.

**Sidelights:** He once said about tinseltown: "You can take all the sincerity in Hollywood, put it in a flea's navel, and have room left over for three caraway seeds and an agent's heart." Witty panelist on TV's quiz show, "What's My Line?" (1954–56). It's ironic that Allen ever agreed to appear on TV, and that he was honored with a TV star on the Walk of Fame. It was a well-known fact that he despised that form of entertainment. "When vaudeville died, TV was the box that they buried it in." Died: 1956.

### George Reeves   *Actor*                                        6709 Hollywood

**Born:** George Besselo; April 6, 1914, in Woodstock, IA.

**Spotlights:** "Faster than a speeding bullet" in "The Adventures of Superman" (1951–57) as Superman Clark Kent.

**Sidelights:** The bank building on the northeast corner of Hollywood and Highland served as Superman's takeoff point. His debut film work? As Brent Tarleton in "Gone With the Wind" (1939). Died: 1959.

### Madeleine Carroll   *Actress*                                   6705 Hollywood

**Born:** Marie O'Carroll; Feb. 26, 1906, in England.

**Spotlights:** Elegant blond beauty. One of the most exquisitely sculptured faces to grace the silver screen. Alfred Hitchcock directed her in comedy thriller *The Thirty-Nine Steps* (1935) and *The Secret Agent* (1936).

**Highlights:** Married to actor Sterling Hayden (1942–46) and *Life* magazine publisher Andrew Heiskel (1950–65).

**Sidelights:** After her sister was killed in World War II, she dedicated countless hours to peace movements and aiding war victims.

### Nils Asther   *Actor*                                           6705 Hollywood

**Born:** Jan. 17, 1897, in Denmark.

**Spotlights:**   Active in silent films, career slowed down with the arrival of sound because of his thick, Scandinavian accent. However, he was extremely popular as the Chinese warlord in Capra's *The Bitter Tea of General Yen* (1933), opposite Barbara Stanwyck. Died: 1981.

## Mary Livingston   Actress                                    6701 Hollywood

**Born:**   Sadie Marks; June 22, 1909, in Seattle, WA.
**Spotlights:**   Mary was girlfriend to the "stingy, vain, always 39-year-old" comic star on "The Jack Benny Show" (CBS, first broadcast 1932). A lot of the show's humor derived from her poking fun at Jack Benny. "Now cut that out!"
**Highlights:**   Married to Jack Benny in 1927 in real life.
**Sidelights:**   Author of *Jack Benny* (1978). Died: 1983.

## Roscoe Arbuckle   Comedian                                   6701 Hollywood

**Born:**   March 24, 1887, in Smith Center, KS.
**Spotlights:**   As a youngster growing up in Santa Ana, California, "Fatty" sold tickets at carnivals and performed in blackface on vaudeville before landing a job ($3 a day) with Mack Sennett's Keystone Cops; audiences roared at his fat cop routine. Working with such all-time comedy greats as Charlie Chaplin, *The Rounders* (1914), Fatty Arbuckle rose to stardom. Wrote and directed comedy shorts. In 1917 joined forces with Joseph M. Schenck and recruited the brilliant, stone-face Buster Keaton — an old vaudeville pal — for *The Butcher Boy* (1917). By 1920 he was on top of the film world, earning $7,000 per week, but the fickle finger of fate pointed in his direction, and by 1921 no one would touch him.
**Sidelights:**   Died: 1933, of a heart attack.

## Mary Astor   Actress                                         6701 Hollywood

**Born:**   Lucille Langhanke; May 3, 1906, in Quincy, IL.
**Spotlights:**   Beautiful brunette active during the silent era; leading lady opposite John Barrymore in *Beau Brummel* (1924). Memorable in *The Maltese Falcon* (1941), opposite Humphrey Bogart.
**Achievements:**   1941 Best Supporting Actress Oscar for *The Great Life*.

## Jean Hersholt   *See page 80.*                               6701 Hollywood

# ⋆ 6689 HOLLYWOOD ⋆

**Faye Emerson**  *See page 76.*      6689 Hollywood

**Ruth Warrick** 🎥 *Actress*
**Born:** June 29, 1915, in St. Louis, MO.
**Spotlights:** One who really loves her work. Debut in *Citizen Kane* (1941); last film, *The Great Bank Robbery* (1969). Stage work on Broadway and many years a top star on ABC's TV soap opera "All My Children" (still on in 1987).

**John Payne** 📺 *See page 171.*      6687 Hollywood

**Myrna Loy** 🎥 *Actress*      6685 Hollywood
**Born:** Myrna Williams; Aug. 2, 1905, in Helena, MT.
**Spotlights:** This petite redhead made 59 movies and was known as the "Oriental Vamp" before her "break" in *The Animal Kingdom* (1932) as "publisher" Leslie Howard's vile wife. MGM paired her with Clark Gable next, *Night Flight* (1933), then very sucessfully with William Powell in sophisticated comedy as a loving, wisecracking couple, *The Thin Man* (1934).
**Sidelights:** Voted "Queen of Hollywood" to Clark Gable's "King" by film-going public in 1936.

**Harry James** 💿 *Jazz trumpeter*      6683 Hollywood
**Born:** May 15, 1916, in Albany, GA.
**Spotlights:** Became a leading member of Benny Goodman's band in 1937. Recorded "Ridin' High" on Goodman's *Jazz Concert, Number 2* album. Formed own big band in 1938, and was very successful. Played throughout the 1970s. Spectacular jazz of the Swing Era. Died: 1983.

**Gene Roddenberry** 📺 *Writer, producer*      6683 Hollywood
**Born:** Aug. 19, 1921, in El Paso, TX.
**Spotlights:** Creator-producer of the sci-fi phenomenon "Star Trek" (1966–69); also *Star Trek—the Motion Picture* (1979), *Star Trek II* (1980), *III* (1984), *IV* (1986), and the voyage continues.

**Gene Lockhart** 📺 *See page 104.*      6681 Hollywood

**George Takei** 📺 *Actor*      6681 Hollywood
**Born:** April 20, in Los Angeles, CA.

**Spotlights:** Attended UCLA. Asian-American actor most famous for his TV and film roles portraying Mr. Sulu on "Star Trek." Takei has appeared on the "Twilight Zone," "Matt Houston," and made other guest appearances.

### Arthur Kennedy 🎥 *Actor* 6681 Hollywood

**Born:** John A. Kennedy; Feb. 17, 1914, in Worcester, MA.
**Achievements:** Nominated for Best Supporting Actor for *Champion* (1949); 1950, nominated for Best Actor for *Bright Victory; Trial* (1955); *Peyton Place* (1957); *Some Came Running* (1958). Five times nominated, but never won. TV: narrator of "F.D.R.," documentary (1965).
**Sidelights:** Who discovered him? "Jimmy the Gent" (James Cagney).

### Mary Carlisle 🎥 *Actress* 6679 Hollywood

**Born:** Feb. 3, 1912, in Boston, MA.
**Spotlights:** Paramount's blond, blue-eyed co-ed in the musical comedy, *College Humor* (1933), also starring Bing Crosby, Jack Oakie, George Burns, Gracie Allen, and Richard Arlen. Retired from show biz in 1943 after marrying.

### Guy Lombardo 🎙 *Bandleader* 6677 Hollywood

**Born:** Gaetano Lombardo, June 19, 1902, in Canada.
**Spotlights:** Radio: Guy Lombardo was a big attraction on "The Robert Burns Panaleta Show." First broadcast in 1932, this comedy-variety show starred George Burns and Gracie Allen, with jokes about Gracie's "missing brother." Lombardo was also famous for his fabulous New Year's Eve broadcasts. TV: "Guy Lombardo and His

*Gene Roddenberry*                    *George Takei*

Royal Canadians" (1954–56) and "Guy Lombardo's Diamond Jubilee" (1956).
**Sidelights:** Orchestrated the big band sound in the 1930s and 1940s with the slogan, "The Royal Canadians, with the sweetest music this side of heaven." His musically talented brothers and sisters often performed with him.

### Robert Guillaume ◼ *Actor*                      6675 Hollywood
**Born:** Robert Williams, Nov. 30, 1937, in St. Louis, MO.
**Spotlights:** Multi-talented, highly regarded celebrity. His role as the uppity servant, Benson (1977–79) on "Soap" was so funny that ABC gave him his own situation comedy "Benson" (1979–). Broadway musicals too.
**Achievements:** 1978–79, Emmy, Outstanding Supporting Actor in a series, "Soap."

### Betty Furness ◼ *Actress*                      6675 Hollywood
**Born:** Jan. 3, 1916, in New York, NY.
**Spotlights:** At 16 years old, she was blond, blue-eyed, 5' 4", 100 lb. sophisticated leading lady on film. Became famous to a nation of television viewers as a spokeswoman: You can "be sure if it's a Westinghouse." She opened hundreds of refrigerator doors betwen 1949–60. That credibility opened official doors, too. Furness became President Johnson's top adviser on Consumer Affairs. Proved intelligent in tracking down safety malfunctions, as well as being concerned with typical consumer rip-offs, such as the amount of water in canned ham. Grew up to be 5' 5½", and is as attractive and as svelte as ever. Is NBC's consumer reporter, a regular on the highly rated "Today" show.
**Sidelights:** Her family's golden rule: "Behave well, apply yourself, and do your very best because nothing else is acceptable."

### George Peppard 🎥 *Actor, producer, director*                      6675 Hollywood
**Born:** Oct. 1, 1928, in Detroit, MI.
**Spotlights:** Abrasive, blue-eyed toughie who briefly dipped into softer roles: *Breakfast at Tiffany's* (1961) and *The Carpetbaggers* (1964).
**Sidelights:** TV fans know him as Colonel John "Hannibal" Smith on "The A-Team" (1983–).

### Ferlin Husky 🎵 *Guitarist, singer, songwriter, comedian*                      6675 Hollywood
**Born:** Dec. 3, 1927, in Flat River, MO.
**Spotlights:** Used other stage names: Simon Crum, and Terry Preston. Ferlin Husky and His Hush Puppies. Hits include: "Fallen Star," "On the Wings of a Dove," "Walkin' and Hummin," "Country Music is Here to Stay" (comic).

### Vin Scully 🎙 *Sportscaster*                      6675 Hollywood
**Born:** Nov. 29, 1927, in New York.
**Spotlights:** Intelligent, enthusiastic super sports fan, who hooked up with the Dod-

gers baseball in the 1950s. Broadcasts golf too. Affiliated with CBS; NBC.
**Achievements:**   1982 Baseball Hall of Fame.

**Tommy Dorsey**   *Jazz trombonist and bandleader*          6675 Hollywood
**Born:**   Thomas Dorsey; Nov. 19, 1905, in Shenandoah, PA.
**Spotlights:**   During the big band era, the Dorsey brothers gained international "boogie woogie" fame via radio and recording. The Tommy Dorsey Orchestra made its debut on "The Kate Smith Evening Hour" in 1951 and became known for rendering ballads at dance tempos. By 1954 Tommy and brother Jimmy had their own musical variety program, "Stage Show." Their theme song: "I'm Getting Sentimental over You." Elvis Presley made his spectacular TV debut on "Stage Show" singing "Heartbreak Hotel." A phenomenal success, Presley appeared on the Dorsey show for the next 6 weeks.
**Sidelights:**   In 1940 at the Apollo Theater in New York City, Dorsey joined Count Basie, Harry James, Coleman Hawkins, Gene Krupa, Benny Goodman, and other jazz greats for the hottest session of all time. Died: 1956.

**Glen A. Larson**   *Writer, producer, director*          6673 Hollywood
**Spotlights:**   A former singer (The Four Preps) who has worked in various capacities creating or producing TV series, including *It Takes A Thief* (1968–70); *McCloud* (1970–77), *Alias Smith and Jones* (1971–73, the show suffered a tragic loss when Peter Deuel "Hannibal Heyes/Joshua Smith" allegedly committed suicide by gunshot); and *The Six Million Dollar Man* (1974–78).
**Sidelights:**   Wrote "B. J. and the Bear" theme song.

**Flora Finch**   *Comedienne*          6673 Hollywood
**Born:**   Feb. 11, 1869, in England.
**Spotlights:**   *A Cure for Pokeritis* (1912); *Bunny's Mistake* (1913), with comedian John Bunny. She was the skinny half of the comedy team, he the fat half. Made over 200 one- and two-reelers; *Bunny Buys a Harem* (1914). Died: 1940.

**Ted Knight**   *Actor*          6673 Hollywood
**Born:**   Tadeus Konopka; Dec. 7, 1925, in Terryville, CT.
**Spotlights:**   He played Ted Baxter, a bumbling, egotistic anchorman at WJM-TV news on "The Mary Tyler Moore Show" (1970–77). Was star Henry Rush on "Too Close for Comfort" (1980–83).
**Achievements:**   Emmy, 1972–73; 1976–76. Died: 1986, from cancer.

**Licia Albanese**   *Opera Singer*          6671 Hollywood
**Born:**   July 22, 1913, in Bari, Italy.
**Spotlights:**   Renowned soprano, performed many lead roles in Italian and French during her long association with the Metropolitan Opera. Recordings: Puccini's *La Boheme*, Verdi's *La Traviata*.

## Jerry Dunphy  *Announcer*

**Born:** June 9, in Milwaukee, WI.

**Spotlights:** "From the desert to the sea, to all of Southern California-good evening." This has been "the Dunph's" catchphrase every weekday evening for over 20 years as the award-winning "Eyewitness News" anchor of Los Angeles' Channel 7. Memorable broadcast "Nixon/Dunphy: 90 Minutes Live" (1979). Enjoys a second career writing lyrics since 1986.

**Achievements:** Has an impressive collection of Emmys and Golden Mikes.

## Patsy Kelly  *Actress*

6669 Hollywood

**Born:** Jan. 10, 1910, in Brooklyn, N.Y.

**Spotlights:** Strong comedienne and pretty good at putting her hooves down: *Pigskin Parade* (1936), *Merrily We Live* (1938), and *Topper Returns* (1941). Died: 1981.

## Andy Williams  *Singer, actor*

6669 Hollywood

**Born:** Howard A. Williams; Dec. 3, 1928, in Wall Lake, IA.

**Spotlights:** Easy listening, smooth, warm, romantic singer whose comfortable manner enhanced his TV programs, 1958–71. Theme song: "Moon River." Songs: "Danny Boy," "Twelfth of Never."

**Achievements:** Emmy, 1966.

## Frank Lloyd  *Director, producer*

6667 Hollywood

**Born:** Feb. 2, 1888, in Scotland.

**Spotlights:** Outstanding job on the original *Mutiny on the Bounty* (1935), starring Charles Laughton and Clark Gable. Directed and produced *Wells Fargo* (1937).

**Achievements:** 1929, Best Director, *The Divine Lady*, 1933, Best Director, *Cavalcade*. Died: 1960.

## John Barrymore  *Actor*

6667 Hollywood

**Born:** John Blythe; Feb. 15, 1882, in Philadelphia, PA.

**Spotlights:** His spellbinding Hamlet on the London stage in 1922, and his discerning performances in the silent *Dr. Jekyll and Mr. Hyde* (1920), in which he transformed himself without makeup.

**Sidelights:** Known as The Great Profile and billed as The Great Lover. Died: 1941, of pneumonia.

## Aaron Spelling  *Producer, executive*

6667 Hollywood

**Born:** April 22, 1928, in Dallas, TX.

**Spotlights:** Highly intelligent, articulate, well-respected individual. So many hit series, difficult to name them all. Successes such as "Charlie's Angels" (1976–81), "The Love Boat" (1977–85), "Fantasy Island" (1978–84), and, my favorite, "Dynasty" (1981–) keep Americans and foreigners alike entertained.

**Buck Owens**  💿  *Singer, musician*                6667 Hollywood
**Born:** Aug. 12, 1929, in Sherman, TX.
**Spotlights:** Colorful country-and-western singer: "Together Again," "Crying Time."
Co-host of TV's "Hee Haw" (1969–71 on CBS; syndicated since 1971).

**Gene Autry**  📺  *See page 312.*                6667 Hollywood

**Quinn Martin**  📺  *Executive, producer*                6667 Hollywood
**Born:** May 22, 1927, in Los Angeles, CA.
**Spotlights:** Keen eye for assembling talent and packages for top shows, including:
"The Fugitive" (1963–67), "The Untouchables" (1959–63), and "The Streets of San
Francisco" (1972–77).

**Harrison Ford**  🎥  *Actor*                6667 Hollywood
**Born:** March 16, 1892, in Kansas City, MO.
**Spotlights:** I know millions of his fans are going to be disappointed to learn that the
Harrison Ford who was immortalized on the Walk of Fame is not the same Harrison
Ford (born July 13, 1942, in Chicago) of *Star Wars* (1977) and *Raiders of the Lost
Ark* (1981). That handsome, light-haired talent deserves one, too, but it does present
a problem. Both actors were christened with the name, both perform in the motion
picture category. It's the first time in the Walk's history that this has happened. The
only solution I can think of for *The Empire Strikes Back* (1980) hero is to include his
middle initial to differentiate himself. The Ford who received a star was a charming,
good-looking, box office attraction of the silent screen: *Passion Flower* (1921),
opposite Norma Talmadge; *Vanity Fair* (1923), with Mabel Ballin, *Little Old New
York* (1923), co-starring Marion Davies. Retired a wealthy man in 1932. Died: 1957.

**William Demarest**  🎥  *Actor*                6667 Hollywood
**Born:** Feb. 27, 1892, in St. Paul, MN.
**Spotlights:** Character actor from vaudeville days. *The Jazz Singer* (1927), *Mr. Smith
Goes to Washington* (1939), *It's a Mad Mad Mad Mad World* (1963).
**Sidelights:** TV's Uncle Charlie O'Casey in "My Three Sons" (1965–72). Died: 1983.

**Freddie Bartholomew**  🎥  *Actor*                6667 Hollywood
**Born:** Frederick Llewellyn; March 28, 1924, in England.
**Spotlights:** Although little Freddie came from a family of modest means, he had a
gentleness about him that indicated he was of aristocratic lineage. His Aunt Cissie
spotted the boy's talent while he was reciting, and it was under her guidance that he
was cast in the title role of *David Copperfield* (1935) and landed a 7-year contract
with MGM. Greta Garbo adored him and he played her son in *Anna Karenina* (1935).
**Sidelights:** The child's salary? One grand per week.

## Mark Serrurier Moviola 🎥 *Inventor, developer of film editing technology* 6667 Hollywood

**Spotlights:** Creator of the Moviola, an editing device. An indispensable piece of equipment, it has a small screen, controlled by a foot pedal, for viewing a film at any speed, slow, normal, or fast. It can also freeze a frame for close examination. Handles sound synchronization.

**Achievements:** 1979, Oscar "for having kept pace effectively to meet the demands of the motion picture technology."

**Sidelights:** His father, Iwan Serrurier, was an inventor and pioneer designer of the Midget, a 1924 film editing bench. The Moviola evolved from this.

## Peter Donald 📺 *Comedian* 6665 Hollywood

**Spotlights:** One of four comedians who told jokes on "Can You Top This?" (1950–51). Panelist (1952–53) on "Masquerade Party," an entertaining show on which the clues for the disguised celebrities were their costumes. Ha! Let them eat cake. A regular on "Pantomine Quiz" (1953–55, 1957).

## Harry Ackerman 📺 *Executive, producer* 6665 Hollywood

**Born:** Nov. 17, 1912, in New York.

**Spotlights:** Creative force associated with Screen Gems. Many success stories include "Dennis the Menace" (1959–63), "Hazel" (1961–65), and "Bewitched" (1964–72).

**Sidelights:** Broke into show biz as a writer.

## Douglas Fairbanks, Jr. 📺 *See page 271.* 6665 Hollywood

## Robert Cummings 🎥 *Actor* 6663 Hollywood

**Born:** Clarence Cummings; June 10, 1908, in Joplin, MO.

**Spotlights:** Ever youthful in *College Swing* (1938); sincere characterization in *Dial M for Murder* (1954). "The Bob Cummings Show" on TV (1955–59) starred him as playboy bachelor photographer, Bob Collins. His infatuated secretary? Charmaine (Shultzy) Schultz.

## Nat "King" Cole 💿 *Singer, pianist* 6655 Hollywood

**Born:** Nathanial Coles; March 17, 1919, in Montgomery, AL.

**Spotlights:** Jazz-rooted. Sung with a "masculine gentleness." Gigantic selling recording singles: "Mona Lisa," "Looking Back," "Ramblin' Rose," "Send for Me," "Too Young," "That Sunday That Summer," "Unforgettable." TV: Made network history in 1953 by becoming the first black entertainer to have his own show: "The Nat 'King' Cole Show" (NBC, 1956–57). Died: 1965, of lung cancer.

## Reginald Denny  *Actor*      6655 Hollywood

**Born:** Reginald Daymore; Nov. 2, 1891, in England.
**Spotlights:** During the silent era, a star whose supporting character roles in talkies were portrayals of slightly silly, dapper Englishmen. Algy in the *Bulldog Drummond* series (1937–39); *The Secret Life of Walter Mitty* (1947). Died: 1967.

## Fritz Kreisler *Musician*      6655 Hollywood

**Born:** Feb. 2, 1875, in Austria.
**Spotlights:** World-famous violinist who played so elegantly he could make people cry. His music also heard in films. Died: 1962.

## Iron Eyes Cody *Actor, consultant*      6655 Hollywood

**Born:** Little Eagle; in 1916, in Bacone, OK.
**Spotlights:** Cherokee Indian. Technical adviser on Indian matters in countless TV and film productions, including Disney's *Westward Ho the Wagons* (1956). For example, Cody explained the cultural tradition of painted faces: "The young Indian man has a vision and paints his face accordingly. The different colors symbolize different things. Green is good, red is war, yellow is sun, and blue is for the clouds and the Great Spirit. After a young man has had his vision, he fasts and meditates. Then he takes a sweat bath to purify himself and dances. Then he is a man." Gained national recognition in the "Pollution: It's a Crying Shame" TV commercials. The "Keep America Beautiful" campaign was launched in 1971. Cody's impact on viewers' minds is staggering. Most people can easily recall his saddened expression as he looks at litter with a tear rolling down his face. Guest actor in "Wagon Train" and "The Virginian" (throughout the 1960s); more. Played a cowboy once in Tony Bill's *Hearts of the West* (1975); 241 movie credits; one of the few living experts in Sioux sign language. Annual Indian representative for decades in both Hollywood Christmas Parade and Rose Parade.

## Dorothy Sebastian  *Actress*      6655 Hollywood

**Born:** April 26, 1903, in Birmingham, AL.
**Spotlights:** Fresh, sexy leading lady of 25 silents who made the transition to talkies for a few years: *Among the Living* (1941). Died: 1957.

## Alan Hale, Jr. *Actor*      6655 Hollywood

**Born:** Alan MacKahn; March 8, 1918, in Los Angeles, CA.
**Spotlights:** The skipper of the charter fishing boat *Minnow* remained robust and merry, even when stranded on "Gilligan's Island" (1964–67). Previously, he was adventurer "Biff Baker U.S.A." (1952–53).
**Highlights:** Talent runs in the family, father was actor Alan Hale.

## Antonio Moreno 🎥 *Actor*

**Born:** Sept. 26, 1886, in Spain.

**Spotlights:** Aristocratic Latin lover, who romanced the loveliest leading ladies of the silent era. Aged gracefully for character roles; sporadically in talkies from 1930 to 1950s. Died: 1967, of a stroke.

## Dean Martin 📺 *See page 77.*

## Phil Harris 🎤 *Actor, musician, orchestra leader*

**Born:** June 24, 1906, in Linton, IN.

**Spotlights:** Formed his own band in 1931, earned orchestra billing in 1932 on radio's "The Jack Benny Show" and was a regular on radio's "Kay Kyser's Kollege of Musical Knowledge" (1938). Teamed with wife (since 1941) on radio's "The Phil Harris-Alice Faye Show," comedy-variety in 1946. Numerous recordings.

## Leonard Nimoy 🎥 *Actor, director*

**Born:** March 26, 1931, in Boston, MA.

**Spotlights:** Screen debut in 1951. Films include the excellent remake of *Invasion of the Body Snatchers* (1978). Best known for his portrayal of the acutely intelligent, humorless (although funny at times), emotionless, science officer Mr. Spock on the starship *U.S.S. Enterprise* on "Star Trek" (1966–69). Continues to explore new box office potential with a series of Paramount pictures. Outstanding job as director of *Star Trek III: The Search for Spock* (1984) and *Star Trek IV: The Voyage Home* (1986).

# · 6633 HOLLYWOOD ·

### Mark Stevens  Actor
6633 Hollywood

**Born:** Richard Stevens; Dec. 13, 1915, in Cleveland, OH.

**Spotlights:** Used the stage name of Steven Richards in early film career. Played the lead in "Martin Kane, Private Eye" (1953–54). Portrayed newspaper editor, Steve Wilson, in "Big Town" (1954–56).

### Anatole Litvak  Director
6633 Hollywood

**Born:** Michael A. Litwak; May 10, 1902, in Russia.

**Spotlights:** Directed Edward G. Robinson and Paul Lukas in Warner's sensational *Confessions of a Nazi Spy* (1939), a heartfelt subject for the Jewish artist forced to flee Nazi Germany. Directed the original suspense thriller, *Sorry Wrong Number* (Paramount, 1948), starring Barbara Stanwyck and Burt Lancaster.

**Sidelights:** Fought in the U.S. military during World War II; was awarded many medals. Died: 1974.

### Dustin Farnum  Actor
6633 Hollywood

**Born:** May 27, 1874, in Hampton Beach, NH.

**Spotlights:** Starred in Cecil B. DeMille's silent, *The Squaw Man*, and in *The Virginian* (both 1914). Played western roles, but retired before the onset of sound pictures. Died: 1929.

### H. C. Potter  Director
6633 Hollywood

**Born:** Henry Codman Potter; Nov. 13, 1904, in New York.

**Spotlights:** Yale educated. A true showman who excelled in light comedies: *Hellzapoppin* (1942), and *The Farmer's Daughter* (1947), Loretta Young's Academy-winning performance. Died: 1977.

### Perry Como  Singer, actor
6631 Hollywood

**Born:** Nick Perido; May 18, 1912, in Canonsburg, PA.

**Spotlights:** Known as 'Mr. C.' Velvety baritone voice with charismatic style. Joined Ted Weems's band as a vocalist in 1936 and sang with them for 6 years. Popularity soared in 1945, with more than 4 million sellers: "Till the End of Time," "A Hubba-hubba-hubba," "Temptation," and a song from Rodgers and Hammerstein's musical, *Carousel*, called "If I Loved You." Radio includes the "Chesterfield Supper Club" (1944); TV: "The Kraft Music Hall" (1958–62), and numerous holiday specials, usually in interesting spots around the world. "It's Impossible" to say enough about one of the world's most successful crooners.

**Achievements:** Emmys: 1954, 1955, 1957, 1959. Grammy: 1958.

### Tex Ritter   *Singer, actor*                              6631 Hollywood

**Born:**   Woodward Ritter; Jan. 12, 1906 in Murvaul, TX.
**Spotlights:**   "America's Most Beloved Cowboy" didn't have to worry about a show-down at "High Noon." His popularity on radio, Broadway, and films rivaled that of the best of them, including Gene Autry.
**Highlights:**   Father of TV actor-comedian, John Ritter. Died: 1974.

### John Ritter   *Actor*                              6632 Hollywood

**Born:**   Sept. 17, 1948, in Burbank, CA.
**Spotlights:**   Played the Reverend Matthew Fordwick (1972–77) on "The Waltons" and Jack Tripper on "Three's Company" (1977–84).
**Achievements:**   Emmy 1983.
**Highlights:**   Son of the late singer-actor Tex Ritter.
**Sidelights:**   In matters of the heart, it was wonderful that John's Walk of Fame star was installed next to his late, beloved father's.

### Fred Zinnemann   *Director*                              6627 Hollywood

**Born:**   April 29, 1907, in Austria.
**Achievements:**   1938, Oscar, *That Mothers Might Live*; 1953, Oscar, *From Here to Eternity*; 1966 Oscar *A Man For All Seasons*.

### Art Carney   *Actor*                              6627 Hollywood

**Born:**   Nov. 4, 1918, in Mount Vernon, N.Y.
**Spotlights:**   Spent a lifetime as best friend and second banana to The Great One on

*Dustin Farnum*                              *John Ritter*

"The Jackie Gleason Show" (1952–57, 1966–70) and "The Honeymooners" (1955–56) as Ed Norton, optimistic sewer worker.

**Achievements:**   1974, Best Actor Academy Award *Harry and Tonto*. Emmys, 1953, 1954, and 1955; special Emmys, 1967 and 1968.

**Sidelights:**   His slightly noticeable limp was caused by a World War II injury (hit by schrapnel).

### Enrico Caruso      *Opera singer*                    6625 Hollywood

**Born:**   Feb. 25, 1873, in Naples, Italy.

**Spotlights:**   One of the greatest tenors of all time. Debut at Metropolitan Opera (1903) in *Rigoletto*. Internationally famous for albums (first opera star to record), and sang in over 50 roles. Died: 1921.

### Angela Lansbury   *Actress*                                      6623½ Hollywood

**Born:**   Oct. 16, 1925, in England.

**Spotlights:**   Perfect performance in debut film, *Gaslight* (1944). Absolutely endearing in *The Picture of Dorian Gray* (1945)and quite lovely too! *The Manchurian Candidate* (1961) cast the final vote that she was a very gifted actress. TV: Jessica Beatrice Fletcher in "Murder, She Wrote" CBS (1984–).

**Achievements:**   1966, 1975, 1979 (two) Tony awards.

### Margaret Whiting   *Singer, actress*                           6623 Hollywood

**Born:**   July 22, 1926, in Detroit, MI.

**Spotlights:**   Said to be "born with a silver tuning fork in her hand." Popular vocalist on radio including "Club Fifteen" with Bob Crosby and the Bobcats and "The Eddie Cantor Show." Singles: "My Ideal," "Moonlight in Vermont," "Come Rain or Come Shine," and 500 other "good old songs." TV: Star of the situation comedy, "Those Whiting Girls" (1955–57); summer replacement for "I Love Lucy." Recorded latest album in 1987. Also published her autobiography *It Might As Well Be Spring*.

**Highlights:**   Daughter of famed composer, Richard (Dick) Whiting — "Hooray for

*Art Carney*                   *Margaret Whiting*                   *Wallace Reid*

Hollywood," "Till We Meet Again," and "Beyond the Blue Horizon." Sister of actress Barbara Whiting.

### Drew Pearson  *Newscaster, columnist, actor* 6623 Hollywood

**Born:** Andrew Pearson; Dec. 13, 1897, in Evanston, IL.
**Spotlights:** Strong, individualized news reporting style — almost prophetic. "I predict ..." Was a regular on the musical variety show, "Calling America" (Mutual, 1939). Died: 1969.

### J. M. Kerrigan *Actor* 6621 Hollywood

**Born:** July 25, 1889, in Louisville, KY.
**Spotlights:** Lady's man during the silent era: *Samson* (1915) and *Captain Blood* (1924); retired a rich man after the latter. Died: 1947.

### Buster Keaton *Comedian, screenwriter* 6621 Hollywood

**Born:** Joseph Keaton; Oct. 4, 1895, in Piqua, KS.
**Spotlights:** Stone-faced, soulful-eyed agile talent from a vaudeville family that had made the circuit with Houdini. Visited pal "Fatty" Arbuckle shooting *The Butcher Boy* (1917) and wound up in the film. Extremely gifted comedian. Two well-loved classics: *The Navigator* (1924) and *The General* (1926). TV: "Comedy Circus" (1951). Guest star.
**Achievements:** 1959, special Oscar. Died: 1966, from lung cancer.

### Peter Lorre *Actor* 6619 Hollywood

**Born:** Laszlo Lowenstein; June 26, 1904, in Hungary.
**Spotlights:** Small, dark-haired, bug-eyed, sinister-looking performer whose talent for adding a touch of humor to the most hardened criminals has never been rivaled: *The Maltese Falcon* (1941) and *Casablanca* (1942). Often paired with huge "evil sidekick, Sydney Greenstreet. An absolute joy to watch in *Arsenic and Old Lace* (released 1942). Made close to 100 films in a career that spanned 40 years. Unique voice and accent often imitated. Died: 1964, of heart failure.

### Wallace Reid *Actor, director* 6617 Hollywood

**Born:** William W. Reid; April 15, 1891, in St. Louis, MO.
**Spotlights:** Acted in and/or directed 100 shorts. Historic participation in D. W. Griffith's *The Birth of a Nation* (1915), probably the only picture he made that remains widely viewed today; at least in history of motion picture classes in college. Died: 1923, from drug addiction.

### Billie Burke *Actress* 6617 Hollywood

**Born:** Mary Burke; Aug. 7, 1885, in Washington, D.C.
**Spotlights:** Played many "bird-witted ladies" for $10,000 a week before landing her

personal favorite role as Glinda the Good Fairy in *The Wizard of Oz* (1939).
**Highlights:** Married former employer, Florenz Ziegfeld, in 1914. Died: 1970.

### Norman Lear  *Producer, director, writer* 6615 Hollywood

**Born:** July 27, 1922, in New Haven, CT.
**Spotlights:** Experienced as a TV writer-director since the mid-1950s, including script material for Dean Martin and Jerry Lewis, Don Rickles, and others. Broke all comedy barriers with his adult approach to humor including "All in the Family" (1971–79), "Archie Bunker's Place" (1979–83), "Maude" (1972–78), "Sanford and Son" (1972–77); more.
**Achievements:** Four Emmys, 1970–71, 1971–72, 1972–73. Many entertainment accolades.

### Cesar Romero *Actor* 6615 Hollywood

**Born:** Feb. 15, 1907, in New York.
**Spotlights:** Handsome, debonair talent in over 100 pictures, including *The Thin Man* (1934), *Return of the Cisco Kid* (1939, series), *Pepe* (1960); more. TV: The villainous Joker in "Batman" (1966–68), and "Falcon Crest" (1986–).

### Lawrence Welk *Bandleader, accordionist* 6613½ Hollywood

**Born:** March 11, 1903, in Strasburg, ND.
**Spotlights:** "Wunnerful, wunnerful," Welk would exclaim on his own television show, 1951–71. He offered viewers and listeners "champagne music" with lots of bubbles.

*Cesar Romero*

Hymn singing, tap and ballroom dancing with emphasis on simple arrangements and melody charmed millions of Americans.

**Sidelights:** Linguists traced his slight accent to his roots in a rural, German- speaking community.

### Hugh O'Brian  *Actor*                                   6613½ Hollywood

**Born:** Hugh Krampke; April 19, 1925, in Rochester, N.Y.

**Spotlights:** For male viewers, he was the sharp shooter with a pair of matching extra-long barreled .45 pistols. For females, he was tall, dark, handsome, and romantic in his western "leathers." He was the Marshal in "The Life and Legend of Wyatt Earp" (1955–61).

### Mildred Dunnock  *Character actress*                   6613 Hollywood

**Born:** Jan. 25, 1906, in Baltimore, MD.

**Achievements:** Nominated for Best Supporting Actress Oscar in *Death of a Salesman* (1951) and *Baby Doll* (1956).

### James Whitmore  *Actor*                                 6611 Hollywood

**Born:** Oct. 1, 1921, in White Plains, N.Y.

**Spotlights:** Stocky, curly-haired, reliable actor who studied drama at Yale. Credible playing Abraham Lincoln Jones in "The Law and Mr. Jones" (1960–62). Also good in light comedy for "Temperatures Rising" (1972–74), as Dr. Vincent Campanelli.

### Kitty Carlisle  *Singer, actress*                       6611 Hollywood

**Born:** Catherine Holzman; Sept. 3, 1915, in New Orleans, LA.

**Spotlights:** Debut in *Murder at the Vanities* (1934). Her clever performance in the zany *A Night at the Opera* (1935), with Groucho, Chico, and Harpo Marx, was also one of her favorite roles.

**Sidelights:** Chairwoman of New York State Council on the Arts (1976).

### Mary Martin  *Actress, singer, dancer*                  6609 Hollywood

**Born:** Virginia Martin; Dec. 1, 1913, in Weatherford, TX.

**Spotlights:** Clear soprano vocalist on "Good News" (NBC, 1939); regular on "Tex and Jinx" (NBC, 1947). Became famous in 1938 when she sang "My Heart Belongs to Daddy" in Cole Porter's *Leave It to Me*. A full-fledged Broadway star by *South Pacific* (1949). Warmth and energy are conveyed in her splendid recordings.

**Achievements:** 1948, special Tony; 1955, Tony for *Peter Pan*; 1960, Tony for *The Sound of Music*. 1955, Emmy.

**Highlights:** Mother of actor Larry Hagman. She frequently took her son to rehearsals with her so that they wouldn't be parted.

### Vincent Lopez  *Bandleader, composer, lyricist*         6609 Hollywood

**Born:** Dec. 30, 1895, in Brooklyn, NY.

**Spotlights:** "Hello, everybody. Lopez speaking from the beautiful Hotel Taft in that grand city New York" is how the pioneer radio man greeted listeners. The year was 1921, just one year after the introduction of American commercial broadcasting! Died: 1979.

### Jane Wyman  *See page 214.* 6607 Hollywood

### Bonita Granville  *Actress* 6607 Hollywood

**Born:** Feb. 2, 1923, in Chicago, IL.
**Spotlights:** As a lying schoolgirl in Samuel Goldwyn's *These Three* (1936), she proved that her talents extended beyond her girlish looks. As she matured, Warners gave her the lead in the *Nancy Drew* series (1938–39). She took *Strike It Rich* (1948) seriously and married an oil-rich Texan. Later her acumen as a businesswoman enhanced the TV production of "Lassie."

### Victor Jory  *Actor* 6605 Hollywood

**Born:** Nov. 23, 1902, in Dawson City, AK.
**Spotlights:** The villian that audiences loved to "boo." Wore more "black hats" than any other character actor. His "bad" face seemed a natural for wicked brutes, which he played in most of his more than 100 movies: *Too Tough to Kill* (1935), *Bad Man of Missouri* (1941), and *Cave of Outlaws* (1951). Died: 1982.

### Marie Wilson  *Actress* 6605 Hollywood

**Born:** Katherine Wilson; Dec. 30, 1916, in Anaheim, CA.
**Spotlights:** Buoyant, beautiful, voluptuous blond. Intelligent off-screen, excelled in playing dingy women on-screen. *Boy Meets Girl* (1938). Lead in *My Friend Irma*, — first a radio show in 1947, a motion picture in 1949, and a TV series (1952–54). Died: 1972, of cancer.

### Edmund Lowe  *See page 93.* 6601 Hollywood

### George Fitzmaurice  *Director* 6601 Hollywood

**Born:** Feb. 13, 1885, in Paris.
**Spotlights:** Made idealistic, pictorial movies during the silent era, with a trend toward realism in the early days of sound. *The Son of Sheik* (1926), with Rudolph Valentino; *The Devil to Pay* (1931) with Ronald Colman; and *As You Desire Me* (1932), with Greta Garbo. Died: 1941.

### Melvyn Douglas  *See page 85.* 6601 Hollywood

# · 6565 HOLLYWOOD ·

**Peggy King**  ☒  *Singer*                                    6565 Hollywood
**Born:**  1931, in Greensburg, PA.
**Spotlights:**  Employed as a secretary before joining a band. Sang on the radio, then landed a recording contract. Featured singer on "The George Gobel Show" (1954–56).

**Clem McCarthy**  ☒  *Pioneer announcer*                       6565 Hollywood
**Spotlights:**  A no-nonsense sportscaster, who knew thoroughbred racing horses. His aggressive delivery was often imitated by comedians in early broadcast years.

**Danny Kaye**  ☒  *Actor*                                      6563 Hollywood
**Born:**  David D. Kaminski; Jan. 18, 1913, in Brooklyn, N.Y.
**Spotlights:**  Comedian on-screen debut in Goldwyn's *Up in Arms* (1944). Wonderful in *The Secret Life of Walter Mitty* (1947). Songs: "The Ugly Duckling," "Thumbelina," and "The Emperor's New Clothes" enhanced the storybook musical *Hans Christian Andersen* (1952). Every holiday season, *White Christmas* (1954) with Kaye and Bing Crosby brings yuletide joy to TV viewers. Radio: "The Danny Kaye Show" (CBS, 1945).
**Achievements:**  1954, special Oscar. 1981, Oscar, Jean Hersholt Humanitarian Award. 1964, Emmy, "The Danny Kaye Show." Widely recognized for his unstinting efforts to help needy children worldwide. Died: 1987.

**Ruth Etting**  ☒  *Actress*                                   6563 Hollywood
**Born:**  Nov. 23, 1896, in David City, NV.
**Spotlights:**  Stage, screen and radio talent. Films: *Ruth Etting Paramount Movietone* (short — 1928); *Ruth Etting The Book of Lovers* (short — 1929). Mainly appeared in shorts, but made a few features through 1936.
**Sidelights:**  The movie *Love Me or Leave Me* (1955) was based on her life. Died: 1978.

**Toby Wing**  ☒  *Actress*                                     6561 Hollywood
**Born:**  Martha Wing; July 14, 1913.
**Spotlights:**  Gorgeous, vivacious, blond girl who enjoyed a 5-year career including *Gold-Diggers of 1933* and *42nd Street* (1933).
**Highlights:**  Retired in 1937 to marry aviator Dick Merrill.

**David Butler**  ☒  *Director, screenwriter*                   6559 Hollywood
**Born:**  Dec. 17, 1894, in San Francisco, CA.

**Spotlights:**   Shirley Temple in *Captain January* (1936) and the Crosby-Lamour-Hope team in *Road to Morocco* (1942) appreciated his direction for light comedy. Started in show biz as an actor in 1919 and remained busy behind the scenes for 46 years. Died: 1979.

## Ozzie Nelson   *Actor, bandleader*                              6555 Hollywood

**Born:**   Oswald Nelson; March 20, 1907, in Jersey City, N.J.

**Spotlights:**   Rarely seen working at a job, but millions of viewers still saw him as an ideal husband, father, and provider on "The Adventures of Ozzie and Harriet" (1952–66). His calm, sensible approach to family problems humorously aided a growing generation.

**Highlights:**   Married singer Harriert Hilliard in 1935. Died: 1975.

## John Cromwell   *Director*                                        6555 Hollywood

**Born:**   Elwood Cromwell; Dec. 23, 1888, in Toledo, OH.

**Spotlights:**   Quality direction of the flag-waving *Abe Lincoln in Illinois* (1940). *Prisoner of Zenda* (1937) is a fascinating, magical adventurous study of a vacationing Englishman who thwarts a rebel's plot by impersonating a kidnapped king. Died: 1979.

## James Dunn   *See page 358.*                                      6555 Hollywood

## Reed Hadley   *Actor*                                             6553 Hollywood

**Born:**   Reed Herring; Jan. 8, 1911, in Petrolia, TX.

**Spotlights:**   He was Captain John Braddock on "Racket Squad" (1951–53), protecting innocent citizens against confidence men. Bart Matthews as *The Public Defender* exonerated innocent people "wrongly accused of crimes." Died: 1974.

## John Forsythe   *Actor*                                           6551 Hollywood

**Born:**   John Freund; Jan. 29, 1918, in Penns Grove, N.J.

**Spotlights:**   Although extremely fond of thoroughbred racehorses, this handsome, wavy-haired actor — capable of comedy or drama — never gambled with his busy career. He was Beverly Hills resident, Bentley Gregg, in "Bachelor Father" (1957–62), guardian of teenage niece Kelly. Linda Evans was one of Kelly's friends! In 1981 he became oil tycoon, Blake Carrington, on "Dynasty." Linda Evans, who played Krystle Jennings Carrington, became his secretary-turned-wife.

**Helen Hayes** See page 193.       6551 Hollywood

**Basil Rathbone**  *Actor*       6551 Hollywood
**Born:** Philip B. Rathbone; June 13, 1892, in South Africa.
**Spotlights:** The screen's best villain: Mr. Murdstone in *David Copperfield* (1935). He was the *Son of Frankenstein* (1939); also best Sherlock Holmes (1943–46); more. Radio: Guest star on Bob Hope, Edgar Bergen, and other comedy varieties. TV: Emcee of "Your Lucky Clue" quiz show (1952) and Suspense (1935). Died: 1967, from a heart attack.

**Penny Singleton** *Actress*       6547 Hollywood
**Born:** Dorothy McNulty; on Sept. 15, 1908, in Philadelphia, PA.
**Spotlights:** Played pretty, feather-brained Mrs. Dagwood Bumstead through most of her career by audience demand. "B-l-o-o-n-d-i-e!" *Blondie* serial from 1938–50. Same comedy role on radio "Blondie" (CBS, 1939).

**Martha Raye** See page 153.       6547 Hollywood

**Jack Warner** *Film pioneer, producer*       6547 Hollywood
**Born:** Aug. 2, 1892, in Canada.
**Spotlights:** Founded the highly successful Warner Brothers studio, along with his three older brothers, Harry, Albert, and Sam. Jack had the artistic sense. Very creative. Significant early productions include *The Gold Diggers* (1923) and *Beau Brummel*

*The Warner Brothers (l. to r.) Harry, Jack, Sam and Abe.*

(1924). Later classics include *Angels with Dirty Faces* (1938) and *Casablanca* (1943); more.

**Highlights:** The magic of the Warner family was that each member had a unique quality to bring to the team. Together, they were an unbeatable force.

**Sidelights:** None of the other studios would touch TV. Warner Brothers broke new ground when they produced for TV. Died: 1978.

**Mickey Rooney**   *See page 142.*     6541 Hollywood

**Bob Hope**   *Comedian, actor*     6541 Hollywood

**Born:** Leslie Hope; May 29, 1903, in England.

**Spotlights:** A hit on vaudeville and Broadway before NBC radio's "The Bob Hope Show" (1934). In his second film, *College Swing* (1938), Hope got third billing behind Burns and Allen and Martha Raye. It was the 1940s "road" pictures that catapulted him to stardom: *Road to Singapore* (1940), with Bing Crosby and Dorothy Lamour; *Road to Zanzibar* (1941); series. TV audiences were impressed by his dedication to entertaining U.S. troops in Vietnam over the Christmas holidays. Dozens of TV specials.

**Achievements:** 1940, 1944, 1952, 1959, and 1965, special Academy Awards. 1966, two Emmys.

**Sidelights:** A wise investor, Hope is worth an estimated $400–$700 million. "Thanks for the Memory."

**Bob Burns**   *See page 248*     6541 Hollywood

**Jose Ferrer**   *Actor, director*     6541 Hollywood

**Born:** Jan. 8, 1909, in Puerto Rico.

**Spotlights:** Cinema debut opposite Ingrid Bergman in *Joan of Arc* (1948). Directed the 1962 remake of *State Fair* starring Pat Boone and Alice Faye.

**Achievements:** 1950, Best Actor Oscar, *Cyrano de Bergerac.*

**Viola Dana**   *Actress*     6541 Hollywood

**Born:** Violet Flugrath; June 28, 1897, in Brooklyn, N.Y.

**Spotlights:** *Cinderella's Twin* (1920) was how she might have felt while she was a screen siren, but the coming of sound was like the clock striking 12 — she dropped out of sight! Died:1987.

**William Fox**   *Executive*     6541 Hollywood

**Born:** Wilhelm Fried; Jan. 1, 1879, in Hungary.

**Spotlights:** Founder of the Fox Film Corporation in 1915. Previously, Fox had started in the entertainment industry by purchasing a penny arcade. He expanded into a theater chain and distributing motion pictures, then in 1912 produced films from his Box Office Attraction Company.

**Sidelights:** An impoverished child who worked long, long days for low pay and with no play, he grossed over $200 million by 1919. Died: 1952.

### Johnny Weissmuller ◤ *Actor* 6541 Hollywood

**Born:** Peter John Weissmuller; June 2, 1904, in Windber, PA.

**Spotlights:** Was *Tarzan the Ape Man* (1932) in the first talkie version. Strong, graceful, and handsome, he acted in 11 more Tarzan pictures before he switched to Columbia Pictures "Jungle Jim" series (1944–55) which were edited for a TV series in 1958.

**Achievements:** Olympic swimming champion. 1924 and 1938 collected 5 gold medals. Set over 60 world records.

**Sidelights:** A recording of Weissmuller's famous Tarzan yell was used on the TV series; TV actor Ron Ely just opened his mouth. Died: 1984.

### David W. Griffith ◤ *Director, film pioneer* 6537 Hollywood

**Born:** David Wark Griffith; Jan. 22, 1874, in La Grange, KY.

**Spotlights:** Known as D. W. Griffith. "Father of modern cinema" who made hundreds of films and invented breakthrough techniques including the first epic films in silent pictures. *The Birth of a Nation* a 3-hour cinematic triumph about the American Civil War (1915), *Intolerance* (1916), and *Orphans of the Storm* (1922). Created the flash-back, intense close-ups, overhead shots, artistic back-lighting, panoramic

*Viola Dana with Tom Moore*

shooting, cross-cutting, and other important techniques.

**Achievements:** Formed United Artists in 1919 with Charlie Chaplin, Douglas Fairbanks, and Mary Pickford.

**Sidelights:** So precise in his shooting techniques, D. W. studied the camera angle of one scene in *The Birth of a Nation* and said, "Move those 10 thousand horses a little to the right." Died: 1948, from a cerebral hemorrhage.

**Duke Ellington**  *Jazz composer, pianist, orchestra*       6535 Hollywood
*leader, radio and screen actor*

**Born:** Edward Kennedy "Duke" Ellington; April 29, 1899, in Washington, D.C.

**Spotlights:** Most prominent figure in big band jazz. Formed own band in 1918. Played the Cotton Club for 5 years starting in 1927. Diversified entertainment included pure instrumental jazz compositions, production numbers, blues, jungle style, popular songs, dance music, and mood music. Extremely productive with 2 thousand compositions — including "Soda Fountain Rag," "Ducky Wucky," and other 3-minute instrumental pieces — LP records, suites, film scores, etc. The creative "Ellington Effect" gave annual concerts at Carnegie Hall from 1943–52. Debut concert was "Black, Brown and Beige," illustrating musically the history of black people in America. Uniquely and perfectly disciplined orchestra caused envy in many jazz greats. His recordings include: "Choo Choo," "Old Man Blues," "Mood Indigo," "Take the 'A' Train," "Satin Doll," and "Sophisticated Lady."

**Achievements:** 1969, Presidential Medal of Freedom Award. Died: 1974.

**Sol Lesser** 🎬 *Producer*       6535 Hollywood

**Born:** Feb. 17, 1890, in Spokane, WA.

**Spotlights:** Produced four Tarzan movies, starting with *Tarzan the Fearless* (1933). Also the serial *Dick Tracy* (1937). Died: 1980.

**Morton Gould**  *Composer, conductor*       6533 Hollywood

**Born:** Dec. 10, 1913, in Richmond Hill, N.Y.

**Spotlights:** A piano prodigy. Conducting and arranging weekly radio programs by age 21, including works "Pavane" and "American Salute." Compositions for symphonies and symphonic band include: "Spirituals for Orchestra"; "Dance Variations for Two Pianos and Orchestra"; "Jekyll and Hyde Variations." Composed musical scores for Broadway, film, the ballet, and television. Works include three major U.S. Bicentennial commissions. Also composed "American Sing" for the Los Angeles Philharmonic — Summer Olympics Concert in the Hollywood Bowl — July, 1984. In 1986 became President of the American Society of Composers, Authors and Publishers (ASCAP).

**Achievements:** 1966, Grammy; 1983 Gold Baton Award.

## Clyde Cook  *Actor*                              6531½ Hollywood

**Born:** Dec. 16, 1891, in Australia.

**Spotlights:** Reliable, diminutive, acrobatic supporting slapstick comic actor, first in Mack Sennett comedies: *For Better, But Worse* (1915). Appeared with Shirley Temple in *Wee Willie Winkle* (1937).

## John Derek  *Actor, director*                    6531 Hollywood

**Born:** Derek Harris; Aug. 12, 1926, in Hollywood, CA.

**Spotlights:** Handsome leading man with wavy, black hair. Then TV: Actor Ronald Reagan narrated the show "A Place in the Sun" (1954), which starred Derek, for Lux Video Theater. Later, he played Ben Travis in the western series "Frontier Circus" (1961–62).

**Highlights:** Married and divorced actresses Ursula Andress and Linda Evans; now married to actress Bo Derek.

## Phyllis Thaxter  *Actress*                        6531 Hollywood

**Born:** Phyllis St. Felix Thaxter; Nov. 20, 1921, in Portland, ME.

**Spotlights:** Pretty brunette presiding in *Thirty Seconds over Tokyo* (1944). Good in Nervous Nellie roles, but breathed fresh life into those characters.

**Sidelights:** Contracted polio in 1952, but courageously continued in her career; *Superman* (1978).

# · 6529 HOLLYWOOD ·

### Alfred Green  *Director*     6529 Hollywood
**Born:** 1889 in Ferns, CA.
**Spotlights:** Creative force behind "America's Sweetheart," Mary Pickford, in *Little Lord Fauntleroy* (1921). Captured the essence of show biz success in *The Jolson Story* (1946, Columbia). Died: 1960.

### Faye Emerson *Actress*     6529 Hollywood
**Born:** July 8, 1917, in Elizabeth, LA.
**Spotlights:** *Wild Bill Hickock Rides* (1941) and *Murder in the Big House* (1942). Known as television's first lady on "The Faye Emerson Show" (1950); "Faye Emerson's Wonderful Town" (1951–52); more.
**Highlights:** Married, later divorced, son of then-president Franklin D. Roosevelt. Died: 1983.

### Liberace *Musician*     6529 Hollywood
**Born:** Wladziv Liberace; May 16, 1919, in West Allis, WI.
**Spotlights:** Attended Wisconsin College of Music at 7. Debuted as a soloist with the Chicago Symphony at 14. Digressed from classical music to play nightclubs during the Depression, using the alias Walter Buster Keys. During this time he added his tongue-in-cheek trademark humor to his show. In 1953, played Carnegie Hall; in 1954, Madison Square Garden. In Las Vegas, 1957, he earned $200 a week at the Riviera Hotel; in 1985, his MGM Grand Hotel contract was valued at over $3 million. Known as "Mr. Showmanship" for his outrageously extravagant costumes and stage sets, including candelabra.
**Achievements:** Emmys (two) 1952; 1953. Also had a successful ABC daytime series. Died: 1987.

### Betty Grable *Actress*     6527 Hollywood
**Born:** Elizabeth Grable; Dec. 18, 1916, in St. Louis, MO.
**Spotlights:** Famous as the World War II, number-one pin-up girl. Films: *Million Dollar Legs* (1940) played off her nickname; *Sweet Rosie O'Grady* (1943); and *Four Jills in a Jeep* (1944) helped to make her the highest paid movie star. Died: 1973.

### Merian C. Cooper *Producer, director, screenwriter*     6525 Hollywood
**Born:** Oct. 24, 1893, in Jacksonville, FL.
**Spotlights:** Produced and co-directed the original *King Kong* (1933); this version remains the best. Co-produced the sentimental western *Fort Apache* (1948).

**Sidelights:** Served in World War I and II. Retired as a U.S. Air Force Brigadier General. Died: 1973.

**Edmond O'Brien**  *See page 117.*     **6525 Hollywood**

**Roland Young** *Actor*     **6525 Hollywood**
**Born:** Nov. 11, 1887, in England.
**Spotlights:** Whimsical character actor in over 100 pictures: the Earl of Burnstead in *Ruggles of Red Gap* (1935); Cosmo Topper in *Topper* (1937). TV: Played suburban husband William in early 1940s on "William and Mary."
**Sidelights:** Trained at the prestigious Royal Academy of Dramatic Arts in London. Died: 1953.

**Harry Von Zell** *Announcer, actor*     **6521 Hollywood**
**Born:** July 11, 1906, in Indianapolis, IN.
**Spotlights:** Robust, happy announcer with a lively personality on "The George Burns and Gracie Allen Show" (first aired on CBS, 1931); "The Eddie Cantor Show" (first aired on NBC, 1931); "The Dinah Shore Show" (first aired on NBC, 1939). Died: 1981.

**Dean Martin** *Actor, comedian, singer*     **6519 Hollywood**
**Born:** Dino Crocetti; June 7, 1917, in Steubenville, OH.
**Spotlights:** Teamed with Jerry Lewis in 1946. Screen debut together in *My Friend Irma* (1949). Their enormous success was attributed to their magical screen pres-

*Liberace*         *Ann Margret*

ence together and "the formula": To take old movies and replace the female lead's role with Jerry Lewis's role. With minor rewriting, this was accomplished easily. Martin played the relaxed, romantic hero and Lewis the feebleminded basket case. After 16 films the duo called it quits in 1956. Martin soloed as a leading man from 1957 on TV: "The Dean Martin Show," comedy- variety (1965–74), another coup for the informal entertainer.

## Leatrice Joy  *Actress*                                      6519 Hollywood
**Born:**   Leatrice J. Zeidler; Nov. 7, 1896, in New Orleans, LA.
**Spotlights:**   Expressive face and control of body movement helped her in *The Slave* (1918) with the sweet, rotund comedian Oliver Hardy. Later, she demonstrated *The Poverty of Riches* (1921).

## Madge Bellamy  *Actress*                                      6517 Hollywood
**Born:**   Margaret Philpott; June 30, 1903, in Hillsboro, TX.
**Spotlights:**   The great beauty in *Blind Hearts* (1921). Romantic leading lady — an outlaw's daughter who is really a kidnapped heiress — in *Lorna Doone* (1922). Worked in the *Charlie Chan* detective series (1934).

## John Howard  *Host, actor*                                      6515 Hollywood
**Born:**   John Cox; April 14, 1913, in Cleveland, OH.
**Spotlights:**   His healing touch as Dr. Wayne Hudson in "Dr. Hudson's Secret Journal" saved broken hearts and battered bodies. Played Dave Welch in "My Three Sons" (1965–67).

## Rochester  *Comedian, actor*                                      6513 Hollywood
**Born:**   Eddie Anderson; Sept. 18, 1905, in Oakland, CA.
**Spotlights:**   Was in a number of films, including *Gone With the Wind* (1939), but the raspy-voiced Anderson became famous in his role as Rochester, Benny's man-servant on "The Jack Benny Program" (CBS radio, 1932; NBC, 1939). When the show moved to TV in 1950, audiences thrilled at Anderson's precision comic style. He enjoyed enormous popularity for the next 15 years.
**Sidelights:**   He took the name "Rochester" off-stage too. Devastated by Jack Benny's death; said that Benny had been one of the warmest, kindest, most loving human beings, and he felt he had been blessed and his life enriched by working with him.

## Clara Kimball Young  *Actress*                                      6513 Hollywood
**Born:**   Sept. 1890, in Chicago, IL.
**Spotlights:**   Film mogul Lewis J. Selznick saw this tall, dark, and beautiful lady's potential; with *Camille* and *Trilby* (both 1915) she shot to superstardom.
**Lowlights:**   Her career took a nosedive when she entrusted it to an incompetent husband. Died: 1960.

## John Sturges 🎥 *Director*
6511 Hollywood

**Born:** Jan. 3, 1911, in Oak Park, IL.

**Spotlights:** Directed tense, action-packed westerns: *The Walking Hills* (1949), *Bad Day at Black Rock* (1954), and *The Magnificent Seven* (1960).

## Art Baker 📺 *Actor, announcer*
6509 Hollywood

**Born:** 1898, in New York.

**Spotlights:** Articulate announcer on radio's "The Bob Hope Show" (first broadcast NBC, 1934). TV: Host on "You Asked For It" (1950-59). Died: 1966.

## Spring Byington 🎥 *Actress*
6507 Hollywood

**Born:** Oct. 17, 1893, in Colorado Springs, CO.

**Spotlights:** Her eyes mirrored a light within that made her a ray of hope as Marmee in David O. Selznick's *Little Women* (1933) starring Katharine Hepburn. It was her first picture, and there was little doubt about her talent and appeal. *You Can't Take It with You* (1938). Star of TV's situation comedy "December Bride" as Lily Ruskin (CBS, 1954–60). Died: 1971.

## Les Brown  *Composer, conductor*
6505 Hollywood

**Born:** Mar. 14, 1912, in Reinerton, PA.

**Spotlights:** Organized his band at Duke University. Later worked for Bob Hope and Steve Allen. "Duckfoot Waddle" and "We Wish You the Merriest" are two of his songs.

## Jimmy Dorsey 🎵 *Musician*
6505 Hollywood

**Born:** James Dorsey; Feb. 29, 1904, in Shenandoah, PA.

**Spotlights:** Jimmy and Tommy, the Dorsey brothers, were classified with the top leaders such as Glenn Miller and Benny Goodman, during the era of the big bands, the 1930s and 1940s. And they kept busy swinging America from the Mocambo in Hollywood, the Trianon and Aragon in Chicago, and hundreds of other ballrooms. These sessions were radio-broadcast, so listeners at home could dance along in their living rooms. Jimmy headed the orchestra on radio's "Kraft Music Hall" with host Bing Crosby in 1936. Numerous recordings. Died: 1957.

## Vincent Price 📺 *See page 165.*
6501 Hollywood

## Ann Margret 🎥 *Actress, singer, dancer*
6501 Hollywood

**Born:** Ann Margret Olsson; Apr. 28, 1941, in Sweden.

**Spotlights:** Ravishing redhead with a perfect figure. Sweet as candy in the musical *Bye Bye Birdie* (1963). MGM's *Viva Las Vegas* (1964) gave Elvis Presley a chance to swing with her. Excellent dramatic talent evident in *Carnal Knowledge* (1971) and *Tommy* (1975).

## Walter Brennan  *Actor*        **6501 Hollywood**

**Born:** July 25, 1894, in Swampscott, MA.

**Spotlights:** With his distinctive voice and punchy face, one of the best supporting actors Hollywood has known.

**Achievements:** Best Supporting Actor Academy Awards for *Come and Get It* (1936); *Kentucky* (1938); and *The Westerner* (1940).

**Sidelights:** Played Grandpa Amos McCoy on "The Real McCoys" (1957–63). Died 1974 of emphysema.

## Julia Faye *Actress*        **6501 Hollywood**

**Born:** Sept. 24, 1896, in Richmond, VA.

**Spotlights:** Worked for half a century in most of Cecil B. De Mille's films, from *The Squaw Man*, a great success in 1914, to *The Ten Commandments* in 1956. Died: 1966.

## Jean Hersholt *Actor*        **6501 Hollywood**

**Born:** July 12, 1886, in Copenhagen, Denmark.

**Spotlights:** Big silent screen star — in U.S. from 1914; became well-known as the kindly Dr. Paul Christian in Fox's *The Country Doctor* (1936), *Meet Dr. Christian* (1939), and four more in the serial. Carried over into radio, where he was star of the show "Dr. Christian" (1937). Made over 400 pictures.

**Achievements:** 1939, special Oscar for humanitarian works, and 1949, special Oscar for distinguished service. The Academy named an award after him (1956), which is presented annually. Died: 1956, of cancer.

# ⋆ 6445 HOLLYWOOD ⋆

### Yma Sumac   *Singer, actress*                                 6445 Hollywood

**Born:** Emperatriz Chavarri; September 10, 1927 in Ichocan, Peru.

**Spotlights:** Soprano, incredible vocal range, over 5 octaves, from a deep contralto to a high coloratura. Won acclaim in the U. S. from her 1949 appearance at the Hollywood Bowl. Known as the "Aztec Princess Reincarnated." Recordings: "Legend of the Sun Virgin," "Mambo," and "Voice of Xtabay." Films: *Secret of the Incas* (1954), *The Loves of Omar-Khayam* (1957).

### Carlton E. Morse   *Writer, announcer*                         6445 Hollywood

**Born:** 1901, in Jennings, LA.

**Spotlights:** Started in radio in 1929. Created radio's most successful serial, "One Man's Family" which was on the air for 27 years (1932–1960). Created and wrote "I Love a Mystery." One of the co-stars was a young actor named Tony Randall. Wrote "His Honor, the Barber" (NBC drama, 1945).

**Sidelights:** His advice to writers? "Be lucky." Owns his own publishing company called Seven Stones Press in Northern California.

### Louis Jordan   *Band leader, saxophone player*

**Born:** 1909.

**Spotlights:** Famous saxophonist, also composed. Was the real band leader in the movie *Follow the Boys* (1944). Died: 1975.

### Barbara Whiting   *Actress, singer*                            6443 Hollywood

**Born:** May 19, 1931, in Los Angeles, CA.

**Spotlights:** Film debut as "Fuffy" in 20th Century-Fox's *Junior Miss* (1945) when she was 13 years old. Played a UCLA co-ed, and her older sister Margaret played a singer on their own TV comedy show, "Those Whiting Girls" (1955–1957).

### Eddie Albert   *Actor*                                         6439 Hollywood

**Born:** Edward Heimberger; April 22, 1908, in Rock Island, IL.

**Spotlights:** Frequent guest star in many dramatic productions. As Oliver Wendell Douglas on "Green Acres" (1965–71), he was the proud owner of a farm near Hooterville.

**Sidelights:** Traveled with the circus as a teenage trapeze artist.

### Harry Warner   *Film pioneer, producer*                       6439 Hollywood

**Born:** Dec. 12, 1881, in Poland.

**Spotlights:**  The business brain of the family. The Warner Brothers, Harry, Albert, Sam and Jack, showed the exciting, 12-minute motion picture, *The Great Train Robbery* (1903), to ecstatic crowds. Made $300 in one week and decided to become even more involved, i.e., make more money by distributing (1907). Filmmaking followed: *My Four Years* (1918) was the first commercial hit.

**Highlights:**  Brother and partner Albert was born July 23, 1884, in Baltimore, MD. Albert died in 1967. Died: 1958.

### Jack Haley   *Actor, comedian, singer*        6435 Hollywood

**Born:**  Aug. 10, 1899, in Boston, MA.

**Spotlights:**  Host of his own variety program, "The Jack Haley Show" (CBS, 1938), which featured a 27-year-old comedienne, Lucille Ball. Frequent guest star on hit comedy-variety shows.

**Sidelights:**  Immortalized in *The Wizard of Oz* (1939) as the Tin Man. Father of producer-director-writer Jack Haley, Jr. Died: 1979.

### Cloris Leachman  *Actress*        6435 Hollywood

**Born:**  Apr. 30, 1930, in Des Moines, IA.

**Spotlights:**  5' 4", 108-lb., blond, grey-green eyes-vivacious positive thinker, youthful-minded. Broadway stage, screen and television star with a perfect sense of comic delivery, she had enhanced such Mel Brooks's movies as *Young Frankenstein* (1974) and *High Anxiety* (1977). Excellent dramatic performer as well. TV: Played the busybody neighbor landlady, Phyllis Lindstrom, on "The Mary Tyler Moore Show" (1970–75). Her own show, "Phyllis," was a spinoff situation comedy (1975–77).

**Achievements:**  1971, Best Supporting Actress Oscar for *The Last Picture Show*. Emmys: 1973, 1974, 1975 (two). Former beauty queen.

### Paul Muni  *Actor*        6433 Hollywood

**Born:**  Muni Weisenfreund; Sept. 22, 1897 in Poland.

**Spotlights:**  Intense, dark-haired, troubled artist, who starred as Al Capone in the

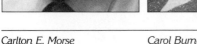

| Carlton E. Morse | Carol Burnett | Hal Mohr |

near-perfect original gangster movie *Scarface* (subtitled *The Shame of a Nation*, 1932), with Ann Dvorak, George Raft, and Boris Karloff.
**Achievements:** 1936, Best Actor Oscar for *The Story of Louis Pasteur*. Died: 1967 of heart failure.

## Carol Burnett ☒ *Comedian, actress, singer* 6433 Hollywood

**Born:** April 26, 1933, in San Antonio, TX.
**Spotlights:** Star of "The Carol Burnett Show," comedy-variety (1967–78). As a youngster, she worked as an usherette at the Hollywood Warner Brothers Theater for 65 cents an hour. Her Walk of Fame star is located at that site (although the theater is gone).
**Achievements:** 1962, Emmy "The Garry Moore Show"; 1963, Emmy "Julie and Carol at Carnegie Hall"; 1972, 1974, 1975, Emmy "The Carol Burnett Show"; 1969, special Tony Award.

## Jesse Lasky 🎥 *Pioneer film producer, executive* 6433 Hollywood

**Born:** Sept. 13, 1880, in San Francisco, CA.
**Spotlights:** Lasky and partners Samuel Goldfish (later Goldwyn) and Cecil B. DeMille made Hollywood's first important film *The Squaw Man* (1914). It was a feature-length western starring Dustin Farnum, cost $15,000, and was made in 18 days. Big success that legitimized the business. The Jesse L. Lasky Feature Play Company merged with Adolph Zuko's Famous Players Corporation in 1916. They purchased the Paramount distributing company and soon moved to the site where Paramount Pictures is located today. Involved with the production of One thousand pictures!
**Highlights:** Samuel Goldfish (Goldwyn) was Lasky's brother-in-law.
**Sidelights:** You can visit "the Barn" where *The Squaw Man* was produced. It's the Hollywood Studio Museum. Died: 1958.

## Lowell Thomas 🎥 *See page 130.* 6433 Hollywood

## Ben Alexander ☒ *See page 294* 6433 Hollywood

## Hal Mohr 🎥 *Cinematographer* 6433 Hollywood

**Born:** Aug. 2, 1894, in San Francisco, CA.
**Spotlights:** Built own camera as a teenager. Began career in 1910, eventually was director of photography on 108 motion pictures, including *The Jazz Singer* (1927).
**Achievements:** 1935, Oscar for *A Midsummer Night's Dream*; 1943, Oscar for *Phantom of the Opera*. Died: 1974.

## Bob Hawk · 🎙 *Emcee* 6433 Hollywood

**Born:** 1908, in Creaton, IA.
**Spotlights:** Host of radio's 1938 "Bob Hawk's Quixie Doodle Quiz." One of the hosts for "Take It or Leave It" in 1940. By 1952, he was pulling in $300,000 a year! Quiz show specialist.

## Melissa Gilbert 📺 *Actress* 6429 Hollywood

**Born:** May 8, 1964, in Los Angeles, CA.
**Spotlights:** Grew up on "Little House on the Prairie" (1974–83) as Laura Ingalls Wilder, the tomboyish farmer's daughter of the struggling Ingalls family in Walnut Grove, Plum Creek, Minn.
**Sidelights:** TV series based on *Little House* books by frontierswoman Laura Ingalls Wilder.

## Jennifer Jones 🎥 *Actress* 6429 Hollywood

**Born:** Phyllis Isley; Mar. 2, 1919, in Tulsa, OK.
**Spotlights:** High-cheekboned, open-faced, dark-haired beauty who was extremely selective (and could afford to be) in what she acted in. In the romantic comedy, *Cluny Brown* (1946), she deliciously partakes in jabbing some of the absurdity of British upper-class society. Her superb acting skills come to life in *Portrait of Jennie* (1948).
**Achievements:** 1943, Best Actress Oscar for *The Song of Bernadette.*
**Highlights:** Second husband was producer David O. Selznick, film wiz who produced *Gone with the Wind* (1939). He also co-wrote many screenplays. Their marriage began in 1949 and ended with his death in 1965. Married third husband, Norton Simon, in 1971.

## Gabby Hayes 🎙 *Actor* 6427 Hollywood

**Born:** May 7, 1885, in Wellsville, N.Y.
**Spotlights:** TV: Red Connors in "Hopalong Cassidy" (1945–48). Radio: regular on "The Roy Rogers Show" (1944-46); regular on "The Andrews Sister Eight-to-the- Bar Ranch" (NBC, 1944).
**Sidelights:** Known as George "Gabby" Hayes. Died: 1969.

## Edward Everett Horton 🎥 *Actor* 6427 Hollywood

**Born:** March 18, 1886, in Brooklyn, N.Y.
**Spotlights:** A nervous Norman-type, he enjoyed great success in supporting comedy roles: *The Gay Divorcee* (1934) with the Astaire-Rogers team and *Arsenic and Old Lace* (released 1944) with Cary Grant. Died: 1970 of cancer.

## Edgar Bergen 📺 *See page 33.* 6425 Hollywood

## Melvyn Douglas  🎥 *Actor* 6425 Hollywood

**Born:** Melvyn Hesselberg; April 5, 1901, in Macon, GA.

**Spotlights:** Brilliant in sophisticated, romantic comedies. A dapper gent with a penciled moustache: *Theodora Goes Wild* (1936), *Ninotchka* (1939), and *I Never Sang for My Father* (1969). Played Benjamin Franklin on TV's "The Statesman."

**Achievements:** Best Supporting Oscars: 1963 *Hud* and 1980 *Being There*; 1967–68 Emmy Award for *Do Not Go Gently into That Good Night*.

**Highlights:** Married to another Walk of Famer, Helen Gahagan, since 1931. Died: 1981.

## Fred MacMurray  🎥 *Actor* 6421 Hollywood

**Born:** Aug. 30, 1908, in Kankakee, IL.

**Spotlights:** Professionally, he started out as a saxophone player and singer. *The Gilded Lily* (1935), with Claudette Colbert, was a sensational lift for his acting career. He played with a light comic flair opposite the witty Carole Lombard in *Hands Across the Table* (1935). Broke away from "Mr. Nice Guy" to be a heel in Billy Wilder's *Double Indemnity* (1944), with murder partner Barbara Stanwyck. Pal Walt Disney starred him in *Shaggy Dog* (1959), the first of 5 pictures with that studio.

**Sidelights:** No *Absent-Minded Professor* (1961) when he invested in Disney stock. Real estate holdings, too, make him one of the world's richest entertainers!

## Carl Reiner  📺 *Comic, writer, producer, director* 6421 Hollywood

**Born:** March 29, 1922, in Bronx, N.Y.

**Spotlights:** Truly versatile talent in front of the cameras, as well as behind the scenes;

*Edward Everett Horton*          *Bert Lytell*

creator of "The Dick Van Dyke Show" (1961–67).
**Achievements:** 1961–62, 1962–63, and1963–64 Emmys for Outstanding Writing, "The Dick Van Dyke Show" (CBS). 1966–67 Emmy for Outstanding Writing Achievement in Variety: "The Sid Caesar, Imogene Coca, Carl Reiner, Howard Morris Special" (CBS).

### Sammy Kaye  *Orchestra, leader, composer* 6419 Hollywood
**Born:** March 13, 1910, in Rocky River, OH.
**Spotlights:** Radio: Host of the long-running musical variety program with his own orchestra, "The Sammy Kaye Show," first aired in 1944, retitled "Sammy Kaye's Sunday Serenade Room" in 1954. TV: "The Sammy Kaye Show" entertained audiences for years with the comic routine "So You Want to Lead a Band?" Kaye would select members of the audience to be guest conductors. The orchestra would musically follow their new leader's baton "instructions" with entertaining results. Kaye and his great dance band had another long run, from 1950–59. Numerous recordings include "Moondust." Died: 1987.

### Bert Lytell  *Actor* 6417 Hollywood
**Born:** Feb. 24, 1885, in New York.
**Spotlights:** A romantic leading man during the silent era. Was an expert at flirting with his heavily lined eyes: *Rupert of Hentzau* (1923). Female audiences sighed at this dreamy, thin-lipped, dimpled-chinned man. Died: 1954.

### Snub Pollard  *Comedian* 6415 Hollywood
**Born:** Harold Fraser; April 2, 1886, in Australia.
**Spotlights:** Small, expressive, slapstick actor from 1914–61; at his peak in the 1920s — including *Luke Laughs Last* (1916), *The Dippy Dentist* (1920), *Are Husbands Human?* (1925). Died: 1962.

### Fanny Brice  *Singer, comedian* 6415 Hollywood
**Born:** Fanny Borach; Oct. 29, 1891, in New York.
**Spotlights:** Sensational star of the Ziegfeld Follies (1910–23) and later repeated her genius on film in *The Great Ziegfeld* (1936) and *Ziegfeld Follies* (1946). NBC radio first aired "The Baby Snooks Show" starring Brice as a playful girl in 1939; it was a hit. **Sidelights:** *Funny Girl* (1968) and *Funny Lady* (1975), based on Brice's life, starred Barbra Streisand. Died: 1951.

### Meredith Willson  *Author, lyricist, conductor* 6413 Hollywood
**Born:** Robert M. Reiniger, May 18, 1902, in Mason City, IA.
**Spotlights:** "May the Good Lord Bless and Keep You" was his mother's traditional Sunday blessing, and later, his title song for Tallulah Bankhead's "The Big Show" (NBC radio 1950). Willson's delightful youth playing piccolo and flute in a marching band inspired his writing the story of a small hometown in America's heartland — *The*

*Music Man.* A hit Broadway musical in 1957, it translated into an Academy-award winning film in 1962. Died: 1984.

**Jack Bailey,**  *Actor*     6411 Hollywood
**Born:** Sept. 15, 1907, in Hampton, IA.
**Spotlights:** TV: Emcee of "Truth or Consequences" (1954–56). Radio: Good-humored announcer on "The Adventures of Ozzie and Harriet" (CBS, 1944).
**Sidelights:** Voice for Disney's Goofy. Died: 1980.

**Slim Summerville** *Actor*     6409 Hollywood
**Born:** George Summerville; July 10, 1892, in Albuquerque, N.M.
**Spotlights:** A lanky, brown-haired talent with a large nose and receding chin. Unique voice had a clangy drawl to it. *Love, Honor, and Oh! Baby* (1933); *Captain January* (1936) Died: 1946, from a stroke.

**Bennett Cerf** *Panelist, editor, publisher,*     6407 Hollywood
*columnist, journalist, lecturer*
**Born:** May 25, 1898, in New York.
**Spotlights:** Was the longest-running panelist (1951–67) on "What's My Line?" Long-time president of Random House, Inc., which he founded in 1927. Died: 1971.

**Graham McNamee** *Announcer, reporter, commentator*   6405 Hollywood
**Born:** July 10, 1888, in Washington, D.C.
**Spotlights:** Called "radio's first reporter." Sports fans can thank the efforts of "the father of sportscasting" for today's personalities who deliver the play-by-play action with expertise, knowledge, and a true love of sports. McNamee permanently took the ball from bored staff announcers, who often had no understanding of the event they were covering, and defined sports broadcasting with sports terminology. Died: 1942.

**Teresa Wright** *See page 205.*     6405 Hollywood

**Del Moore** *Actor*     6405 Hollywood
**Born:** 1917.
**Spotlights:** Cal Mitchell on "Bachelor Father" (1960–62); regular on "The Betty White Show" (1958) and on the talk-variety "The Jerry Lewis Show" (1963). Appeared in humorous movie shorts: *So You Want to Enjoy Life? So You Want to Go to a Nighclub?* (1954); *So You Want to be a Gladiator?* (1955); *So You Want to Be a Vice President? So You Think the Grass is Greener?* (1956). Died: 1970.

**Johnny Maddox** *Pianist*     6401 Hollywood
**Born:** 1929, in Gallatin, TN.
**Spotlights:** A musical prodigy. Performed at concerts at age 5. Late 1950s recordings include: "The Crazy Otto," "Heart and Soul," and "Yellow Dog Blues."

Meredith Wilson                          Will Rogers

## Will Rogers  *Actor, humorist, writer*          **6401 Hollywood**

**Born:** William Rogers; Nov. 4, 1879, in Oologah, Indian Territory, OK.

**Spotlights:** Regarding his birthplace, Rogers remarked, "I usually say I was born in Claremore, for convenience, because nobody but an Indian can pronounce Oologah." His homespun wit, often injected with politics, made him America's folk hero: "The government has never been accused of being a businessman." On education: "Everybody is ignorant, only on different subjects." Of women: "If we can just improve their marksmanship, we can improve civilization. About every fourth fellow you meet nowadays ought to be shot." On foreign government: "For a Latin-American dictator he died a natural death — shot in the back." Extremely well loved ("I never met a man I didn't like"), capable horseback rider, and showman, Rogers's sound pictures were best: *Connecticut Yankee* (1931) and *State Fair* (1933). Radio: comedian and commentator, guest spots on "The Eveready Hour," variety. Died: 1935, in a plane crash.

## Josef von Sternberg  *Director*          **6401 Hollywood**

**Born:** Jonas Jo Sternberg; May 29, 1894, in Austria.

**Spotlights:** As his trademark always wore black riding boots around the studio; his attire hinted at his reputation of being a stern taskmaster. Extravagant, moody; glorious accomplishments include *Underworld* (1927) and making a star out of formerly plump Marlene Dietrich, *The Blue Angel* (1930) and *Shanghai Express* (1932). Died: 1969, from heart disease.

# · 6885 HOLLYWOOD ·

### Lew Ayres 🎥 *Actor, musician*                                          6385 Hollywood

**Born:** Lewis Ayer; Dec. 28, 1908, in Minneapolis, MN.
**Spotlights:** A talented musician on the banjo, guitar, and piano, he was discovered while playing with Ray West's orchestra at the hot Los Angeles nightspot, The Cocoanut Grove. The very next year, he got an amazing Hollywood break when he appeared in one of Universal's best films, *All Quiet on the Western Front* (1930). Next, worked with Edward G. Robinson in *East is West* (1930). Drawing upon his real-life study of medicine, he played *Young Doctor Kildare* (1939) in the original 'B' movie and played the same role on radio's popular "The Story of Dr. Kildare."
**Lowlights:** Ironically, since the war film *All Quiet on the Western Front* had shot him to stardom, the public was outraged by his registering as a conscientious objector during World War II and he became unwelcome at the studios. Later, after a break from Hollywood, he came back to work in films, but never again achieved superstar status.

### Dorothy Gish 🎥 *Actress*                                          6385 Hollywood

**Born:** Dorothy de Guiche; March 11, 1898, in Dayton, OH.
**Spotlights:** Popular silent screen star who was especially good in light comedies. Entered films as a teenager with help from friend Mary Pickford in 1912. *How Molly Made Good* (1915) was one of her more than 90 films. Famed director D. W. Griffith produced a string of comedies for her. Retired at the onset of talkies, with rare appearances until *The Cardinal* (1963).
**Highlights:** Younger sister of dramatic actress Lillian Gish. Died: 1968, of bronchial pneumonia.

### Frankie Laine 💿 *Singer, actor*                                          6385 Hollywood

**Born:** Frank Lo Vecchio; March 30, 1913, in Chicago, IL.
**Spotlights:** Altar-choir boy, 1932 Depression champion marathon dancer, singer in Joe Kaiser's band, soloist on radio and records; "Jezebel" (16 golden records). Voice for film theme songs *Blowing Wild* (1953) and *Gunfight at the O.K. Corral* (1957). TV: Voice for theme songs "Rango" and "Rawhide"; had his own summer show — replacement for "Arthur Godfrey and Friends." "Frankie Laine Time" (1955–56).
**Sidelights:** Known as the "Master of the Ballad."

### Wally Cox 📺 *Actor, comedian*                                          6385 Hollywood

**Born:** Dec. 6, 1924, in Detroit, MI.
**Spotlights:** Bespectacled, nervous Norman-type, who starred as the shy science teacher on "Mr. Peepers" (1952–55). Funny, witty regular on "Hollywood Squares" (1968). Guest star on "Love, American Style" (1969–). Died: 1973.

### Forrest Tucker  *Actor*  **6385 Hollywood**
**Born:** Feb. 12, 1919, in Plainsfield, IN.
**Spotlights:** 6′ 5″ robust character actor who appeared in nearly 100 action films. Film debut in *The Westerner* (1940) starring Gary Cooper. Worked with John Wayne, including *Sands of Iwo Jima* (1949). Gained national popularity as TV's Sgt. Morgan O'Rourke on "F Troop" (1965–67).
**Sidelights:** Collapsed minutes before receiving his star on Walk of Fame, in an Aug. 2, 1986 ceremony. An ambulance took him to the Motion Picture Country Home and Hospital. Battled the big "C" disease for two more months. Died: 1986 from lung cancer.

### Don Murray  *Actor, director, writer*  **6385 Hollywood**
**Born:** July 31, 1929, in Hollywood, CA.
**Spotlights:** Introverted, serious-looking actor, who had the good fortune to play opposite Marilyn Monroe in *Bus Stop* (1956) in his very first picture! Directed and co-wrote the screenplay for *The Cross and the Switchblade* (1970).
**Sidelights:** Follows a strong ethical code in selecting and making movies.

### Vikki Carr  *Singer*  **6385 Hollywood**
**Born:** Florencia Cardona; July 19, 1942, in El Paso, TX.
**Spotlights:** Performed in nightclubs, before TV appearances on all the top-rated programs: "The Ed Sullivan Show," "Jackie Gleason," etc. Albums: *Best of Vikki Carr, Vikki Carr Canta en Español.* Single: "It Must be Him," "The Lesson."

### Gail Davis  *Actress*  **6385 Hollywood**
**Born:** Betty Jeanne Grayson; Oct. 5, 1925.
**Spotlights:** Gene Autry gave this petite (5′ 2″, 95-lb.), wiry actress her break, starring her in over 15 films before TV's western "Annie Oakley" (1953–56).
**Sidelights:** Went behind the scenes to manage other stars' careers.

### Mel Blanc  *Voice specialist*  **6385 Hollywood**
**Born:** Melvin Blanc; May 30, 1908, in San Francisco, CA.
**Spotlights:** Radio characters include the Happy Postman, on "The George Burns and Gracie Allen Show." He'd talk in an extremely depressed voice about the most joyous things; his voice would crack as though he were about to cry. On "The Jack Benny Program" he was the sound of Jack's Maxwell automobile; also Professor LeBlanc, the violin teacher (in reality Blanc was an accomplished violin, tuba, and bass player). TV and films: Does 99% of the voices for Warner Brothers cartoons! Bugs Bunny, Daffy Duck, Sylvester, Porky Pig, Barney Rubble (Flintstones), etc.

### Abbe Lane  *Singer, dancer, actress*  **6385 Hollywood**
**Born:** Dec. 14, 1932, in New York.
**Spotlights:** Co-star "The Xavier Cugat Show" (1957); Latin music. Lane was also Cugat's wife.

*Mel Blanc and friends*

**Anna Magnani**  *Actress*                6381 Hollywood

**Born:** March 7, 1908, in Egypt.
**Spotlights:** Struggled throughout an impoverished childhood and emotionally devastating adulthood. On-screen irregularly for 20 years before being regarded as a true talent. Attractive brunette, but not in conventional screen terms.
**Achievements:** 1955, Best Actress Oscar for *The Rose Tattoo.* Died: 1973, of complications stemming from surgery.

**Sid Grauman**  *Theater owner*                6377 Hollywood

**Born:** March 17, 1897, in Indianapolis, IN.
**Spotlights:** With showmanship genius, he brought Chinese artisans and artifacts to Hollywood to build the world-famous Chinese Theater from his designs. He loved luxury. The opulent theater is known for its unusual architecture, footprints and handprints in cement in its courtyard, and for glamorous premieres. Died: 1950.

**Nathan Milstein** *Musician*                6377 Hollywood

**Born:** Dec. 31, 1904, in Russia.
**Spotlights:** Virtuoso violinist recording artist with a sparkling style.

**Art Linkletter** *See page 221.*                6377 Hollywood

**Harry Carey, Jr.** *Actor*                6363 Hollywood

**Born:** May 16, 1921, in Saugus, CA.
**Spotlights:** Greasepaint runs in the family's veins; screen debut with pop in *Red River* (1948). Like his dad, he also specialized in westerns, *She Wore a Yellow Ribbon* (1949) with John Wayne; also *Mister Rogers* (1955). Movies frequently seen on TV.

**Erroll Garner** *Musician*                6363 Hollywood

**Born:** June 15, 1923, in Pittsburgh, PA.
**Spotlights:** Internationally renowned pianist and composer, on concert and night-club circuit. Film scores, too.

**Victor Young** *Songwriter, arranger,*                6363 Hollywood
*conductor, pianist, violinist*

**Born:** Aug. 8, 1900, in Chicago, IL.
**Spotlights:** Grew up in the tenements of the "Windy City." Involved with over 350 film scores (mostly for Paramount). Selections include: "Love Letters," "Stella by Starlight," and "Around the World in 80 Days."
**Sidelights:** Young surprised everyone with his tough prizefighter looks. Upon first glance it was difficult for studio producers to believe he had been a solo violinist with the Warsaw Philharmonic Orchestra - let alone that he was a musical genius.

## Edmund Lowe  *Actor*  6363 Hollywood

**Born:** March 3, 1890, in San Jose, CA.
**Spotlights:** Handsome, black-haired, mustached, refined, well-dressed leading man in over 100 pictures. Formerly a teacher. On-screen in *The Spreading Dawn* (1917). Surprisingly brilliant in a role that was the antithesis of his personality, as Sergeant Quirt ("a lousy bum") in *What Price Glory?* (1926) and the comedy Hagg and Quirt series that followed. TV: "Front Page Detective" was about newspaper columnist David Chase (1951–53). Died: 1971, from lung disease.

## Guy Lombardo  *See page 54.*  6363 Hollywood

## William S. Hart  *Actor, screenwriter, director*  6363 Hollywood

**Born:** Dec. 6, 1870, in Newburgh, N.Y.
**Spotlights:** Brought the true flavor of the Old West to the screen. *Tumbleweeds* (1925) is one of his realistic works to survive (it was reissued in 1939). Died: 1946.

## Ilka Chase  *Actress*  6361 Hollywood

**Born:** April 8, 1903, in New York, N.Y.
**Spotlights:** Refined, bilingual (French), who was a natural in upper-class roles. *Miss Tatlock's Millions* (1948). TV: Host of "Glamour-Go-Round" (1950). Died: 1978.

## Jack Carson  *See page 224.*  6361 Hollywood

## Charles Ruggles  *See page 195.*  6359 Hollywood

## Jack Lemmon  *Actor*  6357 Hollywood

**Born:** John Lemmon III; on Feb. 8, 1925, in Boston, MA.
**Spotlights:** A shining performer during his college years at Harvard. With his humorous flair for sneering and carping, he emerged as one of the greatest light comedians. Columbia's *It Should Happen to You* (1954), UA's *Some Like It Hot* (1959), and *The Odd Couple* (1968). Enjoyable offbeat performance in *Bell, Book, and Candle* (1958). A fine serious actor too, in *Days of Wine and Roses* (1962), *The China Syndrome* (1979).
**Achievements:** 1955, Best Supporting Actor Oscar, *Mister Roberts*; 1973, Best Actor, *Save the Tiger*.

## Walter Matthau  *Actor*  6357 Hollywood

**Born:** Walter Matuschanskayasky; Oct. 1, 1920, in New York.
**Spotlights:** Lovable, cranky, slouchy, extremely watchable performer in *The Odd Couple* (1968), *Cactus Flower* (1966), *Kotch* (1971), *The Sunshine Boys* (1975); more. He's a one-of-a-kind superstar.
**Achievements:** 1966, Best Supporting Actor Oscar for *The Fortune Cookie*.

**Dave Garroway**  📻  *See page 195.*  **6355 Hollywood**

**Charles Ray**  🎥  *Actor*  **6355 Hollywood**

**Born:** March 15, 1891, in Jacksonville, IL.

**Spotlights:** Early silent screen star — popular until 1919 — in films we wouldn't see today: *A Slave's Devotion* (1913) and *The Clodhopper* (1917). Died: 1943.

**Geraldine Fitzgerald**  📺  *Actress*  **6353 Hollywood**

**Born:** Nov. 24, 1914, in Ireland.

**Spotlights:** This dark-haired lass showed tremendous promise in *Wuthering Heights* (1939) and *The Gay Sisters* (1942). Pal of Bette Davis, but her unreasonable demands at Warner Brothers were responsible for the demise of her career.

**Billie Dove**  📺  *Actress*  **6351 Hollywood**

**Born:** Lillian Bohney; May 14, 1900, in New York.

**Spotlights:** Star of *Polly of the Follies* (1922) and *The Black Pirate* (1926) with dashing Douglas Fairbanks — "in living color!"

**Sidelights:** The master showman — the dazzling Florenz Ziegfeld — discovered this beauty, and famous artist Alberto Vargas painted her.

**Gypsy Rose Lee**  📺  *Stripper, writer, actress*  **6351 Hollywood**

**Born:** Rose Louise Hovick; Feb. 19, 1914, in Seattle, WA.

**Spotlights:** Cool and aloof when she disrobed on the best of the "high-class strip

*Jack Lemmon*

*Fay Wray*

joint" stages, down to her pasties and G-string. The uptown audiences who idolizied her made her rich. Her 12 motion pictures include *Ali Baba Goes to Town* (1937), with Eddie Cantor, and *The Trouble with Angels* (1966) starring Rosalind Russell. Four years earlier, Rosalind Russell starred as Gypsy's mother in the movie based on the burlesque queen's 1957 autobiography, *Gypsy.* Died: 1970.

### Fay Wray  *Actress*          **6349 Hollywood**

**Born:** Vina Fay Wray; Sept. 15, 1907, in Canada.
**Spotlights:** Youthful, beautiful, she burst into stardom in Erich von Stroheim's *The Wedding March*, an incredibly long — 3 hours and 16 minutes — black and white silent (1928). Her niche though was in 1930s horror films. *King Kong* (1933) lifted her to heights beyond her wildest imagination when millions of fans crowned her the new "Screaming Queen of Monster Movies."

### Zachary Scott  *Actor*          **6349 Hollywood**

**Born:** Feb. 24, 1914, in Austin, TX.
**Spotlights:** Dark-haired, mustached, smooth leading man, often cast as a "scoundrel" including: *Danger Signal* (1945), in which he played a two-timing cad with his fiancee and her sister; in *Her Kind of Man* (1946), he played a gangster gambler. In 1947 replaced Bogart on last-minute notice in *Stallion Road* with Ronald Reagan and Alexis Smith. Died: 1965, from a brain tumor.

### Onslow Stevens   *Actor*          **6349 Hollywood**

**Born:** Onslow Stevenson; March 29, 1902, in Los Angeles, CA.
**Spotlights:** Character actor, first signed by Universal: *Once in a Lifetime* (1932), *The Three Musketeers* (1935), *All the Fine Young Cannibals* (1960). Died: 1977.

# ⋆ 6333 HOLLYWOOD ⋆

**Bud Abbott**  📺  *See page 251.*  6333 Hollywood

**Guy Madison**  📺  *Actor*  6333 Hollywood
**Born:**  Robert Moseley; Jan. 19, 1922, in Bakersfield, Calif.
**Spotlights:**  Radio star of "Wild Bill Hickok"; he played the U. S. marshal on this favorite western (first aired, Mutual, 1952). TV: Also lead in "The Adventures of Wild Bill Hickok" as Marshall James Butler Hickok (1951–58).

**Charles Winninger**  🎙  *Actor*  6333 Hollywood
**Born:**  May 26, 1884, in Athens, Wis.
**Spotlights:**  "It's only the beginnin' folks!" Top billing as Captain Henry on "Show Boat," variety (NBC radio, 1932). Dozens of character roles. On-screen, including Universal's *Three Smart Girls* (1936).
**Sidelights:**  Performer in the Winninger Family Novelty Company at the Chicago's World Fair in the late 1890s. Saw the first American appearance of the Little Egypt belly dancing troupe there, too! Died: 1969.

**Jim Lowe**  💿  *Songwriter, recording artist, disc jockey*  6333 Hollywood
**Born:**  May 7, 1927, in Springfield, Mo.
**Spotlights:**  Spent World War II in the army, then educated at the University of Missouri. Wrote hit song "Gambler's Guitar" for the extremely popular country-and-western singer, Rusty Draper. Recordings of the late 1950s include "The Green Door," "Four Walls," and "Talkin' to the Blues." Also a d.j. since the late 1940s; celebrated radio personality at New York station, WNEW.

**Jean Arthur**  🎥  *Actress, comedian*  6333 Hollywood
**Born:**  Gladys Greene; Oct. 17, 1905, in New York.
**Spotlights:**  Pretty, large-eyed, throaty-voiced, peppy blond who excelled in 1930s comedies and was director Frank Capra's favorite actress. Partial Columbia listing includes *The Whole Town's Talking* (1935), opposite Edward G. Robinson; Capra's *Mr. Deeds Goes to Town* (1936), opposite Gary Cooper. A sparkling performance in *The More the Merrier* (1943).
**Sidelights:**  A high school dropout who taught drama at prestigious Vassar!

**Ed Wynn**  🎙  *See page 242.*  6333 Hollywood

## Paul Winchell  *Ventriloquist*     6333 Hollywood
**Born:** Dec. 21, 1924, in New York.
**Spotlights:** His 1944 radio show, "Paul Winchell-Jerry Mahoney Show" went to TV format, comedy-variety (1950–54). Jerry was the dummy. His voice heard on the children's "Smurfs" cartoon show.

## Jetta Goudal   *Actress*     6333 Hollywood
**Born:** July 18, 1898, in France.
**Spotlights:** *Paris at Midnight* (1926) and *The Cardboard Lover* (1928) were two of her silent pictures. Her heavy French accent prevented her from continuing in talkies.

## Richard Carlson   *Actor*     6333 Hollywood
**Born:** April 29, 1912, in Albert Lea, Min.
**Spotlights:** Starred as Herbert Philbrick in the syndicated intrigue series, "I Led Three Lives:" (1) U.S. citizen, (2) Communist party member, and (3) FBI counterspy. Their Red Scare slogan? "Your best friend might be a traitor" (1953–56). Died: 1977.

## Ann Rutherford   *See page 338.*     6333 Hollywood

## Tony Martin   *See page 294.*     6331 Hollywood

## Otto Kruger   *See page 120.*     6331 Hollywood

## Dorothy Kirsten   *Opera singer*     6331 Hollywood
**Born:** July 6, 1919, in New Jersey.
**Spotlights:** Lovely, temperamental soprano prima donna, reigned at Metropolitan Opera for three decades. Films, too.

## Kenny Baker   *Singer, actor*     6329 Hollywood
**Born:** Sept. 30, 1912.
**Spotlights:** "Blue Ribbon Town" (named after the sponsor, Pabst) featured the comedy-musical talents of Baker, Groucho Marx, and others. First aired in 1943. Featured tenor on "The Jack Benny Program."

## Eve Arden   *See page 325.*     6329 Hollywood

## Grace Kelly   *Actress*     6329 Hollywood
**Born:** Nov. 12, 1928, in Philadelphia, Pa.
**Spotlights:** Elegant, graceful blond beauty from a blue-blood family. One of Alfred Hitchcock's favorite actresses: *Dial M for Murder, Rear Window* (both 1954); *To Catch a Thief* (1955).

**Achievements:**   1954, Best Actress Oscar, *The Country Girl*.
**Highlights:**   Married Prince Rainier III in 1956 and retired from the screen. Died: 1982, of heart failure in an automobile accident.

## C. Aubrey Smith   *Actor*                          6327 Hollywood

**Born:**   Charles Aubrey Smith; July 21, 1863, in England.
**Spotlights:**   One of the few knights on the Walk of Fame — Sir Charles Aubrey Smith usually played stately characters. *Little Lord Fauntleroy* (1936) and *A Bill of Divorcement* (1940).
**Sidelights:**   Knighted in 1944. Died: 1948, from pneumonia.

## Henry King   *Director*                          6327 Hollywood

**Born:**   June 24, 1888, in Christianburg, Va.
**Spotlights:**   *State Fair* (1933), starring Will Rogers and Janet Gaynor, *Stanley and Livingston* (1939), starring Spencer Tracy and Cedric Hardwicke, and *The Song of Bernadette* (1943), starring Jennifer Jones are but a few fine examples proving that King's pictures stood up to the test of time. Died: 1982.

## Rosemary Clooney   *Singer, actress*              6327 Hollywood

**Born:**   May 23, 1928, in Maysville, Ky.
**Spotlights:**   Leading lady in *White Christmas* (1954), starring Bing Crosby and Danny Kaye, and *Deep in My Heart* (1955) with her then husband, actor Jose Ferrer. Recorded with Duke Ellington, Harry James, and the Benny Goodman Orchestra.

*Grace Kelly*                          *Rosemary Clooney*

Songs include "Come On-a My House" and "Tenderly." Still a very popular jazz singer in 1987.

**Desi Arnaz**   *See page 192.*  6327 Hollywood

**Lawrence Tibbett** 🎵  *Opera singer*  6325 Hollywood
**Born:** November 16, 1896, in Bakersfield, Calif.
**Spotlights:** American baritone. Debut at the Metropolitan Opera in *Boris Godunov*. Dark, good looks made him a popular figure in films, *The Rogue Song* (1930), *The New Moon* (1931), as well as light opera. Died: 1960.

**Frank Lovejoy**  *Actor*  6325 Hollywood
**Born:** March 28, 1914, in Bronx, N.Y.
**Spotlights:** Appeared in two detective series: Mike Barnett in "Man Against Crime," (1956) and McGraw in "Meet McGraw" (1957–59).

**Gordon Macrae**  *Singer, actor*  6325 Hollywood
**Born:** March 12, 1921, in East Orange, N.J.
**Spotlights:** Comedy-drama star of the long-running music radio show "The Railroad Hour" (NBC, 1948). Busy TV entertainer from 1950–60.

**Lynn Bari**  *See page 180.*  6323 Hollywood

**Rusty Hamer**  *Actor*  6323 Hollywood
**Born:** Russell Hamer; Feb. 15, 1947.
**Spotlights:** He was the 6-year-old son Rusty Williams on "The Danny Thomas Show" (1953–64); literally grew up in front of millions of viewers.

**June Lockhart**  *See page 281.*  6321 Hollywood

**Ann Dvorak**  *Actress*  6321 Hollywood
**Born:** Ann McKim; Aug. 2, 1912, in New York.
**Spotlights:** Dvorak's talent might have been inherited from her silent screen star mother or her studio manager father. In any case, it was apparent, along with her beauty, in *Sky Devils* (1932) and *Scarface* (1932). Died: 1970.

**Sophie Tucker**  *Actress, singer*  6321 Hollywood
**Born:** Sohia Abuza; Jan. 13, 1884, in Boston, Mass.
**Spotlights:** Nicknamed "The Last of the Red-Hot Mamas." *Honky Tonk* (1929), MGM's *Broadway Melody of 1938*. TV: "The George Jessel Show" (1953–54). Died: 1966.

**Laurence Olivier**   *Actor, director, producer*          6321 Hollywood

**Born:**  May 22, 1907, in England.

**Spotlights:**  Widely acclaimed as the greatest actor of the century. "Whether 'tis nobler in the mind" to be a stage or cinema actor, Olivier has dedicated most of his life to the former, but has left an indelible treasury of performances on films, too. *Wuthering Heights* (1939); *Rebecca* (1940); *Sleuth* (1972); *Marathon Man* (1976).

**Achievements:**  Knighted Sir Laurence Olivier (in 1947); 1960, received the honor of a baronetcy, as Lord Olivier. 1946, special Oscar for Shakespearean perfection in *Henry V*; 1948, Best Actor Oscar and Best Picture for *Hamlet*; he also directed both films. 1979, special Oscar.

**Sidelights:**  Friends call Lord Olivier "Larry." Asked, in the 1940s, about TV work, he responded, "TV is here to stay."

**Peggy Lee**  *Singer, actress*          6319 Hollywood

**Born:**  Norma Egstrom; May 26, 1920, in Jamestown, Md.

**Spotlights:**  "Fever" and other tunes have kept Miss Lee's tremendous voice sizzling hot. Co-wrote "It's a Good Day." Formerly with the Benny Goodman band.

**Achievements:**  1969, Grammy, pop vocalist.

*Laurence Olivier*

## Bob Crosby  🎙 *Orchestra leader*  6319 Hollywood

**Born:** Aug. 23, 1913, in Spokane, Wash.

**Spotlights:** Like his older brother, Bing, he began as a singer. After performing with the Jimmy and Tommy Dorsey band, he formed Bob Crosby and the Bobcats band. Listeners enjoyed his swing sound on radio's musical variety, "The Bob Crosby Show" (CBS, 1939; NBC, 1943). Also, radio host of "Club 15" with the Andrews Sisters. TV: Star of his own show on NBC (1958).

## Marjorie Lord  📺 *Actress*  6317 Hollywood

**Born:** July 26, 1922, in San Francisco, Calif.

**Spotlights:** She played Danny Thomas's second wife, Mrs. Kathy Williams-Clancey (1957–64) in "Make Room for Daddy."

## Dick Lane  📺 *Sportscaster, TV pioneer, actor*  6317 Hollywood

**Born:** May 28, 1899, in Rice Lake, Wisc.

**Spotlights:** "Whoa, Nellie!" was Lane's best remembered remark. Spirited announcer of roller derby and wrestling events. Fender-bending, fast-talking TV salesman since 1947. Film credits, vaudeville, and legitimate theater, too. Covered the first news broadcast of an atomic explosion test in the 1950s. Los Angeles Channel 5 newsman in 1964. Died: 1982.

## Mike Gore  🎥 *Pioneer exhibitor, movie magnate*  6315½ Hollywood

**Born:** 1876, in Russia.

**Spotlights:** Arrived in America in 1906. Co-founder of West Coast Theaters in 1923. Involved with the Old First National Pictures Co.

**Highlights:** His daughter was Mrs. Harry Sugarman.

## Bill Cunningham  🎙 *Host, newscaster, interviewer*  6315½ Hollywood

**Spotlights:** Hosted the top-notch interview program called "Meet the Boss." The first telecast on June 10, 1952 set into motion a unique format of interviewing executives about their industrious careers.

## Roland Young  📺 *See page 77.*  6315 Hollywood

## Jack Holt  🎥 *Actor*  6315 Hollywood

**Born:** Charles J. Holt; May 31, 1888, in Winchester, Va.

**Spotlights:** Dark-haired, mustached, tall leading and supporting actor who made over 150 films between 1914 and 1951; *North of the Rio Grande* (1922), *The Littlest Rebel* (1935), and *Cat People* (1942). Died: 1951, of a heart attack.

## W. C. Fields  🎙 *See page 356.*  6315 Hollywood

## Hedda Hopper 🎥 *Gossip columnist, actress* 6315 Hollywood

**Born:** Elda Furry; June 2, 1890, in Hollidaysburg, Pa.

**Spotlights:** "Hollywood's Gossip Queen" whose 35 million daily readers gave her much power. Hopper and archenemy and competitive gossip columnist Louella Parsons had the ability to evaporate careers with their pens, and influence box office receipts by merely hinting a movie was a stinker. Her trademark? A collection of hats.

**Sidelights:** Second v.p. (under president John Wayne) of the anti- communist Motion Picture Alliance for the Preservation of American Ideals. Died: 1966.

## Don Ameche 🎤 *Actor* 6313 Hollywood

**Born:** Dominic Amici; May 31, 1908, in Kenosha, Wisc.

**Spotlights:** Versatile radio talent—as Bob Drake in the dramatic marriage serial "Betty and Bob" (NBC, 1932); John Bickerson in the marriage comedy "The Bickersons" (CBS, 1947); more. TV: Ameche was the refined, cheerful host of "Coke Time with Eddie Fisher," a music show in 1953. Ameche, an accomplished stage and screen actor, was first seen on-screen in 1936.

**Achievements:** 1985, Best Supporting Actor Award for *Cocoon*.

## Al St. John 🎥 *Comedian* 6313 Hollywood

**Born:** Sept. 10, 1893, in Santa Ana, Calif.

**Spotlights:** Clowned around with the silent screen's top funnymen, including Charlie Chaplin, W. C. Fields and Roscoe "Fatty" Arbuckle. *Young and Dumb* (1923), *Stupid but Brave* (1924). Died: 1963.

## Nelson Eddy 🎥 *Singer, actor* 6313 Hollywood

**Born:** June 29, 1901, in Providence, R.I.

**Spotlights:** The 23-year-old baritone won a talent competition to perform with the Philadelphia Civic Opera in *Aida*. Radio: Co-host with Bing Crosby, Al Jolson, and Dorothy Kirsten on "The Kraft Music Hall," variety show (1934).

**Achievements:** On film, his recorded melodic voice was a perfect complement to Jeanette MacDonald's in MGM's *Naughty Marietta* (1935) and *Rose Marie* (1936). Favorite, romantic singing duo of the 1930s screen. Died: 1967, of a stroke after a show.

## Tennessee Ernie Ford  *Singer, songwriter, actor, disc jockey* 6311 Hollywood

**Born:** Feb. 13, 1919 in Bristol, Tenn.

**Spotlights:** Rich bass voice. On radio since 1937 ($10.00 per week) "Hillbilly DJ" on KSLA C & W station in Pasadena, California. Then ABC and CBS radio shows (1950–55), 1955 NBC-TV own daytime show, evening show from 1956 to 1961. ABC-TV 1962–65, then on again, off again. String of hit songs: "Sixteen Tons,"

"Smokey Mountain Boogie," and "Shotgun Boogie"; more. Catchphrase: "Bless your pea- picken hearts!"
**Achievements:** 1964, Grammy, Gospel.

## Joan Blondell  *Actress*

**Born:** Aug. 30, 1909, in New York.
**Spotlights:** Practically born in a vaudeville trunk; both parents were comfortable on the stage. The Blondell family toured worldwide, before the fiesty blond alighted in Texas. She won the Miss Dallas title. James Cagney and she triumphantly performed in the play *Penny Arcade*. Warner Brothers saw them, signed both actor and actress (her 5-year contract started at $200 per week), retitled the play *Sinners' Holiday*, and made a movie (1930). They would be paired together in later films. By 1935 she was enjoying full-fledged star status. The saucy glamor girl made close to 100 films. Died: 1979, from leukemia.

## Van Heflin *Actor*

6309 Hollywood

**Born:** Emmett Evan Heflin, Jr.; on Dec. 13, 1910, in Walters, Okla.
**Spotlights:** Opened career in *A Woman Rebels* (1936), starring Katharine Hepburn. His characterizations in Paramount's stately western *Shane* (1953) and the "sky-scraper jungle" melodrama *Patterns* (1956), written by Rod Sterling, used his superb skills well. TV work includes: "The Dark Side of Earth" (1957), "Rank and File" (1959), and "The Cruel Day" (1960).
**Achievements:** 1942, Best Supporting Actor in *Johnny Eager*. Died: 1971, of cardiac arrest while swimming.

*Tennessee Ernie Ford*                    *Constance Binney*

## Hillary Brooke  *Actress* 6307 Hollywood

**Born:** Beatrice Peterson; Sept. 8, 1914, in Long Island, N.Y.
**Spotlights:** Delightful in the slapstick comedy "The Abbot and Costello Show" (1951–53) as the girlfriend of Lou Costello. A lovely blonde who played love interest Roberta Townsend to the father of "My Little Margie" (1952–55).

## Theda Bara  *Actress* 6307 Hollywood

**Born:** Theodosia Goodman; July 20, 1890, in Cincinnati, Ohio.
**Spotlights:** The screen's very first femme fatale. Rose to goddess stature in the silent film, *A Fool There Was* (1914). The word *vamp* was added to the English language to describe her; she was the first star created entirely by publicity. Made close to 40 silents, mostly playing vamps.
**Sidelights:** Fox's restrictive contract, which prevented her from a normal life — she could not marry and was forced to wear veils in public like a belly dancer- -provided her with many benefits, including a $4,000-a-week job (virtually income-tax free, too!) On stage she pulled in a hefty $6,000 a week. Retired in 1921 upon becoming happily married. Died: 1955, from cancer.

## Mildred Harris  *Actress* 6305 Hollywood

**Born:** Nov. 29, 1901, in Cheyenne, Wyo.
**Spotlights:** Played Dorothy in *The Wizard of Oz* (1914–15) silent series. Also worked in D. W. Griffith's *Intolerance* (1916).
**Highlights:** Married to Charlie Chaplin (1917–20). Died: 1944.

## Ernie Kovacs ■ *Actor* 6305 Hollywood

**Born:** Jan. 23, 1919, in Trenton, N.J.
**Spotlights:** Black-haired, mustached, wacky, cigar-chewing comic in "Ernie in Kovacsland" (1951); his future wife, Edie Adams, was a regular on the show. "The Ernie Kovacs Show" (1952–56); co-host of *Tonight* (1956-57). Quiz show panelist. Died: 1962, in an automobile accident.

## George Sidney *Director* 6303 Hollywood

**Born:** Oct. 4, 1916, in Long Island, N.Y.
**Spotlights:** Excelled in musicals: *Showboat* (1951) and *Bye Bye Birdie* (1960). *Viva Las Vegas* (1964) wasn't a fabulous movie, but it gave Elvis Presley fans another cherished glimpse of the "King."
**Highlights:** 1940, Oscar, *Quicker'n a Wink* (short); 1941, Oscar *Of Pups and Puzzles* (short).

## Gene Lockhart *Actor* 6303 Hollywood

**Born:** July 18, 1891, in Canada.
**Spotlights:** Extremely good playing a scoundrel or a saint. This versatile character

actor played Bob Crachit in *A Christmas Carol* (1938); Regis in *Algiers* (1938); and 80 other pictures. TV: "Fireside Theater," dramatic anthology.
**Highlights:**  Married Kathleen Lockhart; father of actress June Lockhart. Died: 1959.

### Cass Daley  *Comedienne*
6303 Hollywood

**Born:**  Katherine Dailey; July 17, 1915 in Philadelphia, Pa.
**Spotlights:**  "I said it and I'm glad!" was her well-loved catch-phrase on radio's "Maxwell House Coffee Time" comedy-variety program that first aired in 1937. Film debut in *The Fleet's In* (1941). *Red Garters* (1954); more. Popular for a wonderful and crazy song-and-dance routine. TV guest spots. Died 1975, from an accidental fall.

### Marie Wilson  *See page 68.*
6301 Hollywood

### George Montgomery  *Actor*
6301 Hollywood

**Born:**  George M. Letz; Aug. 29, 1916, in Brady, Mon.
**Spotlights:**  Extremely well-built, 6', former champion boxer, who rode high in westerns: *Cimarron City* (1958–60) as Matthew Rockford.
**Highlights:**  Engaged to Ginger Rogers, then Hedy Lamarr, then married Dinah Shore (1943–60).

### Constance Binney  *Actress*
6301 Hollywood

**Born:**  Binney guarded her birth information like a treasure.
**Spotlights:**  Newcomer silent screen bit actress spotted by the keen eye of Adolph Zukor (later president of Paramount); *Sporting Life* (1918), *Erstwhile Susan* (1919), *39 East* (1920). Momentarily in the same league as John Barrymore and Nita Naldi.

### Matt Moore  *Actor*
6301 Hollywood

**Born:**  Jan. 8, 1888, in Ireland.
**Spotlights:**  Appeared in bit parts, supporting, romantic, and character roles in a career that lasted 4½ decades: *Traffic in Souls* (1913) to *An Affair to Remember* (1957).
**Sidelights:**  Both brothers, Owen and Tom, also have stars on the Walk of Fame. Died: 1960.

### Gloria Swanson  *See page 328.*
6301 Hollywood

### Carmen Cavallaro  *Pianist, orchestra leader*
6301 Hollywood

**Born:**  May 6, 1913, in New York.
**Spotlights:**  Showy pianist with exact technique. Credited as "the poet of the piano." Dance music bandleader. Films: *Hollywood Canteen* (1944) and *Diamond Horseshoe*, (1945). Soundtrack for movies, radio shows, concerts. Composed

songs: "Masquerade Waltz" and "Wanda." Records: "My Silent Love" "I'm Getting Sentimental Over You." LPs: *The King and I and Other Rodgers-Hammerstein Songs.*

### Carey Wilson  *Writer, producer*                        6301 Hollywood

**Born:** May 10, 1889, in Philadelphia, Pa.

**Spotlights:** Wrote stories and screenplays from 1921–39; collaborated on the script of *Mutiny on the Bounty* (1935). Produced *The Red Danube* (1949); more.

### Don McNeill  *Host*                                     6301 Hollywood

**Born:** Donald T. McNeill; Dec. 23, 1907, in Galena, Ill.

**Spotlights:** Host of "The Breakfast Club", half a century before it became the title of a popular teenage movie. The variety show was first broadcast on NBC in 1933.

### Archie Mayo  *Director*                                 6301 Hollywood

**Born:** 1891 in New York.

**Spotlights:** At Warner Brothers he directed James Cagney in *The Mayor of Hell* (1933) and Humphrey Bogart in *Black Legion* (1936); at Fox, the Marx Brothers in *A Night in Casablanca* (1946), his last film. Died: 1968.

### Carl Laemmle  *Film pioneer*              Northwest corner of Hollywood and Vine

**Born:** Jan. 17, 1867, in Germany.

**Spotlights:** Founder of Universal in 1912. Brilliant producer-executive. The Universal Studios Tour in Universal City is on a 230-acre parcel of land purchased in 1915 by Laemmle. Died: 1939.

### Neil Armstrong, Edwin E. Aldrin, Jr., Michael Collins

*Astronauts*   *See page 204.*        Northwest corner of Hollywood and Vine

### Jo Stafford  *See page 257.*        Northwest corner of Hollywood and Vine

### Artie Shaw   *Jazz clarinetist, bandleader,*   Northwest corner of Hollywood and Vine
*composer, arranger*

**Born:** Arthur Arshawsky; May 23, 1910, in New York.

**Spotlights:** Formed band in 1936-a string quartet, clarinet, and three rhythm instruments. Swing band formed in 1937 included Billie Holliday. In 1938 recorded Cole Porter's "Begin the Beguine." Other hits included "Frenesi," "Summit Ridge Drive," and "Concerto for Clarinet."

**Sidelights:** In 1939, when he had the hottest band, and the world was getting closer to war he said "Wild dances were reflective of optimism and frenetic happiness."

**Marilyn Miller**  *Actress, singer, dancer*  **Northwest corner of Hollywood and Vine**

**Born:** Mary Ellen Reynolds; Sept. 1, 1898, in Evansville, Ill.

**Spotlights:** Trained as a singer-dancer from age three, on stage by five, and a full-blown Broadway musical star in her early twenties. Films include *Sally; Sunny* (1930) and *Her Majesty Love* (1931).

**Sidelights:** Norma Jean Dougherty liked the soft sound of the double "M" names and borrowed the first name of "Marilyn" from Miller for her own stage name, Marilyn Monroe. Miller was portrayed by Judy Garland in the film biography *Till the Clouds Roll By* (1946) and by June Haver in *Look for the Silver Lining* (1949). Died: 1937.

# ⋆ 1711 VINE ⋆

**Jessica Dragonette**  📱  *Singer, hostess*                    1711 Vine

**Born:** Calcutta, India.
**Spotlights:** Soprano. "The Little Angel" broke new ground being one of radio's earliest female celebrities. "The Cities Service Concert" (1927); star of the "Palmolive Beauty Box Theater" (NBC, 1937).
**Sidelights:** Also known as "Vivian, the Coca-Cola Girl."

**George Stevens**  🎥  *Director*                    1711 Vine

**Born:** Dec. 18, 1904, in Oakland, Calif.
**Spotlights:** *Swing Time* (1936), with Fred Astaire and Ginger Rogers; *Gunga Din* (1939), with Cary Grant; *Shane* (1953), with Alan Ladd.
**Achievements:** 1951, Best Director for *A Place in the Sun*; 1953, Irving Thalberg Memorial Academy Award; 1956, Best Director Oscar for *Giant*. Died: 1975.

**Miriam Hopkins**  🎥  *Actress*                    1711 Vine

**Born:** Ellen M. Hopkins; Oct. 18, 1902, in Bainbridge, Ga.
**Spotlights:** Hopkins's Broadway notoriety earned the testy but chic actress a 7- year Paramount contract beginning at $1,000 a week. Talent emerged in thirties sophisticated comedies: Ernest Lubitsch's *The Smiling Lieutenant* (1931); *Trouble in Paradise* (1932), with Herbert Marshall. *The Old Maid* (1939), starring Bette Davis, was a Civil War weepy woman's movie. TV: Dramatic appearances on "Lux Video Theater" (1954). Died: 1972. of a heart attack.

**Robert Q. Lewis**  📺  *Comedian, host*                    1711 Vine

**Born:** April 5, 1924, in New York.
**Spotlights:** Dual roles as host on "The Robert Q. Lewis Show" (1950–51) and "The Show Goes On", talent hunt. (1950–52). Panelist on quiz shows.

**Deborah Kerr**  🎥  *Actress*                    1711 Vine

**Born:** Deborah Kerr-Trimmer; Sept. 30, 1921, in Scotland.
**Spotlights:** Clark Gable played the lead in MGM's *The Hucksters* (1947), which wasn't a bad start for Kerr's U.S. film debut. Most frequently cast in ladylike roles, with her steamy characterization of an adulteress in *From Here to Eternity* (1953), one of the rare exceptions. Six times nominated for Best Actress Oscar.

**Art Acord**  🎥  *Actor*                    1711 Vine

**Born:** 1890, in Stillwater, Okla.

**Spotlights:** A young, rugged rodeo rider-turned-teenage stuntman. Became Universal's silent screen cowboy in the 1920s with *The Oregon Trail* (1923) (serial) and *Hard Fists* (1927). Like 99 percent of the silent stars, he couldn't make the transition to sound. His last film, *The White Outlaw* (1929), was ominous, as his second career was as a bootlegger and gambler. Died: 1931, of cyanide poisoning, in a Mexican flophouse under mysterious circumstances.

## George Eastman  *Manufacturer* 1711 Vine

**Born:** July 13, 1854, in Waterville, N.Y.

**Spotlights:** Poverty-stricken, forced to leave school at 14 to help support his widowed mother and two older sisters, one crippled by polio. His first job as a messenger boy paid $3 per week; studied accounting and eventually landed a bank clerk job for $800 a year. At 24, he planned to take his first vacation, and an associate suggested he take photographs. The wet-plate photographic equipment he bought to take simple pictures rivaled that of camping gear, with a cumbersome tripod, *big* camera, black tent, chemicals, etc. An inspired Eastman was on the way to several patents, formation of his own company, and pioneering in simplifying photography for the masses.

**Achievements:** Invented numerous photographic processes including an emulsion-coating machine for dry plates, Eastman film, the Kodak camera, flexible film (1889), enabling Thomas Edison to develop the motion picture camera, plates and paper for X-rays (1896), and more! 1952, special Oscar, one of several, for Eastman color motion picture films.

*George Eastman and Thomas Edison*

**Sidelights:** One of the greatest men of the century, Eastman made over $100 million and gave it all away (frequently anonymously) in his lifetime to enable the poor to receive dental treatment, to advance medicine and science, to further education, and to foster the arts. Also, a generous and fair employer, who started profit-sharing. Died: 1932.

**John Bowers**  *Actor*                    1711 Vine

**Born:** Dec. 25, 1899, in Garrett, Ind.
**Spotlights:** Handsome romantic in a slew of silents. Debut film in 1916 with Mary Pickford, *Hilda From Holland*. Career destroyed by talkies.
**Sidelights:** The death scene of the aging, former movie idol in *A Star is Born* (1937) was based on Bowers. Died: 1936, by drowning.

**Slim Whitman** 🎵 *Singer, guitarist*                    1711 Vine

**Born:** Otis Whitman, Jr.; Jan. 20, 1924, in Tampa, Fla.
**Spotlights:** Falsetto-voiced country-and-western entertainer who gained great recognition in the mid-sixties. Songs include: "Casting My Lasso to the Sky," "Rose Marie," "Secret Love," "China Doll," and "Rainbows Are Back In Style." Mega-star.
**Sidelights:** Learned the guitar on the naval ship, *U.S.S. Chilton*, during World War II.

**Robert Sterling** *Actor*                    1711 Vine

**Born:** William Hart; Nov. 13, 1917, in New Castle, Pa.
**Spotlights:** "George Kirby" the friendly ghost, returned to his earthly home to find "Topper" (1953–56) living there.

**Rouben Mamoulian** *Director*                    1711 Vine

**Born:** Oct. 8, 1893, in Russia.
**Spotlights:** A versatile, inventive director who demonstrated his ingenuity in 1932 in directing absolute opposites: the terrifying *Dr. Jekyll and Mr. Hyde*, with Fredric March, and the enchanting musical comedy, *Love Me Tonight*, with Maurice Chevalier. In 1933 Greta Garbo complemented his great style in *Queen Christina*.

**Eddie Heywood** 🎵 *Musician, composer, piano player, jazz*    1711 Vine

**Born:** Dec. 4, 1915 in Atlanta, Ga.
**Spotlights:** Pop style too. Played Harlem Club circuit in 1938. Organized own Jazz sextet in 1943. Gained national acclaim in the 1950s. Big instrumental hit: "Featuring Eddie Heywood."
**Sidelights:** Temporary hand paralysis put his recording career on hold (1947–51).

**Geraldine Farrar** 🎵 *Opera singer, actress*                    1711 Vine

**Born:** Feb. 28, 1882, in Melrose, Mass.
**Spotlights:** Acknowledged internationally as the very finest opera singer of her time

and the first to take her talents to the screen. Although 1915–21 pictures were silent, this beauty used her great skill as a performer to win over surprised audiences. Recorded at the Metropolitan Opera in New York. Died: 1967.

### George Brent   *Actor*
1711 Vine

**Born:**  George B. Nolan; Mar. 15, 1904, in Ireland.
**Spotlights:**  Reliable leading man who played opposite star actresses, such as Greta Garbo in *The Painted Veil* (1934), but most frequently with Bette Davis, *Jezebel* (1938). TV: Co-starred as Dean Evans on "Wire Service" (1956–59).
**Sidelights:**  Was a political criminal in native Ireland. Smuggled out of the country. Died: 1979, of emphysema.

### Elena Verdugo  *Actress*
1711 Vine

**Born:**  April 20, 1926, in Hollywood, Calif.
**Spotlights:**  Pretty, well-groomed Hispanic secretary, Millie Bronson; star of "Meet Willie" (1952–56). Has been in a variety of situation comedies. Also a regular on "Marcus Welby, M.D." (1969–76) as Consuelo Lopez.

### Robert Walker  *Actor*
1711 Vine

**Born:**  Oct. 13, 1918, in Salt Lake City, Utah.
**Spotlights:**  *See Here, Private Hargrove* (1944), *Strangers on a Train* (1951).
**Highlights:**  *Since You Went Away* (1944) was an ominous title for Walker and his beautiful co-star and wife, Jennifer Jones. Their marriage lasted from 1939–45. She left him to marry David O. Selznick.
**Sidelights:**  He became an alcoholic and was institutionalized for a breakdown. Died: 1951, from complications stemming from the use of sedatives.

### Glen Gray  *Bandleader*
1711 Vine

**Born:**  G. G. Knoblaugh; June 7, 1906, in Roanoke, Ill.
**Spotlights:**  Known as "Spike." Together with his Casa Loma Orchestra since 1929; the first all-white band to specialize in jazz albums: "Five Feet of Swing;" more.

### Fred Clark  *Actor*
1711 Vine

**Born:**  March 9, 1914, in Lincoln, Calif.
**Spotlights:**  He was one of the Harry Mortons (1951–53); on "The George Burns and Gracie Allen Show" (1950–58). Regular on the "Pantomime Quiz" in the 1950s. Died: 1968, of a liver ailment.

### Mauritz Stiller  *Director*
1713 Vine

**Born:**  Moshe Stiller; July 17, 1883, in Finland.
**Spotlights:**  Directing since 1912, Stiller was already a respected director in the early Swedish cinema when he discovered Greta Garbo, his claim to American fame. Many

critics consider *Sir Arne's Treasure* (1919) his best work. Stiller cast Garbo in *The Atonement of Gosta Berling* (1924). In 1925 Louis B. Mayer (MGM) lured Stiller to Hollywood. He accepted only with the proviso that Garbo — the actress he had been grooming for stardom — come along too. Mayer thought she was too fat for American beauty standards, but agreed. When Hollywood moguls saw Garbo's rare, mysterious beauty on screen, they ousted Stiller instead.

**Sidelights:** No, dear readers, I did not make a spelling error. But whoever carved the bronze-engraved name "Maurice Diller" certainly did! Died: 1928, of pleurisy, but many say of a broken heart from shattered dreams.

### Walter Catlett   *Actor*     1713 Vine

**Born:** Feb. 4, 1889, in San Francisco, Calif.
**Spotlights:** A former Ziegfeld entertainer, small, thin, balding, bespectacled Catlett was an ideal character for flustery, feebleminded film roles. His eyes played heavily in drama and comedy. *A Tale of Two Cities* (1935), *Mr. Deeds Goes to Town* (1936). Over 50 motion pictures to his credit. Died: 1960.

### John Lupton   *Actor*     1713 Vine

**Born:** Aug. 22, 1926, in Highland Park, Ill.
**Spotlights:** Peacemaker paleface Tom Jeffords befriends Indian Apache Chief Conchise. As blood brothers, they fought injustice on "Broken Arrow" (1956–60).

### Kim Hunter   *See page 254.*     1715 Vine

### Judy Garland   *Actress, singer*     1715 Vine

**Born:** Frances Gumm; June 10, 1922, in Grand Rapids, Mich.
**Spotlights:** A legend. One of the brightest talents of the century. The song- and- dance girl had an unbelievably marvelous, emotionally charged voice. She displayed energy, vulnerability, innocence, and intensity in her roles. Earned immortality for "Somewhere Over the Rainbow," as Dorothy in MGM's *The Wizard of Oz* (1939), in a role intended for Shirley Temple. *Meet Me in St. Louis* (1944) was also a smash hit with her memorable rendition of "The Trolley Song." She gave a warm, sensitive, sparkling performance in *A Star is Born*; theme song: "The Man That Got Away." Millions of records sold.
**Achievements:** 1939, special Oscar.
**Highlights:** Married to actor Vincent Minnelli (third of five) (1945–50). This union was blessed with a daughter, Liza Minnelli. Wed manager-producer Sid Luft (1952–65). The couple had two children, one being the lovely actress Lorna Luft.
**Sidelights:** On stage at age 3, she was signed 10 years later, by Louis B. Mayer to a contract. Her pressured, busy life burned this bright star out. Died: 1969.

### Pee Wee King   *Country-and-western bandleader*     1715 Vine

**Born:** Frank King; Feb. 18, 1914, in Abrams, Wisc.

**Spotlights:** Played harmonica, accordian, and fiddle. Albums: *Blue Ribbon Country, Vol. 3; Best of Pee Wee King, Stars of the Grand Ole Opry, 1926–74.* Singles: "Tennessee Waltz" and "Slow Poke." Pee Wee King and His Golden West Cowboys had their own musical variety TV show in 1955 with King's favorite square dancers.

## John Bunny 🎥 *Actor* 1715 **Vine**

**Born:** Sept. 21, 1863, in New York.
**Spotlights:** America's *original* fat (295-lb.) funny man: *Vanity Fair* (1911), *Pigs Is Pigs* (1914), *Bunny in Bunnyland* (1915). Died: 1915, of a heart condition.

## John Nesbitt 🎥 *Film narrator, producer, radio and* 1717 **Vine**
*television storyteller*

**Born:** Aug. 23, 1910, in Victoria, B.C., Canada.
**Spotlights:** On radio and television called the "top teller of tales." Signed with MGM in 1938 to produce a series of Passing Parade shorts.
**Achievements:** Academy Awards for his one-reel shorts: *That Mothers Might Live* (1938); *Pups and Puzzles* and *Main Street on the March* (both 1941); *Stairway to Light* (1945); and *Goodbye Miss Turlock* (1947).
**Sidelights:** Attributed his "distinctive speaking voice due to the fact I had to talk into my father's close-to-deaf ear." Died: 1960 of a heart attack.

## Verna Felton 📺 *Actress* 1717 **Vine**

**Born:** July 29, 1890, in Salinas, Calif.
**Spotlights:** She was Mrs. Day on "The RCA Victor Show" (1952) and the busybody friend of the unappreciated wife in "Pete and Gladys" (1960–61), a situation comedy. Walt Disney used her voice in many of his animated pictures, including *Dumbo* (1941), *Cinderella* (1950), *Lady and the Tramp* (1955); and *Sleeping Beauty* (1959). Died: 1966.

## James Dean 🎥 *Actor* 1717 **Vine**

**Born:** Feb. 8, 1931, in Marian, Neb.
**Spotlights:** Acclaimed performances in *East of Eden* (1955), *Rebel Without a Cause* (1955), and *Giant* (1956).
**Lowlights:** His proposal of marriage to actress Pier Angeli was a bitter failure. Her mother wouldn't allow the union because he wasn't Catholic, although Dean wanted to convert. She committed suicide 16 years later (1971) "I was only in love once in my life and that was with Jimmy Dean." Died: 1955 at the wheel of his Porsche Speedster in a horrible accident. The "Live Fast, Die Young" line was tagged on him.

## Cesar Romero 📺 *See page 66.* 1719 **Vine**

## Mark Sandrich 🎥 *Director* 1719 **Vine**
**Born:** Aug. 26, 1900, in New York.

**Spotlights:** *The Gay Divorcee* (1934) introduced the Rogers-Astaire team; *Top Hat* (1935). Directed and produced *Holiday Inn* (1942).
**Achievements:** 1932–33, Oscar for *So This Is Harris* (short).

## Charlie Murray   Actor     1719 Vine
**Born:** June 22, 1872, in Laurel, IN.
**Spotlights:** The "Murray" half of the "Murray and Mack" vaudeville team. Joined Biograph Studios in 1912. (A pioneer company located on East 14th Street in New York City). Films include *Soldiers of Misfortune* (1914) and *The Cohens and Kellys in Trouble* (1933), he comically portrayed Mr. Kelly in this series. Died: 1941 of pneumonia.

## Eddie Foy   Vaudeville performer     1719 Vine
**Born:** March 9, 1856, in New York.
**Spotlights:** Best remembered as the father of the "Seven Little Foys." (Bob Hope starred in the movie of the same title in 1955). Foy appeared in one film (with his children), *A Favorite Fool* (1915).
**Sidelights:** "Vaudeville" derived from the French source *Voix de Ville* (voices of the village/street songs). In America it was a popular form of entertainment — variety shows — from the late 1800s to the 1930s. Died: 1928.

## Victor Fleming   Director     1719 Vine
**Born:** Feb. 23, 1883, in Pasadena, CA
**Spotlights:** Brilliant, sensitive experienced director of silent screen stars, such as Clara Bow in *Mantrap* (1926). Also adept at working with strong, leading men, such as Gary Cooper, *The Virginian* (1929). In 1939, he directed MGM's classics *The Wizard of Oz* and *Gone with the Wind*.
**Achievements:** 1939, Best Director, *Gone with the Wind* (although directors George Cukor and Sam Wood put their efforts into it too). Died: 1949.

## Hattie McDaniel   Actress     1719 Vine
**Born:** June 10, 1895, in Wichita, Kan.
**Spotlights:** Over 300 films to her credit, but this versatile performer was immortalized in her role as Mammy in *Gone with the Wind* (1939), *Show Boat* (1936). Radio: First black on the air. "Amos 'n Andy" (first aired in 1926).
**Achievements:** 1939 Best Supporting Actress Academy Award *Gone with the Wind*. First black to win an Oscar. Died: 1952.

## Barbara Britton   Actress     1719 Vine
**Born:** Barbara Brantingham; Sept. 26, 1919, in Long Beach, Calif.
**Spotlights:** Attractive redhead who played wife-turned-sleuth on "Mr. and Mrs. North" (1952–54). She became a spokeswoman for a cosmetics company and spent over a decade making commercials. Died: 1980.

**Harold Peary**  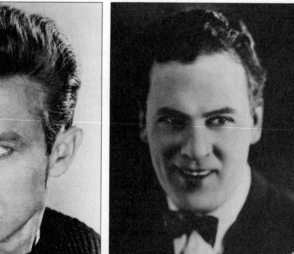 *See page 261.*                     **1719 Vine**

**Thomas Meighan**  *Actor*                                              **1719 Vine**
**Born:**  April 9, 1879, in Pittsburgh, Pa.
**Spotlights:**  Expressive, sometimes risque, silent screen leading man. *The Forbidden City* (1918), *Male and Female* (1919), and *White and Unmarried* (1921). Died: 1936.

**Raymond Massey**  *Actor*                                              **1719 Vine**
**Born:**  Aug. 30, 1896, in Canada.
**Spotlights:**  Tall, thin, not particularly handsome man who earned great cinematic respect as the sixteenth president in *Abe Lincoln in Illinois* (1940); *Fountainhead* (1949). TV: Played Dr. Leonard Gillespie on "Dr. Kildare" (1961–66). Specials. Died: 1983.

**Charles Christie**  *Executive*                                        **1719 Vine**
**Born:**  April 13, 1880, in Canada.
**Spotlights:**  Came to L.A. in 1915. Famous for the "Christie Comedies" from their studio (brother Al handled production; Charles was the administrator). *Charley's Aunt* (1930) starred Charles Ruggles as Lord Babberly. Went broke during the Depression, but later survived quite nicely by selling real estate. Died: 1955.

**Agnes Moorehead**  *Actress*                                           **1719 Vine**
**Born:**  Dec. 6, 1906, in Clinton, Mass.

*James Dean*                          *Thomas Meighan*

**Spotlights:** Her more than 50 films shine like a multifaceted diamond: as the mother in *Citizen Kane* (1941), *The Magnificent Ambersons* (1942), *Mrs. Parkington* (1944), *Johnny Belinda* (1948), *Hush Hush Sweet Charlotte* (1965).

**Sidelights:** TV fans know her as the witch Endora, Samantha's mother, on "Bewitched (1964–72). Died: 1974, of cancer.

### Conrad Nagel  *Actor* 1719 Vine

**Born:** Mar. 16, 1897, in Keokuk, Iowa.

**Spotlights:** 100 films from 1918, *Little Women*, to 1959, including *The Jazz Singer* (1927) and *The Mysterious Lady* (1928). Host of radio's "Silver Theater" (1939). Admired for his resonant voice. "The Silver Theater" appeared on TV (1949–50). TV quiz shows, too.

**Achievements:** 1947, special Academy Award. Died: 1970.

### Tony Martin ▼ *See page 294.* 1719 Vine

### Wendell Niles ▯ *Actor* 1719 Vine

**Born:** Dec. 29, 1904, in Livingston, Mont.

**Spotlights:** Comedy announcer for the salesman who keeps getting doors slammed

*Wendell Niles*

in his face, "Here Comes Elmer" (CBS, 1944); "Ice Box Follies" (ABC, 1945); crime drama announcer on "The Adventures of Philip Marlowe" (NBC, 1947).

## Pierre Monteux  *Conductor*

**Born:**  April 4, 1875, in Paris.
**Spotlights:**  Recordings from San Francisco Symphony (1935–52) and the London Symphony Orchestra (1960–64). Died: 1964.

## Carrol Baker  *Actress*

**Born:**  May 28, 1931, in Johnstown, Pa.
**Spotlights:**  1956 was her brightest year in *Giant,* and as the thumb-sucking girl-wife in *Baby Doll.* She has made a number of European films.

## Edmond O'Brien  *Actor*

**Born:**  Sept. 10, 1915, in New York.
**Spotlights:**  Versatile leading man who appeared in every type of film imaginable including *Fighter Squadron* (1948). Later, character roles, *The Wild Bunch* (1969). TV's Marshal Wyatt Earp on "The Life and Legend of Wyatt Earp" (1955–61). No black hat cowboy could come up against his guns—Buntline Special .45 pistols and dandy extra long barrels. Wasn't packin' no pocket pistol!
**Achievements:**  1954, Best Supporting Actor Oscar for *The Barefoot Contessa.* Died: 1986.

## Marie Doro  *Actress*

**Born:**  Marie Stewart; Feb. 4, 1882, in Duncannon, Pa.
**Spotlights:**  Silent screen only. *Sherlock Holmes, Oliver Twist,* and *The Wood Nymph* (1916). Died: 1956.

## Nancy Carroll  *Actress*

**Born:**  Ann Lattiff; Nov. 19, 1905, in New York.
**Spotlights:**  Dynamic, happy redhead with inviting red lips and a sweet singing voice, who was outrageously popular in the early days of talkies. Considered to be the Clara Bow of sound. Oddly she and Bow worked together in *Paramount on Parade* (1930), as Bow's star was descending and Carroll's ascending. Died: 1965.

## Cecil B. De Mille  *Director, producer, screenwriter*

**Born:**  Cecil Blount De Mille on Aug. 12, 1881, in Ashfield, MA.
**Spotlights:**  Creative genius of film spectaculars (from silents through sound) with the support of partners Jesse L. Lasky and Samuel Goldwyn. Later the company merged with Adolph Zukor's Famous Players to become Paramount. Credits include the celebrated Broadway play *The Squaw Man* (1913) - Hollywood's first film made in "The Barn" and in 18 days; *The Ten Commandments* — De Mille excelled in biblical

and historical stories — (1923 & 1956); *Samson and Delilah* (1949); and *The Plainsman* (1936); host of "Lux Radio Theater" (1936- 45). His premiere show starred Marlene Dietrich and Clark Gable in "The Legionnaire and the Lady." Every superstar jumped at the chance to work with him.

**Achievements:**  1952 Best Picture *The Greatest Show on Earth* (De Mille also directed).

**Sidelights:**  If you're in town, be sure to visit The Hollywood Studio Museum — known as "The Barn." It is an exciting and historical look at the film industry's heritage. For information please call (213)-874-2276. Died: 1959.

### May McAvoy  *Actress*                                    1735 Vine

**Born:**  Sept. 18, 1901, in New York.

**Spotlights:**  Sensitive, pretty 20-year old in the silent *Sentimental Tommy* (1921). Co-starred with Al Jolson in Warner Brothers' *The Jazz Singer*, the first talkie (1927). Retired to marry in 1930. Later, enjoyed bit roles "for the fun of being part of show biz."

### Vic Damone  *Singer, actor*                               1735 Vine

**Born:**  Vito Farinola; June 12, 1928, in Brooklyn, N.Y.

**Spotlights:**  Broke into show biz by winning the Arthur Godfrey talent contest. Album: *We'll Take Romance*. Single: "On the Street."

**Highlights:**  Beat James Dean out in the bid to win Italian actress Pier Angeli's hand in matrimony in 1955. Married beautiful actress Diahann Carroll (1987).

### Marie Dressler  *Actress, comedienne*                     1735 Vine

**Born:**  Leila Von Koerber; Nov. 9, 1869, in Canada.

**Spotlights:**  Described herself as "an overweight, ugly duckling." No matter: She made everyone happy and rose to great heights as America's number one boxoffice attraction in the early 1930s when she was in her sixties! Her first screen appearance was opposite Charlie Chaplin in *Tillie's Punctured Romance* (1914).

**Achievements:**  1930 Best Actress Oscar for *Min and Bill*. Died: 1934.

### William Wyler  *Director*                                 1735 Vine

**Born:**  July 1, 1902, in Germany.

**Spotlights:**  Had a great ability for creating intense emotionalism in his films and cleverly moved his audiences in sweeping sentimentality and presentation: *Jezebel* (1938) and *The Letter* (1940) — both starring Bette Davis. In 1968, directed the musical which introduced Barbra Streisand, *Funny Girl*.

**Achievements:**  1942 Best Director Oscar for *Mrs. Minnver*; 1946 Oscar for *The Best Years of Our Lives*; 1959 Oscar for *Ben Hur*. Died: 1981.

### Roy Rogers  *See page 134.*                               1735 Vine

## Bobby Darin  *Singer, songwriter, actor*    1735 Vine

**Born:**  Robert Cassotto; May 14, 1936, in New York.

**Spotlights:**  Young, handsome, dark-haired entertainer whose song, "Mack the Knife," was a multimillion seller. Nightclub debut with George Burns; then headlined at the Las Vegas Sahara. Other hit songs include "Splish Splash," "Queen of the Hop," and "Dream Lover."

**Achievements:**  Grammys, gold records. 1964, Oscar nomination for Best Supporting Actor for his dramatic performance in *Captain Newman, M.D.*

**Highlights:**  Married to Sandra Dee (1960–67).

**Sidelights:**  He and his mother were welfare recipients. Died: 1973, from complications of heart surgery. Darin, born with a bad heart, gave generously to the American Heart Association.

## Jim Backus  *Actor*    1735 Vine

**Born:**  Feb. 25, 1913, in Cleveland, Ohio.

**Spotlights:**  Delightfully played the long-suffering husband in the series "I Married Joan." His spoiled, childlike portrayal of multimillionaire Thurston Howell III on "Gilligan's Island" and his cartoon voice as Mr. Magoo have made him one of TV's long-standing, most loved, and recognizable personalities.

## Victor McLaglen  *Actor*    1735 Vine

**Born:**  Dec. 10, 1886, in England.

**Spotlights:**  A former heavyweight boxer with a heart of gold, *Beau Geste* (1926), *The Magnificent Brute* (1936).

**Achievements:**  1935, Best Actor in John Ford's *The Informer*. Died: 1959, of a heart attack.

## Lottie Lehmann  *Opera singer*    1735 Vine

**Born:**  Feb. 27, 1888, in Perleberg, Germany.

**Spotlights:**  Dramatic soprano. Prima donna at Metropolitan Opera (1934-45), *Ariadne auf Naxos* and *Der Rosenkavalier*. Later, sought-after coach. Died: 1976.

## Barbara Lawrence  *Actress*    1735 Vine

**Born:**  Feb. 24, 1930, in Carnegie, Okla.

**Spotlights:**  Former child model whose second film, *Margie* (1946), is still enjoyable to watch. Others: *Here Come the Nelsons* (1952), *Oklahoma* (1955). Movies seen on TV frequently.

## Dale Evans  *Actress, singer*    1735 Vine

**Born:**  Frances Smith; Oct. 31, 1912, in Uvalde, Tex.

**Spotlights:**  Host of radio's variety show "Let's Be Crazy" (CBS, 1940); regular on "The Roy Rogers Show" in the late 1940s. "Happy Trails to You" was her theme on

that program (1951–57). The name of her horse? Buttermilk.
**Highlights:**  Married to Roy Rogers since 1947.

### Boris Karloff    *Actor*                          1735 Vine

**Born:**  William Pratt; Nov. 23, 1887, in England.
**Spotlights:**  In real life, Boris Karloff was a nice, sweet guy but on-screen he was a character bad guy until he scared up a frightful following in James Whale's classic *Frankenstein* (1931), a role Bela Lugosi had turned down. Inwardly sensitive, outwardly expressive, Karloff was able to portray the monster with pain and compassion, even through more than 50 pounds of makeup. Among over 100 films are *The Old Dark House* (1932), *The Mask of Fu Manchu* (1932), and *The Bride of Frankenstein* (1935). TV host of "Thriller" (NBC, 1960–62). On Broadway in *Arsenic and Old Lace* (1941), he cracked audiences up with his line, "I killed him because he said I looked like Boris Karloff."
**Sidelights:**  During the shooting of *Frankenstein*, the weight of his costume made it impossible for him to walk any distance, and he had to be carried to the commissary to eat lunch! The "screws" on his neck were put in so deeply they left scars. Died: 1969, of respiratory disease.

### Artur Rubinstein  *Musician*                          1735 Vine

**Born:**  Jan. 28, 1886, in Poland.
**Spotlights:**  One of the world's greatest pianists, who brilliantly played Chopin's *Concerto No. 2 in F Minor, op. 21*, with the NBC Symphony Orchestra under William Steinberg; more. Died: 1982.

### William Boyd  *Actor, producer*                          1735 Vine

**Born:**  June 5, 1898, in Cambridge, Ohio.
**Spotlights:**  The western hero, *Hopalong Cassidy*; by popular demand made over 40 sequels. After purchasing the entire collection, he wisely sold to TV and gained renewed fame and wealth. Died: 1972.

### Otto Kruger  *Actor*                          1735 Vine

**Born:**  Sept. 6, 1885, in Toledo, Ohio.
**Spotlights:**  Elegant character actor who was very good in kindly or villainous roles. Under MGM contract in 1932. *Treasure Island* (1934), *Hitler's Children* (1943), *High Noon* (1952), over 100 pictures. TV playhouse theaters. Died: 1974, on his birthday from heart failure.

### Arlene Francis  *See page 293.*                          1735 Vine

### Groucho Marx  *Comedian, actor*                          1735 Vine

**Born:**  Julius Marx; Oct. 2, 1890, in New York.

**Spotlights:** Radio: "The Groucho Marx Show" (CBS, 1943); host of the quiz show "You Bet Your Life," which was really a comedy platform for Groucho (ABC, 1947); show moved to NBC-TV (1950–61). It gave contestants a chance to win money while Marx quipped a joke at every opportunity (and there were many); it didn't require a high IQ to answer questions such as, "Who was buried in Grant's tomb?"

**Achievements:** 1973, special Oscar; 1950, Emmy for Most Outstanding Personality.

**Sidelights:** Although Groucho, the zany, waddling, mustached, cigar-smoking comedian, is considered the most important figure in the Marx Brothers films, and indeed appeared solo after the family stopped performing together, fans were first introduced to him in Marx Brothers pictures: *Duck Soup* (1933), *A Night at the Opera* (1935), and a *Day at the Races* (1937). The comical clan: Chico (1886-1961); Harpo (1888–1964); and Zeppo (1901–1979). A fifth brother, Gummo (1897–1977) did not appear in their pictures. Died: 1977, from pneumonia.

**Dinah Shore**   *See page 346.*                                    **1749 Vine**

**Ethel Merman**   *See page 380.*                                   **1749 Vine**

**Johnny Carson**   *Host comedian*                                  **1749 Vine**

**Born:** Oct. 23, 1925, in Coring, Iowa.

**Spotlights:** Intelligent, attractive, entertaining host of TVs longest-running late-night program. Its genesis was a Steve Allen vehicle, "Tonight: America After Dark" (1954–57). From 1957–62 it was "The Jack Paar Tonight Show." In 1962, still based in New York, it became "The Tonight Show Starring Johnny Carson." Carson's smooth, easy-going style gained a wide audience. In 1971, he moved the show to Burbank, where glamourous Hollywood celebrities lined up to appear on it.

**Achievements:** Emmys: 1976, 1977, 1978, 1979.

**Sidelights:** Prior to "The Tonight Show," Carson was the emcee of the daytime show "Who Do You Trust?" (with Ed McMahon as his onstage announcer) from 1957–62. The title of the evening version: "Do You Trust Your Wife?"

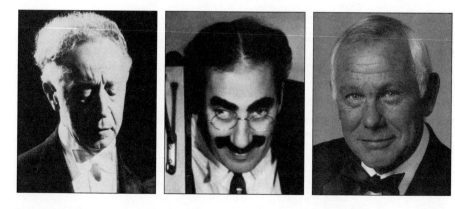

*Artur Rubinstein*          *Groucho Marx*          *Johnny Carson*

## Barbara Stanwyck  🎥 *Actress*  1749 Vine
**Born:**  Ruby Stevens; July 6, 1907, in Brooklyn, N.Y.
**Spotlights:**  This partial listing shows her superb range: a crude wife and mother in *Stella Dallas* (1937); a Christmas shoplifter accepting a holiday invitation to the district attorney's house in *Remember the Night* (1940); a trampy murderess in *Double Indemnity* (1944); the victim of a murder attempt in *Sorry, Wrong Number* (1948). Professional, brilliant, and very nice. Every male superstar jumped at the chance to work with her.
**Achievements:**  1981, honorary Oscar; 1961, Emmy; 1966, Emmy.
**Highlights:**  Second marriage to Robert Taylor (1935–52).
**Sidelights:**  In 1944 Stanwyck made more money than any other woman in the U.S., $400,000.

## Margaret Sullavan  🎥 *Actress*  1749 Vine
**Born:**  May 19, 1911, in Norfolk, Va.
**Spotlights:**  Fair-haired, oval-faced talent of light comedy, *The Moon's Our Home* (1936), and drama *Three Comrades* (1930).
**Highlights:**  Married to Henry Fonda (1931–33).
**Sidelights:**  Died: 1960.

## Virginia Mayo  🎥 *Actress, dancer*  1749 Vine
**Born:**  Virginia Jones; Nov. 30, 1920, in St. Louis, Mo.
**Spotlights:**  Gorgeous blond with an ideal figure, delightful in comedies, but good in dramatic roles too: "Conflict" (1956–57).

## Betty Compson  🎥 *Actress*  1749 Vine
**Born:**  March 18, 1896, in Beaver, Utah.
**Spotlights:**  Bow-lipped, delicate beauty of early silent comedies. Later accepted in dramas as well as in talkies. Two pictures starring with Lon Chaney, *The Miracle Man* (1919) and *The Big City* (1928).

## Elliott Dexter  🎥 *Actor*  1749 Vine
**Born:**  Sept. 11, 1870, in Galveston, Tex.
**Spotlights:**  Played romantic leads in silents, *The Heart of Nora Flynn* (1916) and *Adam's Rib* (1923). Died: 1941.

## Billy Wilder  🎥 *Director, screenwriter, producer*  1749 Vine
**Born:**  Samuel Wilder; June 22, 1906, in Austria.
**Spotlights:**  *Double Indemnity* (1944); *The Seven-Year Itch* (1955); *Some Like It Hot* (1959).
**Achievements:**  1945, Best Director and Best Screenplay (co-written with Charles Brackett), *The Lost Weekend*; 1950 Best Screenplay (co-written with Charles Brack-

ett), *Sunset Boulevard*; 1960, Best Picture, Best Director, Best Screenplay (co-written with A. L. Diamond), *The Apartment.*

## Frankie Carle  *Composer, pianist* 1749 Vine

**Born:** Francis Carlone; March 25, 1903, in Providence, R.I.
**Spotlights:** Composed "Sunrise Serenade." Bandleader in 1940s and 1950s.

## Sarah Bernhardt *Actress* 1749 Vine

**Born:** Henriette-Rosine Bernard on Oct. 25, 1844, in France.
**Spotlights:** Legendary stage star who made an important historical contribution to films as the lead in the European made silent film *Queen Elizabeth* (1912). As a respected performer in the first great literary work brought to the screen, Bernhardt validated motion pictures as a true art form. The film was internationally popular among all classes and brought riches to distributor Adolph Zukor, who started up a production company, later part of Paramount.
**Sidelights:** Made two films after a leg amputation in 1915. Died: 1923.

## Carmel Myers *Actress* 1749 Vine

**Born:** April 4, 1899, in San Francisco, Calif.
**Spotlights:** Romanced one of the best-looking lovers, Rudolph Valentino, in sizzling silent screen performances: *A Society Sensation* (1918), *The Delicious Little Devil* (1919). Died: 1980.

## Virginia Field *Actress* 1749 Vine

**Born:** Margaret Field; Nov. 4, 1917, in England.
**Spotlights:** Beautiful, blond leading lady in *Little Lord Fauntleroy* (1936); *The Sun Never Sets* (1939); dozens more films. TV: guest appearances on "Adam 12" and other series.

## Blanche Sweet *Actresss* 1749 Vine

**Born:** June 13, 1895, in Chicago, Ill.
**Spotlights:** Greatly admired principal character of D. W. Griffith's pictures, *The God Within* (1912) and *Judith of Bethulia* (1914).

## Ray Anthony *Orchestra leader* 1749 Vine

**Born:** Raymond Antonini on January 20, 1922, in Bentleyville, PA.
**Spotlights:** In addition to being a valuable Capitol Records artist for close to two decades, Anthony has done TV and film work. Worked with Glenn Miller band, then Jimmy Dorsey. Hit "Dragnet"; co-composer of "The Bunny Hop." Recordings include: "Sentimental Me/Spaghetti Rag," "True Blue Lou/They Didn't Believe Me," "The Hokey Pokey." Albums: *Big Band Dixieland, Dream Dancing Medley.*

## Stepin Fetchit   *Actor*      1751 Vine

**Born:** Lincoln Perry on May 30, 1892; Key West, FL.

**Spotlights:** Comedian who made his screen debut in *Old Kentucky* (1927). Played sympathetic, lovable characters; tolerant of those who were mean to him. Memorable performances in *Stand Up and Cheer* and *David Harum* (both 1934). Used the professional name of Stepin Fetchit on all screen credits through *Amazing Grace* (1974).

**Sidelights:** Perry said he was the first black actor to walk through the front gate of a movie studio. Died: 1985.

## Ernest Tubb   *Singer, songwriter, guitarist*      1749 Vine

**Born:** Feb. 9, 1914, near Crisp, TX.

**Spotlights:** Deep-voiced drawling performer who helped uplift the image of honky tonk music from hillbilly to country. Debut appearance on the "Grand Ole Opry" in 1942 singing "I'm Walking the Floor Over You." Other hits include "Remember Me, I'm the One Who Loves You," "The Yellow Rose of Texas" "Our Hearts Are Holding Hands," and "Who's Gonna Take The Garbage Out." Films: *Jamboree* (1944) *Hollywood Barn Dance* (1947).

**Sidelights:** Promoted electric guitar because they could be heard in noisy honkytonks. Died: 1984.

## James Arness   *Actor*      1749 Vine

**Born:** James Aurness; May 23, 1923, in Minneapolis, Minn.

**Spotlights:** An impressive 6' 7" of tough, honest Marshal Matt Dillon on "Gunsmoke" (1955–75). John Wayne was originally asked to do the series. He politely declined, but suggested his pal Arness test for it. It just goes to show you, even if you've got the talent, it sure helps to know the right people in the business!

**Sidelights:** Appeared as the alien in the movie *The Thing* (1951). Brother of actor Peter Graves.

## Russ Morgan   *Composer, arranger, bandleader, musician*      1749 Vine

**Born:** April 29, 1904, in Scranton, Pa.

**Spotlights:** With Freddy Martin, created the muted "wah wah" trombone sound. Music in the Morgan manner could be heard in clubs, on films, radio, and TV. Wrote songs: "Somebody Else is Taking My Place," and "You're Nobody Till Somebody Loves You." Recordings: "Does Your Heart Beat for Me?" and "Forever and Ever." Died: 1969.

## Gene Vincent   *Singer, songwriter*      1749 Vine

**Born:** Vincent Craddock; Feb. 11, 1935, in Norfolk, Va.

**Spotlights:** Former choir boy. Formed band, Blue Caps, in 1955. Co-wrote first gigantic hit: "Be-bop-a-lula." Other hits: "Lotta Luvin'" and "Dance to the Bop." Late

1950s became pioneer hard-core rock 'n roller known for breathless, nervous high voice. Died: 1971.

**Mario Lanza**  *See page 31.*    1749 Vine

**Fred Waring**  *See page 303.*    1749 Vine

**Rudolf Serkin** *Musician*    1749 Vine
**Born:**  May 28, 1903, in Bohemia.
**Spotlights:**  Piano virtuoso whose renderings of Brahms, Beethoven, and Bach have immortalized him in the world of music.
**Achievements:**  Recording: Brahms's *Concerto No. 2 in B-flat Major, op. 83*, with the Philadelphia Orchestra under Eugene Ormandy (Columbia); more.

**Jan Peerce** *Opera singer*    1749 Vine
**Born:**  Jacob Perelmuth; June 3, 1904, in New York.
**Spotlights:**  Great dynamic tenor at Radio City Music Hall (1932–39) and Metropolitan Opera (1941). Broadway debut as Tevye in "Fiddler on the Roof" (1971). Recordings: *La Boheme, La Traviata,* and *Fidelio.* Died: 1984.

**Freeman Gosden "Amos"** *Comedian, actor*    1749 Vine
**Born:**  May 5, 1899, in Richmond, VA.
**Spotlights:**   "Holy Mackerel, Andy!" Co-star blackface of "The Amos 'n Andy Show," America's most listened to show in the early 1930s. "Oh wah, oh wah! Oh, wah!"
**Sidelights:**  Andy was played by Charles Correll.

**Earle Williams** *Actor*    1749 Vine
**Born:**  Feb. 28, 1880, in Sacramento, Calif.
**Spotlights:**  A handsome silent screen idol; *Say It with Diamonds* (1927). Died: 1927.

**Charles Correll "Andy"** *Comedian, actor*    1749 Vine
**Born:**  Feb. 1, 1890.
**Spotlights:**  Blackface co-star of "The Amos 'n Andy Show." The two members of the "Mystic Knights of the Sea Lodge" operated the "Fresh Air Taxi Company" and gave audiences a long ride on their comedy show (NBC, 1926); characters established as Sam 'n Henry; names changed to Amos 'n Andy 1929 untill 1960.
**Sidelights:**  Amos was played by another Walk of Famer, Freeman Gosden. The TV series with Alvin Chidress and Spencer Williams aired on CBS (1951–53). Died: 1972.

## John Gilbert  *Actor* 1749 Vine

**Born:** John Pringle; July 10, 1895, in Logan, Utah.

**Spotlights:** The silent screen's number-one lover in 1927, after melting hearts in *Arabian Love* (1922) and *The Merry Widow* (1925). Opposite the one-and-only Greta Garbo in *Flesh and the Devil* (1927) and *Love* (1928). Rumor had it that their love wasn't acted. Died: 1936.

## Jack Perrin  *Actor* 1749 Vine

**Born:** 1896, in Three Rivers, Mich.

**Spotlights:** Silent screen career opened up with his supporting role in Erich von Stroheim's *Blind Husbands* (1919). Later became king of the cow palace in countless westerns, *Ridin' West* (1924). Died: 1967.

## Harry Joe Brown  *Director, producer* 1749 Vine

**Born:** Sept. 22, 1890, in Pittsburgh, PA.

**Spotlights:** Specialized in western action in silents. Established Errol Flynn as a star in his pirate movie *Captain Blood* (1935). Known for impeccable work. Died: 1972.

## Edmund Gwenn  *Actor* 1749 Vine

**Born:** Sept. 26, 1875, in Wales.

**Spotlights:** Character actor whose magical benevolent presence enhanced every film. Oddly delightful in Alfred Hitchcock's *The Trouble with Harry* (1955).

**Achievements:** 1946 Oscar, Best Supporting Actor as Kris Kringle for *Miracle on 34th Street*. This Christmas classic is shown each yuletide season on TV. Died: 1959.

## George Jessel  *Singer, songwriter, actor, producer* 1751 Vine

**Born:** April 3, 1898, in New York.

**Spotlights:** America's "toastmaster general" was singing and dancing when he was a youth. On-screen in 1911, *Widow at the Races*, co-starring Eddie Cantor, his former vaudeville partner. *Four Jills in a Jeep* (1944); more.

**Achievements:** 1969, special Oscar, Jean Hersholt Humanitarian Award. Died: 1981.

## Carole Landis  *Actress* 1777 Vine

**Born:** Frances Ridste; Jan. 1, 1919, in Fairchild, Wisc.

**Spotlights:** Curly blond hair, pin-up girl face and figure who first appeared with the Marx Brothers in *A Day at the Races* (1937). Funny in *Topper Returns* (1941). Died: 1948.

## William Beaudine  *Director* 1777 Vine

**Born:** Jan. 15, 1892, in New York.

**Spotlights:** He directed Mary Pickford in *Little Annie Rooney* (1925) and *Sparrows* (1926), and successfully made the transition to the talkies, directing hundreds of films. Died: 1970.

**John Daly**  *Newsman, host* **1777 Vine**

**Born:** Feb. 20, 1914, in South Africa.

**Spotlights:** CBS news correspondent who moved to ABC for nightly news in 1953, yet simultaneously hosted the CBS game show "What's My Line?" (1950–67). Dozens of other TV appearances, master of ceremonies, actor, moderator.

**Meiklejohn** *Actress* **1777 Vine**

**Born:** Charlotte Meiklejohn; Nov. 5, 1900.

**Spotlights:** Stage and screen actress. Died: 1971.

**Buddy Ebsen** *Actor, dancer* **1777 Vine**

**Born:** April 2, 1908, in Belleville, Tex.

**Spotlights:** His screen debut was in *Broadway Melody of 1936*, but he eventually moved away from musicals into films such as, *Breakfast at Tiffany's* (1961), starring Audrey Hepburn and George Peppard.

**Sidelights:** TV fans remember him as multimillionaire hick Jed Clampett on "The Beverly Hillbillies" (1962–71).

*Buddy Ebsen*

127

## June Haver 🎥 *Actress, singer* 1777 Vine

**Born:** June Stovenour; June 10, 1926, in Rock Island, Ill.
**Spotlights:** Warm, delightful Fox star of the forties musicals. *Irish Eyes are Smiling* (1944), *The Dolly Sisters* (1945), opposite Betty Grable.
**Highlights:** Entered a convent to become a nun in 1953, but was persuaded by lovelorn Fred MacMurray in 1954 to marry him.

## Hoot Gibson 🎥 *Actor* 1777 Vine

**Born:** Edward Gibson; Aug. 6, 1892, in Takamah, Nebr.
**Spotlights:** *Headin' West* (1922) was all this former cowboy wanted to do in films. Often seen with a smile and twinkling eyes, but no guns.
**Sidelights:** As a child, he hunted owls, hence his nickname, "Hoot." Died: 1962.

## Janet Leigh 🎥 *Actress* 1777 Vine

**Born:** Jeanette Morrison; July 6, 1927, in Merced, Calif.
**Spotlights:** With her blond hair and hourglass figure, Leigh is delightful to watch in *Holiday Affair* (1950), a romantic comedy which co-starred Robert Mitchum. She handled comedy easily but is best remembered for her performance in *Psycho* (1959); more.
**Highlights:** Married to actor Tony Curtis (1959–62) and mother of actress Jamie Lee Curtis.

## Marlon Brando 🎥 *Actor* 1777 Vine

**Born:** Apr. 3, 1924, in Omaha, Nebr.

Marlon Brando                                    Dom DeLuise

**Spotlights:** Realistic, original, rebellious qualities that are magnetic on screen. *A Streetcar Named Desire* (1951) and *Viva Zapata!* (1952). Versatile in *Guys and Dolls* (1955).
**Achievements:** Best Actor Oscars: 1954 *On the Waterfront* and 1972, *The Godfather*.
**Sidelights:** Lives part of the time on his 13-island Tahitian atoll.

## Dom DeLuise   *Actor, comedian*     1777 Vine

**Born:** Aug. 1, 1933, in Brooklyn, N.Y.
**Spotlights:** Delightful, funny, winsome talent whose screen debut in *Fail Safe* (1964) assured a lasting career. Works frequently with Mel Brooks and Burt Reynolds: *Blazing Saddles* (1974), *The Adventures of Sherlock Holmes' Smarter Brother* (1975), *Smokey and the Bandit II* (1980), more.

## Richard Hayman   *Conductor, arranger, harmonica player,*     1779 Vine
*composer*

**Born:** Warren Hayman; March 27, 1920, in Cambridge, Mass.
**Spotlights:** When the kleig lights are turned on, he's a quick-witted showman with a taste for extravagant costumes. Orchestrator on MGM musical films: *Girl Crazy* (1943), and *Meet Me in St. Louis* (1944). Became principal arranger for Boston Pops Orchestra in 1950. Musical director for Bob Hope, Johnny Cash, Olivia-Newton John, and others. The song "Ruby" from the soundtrack *Ruby Gentry* (1953) featured his harmonica playing.

## John Huston   *Director, writer, actor*     1779 Vine

**Born:** Aug. 5, 1906, in Nevada, Mo.
**Spotlights:** *The Maltese Falcon* (1941) was the first film he directed. Also wrote the screenplay, a remake with Humphrey Bogart, of *Key Largo* (1948); *The African Queen* (1950); *The Misfits* (1960); more.
**Achievements:** 1948, Best Director and Best Screenplay *The Treasure of Sierra Madre*.
**Sidelights:** Son of the late Walter Huston, father of Angelica Huston. Third wife (of 4) Evelyn Keyes (1946–50). Died: 1987

## Texas Guinan   *Actress, club hostess*     1779 Vine

**Born:** Mary Guinan; in Canada.
**Spotlights:** Screen debut in 1917, *Fuel of Life*; last film 1933, *Broadway Thru a Keyhole*. Died: 1933.

# ⋆ 1770 VINE ⋆

**Jeff Chandler** 🎥 *Actor*                                   1770 Vine
**Born:** Ira Grossell; Dec. 15, 1918, in Brooklyn, N.Y.
**Spotlights:** A dramatic radio actor who was encouraged to pursue films because of his rugged good looks. *Johnny O'Clock* and *The Invisible Wall* (both 1947). Died: 1961, of blood poisoning following routine surgery.

**Eddie Cantor** 📺 *See page 314.*                           1770 Vine

**Heinie Conklin** 🎥 *Actor*                                  1750 Vine
**Born:** Charles Conklin; April 2, 1880, in San Francisco, Calif.
**Spotlights:** Reliable comedian with a walrus mustache whose typical joking always got a laugh. Celebrity from 1915. His last film title embraces the works of his entire career, *Abbot and Costello Meet the Keystone Kops* (1955). Died: 1971.

**Tony Martin** 🎙 *See page 294.*                            1750 Vine

**Lurene Tuttle** 🎙 *See page 369.*                          1750 Vine

**Frank Fay** 🎙 *See page 200.*                              1750 Vine

**Tina Turner** 💿 *Singer*                                    1750 Vine
**Born:** Anna Mae Bullock; Nov. 25, 1941, in Brownsville, Tex.
**Spotlights:** Rhythm-and-blues vocalist with Ike Turner and the Ikettes (from 1958). A string of hits, on the pop and soul charts, included "I Want to Take You Higher" and "Proud Mary." Embarked on a successful solo career since 1974. Hit album: "Private Dancer." Wild spirit with strong spiritual center; a vivacious entertainer. Dramatic roles in films, too.

**Lowell Thomas** 🎙 *Newscaster, narrator, author*            1750 Vine
*(of over 54 books), adventurer, screenwriter, producer*
**Born:** April 6, 1892, in Woodington, Drake County, Ohio.
**Spotlights:** Joined radio almost at its inception. Was host of NBC's "Headline Hunters" (1929), a daily show he closed with, "So long, until tomorrow." CBS broadcast nightly from his 600-acre New York estate for nearly 50 years. Motion Pictures: Narrated and occasionally appeared on screen. *The Blonde Captive* (1932); *Seven Wonders of the World* "Voice" for 20th Century-Fox Movietone News since 1935. Television newscasts and travel series, too. Died: 1981.

## Anne Murray  *Singer* 1750 Vine

**Born:** June 20, 1945, in Nova Scotia.
**Spotlights:** Lovely performer who won American hearts during the 1970s; pop and country. "Let's Keep It That Way."
**Achievements:** 1974, 1979, 1980, Grammys.

## Lee De Forest  *Inventor* 1750 Vine

**Born:** Aug. 26, 1873, in Council Bluffs, Iowa.
**Spotlights:** A genius who invented over 300 useful contraptions to further the technology of motion pictures, radio, and TV. Died: 1961.

## Natalie Cole *Singer* 1750 Vine

**Born:** Stephanie N. Cole; Feb. 6, 1949, in Los Angeles, Calif.
**Spotlights:** *Unpredictable* and *Thankful* are two of this lovely entertainer's albums.
**Achievements:** 1975, Grammy, new artist; 1975, Grammy, rhythm-and-blues vocal; 1976, Grammy.
**Highlights:** Daughter of the late singer and actor Nat "King" Cole.

## Conrad Nagel *See page 116.* 1750 Vine

## Beverly Sills *Opera singer* 1750 Vine

**Born:** Belle Silverman; May 25, 1929, in New York.
**Spotlights:** On radio since age 3. Known as Belle "Bubbles" Silverman on radio's "The Family Hour." Much beloved soprano star of the New York City Opera since debut in 1955; became director in 1980. Films, too. Recordings include: *Barber of Seville, Don Pasquale,* and *Opera's Great Love Duets.*
**Achievements:** 1975, Emmy. 1976, Grammy.

## Vera Ralston *Actress* 1750 Vine

**Born:** Vera Hruba; July 12, 1919, in Czechoslovakia.

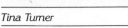

| | | |
|---|---|---|
| *Tina Turner* | *Anne Murray* | *Beverly Sills* |

**Spotlights:** Her film debut in *Ice Capades* (1941) was a natural for this 1936 Olympic contender.
**Highlights:** Married Republic studio head, Herbert J. Yates, in 1952; he personally managed her career.

## Helen Reddy    *Singer*    1750 Vine

**Born:** Oct. 25, 1941, in Australia.
**Spotlights:** "I Am Woman" made her a pop hero with the American female audience during the 1970s. Las Vegas and TV entertainment.
**Achievements:** 1972, Grammy, pop vocal.

## Joe Penner    *Comedian*    1750 Vine

**Born:** Joseph Pinter; Nov. 11, 1905, in Budapest, Hungary.
**Spotlights:** "Wanna Buy a Duck?" Star of the "Joe Penner Show" with vocalists Ozzie Nelson and Harriet Hilliard (CBS 1933–35). Penner was a capable stage, screen, vaudeville and burlesque actor, too. On screen in *A Stuttering Romance* (1930 short); *College Rhythm* (1934). Died: 1941.

## Bruce Humberstone    *Director*    1750 Vine

**Born:** Nov. 18, 1903, in Buffalo, N.Y.
**Spotlights:** Directed a number of the *Charlie Chan* detective series, starting in 1936 with *Charlie Chan at the Racetrack* and *Charlie Chan at the Opera*.

## Beverly Bayne    *Actress*    1750 Vine

**Born:** Nov. 11, 1894, in Minneapolis, MN.
**Spotlights:** Teamed with actor Francis X. Bushman as Hollywood's first romantic couple in a number of silents including *Romeo and Juliet* (1916). Died: 1982.

## Joan Crawford    *Actress*    1750 Vine

**Born:** Billie Cassin; changed to Lucille LeSueur; March 23, 1904, in San Antonio, Tex.
**Spotlights:** MGM labeled her a "jazz baby" in the mid-twenties. *Paid* (1930) proved she survived the transition to the Depression-era thirties, while virtually 99 percent of other female stars dropped out of sight. By *Grand Hotel* (1932), she was the third biggest box office moneymaker (ahead of Greta Garbo by two slots). She surprised everyone when she stormed the next decade in *Mildred Pierce* (1945). Her miraculous staying power to attract audiences and put together deals made the hair on "the old men's club of Hollywood" stand on end. *Sudden Fear* (1952) and *Whatever Happened to Baby Jane* (1962) terrified audiences newly appreciating Crawford's intense, fiery, dominating screen presence.
**Achievements:** 1945, Best Actress Oscar.
**Sidelights:** "Joan Crawford, as much as I dislike the lady, is a star," Humphrey Bogart

once said. Later, other studio personnel showed their aversion to her by flagrantly drinking Coca-Cola around her on the set, while she was married (in 1956) to the head of Pepsi-Cola and doing extensive public relations work for that soft drink. Died: 1977.

## Clarence Brown  *Director*                     1750 Vine

**Born:**  May 10, 1890, in Clinton, Mass.
**Sidelights:**  Directed Greta Garbo in her most triumphant roles: *Anna Christie* (1930), *Anna Karenina* (1935), and *Conquest* (1937). Directed a couple of her silents years earlier. *Ah, Wilderness* (1935), starring Wallace Beery and Lionel Barrymore.

## Rory Calhoun  *See page 369.*                     1750 Vine

## Brian Aherne  *Actor*                     1750 Vine

**Born:**  May 2, 1902, in England.
**Spotlights:**  Handsome, dignified, understated actor of the 1930s and 1940s. In *My Son, My Son* (1940) he starred as a rags-to-riches man who regrets he spoiled his

*Joan Crawford*

son. *My Sister Eileen* (1942). His films shown on TV.
**Highlights:** Married to actress Joan Fontaine (1939–43). Died: 1986.

## George Seaton  *Screenwriter, director* 1750 Vine
**Born:** April 17, 1911, in South Bend, Ind.
**Achievements:** 1947, Oscar for writing *Miracle on 34th Street*; also directed it. 1954, Oscar for *The Country Girl*; also directed it. Died: 1979.

## Roy Rogers *Actor, singer* 1750 Vine
**Born:** Leonard Slye; Nov. 5, 1912, in Cincinnati, Ohio.
**Spotlights:** "King of the Cowboys," in *Sons of the Pioneers* (1942) and *The Yellow Rose of Texas* (1944). Shared spotlight with his horse, *My Pal Trigger* (1946); more. "Happy Trails To You" the theme song on "The Roy Rogers Show" radio (1944 on); TV (1951–57).
**Highlights:** Married to co-star Dale Evans since 1947.

## Donald Meek *Actor* 1750 Vine
**Born:** July 14, 1880, in Scotland.
**Spotlights:** Shy, trembling-voiced, almost bald, funny face character who made

*Roy Rogers*

close to 100 films from the late 1920s until his death, including *The Merry Widow* (1934), *China Seas* (1935), *Young Mr. Lincoln* (1939), and *My Little Chickadee* (1940). Died: 1946.

**Ralph Staub**  *Producer, director, cameraman*  1750 Vine

**Spotlights:**  Began as cameraman in 1920; filmed travel shorts in Alaska. Directed a few features before becoming known for "Screen Snapshots" series at Columbia Pictures. Made 800 shorts (winning several awards) in 20 years at that studio, and not a single "flop." Died: 1969.

**Madge Evans**  *Actress*  1750 Vine

**Born:**  Margherita Evans; July 1, 1909, in New York.

**Spotlights:**  On screen since 1915, she matured in front of the cameras; *The Greeks Had a Word for Them* (1932) with Joan Blondell and Ina Claire. *Dinner at Eight* (1933).

**Highlights:**  Retired to marry New York playwright, Sidney Kingsley, in 1939. Died: 1981.

**Lloyd Nolan**  *Actor*  1750 Vine

**Born:**  Aug. 11, 1902, in San Francisco, Calif.

**Spotlights:**  Cast as a detective (1951–52) in "Martin Kane, Private Eye." In "Julia" (1968–71) he was the employer, Dr. Morton Chegley.

**Achievements:**  1955, Emmy, "The Caine Mutiny Court Martial."

**Sidelights:**  Made 70 films in a 40-year career. Died: 1985.

**Charles Laughton**  *Actor*  1750 Vine

**Born:**  July 1, 1899, in England.

**Spotlights:**  He was thick-lipped, rubbery-faced, and overweight. He was also a brilliant artist who delivered bold, vivid characterizations of each individual he portrayed, whether a king, *The Private Life of Henry VIII* (1933), or a butler, *Ruggles of Red Gap* (1935). One of motion pictures' greatest talents, more proof in 1935: *Les Miserables* and *Mutiny on the Bounty*.

**Achievements:**  1932–33, Best Actor Academy Award for *Henry VIII*. Died: 1962, of cancer.

**Ken Murray**  *Actor, author*  1750 Vine

**Born:**  Don Court; July 14, 1903, in New York.

**Spotlights:**  "The Ken Murray Show," comedy (CBS, 1932); Hollywood-based emcee on variety half hour of "The Texaco Star Theater" (1940).

**Achievements:**  1947, special Oscar for *Bill and Coo*.

**Conrad Nagel**  *See page 116.*  1750 Vine

**Jack Mulhall**   *Actor*                              1750 Vine

**Born:** Oct. 7, 1887, in Wappingers Falls, N.Y.

**Spotlights:** Not many Walk of Famers had the opportunity of working for the world's greatest inventor, Thomas Edison at his very first studio, Black Maria. When Mulhall moved to California, he found sunshine, swimming pools, and an abundance of leading roles throughout the 1920s. Later, character work: *Hollywood Boulevard* (1936). Died: 1979.

**Shelley Winters**  *Actress*                              1750 Vine

**Born:** Shirley Schrift; Aug. 18, 1922, in St. Louis, Mo.

**Spotlights:** Intense, powerful actress. Full-fledged movie star. Dozens of excellent performances including *A Place in the Sun* (1951) and *The Poseidon Adventure* (1972).

**Achievements:** Best Supporting Oscars: 1959, *The Diary of Anne Frank*, 1965, *A Patch of Blue*.

**Marian Nixon**  *Actress*                              1750 Vine

**Born:** Oct. 20, 1904, in Superior, Wisc.

**Spotlights:** Minor lady who made 60 pictures, including *Riders of the Purple Sage* (1925), *Jazz Mad* (1928), and *Silks and Saddles* (1928). Died: 1983.

**Alec Templeton**  *Pianist, composer, host*                              1750 Vine

**Born:** July 4, 1910, in Wales.

**Spotlights:** A musical prodigy who played his first tune before he was 2, composed before he was 4. His own show, *Alec Templeton Time*, was a musical variety treat, which first aired on NBC in 1939. TV show in 1955.

**Sidelights:** His parents never told him that he lacked sight, young Alec thought "everyone lived in darkness and recognized others by the pitch and tone of their voices." His parents never allowed the word "blind" to be said in their house. It was only at the age of 7, when a visitor accidently said the word, that Alec learned he was different. An enthusiastic person who loved life, he said: "What I can't have, I don't think about." Died: 1963.

**Strongheart**  *German shepard dog*                              1750 Vine

**Born:** In Germany.

**Spotlights:** Trained as a World War I military and police dog in his native country. Screenwriter Jane Martin and director Larry Trimble brought him to Hollywood. This highly intelligent, blue-ribboned champion dog made his screen debut in *The Silent Call* (1921) and was remembered in London's *White Fang* (1925).

**Steve Cochran**  *Actor*                              1750 Vine

**Born:** May 25, 1917, in Eureka, Calif.

**Spotlights:** 6', 175-lb., dark-haired, green-eyed, rough-and-tough character cast in hundreds of "heavy" villainous roles. He rejected full-time series work, including the leads in "Mr. Lucky," "Peter Gunn," and "Mike Hammer," preferring to be "captain of my boat" as a guest star. Died: 1965 on his 40' schooner, the *Rogue*, off Guatemala. Three young, female Mexican companions spent 12 awful days drifting until they were rescued.

## Carter De Haven  *Actor, director* 1724 Vine

**Born:** 1896, in Chicago, Ill.
**Spotlights:** Started as an actor in *The College Orphan* (1915); began directing the very next year, *A Gentleman of Nerve* (1916). Died: 1977.

## Lauren Bacall  *Actress* 1724 Vine

**Born:** Betty Perske; Sept. 16, 1924, in New York.
**Spotlights:** This extraordinarily beautiful model made her film debut opposite Humphrey Bogart in Warner Brothers' 1944 production of *To Have and Have Not*. It was the beginning of a beautiful relationship with "Bogie." Played the female lead opposite him many more times — on-screen, and off-screen as wife, and eventually mother of their two children. Their chemistry was magical in *The Big Sleep* (1946),

*Lauren Bacall*

*Dark Passage* (1947), and *Key Largo* (1948). Films up to the late 1970s. Stage work too. Widowed in 1957.Second marriage to Jason Robards (1961–73).

**Eddie Fisher**   ③   *See page 156.*    1724 Vine

**Mary Miles Minter**   🎥   *Actress*    1724 Vine
**Born:**   Juliet Riley; April 1, 1902, in Shreveport, La.
**Spotlights:**   Debut in the silent, *The Nurse* (1912). Pretty, romantic leading lady, until *Drums of Fate* (1923). 24 movies in all. Died: 1984.

**Norman Z. McLeod**   🎥   *Director*    1724 Vine
**Born:**   Sept. 20, 1898, in Grayling, Mich.
**Spotlights:**   Assistant director on *Wings* (1927), the first picture to win an Academy Award, before directing his own film months later. Specialized in comedies: *Monkey Business* (1931), *It's a Gift* (1934), *Topper* (1937), *The Secret Life of Walter Mitty* (1947), and *The Paleface* (1948). Died: 1964.

**Ben Lyon**   🎥   *Actor*    1724 Vine
**Born:**   Feb. 6, 1901, in Atlanta, Ga.
**Spotlights:**   *Open Your Eyes* (1919) introduced this genial young actor to the world, and it liked what it saw. He was his own stunt pilot in his best- remembered film, Howard Hughes's *Hells Angels* (1930). Versatile and immensely popular in England, he did two radio series there as well as serving in the British Royal Air Force during World War II. His career spanned 46 years.
**Achievements:**   Awarded the Order of the British Empire by Queen Elizabeth II. Died: 1979, of a heart attack.

**Lionel Barrymore**   🎥   *Actor, writer, director, composer*    1724 Vine
**Born:**   Lionel Blythe; April 28, 1878, in Philadelphia, Pa.
**Spotlights:**   A dominant character player whose vital presence was felt in over 200 films including *A Free Soul* (1931). His portrayal of Dr. Gillespie was extremely popular in the MGM series *Dr. Kildare* (late thirties to forties), and on radio.
**Achievements:**   1931, Best Actor Oscar for *A Free Soul.*
**Sidelights:**   Confined to a wheelchair in 1937, but continued his busy acting career. Died: 1954.

**Robert Benchley**   🎥   *Screenwriter, actor*    1724 Vine
**Born:**   Sept. 15, 1889, in Worcester, Mass.
**Spotlights:**   Wrote humorous "how to" shorts; *How To Behave* (1936), *How to Become a Detective* (1936), *How to Figure Income Tax* (1938). Character, face, and temperament well suited for the 1930s–1940s. Comedian with a perfect sense of timing.
**Achievements:**   1935, Oscar for *How to Sleep.* Died: 1945, of a cerebral hemorrhage.

**Ida Lupino**  ◾  *See page 29.*                                    **1724 Vine**

**William Faversham**  [1]  *Actor*                                  **1724 Vine**
**Born:**  Feb. 12, 1868, in England.
**Spotlights:**  6' 1", 180-lb., black-haired, green-eyed silent screen player: *The Man Who Lost Himself* (1920), *The Sin That Was His* (1921) Died: 1940.

**Dick Haymes**  ◉  *See page 180.*                                  **1724 Vine**

**Jon Hall**  🎥  *Actor*                                            **1724 Vine**
**Born:**  Charles Locher; Feb. 23, 1913, in Fresno, Calif.
**Spotlights:**  His eastern/western looks enabled him to play roles from *Kit Carson* (1940) to *Ali Baba and the Forty Thieves* (1943). TV: played Dr. Tom Reynolds (Ramar) on "Ramar of the Jungle" (1952–54). Died: 1979, of suicide following cancer surgery, which left him bedridden.

**Lew Ayres**  ▯  *See page 89.*                                     **1724 Vine**

**Deanna Durbin**  🎥  *Actress, singer*                             **1724 Vine**
**Born:**  Edna Mae Durbin; Dec. 4, 1921, in Canada.
**Spotlights:**  A sweet, energetic 15-year old whose box office receipts from *Three Smart Girls* (1936) and other films kept Universal Studios afloat for years; scripts were fashioned around her singing voice, charm, and good- nature.
**Achievements:**  1938, special Oscar for "bringing to the screen the spirit of youth."
**Sidelights:**  Earned all-time top dollar for a leading lady, but moved permanently to France with her husband in 1949.

**Sarah Vaughan**  ◉  *Singer*                                       **1724 Vine**
**Born:**  March 27, 1924, in Newark, N.J.
**Spotlights:**  Dynamic jazz blues singer. Albums: *Count Basie and Sarah Vaughan*; *Billie, Ella, Lena, Sarah Collection*; *Copacabana*.
**Achievements:**  1981, Emmy, Rhapsody and Song, a tribute to George Gershwin.

**Blue Barron**  ◉  *Musician*                                       **1724 Vine**
**Spotlights:**  Orchestra leader Harry Freedlin and the Blue Barron played on big band remote broadcast from nightclubs throughout the country in the 1930s and 1940s.

**George "Gabby" Hayes**  ◾  *See page 84.*                          **1724 Vine**

**Mr. and Mrs. Sidney Drew**  🎥  *Actors, producers, directors;*    **1724 Vine**
*she was also a screenwriter*

**Born:** Mr. Aug. 28, 1864, in New York. Mrs. Jane Morrow; Apr. 18, 1890. (Her stage name before marriage was Lucile McVey.)
**Spotlights:** Comedy team in the popular "Mr. and Mrs. Sidney Drew" series (1915–19). Very funny couple with magical chemistry.
**Sidelights:** He was one of the Drew-Barrymore theatrical tribe. Died: Mr. 1919, of heart failure; Mrs., 1925.

### Irish McCalla  *Actress, artist*  1724 Vine
**Born:** Dec. 25, 1929.
**Spotlights:** Starred as sexy "Sheena" from the comic strip "Sheena, Queen of the Jungle" when it ran on TV from 1955–56. Made 'B' pictures such as *She Demons* (1960), before turning to painting, for which she has achieved acceptance in the art world.

### Ella Mae Morse  *Singer*  1724 Vine
**Born:** Sept. 12, 1924, in Mansfield, Tex.
**Spotlights:** Strong-voiced, charismatic pop jazz singer. Wonderful recordings include "Blacksmith Blues." Album: *Jazz Origin — Behind the Eight Beat.*

### Paul Henreid  *See page 282.*  1724 Vine

### Mark Robson  *Director*  1724 Vine
**Born:** Dec. 4, 1913, in Canada.
**Spotlights:** Boxed his way into directing fame with *Champion* (1949), starring Kirk Douglas. Deceived a husband into thinking he was the father-to-be in *My Foolish Heart* (1949), starring Susan Hayward; *Peyton Place* (1957), starring Lana Turner and Arthur Kennedy; *Valley of the Dolls* (1967), starring Patty Duke. Died: 1978, of heart failure.

### Hoagy Carmichael  *Songwriter, actor, host*  1724 Vine
**Born:** Nov. 22, 1899, in Bloomington, Ind.
**Spotlights:** Starred on the musical variety program "Saturday Night Revue" (1953). Played Jonesy (1959–60) on the western "Laramie."
**Achievements:** 1951, Academy Award for "In the Cool Cool Cool of the Evening" in *Here Comes the Groom*. Died: 1981.

### George Pal  *Producer, special effects*  1724 Vine
**Born:** Feb. 1, 1908, in Hungary.
**Spotlights:** Hollywood's most creative technical artist in the 1950s.
**Achievements:** 1943, special Oscar (technical); Special Effects Awards for 1950, *Destination Moon*; 1951, *When Worlds Collide*; 1953, *War of the Worlds*; 1958, *Tom Thumb*; 1960, *The Time Machine*. Died: 1980.

## Rod Cameron  📺 *Actor* 1724 Vine

**Born:** Nathan Cox; Dec. 7, 1910, in Canada.
**Spotlights:** Handsome, dark-haired he-man who played Trooper Rod Blake on police drama "State Trooper" (1956–59). Died: 1983.

## Vera Vague  🎥 *Actress* 1724 Vine

**Born:** Barbara Allen; Sept. 2, 1905, in New York.
**Spotlights:** "Man-chasing" cast member of "The Bob Hope Show" (first aired, NBC, 1934). Excellent comic timing. On-screen (1940–59): *The Mad Doctor* (1941); *Larceny, Inc.* (1946). Died: 1974.

## Mercedes McCambridge  🎥 *Actress* 1720 Vine

**Born:** Carlotta M. McCambridge; March 17, 1918, in Joliet, Ill.
**Spotlights:** *Giant* (1956) with Rock Hudson, Elizabeth Taylor, and James Dean. TV: Katherine Wells in "Wire Service" (1956–59); more.
**Achievements:** 1949, Best Supporting Actress Oscar for *All the King's Men*; it was her first movie!
**Sidelights:** Provided the scary devil's voice in *The Exorcist* (1973).

## Lillian Gish  🎥 *Actress* 1722 Vine

**Born:** Lillian De Guiche; Oct. 14, 1896, in Springfield, Ohio.
**Spotlights:** Under the direction of D. W. Griffith, she developed into one of the finest silent screen stars, delicate but intense: *Broken Blossoms* (1919), *Orphans of the Storm* (1922).
**Achievements:** 1970, special Oscar.
**Sidelights:** Considered the "First Lady of the Silent Screen."

## Garry Moore  🎙 *Actor* 1722 Vine

**Born:** Thomas Garrison Morfit; Jan. 31, 1915, in Baltimore, Md.
**Spotlights:** Radio: worked as announcer since 1939; "The Jimmy Durante, Garry Moore Show" (1945). TV: "The Garry Moore Show," variety (1958–66; 1967–68). Known as "the Haircut."
**Sidelights:** His delivery of timely tongue-twisters to Durante was especially amazing because he had suffered from stuttering.

## Steve Allen  📺 *Actor, composer, writer* 1720 Vine

**Born:** Dec. 26, 1921, in New York.
**Spotlights:** TV: CBS gave the intelligent, versatile gentleman a nice Christmas present, his own "Steve Allen Show" (1950-52). Original host of "The Tonight Show" (1953, New York local; NBC, 1954-57). Radio: "The Steve Allen Show" was comedy-variety (CBS, 1952).
**Highlights:** Married to actress Jayne Meadows.

## Beulah Bondi  *Actress* 1718 Vine

**Born:** Beulah Bondy; May 3, 1892, in Chicago, Ill.
**Spotlights:** Following her successful stage career, she made close to 70 films. Brilliant characterizations in MGM's drama *The Gorgeous Hussy* (1936), *Of Human Hearts* (1938), and *Mr. Smith Goes to Washington* (1939). Died: 1981.

## Lauritz Melchior *Opera singer* 1718 Vine

**Born:** Lebrecht Hommel; March 20, 1890, in Copenhagen, Denmark.
**Spotlights:** A baritone who became the best heldentenor. Siegfried was one of his most famous roles. Metropolitan Opera debut in 1926. Died: 1973.

## Mickey Rooney *Actor* 1718 Vine

**Born:** Joe Yule, Jr.; Sept. 23, 1920, in Brooklyn, N.Y.
**Spotlights:** Exuberant dancer, singer, comedian, actor. On-screen when he was 6 years old, cast as a midget. Strong screen presence in *A Midsummer Night's Dream* (1935), *A Family Affair* (1937), Hardy serial, 16 more pictures; *Babes in Arms* (1939), *The Last Mile* (1959). Radio: Andy Hardy on "The Hardy Family" (1949). TV: "The Mickey Rooney Show," situation comedy (1954–55).

*Steve Allen*

**Achievements:** 1938, special Oscar; number-one box office star 1939–41; 1981–82 Emmy for "Bill."
**Highlights:** Married 8 times.
**Sidelights:** Dearly loved his late co-star Judy Garland and misses her tremendously.

## Robert Cummings   *See page 59.*     1718 Vine

## Donald Cook   *Actor*     1718 Vine

**Born:** Sept. 26, 1900, in Portland, Ore.
**Spotlights:** Thirties supporting and leading actor with vaudevillian roots. Warner's *The Public Enemy* (1931). Died: 1961.

## Laird Cregar   *Actor*     1718 Vine

**Born:** Samuel L. Cregar; July 28, 1916, in Philadelphia, Pa.
**Spotlights:** Extremely overweight, dark-haired (often seen sporting a goatee) villainous-type actor, who delivered a powerful performance as Jack the Ripper in *The Lodger* (1944). Died: 1944 of a heart attack while on a crash diet.

## Al Jolson   *See page 308.*     1718 Vine

## Lila Lee   *Actress*     1718 Vine

**Born:** Augusta Appel; July 25, 1901, in Union Hill, N.Y.
**Spotlights:** Leading lady in silents: *The Ghost Breaker* (1922), *Woman Proof* (1923). Worked up to 1937, including a good supporting role in MGM's *The Ex-Mrs. Bradford* (1936). Died: 1973.

## Bebe Daniels   *Actress*     1718 Vine

**Born:** Virginia Daniels; Jan. 14, 1901, in Dallas, Tex.
**Spotlights:** The bubbly teenage brunette played adult roles opposite comic Harold Lloyd for $10–$100 per week. At Paramount Rudolph Valentino romanced "the vamp" (at $1,000 per week), but truly she was one of the studio's warm, beautiful comediennes ($5,000 per week). In the thirties her career blossomed in England. Retired in 1955. Died: 1971.

## Delbert Mann   *Director*     1718 Vine

**Born:** Jan. 30, 1920, in Lawrence, Kan.
**Spotlights:** *Lover Come Back* (1961), *Dear Heart* (1964).
**Achievements:** 1955, Academy Award for *Marty*.

## Kay Starr   *Singer*     1708 Vine

**Born:** Katherine Starks; July 31, 1922, in Dougherty, Okla.
**Spotlights:** Diversified style included country music, swing, and blues. Featured on

"The Bob Crosby Show" as an up-and-coming vocalist (CBS, 1939). One of many great voices heard on "The Chesterfield Supper Club" with such orchestras as Sammy Kaye and Glenn Miller in the 1940s. Gold records: "Wheel of Fortune" (1952) and "Rock and Roll Waltz".
**Sidelights:** Born on an Indian reservation.

**Dorothy Malone**   *Actress*     1718 Vine
**Born:** Dorothy Maloney; Jan. 30, 1925, in Dallas, Tex.
**Spotlights:** Lovely blond (sometimes brunette) with large sympathetic eyes. *The Big Sleep* (1946), *Man of a Thousand Faces* (1957).
**Achievements:** 1956, Best Supporting Actress Oscar for *Written on the Wind*.

**Dave Brubeck**   *Composer, musician*     1708 Vine
**Born:** Dec. 6, 1920, in Concord, Calif.
**Spotlights:** Innovator in jazz. *The Light in the Wilderness, Gates of Justice, Take Five.*

**Miriam Hopkins**   *See page 108.*     1708 Vine

**George Shearing**   *Music, composer*     1708 Vine
**Born:** Aug. 13, 1919, in England.
**Spotlights:** Blind since birth. Jazz-rooted. Classical and easy listening pianist, too. Successful in U.S. since 1941. Shearing's arrangement- magnificent instrumental blend-has gently swung the world. Collaboration with other greats: *Nat King Cole Sings/The George Shearing Quintet Plays.* Albums: *Alone Together, Blues Alley Jazz, 500 Miles High,* and *Light, Airy and Swinging.*

**Joan Davis**   *See page 238.*     1708 Vine

**Rosalind Russell**   *Actress*     1708 Vine
**Born:** June 4, 1912, in Waterbury, Conn.
**Spotlights:** Fast and very funny opposite Cary Grant in Howard Hawks's *His Girl Friday* (1940). *My Sister Eileen* (1942); *Auntie Mame* (1958).
**Achievements:** 1972, special Oscar (humanitarian work).
**Sidelights:** "I've played 23 career women, every kind of executive. Except for different leading men, and a switch in title, they were all stamped out of the same Alice in Careerland." Died: 1976.

**Parkyakarkus**   *Comic*     1708 Vine
**Born:** Harry Einstein; in 1904, in Boston, Mass.
**Spotlights:** Uproarious routines. Decades of fame from splitting sides on "The Eddie Cantor Show" (first broadcast in 1931). Led to movie roles *The Life of the Party* (1937) and *Glamour Boy* (1940). Also known as Harry Parke. Died: 1958.

## Alfred Newman  ⊙ *Composer, conductor, music director*                    **1708 Vine**

**Born:** March 17, 1901, in New Haven, Conn.
**Achievements:** Academy Awards: 1938, *Alexander's Ragtime Band*; 1940, *Tin Pan Alley*; 1943, *The Song of Bernadette*; 1947, *Mother Wore Tights*; 1952, *With a Song In My Heart*; 1954, *Call Me Madam*; 1955, *Love is a Many Spendored Thing*; 1956, *The King and I*; 1967, *Camelot*. Worked in over 200 films. Died: 1970.

## Mantovani  ⊙ *Conductor*                    **1708 Vine**

**Born:** Annunzio Mantovani; Nov. 5, 1905, in Venice, Italy.
**Spotlights:** Formed orchestra in 1923. Recordings include "Charmaine," "Dancing with Tears in My Eyes," "It Happened in Monterey," and "Mexicali Rose." Musical Director for Noel Coward in 1945. TV show in 1960s.

## Frazier Hunt  ⍾ *Newscaster*                    **1708 VINE**

**Spotlights:** Began career in New York in the early 1930s. Animated news commentator prior to World War II. Postwar he became an extremely conservative newscaster.

## Frank Morgan  🎥 *Actor*                    **1708 Vine**

**Born:** Francis Wupperman; June 1, 1890, in New York.
**Spotlights:** Under MGM contract for two decades; made close to 100 films including *Tortilla Flat* (1942). Immortalized in *The Wizard of Oz* (1939) as the wizard. He offered his sage advice to the Tin Man: "A heart is not judged by how much you love, but by how much you are loved by others." Radio: Star of "The Maxwell House Coffee Time" (NBC, 1937). Died: 1949.

## Betty Blythe  🎥 *Actress*                    **1702 Vine**

**Born:** Elizabeth Blythe Slaughter; Sept. 1, 1893, in Los Angeles, Calif.
**Spotlights:** Educated at the University of Southern California. Lead in *The Queen of Sheeba* (1921); later played in supporting roles. Died: 1972.

## Jack Bailey  📺 *See page 87.*                    **1702 Vine**

## Perry Como  📺 *See page 62.*                    **1702 Vine**

## Raymond Hatton  🎥 *Actor*                    **1702 Vine**

**Born:** July 7, 1887, in Red Oak, Iowa.
**Spotlights:** Character roles continually in film giant Cecil B. DeMille's early silents; developed into reliable comic or bad guy sidekick in the talkies. *Steamboat Round the Bend* (1935), starring Will Rogers with, among others, Stepin Fetchit, directed by John Ford. Died: 1971.

**Gene Raymond**  *See page 369.*   1702 Vine

**Teresa Brewer** *Singer*   1702 Vine
**Born:** Theresa Breuer; May 7, 1931, in Toledo, Ohio.
**Spotlights:** Frequent radio and TV guest singer. Album: *The Best of Teresa Brewer.*
Songs: "Music, Music, Music," and "Pledging My Love."

**Helen Gahagan** *Actress, politician, writer*   1702 Vine
**Born:** Nov. 25, 1900, in Boonton, N.J.
**Spotlights:** Formerly a Broadway and opera star. Only person on the Walk of Fame
to have only *one* movie credit! She starred in RKO's *She* (1935), about a 50 year-old
woman who cannot die until she falls in love.
**Highlights:** Married to actor Melvyn Douglas (1931, until her death in 1980). He died
less than one year later (1981).
**Sidelights:** 1945–49 congresswoman, U.S. House of Representatives.

**Howard Hawks** *Director, producer, screenwriter*   1702 Vine
**Born:** May 30, 1896, in Goshen, Ind.
**Spotlights:** Skilled in virtually all aspects of filmmaking; excelled in developing
relationships; with piercing insight. *The Criminal Code* (1931), starring Boris Karloff,
was one of his first sound movies, but brilliant as it was, it did not embrace the
emotional aspects of his comedy, *Twentieth Century* (1934), starring Carole Lombard and John Barrymore. Other classics include *To Have and Have Not* (1944),
*Red River* (1946), and *Gentlemen Prefer Blondes* (1953).
**Achievements:** 1975, honorary Oscar. Died: 1977.

**Anna May Wong** *Actress*   Hollywood and Vine
**Born:** Wong Lui Tsong; Jan. 3, 1907, in Los Angeles, Calif.
**Spotlights:** Bright and beautiful in *Red Lantern* (1919). Her portrayal of a Mongol
slave in *The Thief of Bagdad* (1924), starring Douglas Fairbanks, solidified her
celebrity status. Paired with the biggest names, including Laurence Olivier, on stage.
**Sidelights:** Broke into the big time from "extra" work. *Portrait in Black* (1960) was an
ominous title; she died one year later (1961) of a heart attack.

**Kay Kyser** *See page 250.*   Hollywood and Vine

**Eleanor Steber** *Opera singer*   Hollywood and Vine
**Born:** July 17, 1916, in Wheeling, W.Va.
**Spotlights:** Gifted American Metropolitan Opera soprano; especially noted for her
very fine renderings of Mozart and Strauss. Many opera recordings.

**Tom Mix** *Actor*   Hollywood and Vine
**Born:** Jan. 6, 1880, in Mix Run, Pa.

**Spotlights:** Former Oklahoma and Texas sheriff. Dark-haired, tough, number-one cowboy during the silent era, starting in 1909, *On the Little Big Horn*. First cowboy to wear a big, white hat designating him a good guy. Rode the dusty trail — doing his own stunts — in close to 150 quickies (one-to-two reelers) with his horse, Tony. Made over 60 features; *The Miracle Rider* (1935 series).

**Sidelights:** Mix was a real-life colorful cut-up. In front of the cameras he was sweet; off work he was a charming (sometimes) prankster (always). Once he invited a female gossip columnist to an all-male bachelor party. Mix liked being a hellion, and was hired as a bodyguard for Mexican President Madero from 1911–1913. Died: 1940, in a car crash, when his car overturned near Florence, Arizona.

## Molly O'Day 🎥 *Actress*     Hollywood and Vine

**Born:** Molly Noonan; Feb. 11, 1911, in Bayonne, N.J.
**Spotlights:** 'B' picture queen who averaged two features a year (1927–34) including *Sea Devils* (1931).

## Frank Luther 🎵 *Singer, songwriter*     Hollywood and Vine

**Born:** Frank L. Crow in 1900 in Kansas.
**Spotlights:** In 1943, "Americans & Their Songs" made him famous. Familiar to children for recordings of nursery rhymes and song lessons. Died: 1980.

## Joanne Dru 📺 *Actress*     Hollywood and Vine

**Born:** Jan. 31, 1923, in Logan, W.Va.
**Spotlights:** Escaped the skyscraper jungle as Babs Hooten in the situation comedy "Guestward Ho!" (1960–61). Variety guest spots.

## Wendy Barrie 🎥 *Actress*     Northeast corner of Hollywood and Vine

**Born:** Margaret Jenkins; April 18, 1912, in Hong Kong.
**Spotlights:** Her most memorable role was that of saucy Jane Seymour opposite Charles Laughton in the British production, *The Private Life of Henry VIII* (1933). Leading lady in numerous films, including *It's a Small World* (1935), before becoming a favorite hostess for radio and TV shows. Died: 1978.

## Neil Armstrong, Edwin E. Aldrin, Jr., Michael Collins 📺

*See page 204.*     Northeast corner of Hollywood and Vine

## Kirk Douglas 🎥 *Actor*     Northeast corner of Hollywood and Vine

**Born:** Issur Danielovitch (later Demsky); Sept. 9, 1916, in Amsterdam, N.Y.
**Spotlights:** Handsome, forceful actor with a trademark dimpled chin. Made two movies before his role as a prizefighter in *Champion* (1949) made him a winner at the box office. Memorable in *Gunfight at the O.K. Corral* (1957); *Spartacus* (1960); more. Unlike most aging talents, Douglas fought successfuly to continue in leading roles even into his seventies.

**Highlights:** Father of producer-actor Michael Douglas.

### Edward R. Murrow  *Commentator*  Northeast corner of Hollywood and Vine

**Born:** April 25, 1908, in Greensboro, N.C.

**Spotlights:** Highly respected newscaster with CBS since 1935, holding such prestigious positions as director of Talks and Education (1935–37), European director, and World War II correspondent. Broadcast nightly from England (1939–45). Opened with famous intonation: "This is London." Those three words still send chills down the spines of those old enough to recall his dedication to war reporting and his commentaries on the threat of Nazi Germany. Became vice president and director of public affairs at CBS (1945–47).

**Achievements:** Emmys: 1953, 1955, 1956, 1957, 1958–59. Died: 1965.

### James Stewart  *Actor*  Northeast corner of Hollywood and Vine

**Born:** May 20, 1908, in Indiana, Pa.

**Spotlights:** Hedda Hopper urged MGM to screen-test him for his "unusually usual" qualities. With his guileless demeanor and slow, endearing drawl, he quickly became Hollywood's favorite example of the average, all-American boy. Outstanding films include *Mr. Smith Goes to Washington* (1939), and *It's a Wonderful Life* (1947).

**Achievements:** Best Actor Oscar for *The Philadelphia Story* (co-star Cary Grant again missed the golden trophy). Number-one U.S. star in 1955 thanks to Alfred Hitchcock's suspenseful direction in thrillers.

**Highlights:** Happily married to Gloria McLean (since 1949).

**Sidelights:** Holds highest rank in the U.S. Air Force — brigadier general — of any actor.

*Kirk Douglas*                *James Stewart*

# ⋆ 6263 HOLLYWOOD ⋆

### Mike Wallace  📺  *Interviewer, Newsman, host*          6263 Hollywood
**Born:** Myron Wallace; May 9, 1918, in Brookline, Mass.
**Spotlights:** Wallace co-hosted the live interview show "All Around the Town" (1951–52). Emcee of "The Big Surprise" quiz show (1956–57). "Mike Wallace Interviews" (1957–58) established him as a respected, tough newsman. A correspondent on "60 Minutes" (1968–); more.
**Achievements:** Emmys: 1971, 1972, 1973, 1979, 1980. Honored with many other awards, too.

### Billy Gilbert  🎥  *Actor*          6263 Hollywood
**Born:** Sept. 12, 1894, in Louisville, Ky.
**Spotlights:** Rotund comedian who supported Laurel and Hardy in *The Music Box* (1932) and Charlie Chaplin in *The Great Dictator* (1940).
**Sidelights:** Voice of Sneezy on Walt Disney's *Snow White and the Seven Drawfs* (1938). Died: 1971.

### Ruth Chatterton  🎥  *Actress*          6263 Hollywood
**Born:** Dec. 24, 1893, in New York.
**Spotlights:** Oval-faced, brunette beauty who made her screen debut when she was 35! Excellent performance as leading lady in MGM's *Madame* (1929) and Goldwyn's *Dodsworth* (1936).
**Sidelights:** Independent thinker who, upon retiring wrote novels and flew planes. Died: 1961.

### Milton Sills  🎥  *Actor*          6263 Hollywood
**Born:** Jan. 12, 1882, in Chicago, Ill.
**Spotlights:** Handsome star in the silent era; *Flaming Youth* (1923). Last film was *The Sea Wolf* (1930). Died: 1930, of a heart attack.

### Milton Berle  📺  *Comedian*          6263 Hollywood
**Born:** Milton Berlinger; July 12, 1908, in New York.
**Spotlights:** Radio: Host-judge of fighting married couples on "Kiss and Make up" (CBS 1946). "The Milton Berle Show" (NBC, 1939). TV: In the early days of black and white commercial TV broadcasting (begun in 1941), few people owned sets, but if they did, they could count on curious relatives and neighbors dropping in to view the newfangled thing. Many predicted TV wouldn't last, and stubbornly refused to buy one. It was crazy, slapstick Berle on "The Texaco Star Theater" and later "The Milton

149

Berle Show" (1948–56), whose outrageous vaudevillian-type costumes and gags sold more TV sets than anyone else. "Mr. Television" became a household word and the most talked about comedian for "people in the know." Known as the "Thief of Badgags."

**Achievements:** 1949, most outstanding Kinescope Personality; 1950 special Emmy to "Mr. Television".

### Allan Dwan  *Director*

6263 Hollywood

**Born:** April 3, 1885, in Canada.

**Spotlights:** Inventor of shooting techniques, e.g., the dolly shot. 400 films including *Robin Hood* (1922), starring Douglas Fairbanks; *Heidi* (1937), starring Shirley Temple; *Sands of Iwo Jima* (1949), starring John Wayne. Died: 1981.

### Helen Parrish  *Actress*

6263 Hollywood

**Born:** March 12, 1922, in Columbus, Ga.

**Spotlights:** Born with grease paint in her veins, this child star was a baby- faced joy in *Our Gang* (1927) — many shorts in this comedy series. They are seen on TV as "The Little Rascals." Supporting actress in a Universal, Deanna Durbin vehicle, *Mad About Music* (1938), where she played a jealous roommate. Died: 1959, of cancer.

*Milton Berle and Sir Michael Teilmann*

## Helen Twelvetrees  *Actress*    6263 Hollywood

**Born:** Dec. 25, 1907, in Brooklyn, N.Y.

**Spotlights:** Alluring blond leading lady of the thirties who was mainly cast in woeful roles. *A Bedtime Story* (1933), opposite Maurice Chevalier; *Now I'll Tell* (1934) co-starring Spencer Tracy. Died: 1958.

## Barry Nelson, *Actor*    6263 Hollywood

**Born:** Robert Haakon Nielson; April 16, 1920, in Oakland, Calif.

**Spotlights:** Best known as George Cooper in "My Favorite Husband" situation comedy (1953–57).

## Betty Hutton *Singer, actress*    6253 Hollywood

**Born:** Betty Thornburg; Feb. 26, 1921, in Battle Creek, Mich.

**Spotlights:** Raised in the depths of poverty, Hutton earned a fortune in motion pictures including the lead in MGM's *Annie Get Your Gun* (1950) and Paramount's *The Greatest Show on Earth* (1952).

**Sidelights:** After she walked out on her Paramount contract and ran out of money, she moved into St. Anthony's Rectory in Rhode Island as a domestic.

## Joi Lansing *Actress*    6253 Hollywood

**Born:** Joyce Wassmansdoff; April 6, 1928.

**Spotlights:** Wonderful character talent. Cast as Shirley Swanson (1956–59) on "The Bob Cummings Show." Played Gladys Flatt (1962–68) on "The Beverly Hillbillies."

## Howard Keel *Singer, actor*    6253 Hollywood

**Born:** Harold Leek; April 13, 1917, in Gillespie, Ill.

**Spotlights:** *Annie Get Your Gun* (1950), *Show Boat* (1951), and *Seven Brides for Seven Brothers* (1954) were MGM musicals that put his big, baritone singing voice to good use.

**TV:** Plays handsome Clayton Farlow (since 1981) on "Dallas."

## Jerome Cowan *Actor*    6253 Hollywood

**Born:** Oct. 6, 1897, in New York.

**Spotlights:** This dapper character actor might be difficult to identify by name; in Blondie films (based on the comic strip) he's identifiable as Dagwood's boss. Played company president Herbert Wilson on "The Tycoon" (1964–65). Died: 1972.

## Jack Albertson *Actor*    6253 Hollywood

**Born:** June 16, 1910, in Lynn, Mass.

**Achievements:** 1968 Best Supporting Actor Oscar, *The Subject was Roses*. 1975–76, Emmy, Outstanding Lead Actor in a comedy series, "Chico and the Man," as Ed Brown ("the Man"). Died: 1981.

## Robert Casadesus 💿 *French pianist* 6251 Hollywood

**Spotlights:** His renderings of French music were magnificent. Recordings include *Ravel Piano Music* (Columbia) and *Saint-Saens Concerto No. 4 in C Minor, op. 44.*

## Anthony Quinn 🎥 *Actor* 6251 Hollywood

**Born:** April 21, 1915, in Mexico.
**Spotlights:** In 1936 Mae West gave the 21-year-old "kid" a break by casting him as a 65-year-old man in her play *Clean Beds*. Then, in true acting form, he told director Cecil B. DeMille he was a Cherokee Indian and landed a role in *The Plainsman* (1936). (Quinn's mother was Mexican, his father Irish.)
**Achievements:** 1952, Best Supporting Actor, *Viva Zapata!*; 1956, *Lust for Life.*
**Highlights:** Married Katharine, adopted daughter of Cecil B. DeMille, in 1937, divorced in 1965.
**Lowlights:** 1941, a horrible tragedy occurred — Quinn's 3-year-old son drowned in a lily pond at W. C. Fields's house; a horrified Fields immediately sold the property.

## Dave O'Brien 🎥 *Actor* 6251 Hollywood

**Born:** David Barclay; May 31, 1912, in Big Springs, Tex.
**Spotlights:** Made the comedy series, *Pete Smith*, shorts, then 'B' vehicles: *The Ghost Creeps* (1940) and *The Spider Returns* (1941).
**Highlights:** 1960–61 Emmy, Outstanding Writing Achievement in Comedy: "The Red Skelton Show." Died: 1969.

## Laura Hope Crews 🎥 *Actress* 6251 Hollywood

**Born:** Dec. 12, 1879, in San Francisco, Calif.
**Spotlights:** Delighted in playing feebleminded Aunt Pitty-Pat to Scarlett in *Gone with the Wind* (1939). Slightly scatterbrained in *The Flame of New Orleans* (1941). Died: 1942.

## Sabu 🎥 *Actor* 6251 Hollywood

**Born:** Savu Dastagir; Jan. 27, 1924, in India.
**Spotlights:** A British director discovered this beautiful, mystical boy working in the stables of a maharaja and made him the star of *Elephant Boy* (1937), a natural role for Sabu, the son of an elephant driver, 22 typecast adventure flicks followed before the popularity of exotic themes waned. *The Thief of Bagdad* (1940), *Jungle Book* (1942).
**Achievements:** A decorated war hero. Died: 1963, of a heart attack.

## Hugh Herbert 🎥 *Actor, writer* 6251 Hollywood

**Born:** Aug. 10, 1887, in Binghamton, N.Y.
**Spotlights:** His comic antics — excitedly waving his hands and crying "Woo Woo!"--appeared in countless films and always got a laugh. His film career consisted of both

character and lead roles: *Husbands for Rent* (1928); *Havana Rose* (1951), his last film. Died: 1952, of a heart attack.

## Wayne King  *Composer, conductor, clarinetist*     6251 Hollywood
**Born:** Feb. 16, 1901, in Savannah, Ill.
**Spotlights:** "The Waltz King" received orchestra billing on "Lady Esther Serenade," which featured Bess Johnson (1940s). Songs: "Baby Shoes" and "Blue Hours." Died: 1985.

## Susan Hayward *Actress*     6251 Hollywood
**Born:** Edythe Marrener; June 30, 1918, in Brooklyn, N.Y.
**Spotlights:** Courageous portrayals of phoenixlike characters rising from the ashes: *Smash Up: The Story of a Woman* (1947), *With a Song in My Heart* (1952).
**Achievements:** 1958, Best Actress Oscar, *I Want to Live*. Received four Oscar nominations. Died: 1975, from a brain tumor.

## William Bendix *See page 210.*     6251 Hollywood

## Martha Raye *Actress*     6251 Hollywood
**Born:** Margaret O'Reed; Aug. 27, 1916, in Butte, Mont.
**Spotlights:** Boundless energy gave viewers the impression this wide-mouthed comedienne could sing her lungs out. *Mountain Music* (1937), *The Boys from*

*Anthony Quinn*        *Connie Stevens*

*Syracuse* (1940), *Four Jills in a Jeep* (1944). TV: Carrie Sharples (1982–84) on "Alice".
**Achievements:**  1969, special Oscar for wartime efforts.

### Connie Stevens  *Actress, singer* 6249 Hollywood

**Born:**  Concetta Ann Ingolia; Aug. 8, 1938, in Brooklyn, N.Y.
**Spotlights:**  One of the friendliest, perkiest ladies in Hollywood, she starred in "Hawaiian Eye" (1959–63) and makes numerous guest appearances.

### Hedy Lamarr  *Actress* 6249 Hollywood

**Born:**  Hedwig Kiesler; Nov. 9, 1913, in Austria.
**Spotlights:**  At 19, Lamarr signed a movie contract in Europe, which required her to bathe and run through a forest in *Ecstasy* (1933); She immediately won audiences hearts. On a boat to the States, she wooed a long-term contract out of Louis B. Mayer. Billed as "the most beautiful girl in Hollywood." Many starring roles include *Algiers* (1938), *Samson and Delilah* (1949).

### June Knight *Actress* 6247 Hollywood

**Born:**  Margaret Vallikett; in 1908, in Los Angeles, Calif.
**Spotlights:**  Singer-dancer who came into prominence in the 1930s under contract to MGM. A pretty blond with a cute, turned up nose, she melted Robert Taylor's heart in *Broadway Melody of 1936*. Vivacious, energetic, and charming, she retired too soon upon marrying (first a wealthy oilman, then an industrialist).

### Phil Baker *Comedian, composer, accordianist* 6247 Hollywood

**Born:**  Aug. 24, 1898, in Philadelphia, Pa.
**Spotlights:**  Former top vaudeville celebrity whose own comedy-variety program brought him fame, "The Phil Baker Show" (1933–40). Popular for playing the accordian. Emcee on "Take It or Leave It" quiz show (debut on CBS, 1940). Also seen in films. Died: 1963.

### Sylvia Sidney *Actress* 6245 Hollywood

**Born:**  Sophia Kosow; Aug. 8, 1910, in Bronx, N.Y.
**Spotlights:**  Pretty, round-faced brunette of 30 films at Paramount, usually as a working-class heroine; *Jennie Gerhardt* (1933). Co-starred with Cary Grant in *Thirty-Day Princess* (1934). Appeared in films sporadically through the seventies.

### Randolph Scott *Actor* 6245 Hollywood

**Born:**  Randolph Crane; Jan. 23, 1898, in Orange Co., Va.
**Spotlights:**  Tall, fair-haired, square-jawed, serious-looking cowboy star: *Abilene Town* (1946), *Colt .45* (1950). Made 96 movies; mostly played the cowboy hero. Died: 1987.

## Gary Cooper  *Actor* 6245 Hollywood

**Born:** Frank James Cooper; May 7, 1901, in Helena, Mont.

**Spotlights:** "That fellow is the world's greatest actor. He can do, with no effort, what the rest of us spend years trying to learn: to be perfectly natural," John Barrymore stated. Humphrey Bogart said, "Coop is a star." The entire industry admired Cooper's honest, strong, silent style. A man of few words, "Yup; nope." Ironic, because his intention in moving to Los Angeles was to draw cartoons! Obtained extra work in westerns in 1925 because he could ride a horse; was paid $50 per week for second lead in *The Winning of Barbara Worth* (1926). By 1939, the highest contracted actor at $500,000 per year.

**Achievements:** 1941, Best Actor Oscar, *Sergeant York* (he had turned down the offer of making this movie three times); 1952, *High Noon*; and 1960, honorary Oscar.

**Sidelights:** His "Yup" from *The Virginian* (1929, Cooper's first all-talkie) has been imitated countless times. Died: 1961, of cancer.

## Maurice Tourneur  *Director* 6243 Hollywood

**Born:** Maurice Thomas; Feb. 2, 1876, in France.

**Spotlights:** He put on film for the first time the macabre work of Edgar Allan Poe. *The System of Doctor Tarr* and *Professor Fether* (1912). A strong stylist who captured wondrous depth and beauty in his pictures.

**Sidelights:** Retired in 1949 after losing a leg in a car accident in his native country. Died: 1961.

*Gary Cooper*

**Mercedes McCambridge**  📺  *See page 141.*  6243 Hollywood

**Edward Dmytryk**  🎥  *Director*  6241 Hollywood
**Born:**  Sept. 4, 1908, in Canada.
**Spotlights:**  Started off in the mailroom and worked his way up to such thrillers as *Murder, My Sweet* (1945) and *The Caine Mutiny* (1954), starring Humphrey Bogart.
**Sidelights:**  Political involvement in the late 1940s caused his career to slip.

**Lana Turner**  🎥  *Actress*  6233 Hollywood
**Born:**  Julia Turner; Feb. 8, 1920, in Wallace, Idaho.
**Spotlights:**  Plantinum blond love goddess with penciled eyebrows — she lost them permanently when they were shaved for her fourth film, *Adventures of Marco Polo* (1938); big box office attraction in late 1940s through early 1950s; *The Postman Always Rings Twice* (1946); *Peyton Place* (1957). Still looks great.

**Henry Winkler**  📺  *Actor*  6233 Hollywood
**Born:**  Oct. 30, 1945, in New York.
**Spotlights:**  When Arthur "Fonzie" Fonzarelli said "aaayyh!" and turned his thumbs up, the "Happy Days" (1974–84) audience went crazy with applause. A sensitive, compassionate performer; involved behind the scenes as a producer too.
**Sidelights:**  A far cry from being undereducated, he studied at Yale.

**Joel McCrea**  🎙  *See page 26.*  6233 Hollywood

**Eddie Fisher**  💿  *Singer, actor*  6233 Hollywood
**Born:**  Edwin Fisher; Aug. 10, 1928, in Philadelphia, Pa.
**Spotlights:**  Born with a golden throat, the skinny, little 12-year-old was picked out of Thomas Junior High School by a talent scout to sing "The Army Air Corps Song" on local radio. He was on his way to becoming the biggest teen idol of the fifties, a full-blown star by 22. He hosted "Coke Time" (NBC, TV), a top-rated show. "Every new song I recorded became an instant best-seller." "With These Hands," "How Do You Speak to an Angel?" and "Oh! My PaPa." Earned $25,000 a week.
**Highlights:**  Four marriages to actresses ended in divorce; talented Debbie Reynolds, the ever-gorgeous superstar Elizabeth Taylor, vivacious Connie Stevens, lovely Terry Richard.
**Sidelights:**  Born dirt poor with 6 brothers and sisters, he went on to earn over $20 million (and lose it).

**Carol Channing**  📺  *Actress, singer, comedienne*  6233 Hollywood
**Born:**  Jan. 31, 1925, in San Francisco, Calif.
**Spotlights:**  "Aren't I the Luckiest?" Tall, blonde "Kewpie" with king-sized brown eyes

and giant smile who made it big in a revue show called "Lend an Ear" in a little theater off Hollywood Boulevard. Played Lorelei in *Gentlemen Prefer Blondes* (Anita Loos's stage musical) in 1962 for a two-year run. Countless TV guest spots.

**Sidelights:** Worried about doing justice to child-genius composer's music for "Hello, Dolly!" (on Broadway), she called "family mentor" George Burns and asked him, "George, do you think I am up to singing this Jerry Herman score?" And George replied, "Carol, what are you worried about? Your voice is as good as mine." Now, doesn't that give you *confidence*.

**Barry Manilow**  *Singer, songwriter*    6233 Hollywood

**Born:** June 17, 1946, in Brooklyn, N.Y.

**Spotlights:** Someone persuaded a young Manilow to start in the CBS mailroom and work his way up. When his dream of recording was realized, he might have asked himself, "Could It Be Magic?" "Even Now" holding onto superstar status, he gives thanks for this "Sweet Life."

**Mitchell Leisen** 🎥 *Director*    6233 Hollywood

**Born:** Oct. 6, 1897, in Menominee, Mich.

**Spotlights:** Associated with Paramount for two decades, including *Death Takes a Holiday* (1934), starring Fredric March; *Murder at the Vanities* (1934), a comedy-mystery starring Jack Oakie; *Hands Across the Table* (1935), a romantic comedy starring Carole Lombard and Fred MacMurray. Died: 1972.

*Henry Winkler*                    *Carol Channing*

## James Nederlander  *Broadway producer*          6233 Hollywood

**Born:** 1922, in Detroit, Mich.

**Spotlights:** He once said, "There are no bad theaters, just bad plays." His productions include *Whose Life Is It Anyway?, Annie, Lena Home: The Lady and Her Music.* Owner of 7 west coast theaters, and 11 theaters on Broadway; head of one of the largest chains of legitimate theaters. Responsible for revivals of such stage winners as "Hello, Dolly!" "Porgy and Bess," and "Fiddler on the Roof."

## Marshall Neilan  *Director*          6233 Hollywood

**Born:** April 11, 1891, in San Bernardino, Calif.

**Spotlights:** At his best with "America's Sweetheart," Mary Pickford, in *Rebecca of Sunnybrook Farm* (1917) and *A Little Princess* (1917).

**Sidelights:** Got into show biz, acting first, when he was a chauffeur to a great director! Died: 1958, of cancer.

## Kathleen Lockhart  *Actress*          6233 Hollywood

**Born:** Kathleen Arthur; in 1894, in England.

**Spotlights:** Pretty character actress. Screen debut in 1936. Co-starred with her husband in *A Christmas Carol* (1938).

**Highlights:** Married to actor Gene Lockhart. Mother of actress June Lockhart. Died: 1978.

## Edward G. Robinson  *Actor*          6233 Hollywood

**Born:** Emmanuel Goldenberg; Dec. 12, 1893, in Bucharest.

**Spotlights:** Hit it big as the tough gangster in *Little Caesar* (1931). As a criminal, he became more than *The Little Giant* (1933), and one of the most powerful players of 1940s *film noir, Double Indemnity* (1944). Brilliant in dozens of movies spanning decades.

**Achievements:** 1973, special Oscar. Died: 1973.

## Joshua Logan  *Director, writer*          6233 Hollywood

**Born:** Oct. 5, 1908, in Texarkana, Tex.

**Spotlights:** Wrote *Mister Roberts* (1955), screenplay with Frank Nugent (from a play he wrote with Thomas Heggen). Henry Fonda, one of the movie's stars, worked with Logan 27 years earlier, with the University Players (Princeton). Logan directed Marilyn Monroe in the critically acclaimed *Bus Stop* (1956), a simple story about a singer and a cowboy set in a rodeo town.

## Arthur Godfrey  *News commentator, writer, host*          6233 Hollywood

**Born:** Aug. 31, 1903, in New York.

**Spotlights:** Completed one and one-half years of high school with additional home correspondence courses before becoming one of America's most treasured entertainers. Godfrey's style was friendly and casual, like a next-door neighbor. Radio: He cried describing President Franklin Roosevelt's funeral, and America wept along. "Arthur Godfrey Time" (first broadcast in 1945); "Arthur Godfrey's Digest" (broadcast in 1950); and "Arthur Godfrey's Talent Scouts" (1946; also produced on TV, 1948–58); many celebrities were discovered: Connie Francis, Tony Bennet, Patsy Cline, et al. "Arthur Godfrey and Friends" ran on TV from 1949–59. Died: 1983.

**Bette Davis** *See page 160.*   6233 Hollywood

**Spring Byington** *See page 79.*   6233 Hollywood

**Jane Froman** *Singer*   6231 Hollywood
**Born:** Ellen J. Froman; Nov. 10, 1907.
**Spotlights:** Radio and recording regular on "The Andrews Sisters Show" (1945); star of the show "Yours for a Song," (1948). Hit records: "With a Song in My Heart" and "I Believe." TV: "Jane Froman's USA Canteen" (1952–55).

**Constance Collier** *Actress*   6231 Hollywood
**Born:** Laura C. Hardie; Jan. 22, 1878, in England.
**Spotlights:** Silent screen debut in D. W. Griffith's *Intolerance* (1916). Her sporadic career continued into the talkies; Paramount's slapstick *The Perils of Pauline* (1947). Died: 1955.

**Karl Malden** *Actor*   6231 Hollywood
**Born:** Mladen Sekulovich; March. 22, 1914, in Gary, Ind.
**Spotlights:** *On the Waterfront* (1954); *One-Eyed Jacks* (1960).
**Achievements:** 1951, Best Supporting Actor Oscar for *A Streetcar Named Desire*.
**Sidelights:** TV buffs know him as Detective Lieutenant Mike Stone on "The Streets of San Francisco" (1972–77).

**Jackie Gleason** *See page 268.*   6225 Hollywood

**Buster Keaton** *See page 65.*   6225 Hollywood

**Anthony Mann** *Director*   6225 Hollywood
**Born:** Emil A. Bundesmann; June 30, 1906, in San Diego, Calif.
**Spotlights:** Handled nervous hopefuls — aspiring actresses and actors — by directing their screen tests, before his biggest box office successes with James Stewart: *Winchester 73* (1950), *The Far Country* (1954), and *The Man from Laramie* (1955). Died: 1967.

**Nat "King" Cole** *See page 59.*   6225 Hollywood

## Quentin Reynolds  🖉  *Actor*                    **6225 Hollywood**

**Born:**  1903.
**Spotlights:**  Radio newscaster, film director, writer and screen actor. Narrator of films: *Naked Africa* (1959); *Justice and Caryl Chessman* (1960). Died: 1965.

## Bette Davis  🎥  *Actress*                    **6225 Hollywood**

**Born:**  Ruth Elizabeth Davis; April. 5, 1908, in Lowell, Mass.
**Spotlights:**  "The First Lady of the Screen" earned that title through sheer determination and talent. It was a good thing she had more acting ability than Hollywood had ever seen, because she was competing with the most glamorous women in the world — Greta Garbo, Marlene Dietrich, Hedy Lamarr. *All About Eve* (1950); *What Ever Happened to Baby Jane?* (1962); more. TV: In addition to playhouse theaters, made a rare guest appearance on the first episode of "Hotel" (1983).
**Achievements:**  Best Actress Academy Awards: 1935, *Dangerous*, 1938, *Jezebel*. 1978–79, Emmy, "Stranger: The Story of a Mother and Daughter." 1977, first woman recipient of the American Film Institute Life Achievement Award.
**Sidelights:**  Her strong, gutsy personality kept her going, even after she was fired by George Cukor from her first acting job in a stock company. "Flunked" a screen test at Goldwyn. Was told by studio head (Universal) that she had no sex appeal, then was signed by that same studio only to be dropped a year later. Warner Brothers picked her up, and the rest is history.

## Eddy Arnold  🎵  *Singer, musician*                    **6225 Hollywood**

**Born:**  May 15, 1918, in Henderson, Tenn.

*Bette Davis*                                   *Irene Rich*

160

**Spotlights:** Known as "The Tennessee Playboy" on "The Grand Ole Opry" musical program, which had its debut in 1925 out of Nashville; the studio auditorium became The Grand Ole Opry House in 1961. Host of the "Opry House Matinee" (1946 debut), a country-western musical variety program.

**Irene Rich** 🔘 *Actress*                    6225 Hollywood

**Born:** Irene Luther; Oct. 13, 1891, in Buffalo, N.Y.
**Spotlights:** *Jes' Call Me Jim* (1920); *They Had to See Paris* (1929), both with Will Rogers. On-screen 1918–48. Radio: Host of "Dear John" (1933).

**Red Foley** 🔘 *Singer, songwriter*              6225 Hollywood

**Born:** Clyde Julian; June 17, 1910, in Blue Lick, Ky.
**Spotlights:** Smooth baritone voice which enhanced country-western music. Radio: "Avalon Time" in 1939 (first network show with country music) co- starring Red Skelton. TV: Emcee for "Ozark Mountain Jubilee" (1954-61). Recordings include: "Blues in My Heart," "Peace in My Valley" (gospel), and "Chattanoogie Shoe Shine Boy." Died: 1968.

**Tod Browning** 🎥 *Director, screenwriter*          6225 Hollywood

**Born:** Charles Browning; July 12, 1882, in Louisville, Ky.
**Spotlights:** He was the behind-the-scenes horror king of the thirties, specializing in fear and terror; Universal released the powerful *Dracula* (1931) with the threatening Bela Lugosi in the lead role. *Freaks* (1932) was his most eccentric, grotesque work. Died: 1962.

# ⋆ 6211 HOLLYWOOD ⋆

## Sir Cedric Hardwicke 🎥 *Actor*
6211 Hollywood

**Born:** Feb. 19, 1883, in England.
**Spotlights:** "I believe God felt sorry for actors, so he created Hollywood to give them a place in the sun and a swimming pool." Dark-haired, aristocratic, intelligent, sad-looking performer versatile in villainous or gentle roles: *Les Miserables* (1935); *The Moon Is Down* (1940). TV Playhouse work in the sixties.
**Achievements:** Knighted in 1934. Died: 1964.

## Johnnie Ray 📀 *Singer*
6211 Hollywood

**Born:** John Ray; Jan. 10, 1927, in Dallas, Ore.
**Spotlights:** Famous for his song "Cry." Supporting actor in *There's No Business Like Show Business* (1954). Active on the club circuit.

## Alice Brady 🎥 *Actress*
6211 Hollywood

**Born:** Nov. 2, 1892, in New York.
**Spotlights:** Accomplished singer and stage actress who was very good in both comedies and dramas: *The Gay Divorcee* (1934) and *In Old Chicago* (1938,).
**Achievements:** 1938 Best Supporting Actress Oscar. Died: 1939, of cancer.

## Carol Lawrence 🎤 *Actress*
6211 Hollywood

**Born:** Sept. 5, 1934, in Melrose Park, Ill.
**Spotlights:** Exuberant dancer-singer whose glowing performances on Broadway culminated in numerous hit shows, including *Guys and Dolls*, *South Pacific*, *West Side Story*, *Funny Girl*; more. Also appears on TV.

## Constance Cummings 🎥 *Actress*
6211 Hollywood

**Born:** Constance Halverstadt; May 15, 1910, in Seattle, Wash.
**Spotlights:** Intelligent, determined, high-cheekboned 21-year-old brunette who fought back to become a star after being fired from her first film. Kept pace with Spencer Tracy and Jack Oakie in William A. Wellman's *Looking for Trouble* (1934).

## Joseph L. Mankiewicz 🎥 *Director, screenwriter*
6211 Hollywood

**Born:** Feb. 11, 1909, in Wilkes-Barre, Pa.
**Achievements:** 1949, Best Screenplay and Best Director Oscars for *A Letter to Three Wives*. 1950, two Oscars — Screenwriter and Director — *All About Eve*.

## Frank Faylen 📺 *Actor*
6211 Hollywood

**Born:** Frank Rufin; in 1907, in St. Louis, Mo.

**Spotlights:** Thin character actor in films (1936–68); as Herbert T. Gillis had to contend with the "Many Loves of Dobie Gillis" (1959–63).

### Marie Prevost  *Actress* 6211 Hollywood

**Born:** Mary Dunn; Nov. 8, 1898, in Canada.
**Spotlights:** One of Mack Sennett's bathing beauties. *Her Nature Dance* (1917) went into stardom during the mid-twenties, *Kiss Me Again* (1925). Died: 1937, from anorexia nervosa (starved herself to death).

### Earl Godwin  *Correspondent, newscaster* 6207 Hollywood

**Born:** 1881.
**Spotlights:** Washington radio correspondent. President of White House Correspondents Assoc., from 1938–40. Wrote for the *Milwaukee Sentinel* and *Montreal Star.* Died: 1956.

### Ann Harding  *Actress* 6207 Hollywood

**Born:** Dorothy Gatley; Aug. 7, 1901, in Houston, Tex.
**Spotlights:** Portrayed long-suffering, teary roles; so good at it that she was typecast as

*Carol Lawrence with Robert Goulet*

such in the 1930s. *Holiday* (1930); *Gallant Lady* (1934). TV appearances on the "Dr. Kildare" series; more. Died: 1981.

### Pinky Lee  *Actor, entertainer*                6207 Hollywood

**Born:** Pincus Leff; in 1916, in St. Paul, Minn.
**Spotlights:** "The Pinky Lee Show" (1950), a situation comedy; "Those Two" (1952–53); various morning children shows (1954–57).

### George O'Brien *Actor*                6207 Hollywood

**Born:** April 19, 1900, in San Francisco, Calif.
**Spotlights:** Big, strong cowboy star of the silent era. Women melted over his muscles in John Ford films: *The Iron Horse* (1924); still handsome in *She Wore a Yellow Ribbon* (1949) starring John Wayne. Died: 1985.

### Philip Ahn *Actor*                6207 Hollywood

**Born:** March 29, 1911, in Los Angeles, Calif.
**Spotlights:** In the 1940s and 1950s he was usually a cruel, villainous Japanese or Chinese man. Busy in war pictures. In real life he was Korean. On-screen 1936 through 1975: *The General Died at Dawn* (1936); *China Girl* (1943); *Japanese War Bride* (1952); more.
**Sidelights:** TV's Master Kan on "Kung Fu." Died: 1978.

*Vincent Price*

## Vincent Price 🎥 *Actor*                                    6207 Hollywood

**Born:** May 27, 1911, in St. Louis, Mo.

**Spotlights:** Tall, well-educated, articulate actor with a unique voice; roles in *The Mad Magician* (1954); *The Fly* (1958); *The House of Usher* (1960), and *The Pit and the Pendulum* (1961) made him the "Master of Horror." TV: "The Chevy Mystery Show" (1960). Specials. Busy into the 1980s hosting mystery and playhouse shows.

## Henry B. Walthall 🎥 *Actor*                               6207 Hollywood

**Born:** March 16, 1878, in Shelby City, Ala.

**Spotlights:** Leading man in *The Sorrows of the Unfaithful* (1910), *The God Within* (1912), *The Wedding Gown* (1913), *The Birth of a Nation* (1915), *The Raven* (1915). Worked up until his death. Died: 1936.

## Sam Warner 🎥 *Film pioneer, producer*                     6207 Hollywood

**Born:** Aug. 10, 1888, in Baltimore, Md.

**Spotlights:** Of Warner Brothers studio fame; the brother with foresight. Recognized the big business potential of the Edison Kinetoscope motion picture industry. Persuaded his near-poverty family to sell their few prized possessions (e.g., an old horse) to buy a projector. Later, when Warner Brothers was already succeeding in the silents — Rin-Tin-Tin and John Barrymore were its biggest stars, Sam's dream was to produce a talking picture. Brother Harry thought it was a lousy idea. Who'd want to hear actors talk? Others thought it was plain stupid. Sam persuaded Harry it would work, and Warner Brothers made history with the first talkie, *The Jazz Singer* (1927). Died: 1927 from a cerebral hemorrhage the night before *The Jazz Singer* opened. It was a horrible twist of fate that the man who instigated the first sound pictures as well as his mourning brothers-business partners, could not attend its debut. The audience went wild with joy, realizing they were part of history when Al Jolson opened his mouth on-screen and said, "You ain't heard nothing yet."

# ⋆ 6100 HOLLYWOOD ⋆

## Jeanette MacDonald  🎥  *Actress, singer*                6161 Hollywood

**Born:**  June 18, 1901, in Philadelphia, Pa.

**Spotlights:**  Pretty operetta singer who sang her way through romantic comedies. A clever comedienne. Teamed with Maurice Chevalier in *Love Parade,* her very first film (1929); *Love Me Tonight* (1932); *The Merry Widow* (1934); more. Highly successful with baritone Nelson Eddy in *Naughty Marietta* (1935), *Maytime* (1937), six more. Died: 1965.

## Paul Whiteman  💿  *Music, bandleader*                6161 Hollywood

**Born:**  March 28, 1891, in Denver, Colo.

**Spotlights:**  America danced, danced, danced to his music in the 1920s and 1930s. Album: *Legendary Performer and Composer Paul Whiteman and His Orchestra.* Extremely popular for his jazz arrangements. Led the orchestra on radio's "Burns and

*Jeanette MacDonald*

Allen"; worked with star Al Jolson on "Kraft Music Hall." Recordings: "Whispering" and "Japanese Sandman." Died: 1967.

### House Peters   *Actor*                                    6161 Hollywood
**Born:** March 28, 1880, in England.
**Spotlights:** Worked as a leading man in the pioneer days of filmmaking: *In the Bishop's Carriage* (1913). Appeared in 45 pictures before retiring with the advent of sound. Died: 1967.

### Herbert Kalmus   *Inventor*                              6161 Hollywood
**Born:** Nov. 9, 1881, in Chelsea, Mass.
**Spotlights:** Every filmgoer has seen his work: "Color by Technicolor," "Photographed in Technicolor," or "In Technicolor." Patented the process that turned a black-and-white movie world into "living color." Died: 1963.

### Kate Smith   *Singer, hostess, commentator*             6161 Hollywood
**Born:** Kathryn Smith; May 1, 1909, in Greenville, Va.
**Spotlights:** In Broadway musicals before starting in radio in 1931. Especially famous for her rendition of "God Bless America," which she first sang in 1938. "The Kate Smith Show," variety, featured Broadway and movie stars, comedians, jazz greats, and others. Her theme song, "When the Moon Comes Over the Mountain," was a treat each show. She also had daytime and evening TV shows; films. Recorded another Americana turn: "Star Spangled Banner." Album *This is Christmas* still sells well.
**Sidelights:** Affectionately known as the "Songbird of the South." Died: 1986.

### Jan Murray   *Emcee*                                     6161 Hollywood
**Born:** 1917, in New York.
**Spotlights:** Popular game show host of the 1950s: "Blind Date" (1953); "Dollar a Second" quiz show (1953–57); actor on "Treasure Hunt" (1956–58).

### Helen Ferguson   *Actress*                               6161 Hollywood
**Born:** July 23, 1901, in Decatur, Ill.
**Spotlights:** Intelligent silent screen star: *The Famous Mrs. Fair* (1923), *The Scarlet West* (1925).

### Walter O'Keefe   *Author, actor*                         6161 Hollywood
**Born:** Aug. 18, 1900, in Hartford, Conn.
**Spotlights:** Quiz show host of "The Battle of the Sexes" (NBC, early 1940s); "Double or Nothing," a contestant had the chance to win as much as $10 to $40! (Mutual, 1940; CBS, 1947). Also radio producer.

## Louis Jourdan   *Actor*     6161 Hollywood

**Born:** June 19, 1921, in Marseille, France.

**Spotlights:** Handsome, debonair leading man of French and American cinema; adored for his role in *Gigi* (1958). Partial TV movie listings: "To Die in Paris" (1968), "Run a Crooked Mile" (1969), "The Count of Monte Cristo" (1974). Albums: *Babar Comes to America/Babar's Birthday Surprise* (the Babar Series); *Gigi; Little Prince.*

**Sidelights:** In Paris Underground during World War II after the Nazis captured his father. (His name is misspelled on the star. It's *Jourdan.*)

## Gene Kelly   *Dancer, choreographer, actor*     6161 Hollywood

**Born:** Eugene Kelly; Aug. 23, 1912, in Pittsburgh, Pa.

**Spotlights:** One of America's two top dancing sensations, the other being Fred Astaire. Magnificent MGM musical star who beautifully choreographed the films he appeared in: *An American in Paris* (1951); *Singin' in the Rain* (1952) — also co-directed. Genius talent.

**Achievements:** 1951, special Oscar.

## Bill Williams   *Actor*     6161 Hollywood

**Born:** William Katt; in 1916, in Brooklyn, N.Y.

*Gene Kelly with Ronald Reagan, George Murphy, and William Holden*

**Spotlights:** This rugged, all-American type got his start after serving in World War II, *Murder in the Blue Room* (1944). Gained TV fame as the lead in "The Adventures of Kit Carson" (1951–55).

**Jack Smith**  *Singer, actor*                    6141 Hollywood
**Born:** 1900.
**Spotlights:** Regular on "The Fred Allen Show," comedy-variety (first aired on CBS, 1932). The baritone Whispering Jack Smith on "The Jack Smith Show," variety (CBS, 1946).

**Stan Freberg** *Comedian*                    6141 Hollywood
**Born:** Aug. 7, 1926, in Los Angeles, Calif.
**Spotlights:** His off-screen voice was heard in the *Looney Looney Looney Bugs Bunny Movie*; developed "Time for Beany" (1949–54), puppet series.
**Achievements:** 1958, Grammy, spoken word.

**Jane Froman** *See page 159.*                    6141 Hollywood

**Dan Duryea** *Actor*                    6141 Hollywood
**Born:** Jan. 23, 1907, in White Plains, N.Y.
**Spotlights:** Slim, tough, silent type whose intense characterizations worked in motion pictures and TV: "China Smith" (1932–55) and as Eddie Jacks in "Peyton Place" (1967–68). Died: 1968.

**J. Carrol Naish** *Actor*                    6141 Hollywood
**Born:** Joseph C. Naish; Jan. 21, 1897, in New York.
**Spotlights:** Dark-haired Irishman with over 200 films to his credit; portrayed, with correct accents, Italians, Japanese, Jews, Arabs, etc! Small screen fame for "The New Adventures of Charlie Chan" (1956–57) as the deadly accurate sleuth. Died: 1973.

**Hildegarde** *Singer, pianist*                    6141 Hollywood
**Born:** H. Sell; Feb. 1, 1906, in France.
**Spotlights:** "The Incomparable Hildegarde" was musical hostess of the quiz show "Beat the Band" (NBC, 1940). Previously, she had been a cabaret star in her native country. Many recordings including "Eeny Meeny Miney Mo" and "When I'm With You."

**Bob Hope** *See page 72.*                    6141 Hollywood

**Tallulah Bankhead** *Actress*                    6141 Hollywood
**Born:** Jan. 31, 1902, in Huntsville, Ala.
**Spotlights:** Her wealthy congressman father indulged her every whim, including

169

opening doors in Hollywood. The beauty worked on stage and in silent films in both the U.S. and England. Later (ca. 1931), her unique, low raspy voice ("Hello Dahlinks") was worth $50,000 per talkie film, although most critics considered her acting better suited for stage. When she portrayed a journalist in Alfred Hitchcock's *Lifeboat* (1944), the critics changed their tune and called her the year's best actress. Made only four more films before shunning Hollywood for stage work. Died: 1968.

### Lloyd Hamilton  *Actor*     6141 Hollywood

**Born:** Aug. 19, 1891, in Oakland, Calif.

**Spotlights:** Very successful comedian in one- and two-reelers. One title hints at the light, crazy content: *Ham at the Garbage Gentlemen's Ball* (1915). Died: 1935.

### W. S. Van Dyke  *Director*     6141 Hollywood

**Born:** Woodbridge Strong Van Dyke III; in 1887, in Seattle, Wash.

**Spotlights:** He thrilled audiences with *Tarzan the Ape Man* (1932). Superlative directing of *The Thin Man* (1934), an exciting film starring William Powell and Myrna Loy. His nickname was "One Shot Woody" for his efficiency.

**Sidelights:** Hollywood isn't all glamor; Van Dyke contracted malaria while shooting *Trader Horn* (1931) on location in Africa. Died: 1943, of a heart attack.

### Raoul Walsh  *Director*     6141 Hollywood

**Born:** March 11, 1887, in New York.

**Spotlights:** Walsh's 'A' list of rugged male action stars included Errol Flynn, John Wayne, James Cagney, and Humphrey Bogart. Films include *The Big Trail* (1930), *High Sierra* (1941), *White Heat* (1949).

**Sidelights:** An accident cost him his right eye while shooting *In Old Arizona* (1928). Died: 1981.

### Buddy Rogers  *Actor, orchestra leader*     6141 Hollywood

**Born:** Charles Rogers; Aug. 13, 1904, in Olathe, Kan.

**Spotlights:** Very handsome and gracious. Entered movies during the transitional phase; the technology of sound was destroying many careers, and the oncoming Depression altered what audiences wanted to view. He co-starred in *Wings*, a Paramount silent, in 1927, his second year as a film actor; Clara Bow had the female lead. The movie won the very first Best Picture Academy Award. It also secured Rogers's career as a leading man; *Wings* was re-released in sound in 1929.

**Highlights:** Married Mary Pickford in 1937, the marriage lasted until her death in 1979.

### Warren Hull  *See page 196.*     6141 Hollywood

### Loretta Young  *See page 179.*     6141 Hollywood

## John Payne  *Actor*                    6125 Hollywood

**Born:** May 23, 1912, in Roanoke, Va.
**Spotlights:** Tall, dark, handsome leading man in *To the Shores of Tripoli* (1942); *Hello Frisco Hello* (1943). TV: "The Restless Gun" (1957–59).

## Virginia Valli *Actress*                    6125 Hollywood

**Born:** Virginia McSweeney; June 10, 1895, in Chicago, Ill.
**Spotlights:** Gorgeous bit player (1915) who rose to stardom slowly but surely within 9 years; *A Lady of Quality* (1924).
**Highlights:** Retired in 1932 to marry true love, actor Charles Farrell; marraige lasted until her death. Died: 1968.

## Gene Tierney *Actress*                    6125 Hollywood

**Born:** Nov. 20, 1920, in Brooklyn, N.Y.
**Spotlights:** Exquisitely sculptured face with high cheekbones, full lips, and thick dark hair made her one of the screen's greatest beauties. *Tobacco Road* (1941), *Laura* (1944), *Leave Her to Heaven* (1945).

*Buddy Rogers and Mary Pickford*

### Smiley Burnette   *Actor*     6125 Hollywood

**Born:** Lester Burnette; March 18, 1911, in Summum, Ill.
**Spotlights:** Round comic sidekick for Gene Autry from 1934–42. Played Frog Milhouse, who rode alongside the hero in close to 90 cowboy pictures. Made over 100 westerns; always box office material. Songwriter, too. Died: 1967.

### Van Heflin   *See page 103.*     6125 Hollywood

### William Wellman   *Director*     6125 Hollywood

**Born:** Feb. 29, 1896, in Brookline, Mass.
**Spotlights:** His career was flying high with *Wings* (1927). Directed James Cagney in a vicious, dynamic characterization in *The Public Enemy* (1931), making Cagney number one. Carole Lombard, Fredric March, and Walter Connolly played brilliantly in Wellman's funny, funny satire, *Nothing Sacred* (1937). *A Star is Born* (1937) was the original Hollywood melodrama (in Technicolor) and is still the best version.
**Achievements:** 1937, Academy Award for story *A Star is Born.* Died: 1975.

### Pauline Starke   *Actress*     6125 Hollywood

**Born:** Jan. 10, 1900, in Joplin, Mo.
**Spotlights:** Screen debut in 1919. *Dante's Inferno* (1924), adapted from the great poem, was one of her triumphant silents; *$20 a Week* (1935) — a talkie, was her last picture.

### Jane Withers   *Actress*     6125 Hollywood

**Born:** April 12, 1926, in Atlanta, Ga.
**Spotlights:** "Baby W" was on vaudeville virtually from day one. Cast as the mean brat who antagonized sweet Shirley Temple in *Bright Eyes* (1934), Withers established herself as the antithesis of childlike innocence. Nicknamed "Dixie's Dainty Dewdrop," she portrayed a fiesty, mischievous, spoiled girl; *The Holy Terror* (1937); *Always in Trouble* (1938). Popularity waned in teen years.
**Sidelights:** TV viewers might recall her commercial work as Josephine the Plumber.

### John Conte    *Host, actor, singer*     6125 Hollywood

**Born:** Palmer, MA.
**Spotlights:** Actor at Pasadena Playhouse, then specialized in musical comedies: *Carousel.* Also TV host of "John Conte's Little Show" (1950–51) and "Montovani Welcomes You" (1958–59). Became president of KMIR-TV, Channel 36, in Palm Springs, California.

### Gale Storm   *Actress, singer*     6125 Hollywood

**Born:** Josephine Cottle; April 5, 1922, in Bloomington, Tex.
**Spotlights:** Radio: Played the lead in the comedy "My Little Margie" (first broadcast, 1952). At the same time the show ran on TV (1952–55) but with different episodes!

On TV's "The Gale Storm Show" (1956–1960) she played Susanna Pomeroy, who worked on the luxury liner *S.S. Ocean Queen*. Recorded too.

### Thomas L. Tully  🎥 *Actor*                                6125 Hollywood
**Born:** Aug. 21, 1896, in Durango, Colo.
**Spotlights:** A seasoned professional with over 2,500 national radio broadcasts and Broadway performances to his credit before coming to Hollywood in the early 1940s. *June Bride* (1948), *The Caine Mutiny* (1954).
**Sidelights:** His early break in radio came because he could bark like a dog for "Renfrew of the Mounted." Died: 1982.

### Genevieve Tobin  🎥 *Actress*                                6125 Hollywood
**Born:** Nov. 29, 1901, in New York.
**Spotlights:** Lively in Warner's *Goodbye Again* (1933); the stubborn wife of Edward G. Robinson in *I Loved a Woman* (1933); played perky secretary Della Street in the thriller *The Case of the Lucky Legs* (1935); part of all-star cast — Humphrey Bogart, Leslie Howard, and Bette Davis, in *The Petrified Forest* (1936). Retired in 1941.

*Jane Withers*

**Sidney Lanfield**  🎥  *Director*                          6125 Hollywood

**Born:**   April 20, 1898, in Chicago, Ill.
**Spotlights:**   Joined a new film arena — sound. His early films spoke of confidence, *Cheer Up and Smile* (1930), and soothed audiences during the Depression. As America moved closer to the war, he entertained fans with the mystery thriller *The Hound of the Baskervilles* (1939). Died: 1972.

**Don Ameche**  📺  *See page 102.*                          6125 Hollywood

**George Meeker**  🎥  *Actor*                          6125 Hollywood

**Born:**   March 5, 1904, in Brooklyn, N.Y.
**Spotlights:**   Graduate of the American Academy of Dramatic Arts in 1921. Tall, slightly balding character performer often cast in villainous roles. Debut in 1928, *Four Sons*; *Back Street* (1932), with Irene Dunne; 11 more films. Died: 1963.

**Johnny Mack Brown**  🎥  *Actor*                          6125 Hollywood

**Born:**   Sept. 1, 1904, in Dothan, Ala.
**Spotlights:**   Athletic, square-jawed, dark-haired, former football hero who played opposite Greta Garbo twice in 1928: *The Divine Woman* and *A Woman of Affairs*. *Billy the Kid* (1930) established him in westerns, which he concentrated on afterward. Died: 1974.

**John Hodiak**  🎙  *Actor*                          6125 Hollywood

**Born:**   Apr. 16, 1914, in Pittsburgh, PA.
**Spotlights:**   Davie Lane on the serial drama "Bachelor's Children" (CBS, 1935); hillbilly star of "Li'l Abner" (ABC, 1939). Moved on to the big screen and the lights of Broadway. Died: 1955.

**William DeMille**  🎥  *Director, screenwriter*                          6125 Hollywood

**Born:**   July 25, 1878, in Washington, D.C.
**Spotlights:**   *The Ragamuffin* (1916) and *Miss Lulu Bett* (1921) were two of the many silent movies he directed in the shadow of his younger but more talented brother, Cecil B. DeMille. Died: 1955.

**Danny Kaye**  🎙  *See page 69.*                          6125 Hollywood

**Sonja Henie**  🎥  *Actress*                          6125 Hollywood

**Born:**   April 8, 1912, in Oslo, Norway.
**Spotlights:**   20th Century-Fox guided this pretty Olympic ice skating champion on the silver screen in lightweight musicals: *Happy Landing* (1938), with Don Ameche, Cesar Romero, and Ethel Merman; and *Second Fiddle* (1939), with Tyrone Power and Rudy Vallee. Died: 1969.

**Ed Sullivan**   *Host, columnist*　　　　　**6125 Hollywood**

**Born:** Edward Sullivan; Sept. 28, 1902, in New York.
**Spotlights:** Every Sunday night, millions of American families tuned in to hear, "It's a Really Big SHEW Tonight!" His variety program, "The Ed Sullivan Show" (1948–71), provided audiences with the best talent from the Bolshoi Ballet to the Beatles.
**Achievements:** 1955, Emmy, best variety show. Died: 1974.

**Marvin Miller**　 *Actor, narrator, writer*　　　　　**6125 Hollywood**

**Born:** Marvin Mueller; July 18, 1913, in St. Louis, Mo.
**Spotlights:** Children pushed ABC's button to watch him as Mr. Proteus on "Space Patrol" (1951–52). As Michael Anthony on "The Millionaire," he led adults to fantasize about money: "What would you do if you had a million dollars?" From 1955–60 he had the fortune to find out.
**Sidelights:** His voice was used for various characters on the Mr. Magoo cartoon show.

**Bill Boyd**　 *Actor, producer*　　　　　**6125 Hollywood**

**Born:** June 5, 1898, in Cambridge, Ohio.
**Spotlights:** In "Hopalong Cassidy" he was "feared, respected, and admired, for this

*Ed Sullivan with Henry Fonda*

175

great cowboy rides the trails of adventure and excitement." His ranch was called "The Bar 20." Always wore black. Horse's name? Topper. Boyd played Hopalong on films and TV, too. Died: 1972.

**Richard Thorpe**  *Director*                              6125 Hollywood

**Born:**  Rollo Thorpe; Feb. 24, 1896, in Hutchinson, Kan.

**Spotlights:**  Holds the directors' record at MGM for longevity. Joined in 1935 and stayed until 1968. Film credits include the Tarzan series, starting with *Tarzan Escapes!* (1936); swashbucklers, starring Robert Taylor, *Ivanhoe*, *Knights of the Round Table* (both 1953); *Jailhouse Rock*, starring Elvis Presley (1957).

**Benny Goodman**  *Musician, bandleader*                   6125 Hollywood

**Born:**  Benjamin Goodman; May 30, 1901, in Chicago, Ill.

**Spotlights:**  "The King of Swing" was an outstanding clarinetist. Goodman formed his own band in 1933. The hot, jazzy period of the 1930s and 1940s sizzled with his virtuoso playing and conducting. Extremely popular worldwide in concert, on radio, and film. Died: 1986.

# · 6100 HOLLYWOOD ·

### Stanley Kramer *Producer, director*          **6100 Hollywood**

**Born:** Sept. 29, 1913, in New York.

**Spotlights:** Produced *Cyrano de Bergerac* (1950), *Death of a Salesman* (1952), *High Noon* (1952), and *The Caine Mutiny* (1954). Directed and produced the critically acclaimed *The Defiant Ones* (1958), which raised racial issues between blacks and whites, and the looney *It's a Mad Mad Mad Mad World* (1963).

### Gregory Peck  *Actor*          **6100 Hollywood**

**Born:** Eldred G. Peck; April 5, 1916, in La Jolla, Calif.

**Spotlights:** Handsome, trustworthy, in-demand leading man: *The Keys of the Kingdom* (1944), *Duel in the Sun* (1946), *Twelve O'Clock High* (1949), *The Gunfighter* (1950), *The Big Country* (1958), *The Omen* (1976), more.

**Achievements:** 1962, Best Actor Oscar, *To Kill a Mockingbird*; 1967, Jean Hersholt Humanitarian Academy Award. Medal of Freedom Award.

*Gregory Peck*

**Thomas Mitchell**  *See page 263.* *See page 263.* 6100 Hollywood

**Allan Jones** *Singer, actor* 6100 Hollywood
**Born:** Oct. 14, 1907, in Scranton, Pa.
**Spotlights:** Romantic leading man in *Show Boat* (1936) and other 1930s and 1940s films, including a Marx Brothers comedy *A Day at the Races* (1937). Albums include *Allan Jones Sings Friml Favorites; This is the Decade of the 30s; World's Greatest Operettas.*
**Highlights:** His marriage to Irene Hervey produced a son, singer Jack Jones.

**Audrey Meadows** *Comedienne, actress* 6100 Hollywood
**Born:** Audrey Cotter; Feb. 8, 1924, in China.
**Spotlights:** Beautifully complemented *The Jackie Gleason Show* (1952–57) as the most understanding wife imaginable. Alice Kramden in "The Honeymooners" (1955–56).
**Achievements:** 1954–55, Emmy.

**Gregory Ratoff** *Actor, director* 6100 Hollywood
**Born:** April 20, 1897, in Russia.
**Spotlights:** Supporting role in *All About Eve* (1950), starring Bette Davis and George Sanders; another supporting player, Marilyn Monroe, later reflected that it was one of her first good parts. Directed *Intermezzo* (1939), which made Ingrid Bergman an international star. Died: 1960.

**Montgomery Clift** *Actor* 6100 Hollywood
**Born:** Edward M. Clift; Oct. 17, 1920, in Omaha, Nebr.
**Spotlights:** Dark-haired, young-looking, extremely handsome leading man whose intensity was apparent in his first role as an American soldier in *The Search*; this postwar drama (released in 1948) had audiences weeping and earned him an Academy nomination.
**Sidelights:** Permanently disfigured in an automobile accident in 1957. *The Misfits* (1960) with Marilyn Monroe and Clark Gable was one of his last films. Died: 1966, of a heart attack, although suicide was rumored.

**Lucille Ball** *Actress, comedienne, producer* 6100 Hollywood
**Born:** Aug. 6, 1911, in Jamestown, N.Y.
**Spotlights:** A Goldwyn chorus girl in her third film, *Roman Scandals* (1933). Finally, after 5 years of hard knocks, she was *Having a Wonderful Time* (1938), with Ginger Rogers and Red Skelton. In 1951 she starred with hubby Arnaz in the still popular "I Love Lucy" series and became the undisputed queen of TV. In 1954 Lucy and Desi were paid $250,000 to make *The Long, Long Trailer* (1954) for MGM, directed by Vincent Minnelli. Film audiences roared with delight at this zany comedy.
**Highlights:** Her marriage to Desi Arnaz (1940–60) resulted in two showbiz kids.

**Sidelights:** For the unimpeachable authority on this glamorous redhead, pick up a copy of *The "I Love Lucy" Book* by Bart Andrews, published by Doubleday/Dolphin in 1985.

## Loretta Young  *Actress* 6100 Hollywood

**Born:** Gretchen Belzer; Jan. 6, 1913, in Salt Lake City, Utah.

**Spotlights:** Grew up surrounded by actor hopefuls in the Los Angeles boarding house run singlehandedly by her mother. Loretta and her three sisters were sent to "cattle calls" (casting calls for extras in motion pictures) to help supplement the family income so they could afford a formal Catholic education (convent). In 1927 one of Loretta's sisters, Polly Ann, landed a role in *Naughty but Nice*. She wasn't able to take it, however, so director Mervyn Le Roy used pretty Loretta as her replacement. Other pictures include *Laugh Clown Laugh* opposite Lon Chaney (1928). Douglas Fairbanks, Jr., paired with her in *The Fast Life* (1929); it was the first in a series of pictures together. *The Hatchet Man* (1932), co-starring Edward G. Robinson, earned the glamorous brunette a $1,000-a-week salary. TV: Her own show was a dramatic anthology series, 1953–61; best remembered for her sweeping fashion-model appearances.

**Achievements:** 1947, Best Actress Oscar for *The Farmer's Daughter*.

*Lucille Ball*

179

**Will H. Hays**  *Business executive*   6100 Hollywood

**Born:** Nov. 5, 1879, in Sullivan, Ind.

**Spotlights:** Head of the Motion Pictures Producers and Distributors of America, Inc., founded in 1922 to keep film executives in line. To placate the American public amid recent Hollywood scandals, the "Hays Office" enacted strict regulations — the "Hays Code" — to uphold American morals. Its rulings covered sex, violence, language, religion, and racial issues and, because of relentless monitoring, the course of American filmmaking was irrevocably altered. The code was revised in 1966. Filmgoing audiences today can recognize a continuation of the Hays Office in the motion pictures ratings: G, PG, PG 13, R, X. Died: 1954.

**Sigmund Lubin** *Producer*   6100 Hollywood

**Born:** 1851 in Germany.

**Spotlights:** Was the early creator of filmed boxing events. His production, *The Battle of Gettysburg* (1912)simulating an 1897 prizefight made a bundle of money. Died: 1923.

**Anita Page** *Actress*   6100 Hollywood

**Born:** Anita Pomares; Aug. 4, 1910, in Flushing, N.Y.

**Spotlights:** Enjoyed a decade-long 'B' career including *Love 'Em and Leave 'Em* (1926), *Night Court* (1932), *Jungle Bride* (1933), and *Hitchhike to Heaven* (1936).

**Lynn Bari** *Actress*   6100 Hollywood

**Born:** Marjorie Fisher; Dec. 18, 1915, in Roanoke, Va.

**Spotlights:** A pretty, slender chorus girl whose on-screen appearance in low- budget flicks earned her 20th Century-Fox's title of "Queen of the B's" (although you wouldn't know it from her gigantic paychecks). Frequently cast as "the other woman." *The Return of the Cisco Kid* and *Charlie Chan in City of Darkness* (both 1939). TV: Gwen F. Allen on "Boss Lady" (1952).

**Dick Haymes** *Singer, actor*   6100 Hollywood

**Born:** Richard Haymes; Sept. 13, 1916, in Argentina.

**Spotlights:** Broke into showbiz while trying to sell some of his songs to bandleader Harry James. James said: "Your songs don't jell, but I'll buy your voice." Tall, blonde and handsome, the high baritone became the start of 20th Century-Fox's musical *Carnival in Costa Rica* (1947). By 1948 half of the population of American women swooned when they heard his smooth singing voice with its warm quality. That year he sold over 7 million records — more than Frank Sinatra, Perry Como or Bing Crosby — and earned $230,000 in royalties. Radio: Host of "Everything for the Boys" (servicemen, that is) in 1944. Star of the adventure show "I Fly Anything" (1950).

**Sidelights:** "In 1946 I lost 500 handkerchiefs a year to souvenir-grabbing fans." Died: 1980.

## Ralph Edwards   *Actor, producer*     6100 Hollywood

**Born:** June 13, 1913, in Merino, Colo.

**Spotlights:** Radio announcer from 1936–40. Created, produced and hosted "Truth or Consequences" (first broadcast in 1940) and "This is Your Life" (first broadcast in 1948). Both shows became popular TV series.

**Achievements:** Emmys; 1950, 1953, and 1954.

## Rock Hudson   *Actor*     6100 Hollywood

**Born:** Roy Scherer, Jr.; Nov. 17, 1925, in Winnetka, Ill.

**Spotlights:** Introduced in a World War II Warner's picture, *Fighter Squadron* (1948), starring Edmond O'Brien and Robert Stack. His acting skills had improved considerably by *Giant* (1956), with Elizabeth Taylor and James Dean. Huggable, beefcake hunk image with a soft heart opposite Doris Day endeared him to millions: *Pillow Talk* (1959), *Man's Favorite Sport?* (1963). Died: 1985.

## William N. Selig   *Studio head*     6100 Hollywood

**Born:** March 14, 1864, in Chicago, Ill.

**Spotlights:** Founder of Selig Polyscope Company whose first film was *The Tramp and the Dog* in 1896! His "garage room" operation blossomed for the next two decades with pictures such as *Dr. Jekyll and Mr. Hyde* (1908).

**Sidelights:** Los Angeles owes its thanks to Selig, whose studio was one of the first to move here in 1909. By the 1920s Hollywood was the Boom Town. Died: 1948.

## Raymond Griffith   *Actor, producer*     6124 Hollywood

**Born:** Jan. 23, 1890, in Boston, Mass.

**Spotlights:** Side-splitting, hilarious silent screen comedian, *Hands Up* (1926). Surprisingly powerful dramatic performance as the dying French soldier in *All Quiet on the Western Front* (1930). Later produced. Died: 1937.

## Edna Best   *Actress*     6124 Hollywood

**Born:** March 3, 1900, in England.

**Spotlights:** Fair-haired with a soft, charming accent, she appeared opposite Leslie Howard and Ingrid Bergman in *Intermezzo* (1939) and opposite Gene Tierney and Rex Harrison in *The Ghost and Mrs. Muir* (1947). Died: 1974.

## Yvonne De Carlo   *Actress*     6124 Hollywood

**Born:** Peggy Middleton; Sept. 1, 1922, in Canada.

**Spotlights:** Star of Universal's exotic harem girl movies, *Salome Where She Danced* (1945); *Song of Scheherazade* (1947). She belly-danced into the hearts of many male picturegoers. Cecil B. DeMille cast her in *The Ten Commandments* (1956); more. TV series: Starred as the vampire like Lily Munster in "The Munsters" from 1313 Mockingbird Lane (1964–66).

### Art Lund ⊙ *Singer, actor* 6126 Hollywood

**Born:** April 1, 1920, in Salt Lake City, Utah.

**Spotlights:** Character actor on-screen in 1968. Previously Broadway and London Stage entertainer: *Most Happy Fella.*

### Gracie Fields ▯ *Comedienne, actress, singer* 6126 Hollywood

**Born:** Gracie Stansfield; Jan. 9, 1898, in England.

**Spotlights:** Great Britain's pride and joy. They adored her irreverent sense of humor. Hollywood recruited her for films, but the vehicles were ill- structured for her. She preferred BBC radio and the London Palladium audiences. Died: 1979.

**Sidelights:** Born over a fish and chip shop in Rochdale, Lancashire.

### Jimmie Fidler ▯ *Gossip columnist* 6128 Hollywood

**Born:** Aug. 26, 1898, in St. Louis, Mo.

**Spotlights:** "Jimmie Fidler in Hollywood" was first broadcast in 1932. His breathless, rapid-fire style of delivery won him 9 million listeners weekly by 1934. Touted as the "reliable, authentic gossip," his reputation suffered greatly in 1941 when *The Hollywood Reporter* ran a front- page story with the headline: "Gossiper admits reviewing pictures he has not seen."

**Sidelights:** What did he do with his first professionally earned $50? "I bought a tin of caviar."

### Raymond Knight ▯ *Actor* 6128 Hollywood

**Spotlights:** Ambrose J. Weems actor and star of the comedy, "The Cuckoo Hour" (NBC, 1930). The shopkeeper in the drama *A House in the Country* (NBC, 1941).

### Evelyn Knight ⊙ *Singer* 6128 Hollywood

**Spotlights:** Featured as a regular vocalist on radio's "Club 15" with host-bandleader Bob Crosby (1947 on). Guest vocalist on radio's "Sing It Again," music and quiz show. (1948 on).

### Bill Leyden ▮ *Host* 6140 Hollywood

**Spotlights:** Moderator of "Musical Chairs" (1955). Emcee of the popular audience participation show "It Could Be You" (1956–61).

### Don Cornell ⊙ *Singer* 6140 Hollywood

**Born:** Louis Varlaro; April 21, 1919, in New York.

**Spotlights:** Sang with other vocalists on "The Chesterfield Supper Club" (radio) to the music of Glenn Miller. Other bands and noted celebrities such as Perry Como, also performed on this music show. Theme songs: "A Cigarette, Sweet Music, and You," and "Smoke Dreams." Had a high baritone voice.

### Mona Barrie  *Actress* 6140 Hollywood

**Born:** Mona Smith; Dec. 18, 1909, in England.
**Spotlights:** Refined, gentle performer in films for two decades (1933–1953). *Charlie Chan in London* (1934), *Never Give a Sucker an Even Break* (1941).

### Karl Dane  *Actor* 6140 Hollywood

**Born:** Karl Daen; Oct. 12, 1886, in Denmark.
**Spotlights:** Life was *The Big Parade* in 1925, for this up-and-coming actor. But it painfully fizzled out by *Whispering Shadows* (1933) because of his thick Danish accent. Died: 1934.

### Eileen Heckart  *Actress* 6140 Hollywood

**Born:** March 29, 1919, in Columbus, Ohio.
**Spotlights:** Outstanding performance in *The Bad Seed* (1956). Strong characterization in *Bus Stop* (1956), starring Marilyn Monroe.
**Achievements:** 1972, Best Supporting Actress Oscar for *Butterflies Are Free*.

### Nazimova *Actress* 6140 Hollywood

**Born:** Alla Nazimoffa; June 4, 1879, in Russia.
**Spotlights:** At least half of today's movie and TV stars practice "method" acting and attribute their success to its techniques. Nazimova was one of the only Walk of Famers who studied with the master who started the movement, Stanislavsky. *War Brides* (1916), *Camille* (1921), *Salome* (1923). Died: 1945.

### Don Haggerty *Actor, animal trainer* 6140 Hollywood

**Born:** Nov. 19, 1941, in Hollywood, Calif.
**Spotlights:** A natural at sharing the cameras with Ben the Bear on "The Life and Times of Grizzly Adams" (1977–78); starred in the movie version.

# · 6150 HOLLYWOOD ·

## Roy Del Ruth    *Director*          6150 Hollywood

**Born:** Oct. 18, 1895, in Philadelphia, Pa.

**Spotlights:** Directed the original *Maltese Falcon* (1931), which the New York Times claimed was "the best mystery thriller of the year," with Ricardo Cortez in the lead. (Humphrey Bogart starred in the 1941 remake directed by John Huston.) Also directed the delightful *Topper Returns* (1941). Died: 1961.

## Jerry Lewis    *See page 32.*          6150 Hollywood

## George Raft    *Actor*          6150 Hollywood

**Born:** George Rauft; Sept. 26, 1895, in New York.

**Spotlights:** Audiences liked him best as a criminal. In *Scarface* (1932), director Howard Hawks had steely-eyed, tough guy Raft flip a coin with such menacing style that he became a superstar overnight. Even now, that powerful image lingers in filmgoers' minds. *Bolero* (1934), with Carole Lombard; *Manpower* (1941) with Edward G. Robinson. TV: Lieutenant George Kirby in "I'm the Law" (1952–53). Died: 1980.

## Irene Rich    *See page 161.*          6150 Hollywood

## Art Mooney    *Big band leader*          6150 Hollywood

**Spotlights:** Albums: *This Is the Decade of the 30s, Decade of the 40s*. Big orchestra hit: "I'm looking Over a Four-Leaf Clover."

## Anna Q. Nilsson    *Actress*          6150 Hollywood

**Born:** March 30, 1890, in Sweden.

**Spotlights:** Debut screen appearance in *Molly Pitcher* (1911) was successful enough to keep her active in silent films through 1927. Rare supporting role in Paramount's *Sunset Boulevard* (1950), starring Gloria Swanson and William Holden. Died: 1974.

## Mary Boland    *Actress*          6150 Hollywood

**Born:** Jan. 28, 1880, in Philadelphia, Pa.

**Spotlights:** Paramount's Anglo-American comedy, *Ruggles of Red Gap* (1935) opposite Charles Laughton. Talent in dramatic roles on stage, yet delightful in a series of fluttery, dim-witted roles. Died: 1965.

## Jeanie MacPherson   *Screenwriter*   6150 Hollywood

**Born:** 1884, in Boston, Mass.

**Spotlights:** A lovely, brunette actress who turned to the pen for her creative outlet. For Cecil B. DeMille, she wrote the hits *The Affairs of Anatol* (1921), *Adam's Rib* (1923), *The Ten Commandments* (1923), *The King of Kings* (1927), more. Died: 1946.

## Herbert Rawlinson  *Actor*   6150 Hollywood

**Born:** Oct. 13, 1885, in England.

**Spotlights:** Started in 1911 accurately enough in *The Novice*. Made 50 silents, often as the tall, handsome lead; *Playthings of Destiny* (1921). Last movie was *Gene Autry and the Mounties* (1951). Died: 1953.

## Bud Collyer  *Actor, TV host*   6150 Hollywood

**Born:** June 18, 1908, in New York.

**Spotlights:** Cast as the man "more powerful than a speeding bullet" and, of course, the *Daily Planet*'s reporter, Clark Kent in "The Adventures of Superman" (first aired on Mutual in 1940). Also host and announcer of the quiz show, "Break the Bank" (Mutual, 1945); more.

## Ina Claire  *Actress*   6160 Hollywood

**Born:** Ina Fagan; Oct. 15, 1892, in Washington, D.C.

**Spotlights:** *The Greeks Had a Word for Them* (1932), opposite Joan Blondell; and MGM's *Ninotchka* (1939) directed by Ernst Lubitsch with Greta Garbo, Melvyn Douglas, and Bela Lugosi.

**Highlights:** Briefly married to actor John Gilbert (1929–31).

## Barry Sullivan  *Actor*   6160 Hollywood

**Born:** Patrick Barry; Aug. 29, 1912, in New York.

**Spotlights:** Versatile character talent *The Gangster* (1947), *Oh God* (1977). TV: Deputy Sheriff Pat Garrett on "The Tall Man" (1960–62).

## Yul Brynner  *Actor*   6160 Hollywood

**Born:** Youl Bryner; July 12, 1915, in Sakhalin, Russia.

**Spotlights:** Bald-headed, intense leading man. Usually played "heavy" characters, including his role in *The Magnificent Seven* (1960).

**Achievements:** 1956, Best Actor Oscar for *The King and I* (he was immortalized as the King of Siam).

**Sidelights:** Descent of half-gypsy blood. While a teenager worked as a trapeze artist with a French circus. Later, worked as a French radio commentator for the U.S. during World War II. Died: 1985, of cancer. During his last years he spoke out against cigarette smoking, which he believed caused his cancer.

## Gower Champion *Dancer, choreographer*    **6162 Hollywood**

**Born:**  June 21, 1921, in Geneva, Ill.

**Spotlights:**  Enjoyed great success as a husband and wife team with Marge Champion on Broadway and in films before TV's "Admiral Broadway Revue" (1949), a variety show starring Sid Caesar and Imogene Coca, and their own situation comedy "The Marge and Gower Champion Show" (1957).

**Highlights:**  Married to Marge Champion in 1947; divorced 1973. Died: 1980.

## Tommy Riggs and Betty Lou *Ventriloquist, comedy*    **6166 Hollywood**

**Born:**  Oct. 21, 1908, in Pittsburgh, Pa.

**Spotlights:**  Tommy Riggs was a ventriloquist and his alter ego was Betty Lou. "Tommy Riggs and Betty Lou" (NBC, 1938). Died: 1967.

## Rudolph Valentino *Actor*    **6166 Hollywood**

**Born:**  Rodolfo Guglielmi di Valentina d'Antonguolla; May 6, 1895, in Italy.

**Spotlights:**  The silent screen's greatest lover. Female filmgoers fainted at the erotic sight of his bejeweled bare chest in *The Young Rajah* (1922), sequel to the smash *The Sheik* (1921). Valentino unleashed a flood of sensuous fantasies that Victorian women had kept locked away. Women daydreamed about being master or slave to

*Rudolph Valentino*

the dark, handsome lover, who wore a prominently displayed slave bracelet. Most men disliked him. The beautiful Nita Naldi, famous Alberto Vargas model, co-starred in *Blood and Sand* (1922). Died: 1926.

**Sidelights:** His Arabian movies started a fashion and interior decorating Middle Eastern craze. Died: 1926, of complications from a bleeding ulcer. His death caused riots in the streets. Ironically, he was born poor, made $5 million (when a million was worth a million) during his brief stardom, yet died almost a quarter-of-a-million dollars in debt!

## Theodore Roberts 🎥 *Actor*      6166 Hollywood

**Born:** Oct. 2, 1861, in San Francisco, Calif.

**Spotlights:** A distinguished-looking man, he entered the adolescent film scene when he was in his fifties. Within two decades he had made over 60 pictures, including Moses in *The Ten Commandments* (1923). Died: 1928.

*Note to my readers: The block physically continues here in front of stuntman Jay Ohrberg's Show Car Museum, but the numbers break from 6166 to 6200. Please continue with Block 19. Thank you.*

# ⋆ 6200 HOLLYWOOD ⋆

## Jan Clayton 📺 *Actress*
**Born:** Aug. 26, 1917, in Tularosa, N.Mex.
**Spotlights:** Played the widowed mother Ellen Miller (1954–57) on "Lassie." Was a regular on "Pantomime Quiz" (1953–54; 1962–63). Mini-series "Scruples" (1980).

## Leonard Bernstein 💿 *Conductor, composer*
**Born:** Aug. 25, 1918, in Lawrence, Mass.
**Spotlights:** Musical genius. Educated at Harvard. Became the assistant conductor for the New York Philharmonic (1943–44); conductor of New York Symphony (1945–48). Nominated for an Academy Award for his music for *On the Waterfront* (1954), starring Marlon Brando.
**Achievements:** Tonys: 1953 and 1959. Emmys: 1956, 1957, 1960, 1961, 1965, 1972, 1976. Grammys: 1961 (9 awards), 1962, 1963, 1964, 1967, 1977!

## Gordon Hollingshead 🎥 *Actor, director*
**Born:** Jan. 8, 1892, in Garfield, N.J.
**Spotlights:** On-screen in 1914, silent screen actor, later director. Died: 1952.

## John Nesbitt 🎙 *See page 113.*

## Rochelle Hudson 🎥 *Actress*
**Born:** March 6, 1914, in Oklahoma City, Okla.
**Spotlights:** Dark-haired American beauty. *She Done Him Wrong* (1933); in *Les Miserables* (1935), she turned in a superb performance. In the film that made James Dean famous, *Rebel Without a Cause* (1955). Died: 1972.

## Herbert Marshall 🎥 *Actor*
**Born:** May 23, 1890, in England.
**Spotlights:** Paramount's *The Letter* (1929) sent his career soaring. He was handsome, elegant, sensitive, good in comedy or drama, and well liked by his female co-stars — Garbo, Dietrich, Davis, Colbert, and Hepburn. *A Bill of Divorcement* (1940).
**Sidelights:** Lost his right leg in World War I service but trained himself to walk well, with only the slightest stiffness. Always wore long pants. Died: 1966, from a heart attack.

## Jack Paar 📺 *TV host, comic*
**Born:** May 1, 1918, in Canton, Ohio.

**Spotlights:** He worked both daytime (including quiz shows) and nighttime programs, before his best-remembered work as the temperamental TV personality on "The Tonight Show" (1957–62). Johnny Carson succeeded him in 1962.

### Jean Negulesco 🎥 *Director* 6200 Hollywood
**Born:** Feb. 29, 1900, in Rumania.
**Spotlights:** Parisian painter-turned-director: *The Mask of Dimitrios* (1944), starring Peter Lorre and Sidney Greenstreet; *Road House* (1948), starring Ida Lupino.

### Gigi Perreau 📺 *Actress* 6200 Hollywood
**Born:** Ghislaine Perreau-Saussine; Feb. 6, 1941, in Los Angeles, Calif.
**Spotlights:** Played teenager Pat Strickland on "The Betty Hutton Show" (1959–60); Katharine Ann Richards on "Follow the Sun" (1961–62).
**Sidelights:** Parents fled Nazi-occupied France.

### Jean Renoir 🎥 *Actor, director, screenwriter* 6200 Hollywood
**Born:** Sept. 15, 1894, in Paris.
**Spotlights:** Acutely perceptive of the beauty of nature and the flowing movement of his pictures; *Grand Illusion* (1937) and *The Rules of the Game* (1939) reached the highest level of that art.
**Achievements:** 1975, honorary Oscar.
**Highlights:** First wife Catherine Hessling, was his father's model and star of his first production, *Life Without Joy Catherine* (1924).
**Sidelights:** *Mais oui*, he is the son of the French Impressionist painter, Pierre Auguste Renoir (1841–1919). Died: 1979.

### Dorothy Lamour 🎤 *See page 275.* 6200 Hollywood

### William Seiter 🎥 *Director* 6240 Hollywood
**Born:** June 10, 1892, in New York.
**Spotlights:** Worked on countless silents and talkies, including the following for Warner Brothers: *Delightful Daddies* (1942), about six confirmed bachelors caring for orphans; *The Truth About Youth* (1930), with Myrna Loy making some decisions about marriage; *Going Wild* (1931), starring zany Joe E. Brown; and *Big Business Girl* (1931), starring Loretta Young, Ricardo Cortez, and Jack Albertson. Died: 1964.

### John Carradine 🎥 *Actor* 6240 Hollywood
**Born:** Richmond Carradine; Feb. 5, 1906, in Greenwich Village, N.Y.
**Spotlights:** His resonant voice and eastern/western face helped him earn over 100 film credits playing a variety of characters. Best under the direction of John Ford in *Stagecoach* (1939) and *The Grapes of Wrath* (1940).

**Robert Mitchum**  *Actor*                    6240 Hollywood

**Born:**  Aug. 6, 1917, in Bridgeport, Conn.

**Spotlights:**  Tough, strong, man of action in *The Story of G.I. Joe* (1945), *River of No Return* (1954), *The Hunters* (1958), *The Big Sleep* (1978); more.

**Cecil B. DeMille**   *See page 117.*          6240 Hollywood

**Pat O'Brien**   *See page 240.*              6240 Hollywood

**Nunnally Johnson**  *Screenwriter, producer*  6240 Hollywood

**Born:**  Dec. 5, 1897, in Columbus, Ga.

**Spotlights:**  Many years associated with 20th Century-Fox: *The House of Rothschild* (1934), *The Grapes of Wrath* (1940), *How to Marry a Millionaire* (1953). *The Dirty Dozen* (MGM, 1967). Turned to directing in the 1950s: *The Three Faces of Eve* (1957), starring Joanne Woodward. Died: 1977.

# ⋆ 6250 HOLLYWOOD ⋆

**Lena Horne**  *See page 199.*  6250 Hollywood

**Ona Munson** 🎥 *Actress*  6250 Hollywood
**Born:** June 16, 1906, in Portland, Ore.
**Spotlights:** Made 7 films before landing the role of Belle in David O. Selznick's *Gone with the Wind* (1939). Co-starred with John Wayne in *Lady from Louisiana* (1941). Died: 1955.

**Arlene Harris** 📻 *Actress*  6250 Hollywood
**Born:** 1899, in Toronto, Canada.
**Spotlights:** Delightful comedienne, "The Human Chatterbox," on "Al Pearce and His Gang" (first aired on NBC, 1933); Mummy/Mrs. Higgins on Fanny Brice's "The Baby Snooks Show" (NBC, 1939); "The puny Plaza Hotel's switchboard operator" on "Here Comes Elmer" (1944). Died: 1976.

**Constance Bennett** 🎥 *Actress*  6250 Hollywood
**Born:** Oct. 22, 1904, in New York.
**Spotlights:** A witty, lovely blond with a husky voice who enhanced sophisticated comedies: *Topper* (1937), with Cary Grant. Previously she was in silents: *Reckless Youth* (1922).
**Sidelights:** Older sister of Joan Bennett. Died: 1965.

**Bob Crosby** 📺 *See page 101.*  6252 Hollywood

**Barry Fitzgerald** 🎥 *Actor*  6252 Hollywood
**Born:** William Shields; March 10, 1888, in Ireland.
**Spotlights:** Character Irish actor with bright, blue eyes. Versatile, he played rogues to near-saints to villains *Bringing Up Baby* (1938); *How Green Was My Valley* (1941). TV: "General Electric Theater" hosted by Ronald Reagan (1954–62).
**Achievements:** 1944, Best Supporting Actor Oscar as priest in *Going My Way*. Ironically, in real Irish life, he was a Protestant! Died: 1961, from complications stemming from brain surgery.

**Everett Sloane** 📺 *Actor*  6252 Hollywood
**Born:** Oct. 1, 1909, in New York.
**Spotlights:** Planned a financial career on Wall Street until the crash of 1929 discouraged him. Evidently the gambling persona remained, and he pursued an acting career. His first film, with Orson Welles, was *Citizen Kane* (1941). He usually played

tough-type characters, which was unusual because he was small, almost bald, and wore round, wire- rimmed glasses. TV dramatic work included "The Loretta Young Show" (1953–61). Died: 1965, of suicide by sleeping pills.

## Everett Mitchell  Host
6254 Hollywood

**Spotlights:**  Red, white, and blue flag waver on "The National Farm and Home Hour," variety program, with Don Ameche as a forest ranger (NBC, 1928); made with the approval of the U.S. Department of Agriculture. Emcee on other radio programs.

## Sammy Davis, Jr.  Singer, dancer, actor
6254 Hollywood

**Born:**  Dec. 8, 1925, in New York.
**Spotlights:**  His first year on earth was the only year he did not perform. As soon as he could walk, he was put on stage with his father and uncle, Will Mastin. Davis is an energetic entertainer on Broadway, films, and TV. Albums: *Hey There (It's Sammy Davis, Jr., at His Dynamite Greatest)*. Singles: "Candy Man," "People Tree."
**Sidelights:**  Lost his left eye in an automobile accident in 1954.

## Desi Arnaz  Actor, singer, musician, bandleader
6254 Hollywood

**Born:**  Desiderio Alberto Arnaz y de Acha III; Mar. 2, 1917, in Cuba.
**Highlights:**  Moved to America at age 16. Playing the rumba and conga sounds to delighted audiences, Arnaz cha-cha-cha'd his way onto the silver screen and into co-star (and future wife) Lucille Ball's heart. Film debut in RKO's *Too Many Girls* (1940) wasn't their most memorable film together, but it united a couple who would create TV's all-time most popular series, "I Love Lucy" (1951). Arnaz also pioneered TV's three-camera technique. Desilu Productions "babalued" all the way to the bank. Died: 1986, from cancer.

## Imogene Coca  Comedienne
6256 Hollywood

**Born:**  Nov. 18, 1908, in Philadelphia, Pa.
**Spotlights:**  Saturday night live comedy series "Your Show of Shows" (1949–54), where she co-starred with Sid Caesar. "The Imogene Coca Show" (1954–55) struggled with format and folded.
**Achievements:**  1951, Best Actress Emmy.

## Henry Wilcoxon  Actor
6256 Hollywood

**Born:**  Sept. 8, 1905, in the West Indies.
**Spotlights:**  Dark-haired British stage and screen star. American debut as Marc Antony in Cecil B. DeMille's *Cleopatra* (1934). Last film credit, *F.I.S.T.* (1978), starring Sylvester Stallone. Died: 1984.

## Fulton Lewis  Commentator, columnist
6258 Hollywood

**Born:**  F. Lewis, Jr.; in 1903, in Washington, D.C.

**Spotlights:** Began career as a newspaper reporter. His outspokeness against liberal causes won him radio work in 1926. For over 30 years he was known for his conservative philosophies and his closing statement: "...and that's the top of the news as it looks from here."
**Sidelights:** Instrumental in securing a radio gallery in the U.S. Senate and House. Died: 1966.

**Andy Devine**     *See page 282.*                          **6258 Hollywood**

**Helen Hayes**   *Actress*                                                    **6258 Hollywood**
**Born:** Helen H. Brown; Oct. 10, 1900, in Washington, D.C.
**Spotlights:** "The Helen Hayes Theater" dramatic presentations (NBC radio, 1935).
**Achievements:** 1931, Best Actress Academy Award *The Sin of Madelon Claudet*; 1970, Best Supporting Actress Academy Award, *Airport*. Acknowledged as the "First Lady of the American Theater."

**Ozzie and Harriet Nelson**   *Actor, bandleader,*      **6260 Hollywood**
*producer, director*

*Desi Arnaz*

**Born:**   Oswald Nelson; March 20, 1906, in Jersey City, N.J; Harriet Hilliard; July 18, 1914, in Des Moines, Iowa.
**Spotlights:**   "America's favorite young couple." Ideal domestic life. Originally titled "The Ozzie Nelson, Harriet Hilliard Show" radio broadcast in 1944; later changed to "The Adventures of Ozzie and Harriet." In earlier years Ozzie was a bandleader-vocalist and Harriet a vocalist with his band. She was one hot number, too! Performed on numerous shows, "Believe It or Not." (1930). Died: (Ozzie) 1975.

### Donald Woods,  *Actor* 6260 Hollywood
**Born:**   Ralph L. Zink; in New York.
**Spotlights:**   Alternated with then-emcee Ronald Reagan in "The Orchid Award" (1953–54), a musical variety program. "Tammy" (1965–66) was employed as a secretary to Woods' John Brent, her sophisticated but good-humored boss.

### Ruth Roland   *Actress* 6260 Hollywood
**Born:**   Aug. 26, 1892, in San Francisco, Calif.
**Spotlights:**   Hard-working, busy leading lady in 12 western serials (1915–23); *The Neglected Wife* (1917). Died: 1937.

### Thelma Todd   *Actress* 6262 Hollywood
**Born:**   July 29, 1905, in Lawrence, Mass.
**Spotlights:**   Peaches-and-cream blonde with penciled eyebrows and a contagious smile. *Horse Feathers* (1932) with the Marx Brothers; *The Devil's Brother* (1933) with Laurel and Hardy. Died: 1935.

### Ralph Edwards   *See page 181.* 6262 Hollywood

### Marian Anderson   *Opera singer* 6262 Hollywood
**Born:**   Feb. 17, 1902, in Philadelphia, Pa.
**Spotlights:**   Contralto. International concert celebrity. First black singer at Metropolitan Opera, in *Il Trovatore* in 1955. Albums: *Snoopycat, Spirituals*.
**Achievements:**   1963, Presidential Medal of Freedom.

### Una Merkel   *Actress* 6262 Hollywood
**Born:**   Dec. 10, 1903, in Covington, Ky.
**Spotlights:**   Smart-aleck supporting actress with red-gold hair whose career of approximately 125 films spanned more than 4 decades, with the 1930s being the busiest: *The Merry Widow* (1934), *Some Like It Hot* (1930), *Destry Rides Again* (1939).

### Carmen Miranda   *Singer, dancer, actress* 6262 Hollywood
**Born:**   Maria de Carmo de Cunha; Feb. 9, 1909, in Portugal.
**Spotlights:**   Fox allowed Miranda to be her energetic self in *Down Argentine Way*

(1940) — her U.S. debut. Americans liked her colorful costumes and wild foot-high headdresses. Performed a spicy rendition of "Chica, Chica, Boom, Chic" in *That Night in Rio* (1940), with Don Ameche. By 1943 audiences expected the craziest entertainment from "The Lady in the Tutti-Fruiti Hat." In *The Gang's All Here* 30 feet of bananas topped her head!

**Sidelights:** Her father was in the fruit business. Died: 1955, from a heart attack following an energetic performance.

## Peggy Knudsen    *Actress*                                      6262 Hollywood

**Born:** April 27, 1923, in Duluth, Minn.

**Spotlights:** Very pretty blond. She played April Adam in "So This is Hollywood" (1955), a situation comedy about two female hopefuls trying to break in. Previously in Warner Brothers films. Died: 1980.

## Ogden Nash    *Panelist*                                        6262 Hollywood

**Born:** Frederich O. Nash; Aug. 19, 1902.

**Spotlights:** Attended Harvard University. Cleverly queried disguised celebrity contestants on the madly successful quiz-audience participation program "Masquerade Party" (1953–57).

**Sidelights:** Author, poet; radio host on "Author, Author" (1939); regular on "Guy Lombardo Time" (1939–50). Composer of Broadway stage scores. Died: 1971.

## Charles Ruggles    *Actor*                                      6262 Hollywood

**Born:** Feb. 8, 1886, in Los Angeles, Calif.

**Spotlights:** Dapper leading and supporting character in 100 films (1915–66); *Charley's Aunt* (1930); *Ruggles of Red Gap* (1935). Small, meek, and mustached, hilarious opposite larger, domineering Mary Boland in *Early to Bed* (1936). Radio: "The Charlie Ruggles Show," comedy-variety (1944). TV: The off- screen voice of Aesop on "The Bullwinkle Show," cartoon (1961–62); more. Died: 1970, of cancer.

## Dave Garroway    *Radio and TV personality*                     6262 Hollywood

**Born:** July 13, 1913, in Schenectady, N.Y.

**Spotlights:** Host of "The Dave Garroway Show," variety (NBC radio, first broadcast in 1947). TV: "Garroway at Large," variety show (NBC, 1948–51); 1951 pioneer star of "The Today Show."

**Sidelights:** Closed each TV show with one quiet, word, "Peace." Died: 1982.

## Peggie Castle    *Actress, singer*                              6262 Hollywood

**Born:** Dec. 22, 1927, in Appalachia, Va.

**Spotlights:** Made several western films before becoming the Birdcage saloonkeeper, Lily Merril, on "The Lawman" (1959–62). Died: 1973.

## Charles Coburn    *Actor*                                       6262 Hollywood

**Born:** June 19, 1877, in Savannah, Ga.

**Spotlights:** He was nearly 60 years old when he entered films. Aristocratic, cigar-smoking, monocled, thick-lipped American character, who delighted audiences with his old-school gentleman manners. *Of Human Hearts* (1938). Versatile performance in *King's Row* (1941). Made over 63 pictures.
**Achievements:** 1944, Best Supporting Actor for *The More the Merrier*. Died: 1961, of a heart attack.

## Pat Boone  ⚊  *See page 258.*                    6262 Hollywood

## Mitzi Gaynor  🎥  *Actress*                    6262 Hollywood
**Born:** Francesca M. Gerber; Sept. 4, 1930, in Chicago, Ill.
**Spotlights:** Co-starred with the most popular leading men: Bing Crosby in *Anything Goes* (1946), Frank Sinatra in *The Joker Is Wild* (1957), Gene Kelly in *Les Girls* (1957). Musical fans adored her in *South Pacific* (1958).

## Mel Ferrer  🎥  *Actor, director, producer*                    6262 Hollywood
**Born:** Aug. 25, 1917, in Elberton, N.J.
**Spotlights:** Acted opposite Leslie Caron in MGM's *Lili* (1953). Directed Audrey Hepburn in *Wait Until Dark* (1967).

## Jo Stafford  ⚊  *See page 257.*                    6270 Hollywood

## Constance Moore  🎥  *Actress, singer*                    6270 Hollywood
**Born:** Jan. 18, 1909, in Sioux City, Iowa.
**Spotlights:** 5' 4", 110-lb., Columbia Broadcasting staff singer. Signed next with Universal Studios, then Paramount Pictures. Three decades of films include: *You Can't Cheat an Honest Man* and *Charlie Chan — Detective* (both 1939).

## Warren Hull  🎙  *Actor, singer*                    6270 Hollywood
**Born:** Jan. 17, 1903, in Gasport, N.Y.
**Spotlights:** Host of radio's popular quiz-audience participation show, "Strike It Rich" (first broadcast in 1947). Extremely needy people were the only contestants allowed on the show. These long-suffering destitutes told their woeful stories on the air, and then were asked simple questions. One would be chosen "the winner" and would be helped with medical expenses or whatever else he or she was in dire need of. "The losers" still had a chance at help, when Hull asked the listening audience to chip in "some charity." This was the basis for the equally successful TV series (1951–55). Died: 1974.

## Ernest Schoedsach  🎥  *Director*                    6270 Hollywood
**Born:** June 8, 1893, in Council Bluffs, Iowa.
**Spotlights:** Directed, with Merian C. Cooper, the biggest monster of them all, *King*

*Kong* (1933), a classic. *Dr. Cyclops* (1940) thrilled audiences with its South American setting and mad scientist.

## Grace Moore 🎥 *Opera singer, actress*                    6274 Hollywood
**Born:** Dec. 5, 1901, in Slabtown, Tenn.
**Spotlights:** Soprano singing sensation; Metropolitan Opera debut in 1928. Seven films to her credit, including *New Moon* (1931) and *One Night of Love* (1934). Died: 1947, in a plane crash.

## Stu Erwin 📺 *Actor*                    6274 Hollywood
**Born:** Feb. 14, 1902, in Squaw Valley, Calif.
**Spotlights:** Bumbling, innocent lead in the situation comedy "The Stu Erwin Show"; "The Trouble with Father" (1950–55). Died: 1967.

## Merle Oberon 🎥 *Actress*                    6274 Hollywood
**Born:** Estelle M. Thompson; Feb. 19, 1911, in Tasmania.
**Spotlights:** Her career existed because she had great beauty — a brown-eyed brunette with an oval face — great men behind her (husband Alexander Korda, Samuel Goldwyn), and a great style. Remembered for *Wuthering Heights* co-starring Laurence Olivier.
**Highlights:** Married Alexander Korda (1939–45), first of four husbands. Died: 1979.

## Arthur Treacher 🎥 *Actor*                    6274 Hollywood
**Born:** Arthur Veary; July 23, 1894, in England.
**Spotlights:** His English accent and well-bred manners had David Niven saying, *Thank you, Jeeves* (1936). He was "supercalifragilisticexpealedocious" in *Mary Poppins* (1964). Died: 1975.

## Lou Costello 📺 *See page 294.*                    6278 Hollywood

## Richard Basehart 🎥 *Actor*                    6278 Hollywood
**Born:** Aug. 31, 1915, in Zanesville, Ohio.
**Spotlights:** Followed in his father's journalistic footsteps before he opted for the bright lights of Broadway at 24. Launched his film career when he won the 1945 New York Drama Critics Award. Hollywood welcomed his *Repeat Performance* (1947) and later *He Walked by Night* (1948) before portraying Ishmael in *Moby Dick* (1956); *La Strada* (1954). Died: 1984.

## Jack Webb 📺 *Actor, director, producer*                    6278 Hollywood
**Born:** April 2, 1920, in Santa Monica, Calif.
**Spotlights:** Radio: He was tough stuff, private eye, "Pat Novak for Hire" (1949). TV: "My name's Friday, I'm a cop," Sergeant Joe Friday on "Dragnet" (1952–59; 1967–70). "Just the facts, ma'am."

**Sidelights:** What was Friday's badge number? 714. Died: 1982.

## Doris Day 🎵  *Actress, singer*                                    6278 Hollywood

**Born:** Doris Von Kappelhoff; April 3, 1924, in Cincinnati, Ohio.
**Spotlights:** Blonde, sparkling eyes, toothpaste smile, girl next door. Accumulated experience as a dancer and band singer on the road and radio. Debut in Warner's *Romance on the High Seas*, "It's Magic," (1948). Fine dramatic performance in Hitchcock's *The Man Who Knew Too Much*, "Que Sera Sera," (1956). Truly wonderful in Warner's production of the fun musical *The Pajama Game* (1957). Teamed with Rock Hudson in *Pillow Talk* (1959).

## Jean Muir 🎥  *Actress*                                           6280 Hollywood

**Born:** J. M. Fullerton; Feb. 13, 1911, in New York.
**Spotlights:** Sought-after, pretty performer during the 1930s. Wonderful in Warner's *A Midsummer Night's Dream* (1935), with James Cagney, but not selective enough with later works.

## Mary Pickford 🎥  *Actress, executive*                            6280 Hollywood

**Born:** Gladys Smith; April 8, 1892, in Canada.
**Spotlights:** On stage at age 5, as Baby Gladys Smith, this impoverished child developed a shrewdness that made her one of the keenest financial minds the industry has ever confronted. An example of this trait in early childhood was seen when she approached Biograph Studios in 1909. Director D. W. Griffith thought she was "too little and too fat," but had her work on film that day, anyway. When he asked

*Doris Day*                          *Mary Pickford*

her to return the next day for $5, she insisted on $10, and got it! In the pioneer film days, actors did not receive credit. In *The Little Teacher* (1910) the subtitle, "Little Mary," finally identified her; "The Girl with the Curls" became a household name. "America's Sweetheart," who enchanted viewers with her innocence and purity and smiled through the darkest hour to come out a winner, was the first truly recognizable famous person. She used her popularity to drive her salary up past $500,000 a year, plus percentage, plus extensive creative control. Then, when she found out Charlie Chaplin was paid more, she insisted on another raise to top him and got it!

**Achievements:**  In 1919 she formed United Artists with Charlie Chaplin, D. W. Griffith, and Douglas Fairbanks. Their first film, *Pollyanna* (1920), was a commercial success. It starred the 27-year old Pickford who apparently convinced audiences that she was a 12-year-old. Ticket buyers worldwide liked her in little girl roles, and when talkies arrived, her two attempts to do adult roles failed. She retired a very wealthy lady (worth over $50 million).

**Achievements:**  1929, Best Actress Academy Award, *Coquette*. 1975, special Oscar.

**Highlights:**  Married to Douglas Fairbanks (1920–36) and Charles "Buddy" Rogers (1937 on). Died: 1979.

## Marge Champion  📺  *Dancer, actress*                     6280 Hollywood

**Born:**  Marge Belcher; Sept. 2, 1923, in Hollywood, Calif.

**Spotlights:**  Charming dancing star, along with her partner-husband, Gower Champion, in 1950s musicals, including *Everything I Have is Yours* (1952). Off- screen voice of the Blue Fairy in Disney's *Pinocchio* (1940). Also a capable actress.

**Achievements:**  1975, Emmy, choreographer of "Queen of the Stardust Ballroom." Walt Disney chose her for the "fairest of them all" model of *Snow White and the Seven Dwarfs* (1937).

**Highlights:**  Married to Gower Champion (1947–73).

## Ben Bernie  🎻  *Composer, violinist, orchestra conductor*       6280 Hollywood

**Born:**  May 30, 1891, in New York.

**Spotlights:**  On the air for 20 years. "The Ben Bernie Show" (1936) provided CBS listeners with relaxing music and light comedy. Songs: "Who's Your Little Whoosis?" and "Sweet Georgia Brown." Died: 1943.

## Lena Horne  🎥  *Singer, actress*                           6280 Hollywood

**Born:**  June 30, 1917, in Brooklyn, N.Y.

**Spotlights:**  Beautiful, elegant performer. Started off in the floor show at Harlem's Cotton Club when she was a teenager. Went on to perform at trendy nightclubs: Cafe Society, Little Troc, and others. Appeared on film in *The Duke is Tops* (1938). Other pictures include *Stormy Weather* and *Swing Fever* (both 1943); more. Broadway shows include *Blackbirds, Jamaica, Lena Horne — the Lady and Her Music*, others.

**Achievements:**  1980, special Tony; 1981, Grammy, pop vocalist.

**Frank Fay**  *Supporting actor, comedian*  6280 Hollywood

**Born:** Nov. 17, 1894, in Ireland.

**Spotlights:** Wonderful in a supporting role in David O. Selznick's comedy *Nothing Sacred* (1937), starring Carole Lombard and Fredric March. Radio: "The Frank Fay Show" was an effort on Fay's part to be star comedian, emcee, writer, director, etc. It lasted about 3½ months. Died: 1961.

**Janet Gaynor** *Actress*  6280 Hollywood

**Born:** Laura Gainer on Oct. 6, 1906, in Philadelphia, Pa.

**Spotlights:** Sweet and optimistic in the face of the Depression: *Lucky Star* and *Sunny Side Up* (both 1929); *Happy Days* (1930). Commanding performance in David O. Selznick's original *A Star is Born* (1937).

**Achievements:** Won the first ever Academy Award presented to Best Actress: 1927–28 *Seventh Heaven, Street Angel*, and *Sunrise*. At that time, the Academy presented one award for an entertainer's performances in several films.

**Paderewski** *Composer, musician*  6280 Hollywood

**Born:** Ignacy Jan Paderewski; Nov. 6, 1860, in Poland.

**Spotlights:** Eminent concert pianist and composer.

**Achievements:** Polish prime minister (1919). Died: 1941.

**Monte Blue** *Actor*  6280 Hollywood

**Born:** Jan. 11, 1890, in Indianapolis, Ind.

**Spotlights:** Onscreen from 1915 — *The Birth of a Nation* — to 1954, in *Apache*. (He was part Indian.) Made 200 films as star and character actor. Died: 1963.

**Katharine Hepburn** *Actress*  6280 Hollywood

**Born:** Nov. 9, 1907, in Hartford, Conn.

**Spotlights:** Fiercely independent, private, intelligent heroine. Brilliant debut in *A Bill of Divorcement* (1932), with John Barrymore. Exalted performances in *Little Women* (1933), *Bringing Up Baby* (1938), *The Philadelphia Story* (1940), and *Adam's Rib* (1949).

**Achievements:** Record-breaking Best Actress Academy Awards for *Morning Glory* (1933), *Guess Who's Coming to Dinner* (1967), *The Lion in Winter* (1969); *On Golden Pond* (1981).

**Highlights:** Met her love match on the set of *Woman of the Year* (1942). "I'm afraid I'm a little tall for you, Mr. Tracy," Hepburn remarked. Spencer Tracy responded, "Don't worry, Miss Hepburn, I'll soon cut you down to my size." Their romance endured for 25 years.

**Jim Davis** *Actor*  6280 Hollywood

**Born:** Aug. 26, 1915, in Edgerton, Mo.

**Spotlights:** Appeared in a couple of short-lived series before striking oil on "Dallas" as John Ross "Jock" Ewing (1978–81). Died: 1981.

## Clifton Fadiman  *Literary critic*

**Born:** May 15, 1904.
**Spotlights:** Host of the quiz show "Information Please" (NBC, 1938–52). "Stump the Experts!" contestants won a set of *Encyclopaedia Britannica*.

## Jonathan Winters ◼ *Actor*

**Born:** Nov. 11, 1925, in Dayton, Ohio.
**Spotlights:** Had been a comedian host on several shows before "The Jonathan Winters Show" (1967–69). The round-faced, quick-witted comedian amused audiences on "The Wacky World of Jonathan Winters" (1972–74), before becoming Mearth (1981–82), the 225-lb. baby of "Mork and Mindy." Films include: *It's a Mad Mad Mad Mad World* (1963).

## Warner Baxter 🎥 *Actor*

**Born:** Mar. 29, 1889, in Columbus, Ohio.
**Spotlights:** Handsome, gentlemanly, extremely popular talent of 100 films including *The Cisco Kid* (1931), *The Prisoner of Shark Island* (1936).
**Achievements:** 1928–29, Best Actor Academy Award, *In Old Arizona* (Fox's first outdoor all-talkie).

*Katharine Hepburn*

**Sidelights:** Father died when he was 6 months old, and when his mother moved to San Francisco, they lost all of their possessions in the great earthquake of 1906. Died: 1951.

**Tom Breneman**  *Emcee*                    6280 Hollywood

**Spotlights:** Emcee on "Breakfast in Hollywood" (NBC, 1942; ABC, 1948).

**Jessica Tandy**  *Actress*                    6280 Hollywood

**Born:** June 7, 1909, in England.
**Spotlights:** Veteran stage artist who has graced the American screen fewer than a dozen times; *The Birds* (1963).

**Spike Jones**  *See page 233.*                    6280 Hollywood

**Marguerite Chapman**  *Actress*                    6280 Hollywood

**Born:** March 9, 1920, in Chatham, N.Y.
**Spotlights:** On-screen from 1940 to 1960, including *The Seven Year Itch* (1955). TV: Dramatic anthology playhouse works.

# · 1680 VINE ·

### Gladys Swarthout  *Opera Singer*      1680 Hollywoood

**Born:** Dec. 25, 1904, in Deepwater, MO.

**Spotlights:** American contralto. Metropolitan Opera debut in *La Gioconda* in 1929. Beautiful leading lady in four Paramount musicals including *Champagne Waltz* (1937). Retired to Florence, Italy, in 1954. Died: 1969.

### Donald O'Connor  *Actor*      1680 Hollywood

**Born:** Aug. 28, 1925, in Chicago, Ill.

**Spotlights:** Happy-go-lucky dancer, singer, comedian. On-screen in *Melody for Two* (1937); *Singin' in the Rain* (1952). The *Francis* talking mule series ran from 1950–55; *Francis in the Haunted House*, 1956, starred Mickey Rooney.

**Achievements:** 1953, Emmy "The Donald O'Connor Show."

*Neil A. Armstrong, Michael Collins and Edwin E. Aldrin, Jr.*

## Neil A. Armstrong, Edwin E. Aldrin, Jr., Michael Collins

*Astronauts*  **Southeast Corner of Hollywood and Vine**

**Born:**  Armstrong, Aug. 5, 1930; Aldrin, Jr. (Buzz), Jan. 20, 1930; Collins, Oct. 31, 1930.

**Spotlights:**  Armstrong, Aldrin and Collins participated equally on that historic Apollo XI mission to the moon (July 20, 1969). When Armstrong became the first man to walk on the moon, hundreds of millions of TV viewers watched. This was the single most important live TV broadcast ever: "One small step for man, one giant leap for mankind." So many people watched this event, that the streets throughout the entire country were silent and empty. The astronauts were honored with TV stars on the four corners of Hollywood and Vine to represent their reach to the four corners of the earth.

**Sidelights:**  This was the second longest continuous live TV coverage in history (31 hours).

## Julius La Rosa  *Singer*  **Southeast corner of Hollywood and Vine**

**Born:**  Jan. 2, 1930, in New York.

**Spotlights:**  Appeared in the musical variety "Arthur Godfrey and His Friends" (1952–53) and "The Julius La Rosa Show" (1956–57).

## Maria Callas  *Opera singer*  **Southeast corner of Hollywood and Vine**

**Born:**  Cecilia Maria Calogeropoulous; Dec. 3, 1923, in New York.

**Spotlights:**  Temperamental prima donna. Metropolitan Opera debut in 1957. Soprano whose range, technique and acting talent spanned a wide range of emotions: remembered for her brilliant dramatic voice.

**Highlights:**  Close friend of Greek tycoon, Aristotle Onassis. Died: 1977.

## Gale Storm  *See page 172.*  **1680 Vine**

## Vladimir Horowitz  *Virtuoso pianist*  **1680 Vine**

**Born:**  Oct. 1, 1904, in Russia

**Spotlights:**  Began playing piano at age 6 in the Ukraine. Attended the Kiev Conservatory of Music at age 12. Within 5 years he was performing, and his successful concert debut in 1922 enabled him to obtain a visa. He never returned to Russia from his 6-month study in Germany. His first concert in America in 1928 was a great event. It was the beginning of a long list of top classical recordings, sold-out concerts, White House invitations, and enrichment of radio programming.

**Achievements:**  Collected an impressive 18 Grammy awards.

**Sidelights:**  Became a U.S. citizen in 1944. Returned to his homeland for well-received concerts in Moscow and Leningrad in 1987.

## Joe E. Brown  *Actor*  **1680 Vine**

**Born:**  July 28, 1892, in Holgate, Ohio.

**Spotlights:**  Joined the circus in 1902 and made audiences laugh uproariously ever after. He had a lovable mug with the widest mouth in show biz. *The Lottery Bride* (1930), *Some Like It Hot* (1959). Died: 1973.

### Duncan Renaldo  *Actor*                1680 Vine

**Sidelights:** Abandoned by both parents, his birthdate and place remain a mystery. Renaldo guessed he was born between 1903 and 1906.
**Spotlights:** He was "The Cisco Kid" (1950–56) and amigo of Pancho in one of the first syndicated series. Over 50 films from 1928 to 1959. Died: 1980.

### Ted Weems  *Bandleader*                1680 Vine

**Born:** Sept. 26, 1901, in Pitcairn, PA.
**Spotlights:** Musical director on radio's "Beat the Band" quiz show, first broadcast in 1940. Bandleader of 1930s and 1940s; heard on "The Jack Benny Show"; more. Died: 1963.

### Garry Moore  *See page 141.*                1680 Vine

### Teresa Wright  *Actress*                1680 Vine

**Born:** Muriel T. Wright; Oct. 27, 1918, in New York.
**Spotlights:** Film career peaked during the 1940s and 1950s: *The Little Foxes* (1941); *The Pride of the Yankees* (1942,). TV: Annie Sullivan in "The Miracle Worker"; more.
**Achievements:** 1942 Best Supporting Actress Oscar in *Mrs. Miniver.*

### Michael O'Shea  *Actor*                1680 Vine

**Born:** Edward O'Shea; March 17, 1906, in Hartford, Conn.
**Spotlights:** Red-haired, friendly, former vaudeville and film performer who starred as Denny David in "It's a Great Life" (1954–56). Died: 1973.

### Jimmy Wakely  *Singer, actor*                1680 Vine

**Born:** James Wakely; Feb. 16, 1914, in Mineola, Ariz.
**Spotlights:** Country and western hit singer, "Cimarron, Roll On," of the 1930s and 1940s who easily made the transition to the silver screen — an early rhinestone cowboy. Film debut in *Saga of Death Valley* (1939); *The Tulsa Kid*; more. Died: 1982.

### Louis Hayward  *See page 227.*                1680 Vine

### Arthur Spiegel  *Executive*                1680 Vine

**Born:** 1885.
**Spotlights:** With boundless energy, this enterprising youth sold the mail-order world prestige with Spiegel catalogue. With profits and fame, became president of the

Equitable Motion Pictures Corporation, and was taking hold of another film corporation when he suddenly died at age 31. Died: 1916.

**Jack Pearl**  📷  *Comedian, quiz show host*                    **1680 Vine**
**Born:** Jack Pearlman; in New York.
**Spotlights:** Professional start in 1913. Remembered for his comic portrayal of a German baron — "Oh shure, I vass in a much bigger vun" — on "The Jack Pearl Show." (It first aired on NBC, 1933.) Another favorite character was that of Peter Pfeiffer in his Frigidaire series. Hosted "The Baron and the Bee" spelling bee (NBC, 1953).

**Morton Downey**  📷  *Composer, singer*                    **1656 Vine**
**Born:** Nov. 14, 1901, in Wallingford, Conn.
**Spotlights:** Featured tenor with a "romantic voice" on "The Coke Club" (Mutual, 1946). Vocalist with Paul Whiteman Orchestra in 1927. Songs: "Wabash Moon," and "Now You're in My Arms."
**Sidelights:** Opened own New York nightclub — The Delmonico — in 1930s.

**Jackie Coogan**  🎥  *Actor*                    **1654 Vine**
**Born:** Oct. 24, 1914, in Los Angeles, Calif.
**Spotlights:** The all-time most successful 1½-year-old to enter films, debuting in *Skinner's Baby* (released 1917). Cast by director-star Charlie Chaplin in *A Day's Pleasure* (1919) and *The Kid* (1920) for his engaging smile and sandy blonde tousled hair. "The Tramp" could not persuade sensitive Coogan to smack him, as required in a scene. Chaplin tricked him into thinking that hitting was a game. Convinced, gentle Jackie finally cuffed him. Much later in Coogan's career, TV buffs recall him as Uncle Fenster in the "Addams Family" (1964–66).
**Achievements:** His suffering paved ground for the California Child Actors Bill. The "Coogan Act" was passed to protect children (it was already too late for him) from having their earnings stolen by greedy parents, abusive guardians, etc. Unfortunately, Coogan's court battle to recover $4 million yielded him only $125,000.
**Highlights:** Married to *Million Dollar Legs* (1939) co-star Betty Grable (1937–39). Money problems were cited in divorce proceedings. Died: 1984.

**Hal Roach**  🎥  *Movie pioneer, screenwriter, actor, director, producer* **1654 Vine**
**Born:** Jan. 14, 1892, in Elmira, N.Y.
**Spotlights:** "When I first came to L.A. in 1912, I read an ad in the paper: 'Men wanted in western costume. Be in front of the post office at 7 a.m.' A dollar, carfare and lunch was the pay." Later, when he went behind-the-scenes, he made stars out of comedian Harold Lloyd and Laurel and Hardy. Over 100 films include: *Our Gang* (1922) — this series is shown on TV as "The Little Rascals"; and *Topper* (1937).
**Achievements:** 1932, Academy Award for *The Music Box* (Laurel and Hardy classic short); 1936, Academy Award for *Bored of Education* (Our Gang); 1983, special Oscar. Founder of Hal Roach Studios.

## Paulette Goddard  *Actress*      1650 Vine

**Born:** Marion Levy; on June 3, 1911, in Long Island, N.Y.

**Spotlights:** Very pretty former Ziegfeld showgirl who later came to Hollywood. Four of her better films include: *Modern Times* (1936), with her then-husband Charlie Chaplin; *Nothing but the Truth* (1941), with Bob Hope; *Second Chorus* (1941), with Fred Astaire; and *Diary of a Chambermaid* (1941), with then-husband Burgess Meredith.

**Highlights:** Notorious first marriage when she was just 14 to timber magnate, Edgar James. He spotted her in Ziegfeld's Follies. She retired upon marrying him. Second marriage to Charlie Chaplin (1936–42). Third of four husbands, Burgess Meredith (1944–49).

## Vera Miles  *Actress*      1650 Vine

**Born:** Vera Ralston; on Aug. 23, 1930, in Boise City, Okla.

**Spotlights:** Professional, well-liked beauty with blonde hair and green eyes who made comedies and dramas. Appeared on the "Pepsi-Cola Playhouse" (early 1950s) and "Twilight Theater" (late 1950s). Made for TV movies 1960s, 1970s. 25 films.

*Audrey Hepburn*

### Audrey Hepburn 🎥 *Actress*                   1650 Vine

**Born:** Edda Hepburn van Heemstra; May 4, 1929, in Belgium.
**Spotlights:** Flawless performance in first U.S. film, *Roman Holiday* (1953) opposite Gregory Peck. Fluid, rich, engaging as the free-spirited, happy-go- lucky heroine in *Breakfast at Tiffany's* (1961). Brilliant as Eliza Doolittle in *My Fair Lady* (1964).
**Achievements:** 1953, Best Actress Oscar for *Roman Holiday*. Nominated 4 more times.
**Sidelights:** Put her acting talents on the line when she smuggled messages past Nazi soldiers during World War II.

### Scott Forbes 📺 *Actor*                   1650 Vine

**Spotlights:** The rugged western lead in "The Adventures of Jim Bowie" (1956– 58). Formerly in "The Seeking Heart" (1954).

### Al Hibbler 💿 *Singer*                   1650 Vine

**Born:** Aug. 16, 1915, in Little Rock, Ark.
**Spotlights:** Blind vocalist with the giant of jazz and soul, Duke Ellington (1943–51).

### Jimmy Durante 📺 *See page 217.*                   1650 Vine

### Tom Brown 🎥 *Actor*                   1648 Vine

**Born:** Jan. 6, 1913, in New York.
**Spotlights:** All-American, innocent-looking child actor in the silent, *The Hoosier Schoolmaster* (1924); matured into military roles (after serving in World War II), then on TV's long-running series, "Gunsmoke" as Ed O'Connor.

### Paul Douglas 🎥 *Actor*                   1648 Vine

**Born:** Nov. 4, 1907, in Philadelphia, Pa.
**Spotlights:** A 42-year old latecomer to Hollywood. *Love That Brute* (1950) aptly describes his effect on audiences. A big kindly (sometimes mean) stooge. Host of TV's "Adventure Theater" (1956); numerous roles on playhouse theaters. Died: 1959, of a heart attack.

### Richard Crooks 💿 *Opera singer*                   1648 Vine

**Born:** June 26, 1900, in Trenton, N.J.
**Spotlights:** Tenor. Metropolitan Opera debut in 1933. "The Voice of Firestone" (first aired in 1928), one of the longest-running shows on radio.

### Eric Linden 🎥 *Actor*                   1648 Vine

**Born:** Sept. 15, 1909, in New York.
**Spotlights:** Supporting talent in the action picture, *Robin Hood of El Dorado* (1936), starring Warner Baxter and Bruce Cabot. Worked with Lionel Barrymore and Mickey Rooney in the Hardy series, *A Family Affair* (1937), a well-loved American movie.

## Rosemary De Camp  *Actress*

1642 Vine

**Born:** Nov. 14, 1914, in Prescott, Ariz.

**Spotlights:** The confused sister, Margaret McDonald, of bachelor Bob on "The Bob Cummings Show" (1955–59); and mother Helen Marie (1966–70) on "That Girl." Commercials for 20-Mule Team Borax on "Death Valley Days" (1952–75). 18 motion pictures.

## John Ford  *Director*

1642 Vine

**Born:** Sean O'Feeney; Feb. 1, 1895, in Cape Elizabeth, Maine.

**Spotlights:** Sensitive genius whose work was good when he started in 1917, and improved, with masterpiece after masterpiece: *Stagecoach* (1939), *Young Mr. Lincoln* (1939), and *Wagonmaster* (1950).

**Achievements:** Oscars: 1935, *The Informer*; 1940, *The Grapes of Wrath*; 1941, *How Green Was My Valley*; 1952, *The Quiet Man*, which he also co-produced.

**Sidelights:** Hollywood nicknamed the scenic Monument Valley (Arizona/Utah border) "Ford Country" because he shot many films there. He wanted his epitaph to read: "He made westerns." Died: 1973.

## Tom Moore  *Actor*

1642 Vine

**Born:** Nov. 14, 1884, in Ireland.

**Spotlights:** Big and handsome, he melted many hearts in silent films such as *The Cinderella Man* (1917) and *A Man and His Money* (1919). Worked in horror films and westerns, too. Died: 1955.

## Portland Hoffa  *Actress, comedienne*

1642 Vine

**Spotlights:** Co-starred on "The Fred Allen Show," one of the wittiest, funniest, longest-running comedy programs (1932–1949).

**Highlights:** Married to the famous radio personality, Fred Allen.

## Hanley Stafford  *Actor*

1640 Vine

**Born:** Sept. 22, 1898, in England.

**Spotlights:** Played Daddy/Mr. Higgens on "The Baby Snooks Show" (singer- comedienne Fanny Brice was Baby Snooks) (NBC, 1939). Played Irma's father on "The Fanny Brice Show" (Fanny Brice played teenager Irma) (CBS, 1944). Died: 1968.

## Henry Hathaway  *Director*

1640 Vine

**Born:** March 13, 1898, in Sacramento, Calif.

**Spotlights:** Specialized in westerns in the early thirties, diversified into drama, romance, and thrillers. Brought out Marilyn Monroe's acting talents as a femme fatale in her first big role, *Niagara* (1952), and directed John Wayne in his only Academy Award-winning performance, *True Grit* (1969).

## Lee Tracy  *Actor*

1638 Vine

**Born:** William L. Tracy; April 14, 1898, in Atlanta, Ga.
**Spotlights:** Fair-haired, fast-talking wise guy star reporter: *Advice to the Lovelorn* (1933), *Dinner at Eight* (1933). Died: 1968, from liver cancer.

## William Bendix   🎙 *Actor*                                   1638 Vine

**Born:** Jan. 4, 1906, in New York.
**Spotlights:** Radio: Starred as Chester A. Riley on "The Life of Riley" (last aired on NBC, 1931). TV: "What a revoltin' development this is!" The success of the radio show encouraged NBC to put newcomer Jackie Gleason in as Chester A. Riley. It flopped (1949–50; one season). NBC tried again, starring the only member from the radio show, William Bendix, in his original role. Instant hit (1953–58). Died: 1964.

## William Powell   🎥 *Actor*                                   1636 Vine

**Born:** July 29, 1892, in Pittsburgh, PA.
**Spotlights:** Intelligent, refined, elegant, sparkling leading man in screwball comedies or in fast, witty suspense comedies, *The Thin Man* (MGM, 1934) co- starring Myrna Loy. Five sequels starring the same duo followed (1936–47). *My Man Godfrey* (1936), opposite his close friend, ex-wife (married 1931–33), and equally popular wit, Carole Lombard.
**Highlights:** His third fiancee, Jean Harlow, died during their engagement (1937). Died: 1984.

## George Sanders   🎥 *Actor*                                   1636 Vine

**Born:** July 3, 1906, in Russia.
**Spotlights:** Worldly, dry, leading man, and supporting actor: *The Ghost and Mrs. Muir* (1947); his last film was ominously titled *Psychomania* (1972).
**Achievements:** 1950, Best Supporting Oscar, *All About Eve.*
**Highlights:** Second of his 5 wives was Zsa Zsa Gabor (1949–57). Died: 1972.

## Ann Sothern   📺 *See page 215.*                              1634 Vine

## Ezra Stone   🎙 *Actor, director*                             1634 Vine

**Born:** Dec. 2, 1917, in New Bedford, Mass.
**Spotlights:** "The Aldrich Family" had a fun-loving prankster son, Henry Aldrich," co-star of the show (NBC, 1939). Broadway, TV, and author of books, too.
**Sidelights:** Educated at the American Academy of Dramatic Arts.

## Delmer L. Daves   🎥 *Director, screenwriter*                 1634 Vine

**Born:** July 24, 1904, in San Francisco, Calif.
**Spotlights:** Co-wrote *Love Affair* (1939), comedy hit, starring Charles Boyer and Irene Dunne, for Paramount. Wrote and directed *The Red House* (1947), a scary suspense film starring Edward G. Robinson. Died: 1977.

**Fred Stone**  *Actor* 1634 **Vine**
**Born:** Aug. 19, 1893, in Denver, Colo.
**Spotlights:** Veteran vaudeville and Broadway performer. Made a dozen films; *Life Begins in College* (1957). Died: 1959.

**Akim Tamiroff** *Actor* 1634 **Vine**
**Born:** Oct. 29, 1899, in Russia.
**Spotlights:** Small, round, slightly bald, mustached, distrustful-looking character who frequently played scoundrels. *For Whom the Bell Tolls* (1943). Died: 1972.

**Jane Greer** *Actress* 1634 **Vine**
**Born:** Bettejane Greer; Sept. 9, 1924, in Washington, D.C.
**Spotlights:** George White's *Scandals* (1945) and *The Falcon's Alibi* (1946) were two of her first movies that seemed to indicate a much brighter career, but within a decade it had fizzled out.
**Highlights:** Married briefly to crooner Rudy Vallee (1943–44).

**Ray Milland** *See page 255.* 1634 **Vine**

**Margaret O'Brien** *See page 306.* 1628 **Vine**

**Charlie Ruggles** *See page 195.* 1628 **Vine**

**Rudy Vallee** *Singer, saxophone player, actor* 1628 **Vine**
**Born:** Hubert Vallee; July 28, 1901, in Island Point, Vt.
**Spotlights:** Host of "Fleischmann's Yeast Hour"; listeners got a rise out of it (NBC, 1935–39). "Heigh-ho everybody" star of "The Rudy Vallee Show" (NBC, 1938). On-screen as *The Vagabond Lover* (1929); 33 more pictures, mostly light romantic, musical comedies.
**Sidelights:** Sang the salute "There's a New Star in Heavan Tonight, R-u-d-y V-a-l-e-n-t-i-n-o," after the silent screen star's unexpected death. Died: 1986.

**Grantland Rice** *Sportscaster, writer, short subjects commentator* 1628 **Vine**
**Born:** Nov. 1, 1880, in Murfreesboro, Tenn.
**Spotlights:** Began career as sportswriter in 1909. Handled the World Series and other major sports events (from the twenties on); football spots on "The Cities Service Concert" (NBC, late 1920s). Died: 1954.

**Joe Kirkwood, Jr.** *Actor* 1628 **Vine**
**Born:** March 22, 1897.
**Spotlights:** Became the leading man created from a comic strip in a successful movie series, *Joe Palooka — Champ* (1946), *Joe Palooka in the Big Fight* (1949),

and six others. Was the basis for syndicated TV show in 1954, co- starring Cathy Downs.

## Emil Jannings    *Actor*      1628 Vine

**Born:** Theodor E. Janenz; July 22, 1884, in Switzerland.

**Spotlights:** Big, powerful, tragic characterization of authoritative rulers in history, in *Anne Boleyn* (1920) and *Peter the Great* (1922). Moved to Hollywood in 1927. He was "Falling in Love Again" with Marlene Dietrich in *The Blue Angel* (1930).

**Achievements:** 1927–28, Academy Award, first ever presented to a best actor, *The Last Command* and *The Way of All Flesh*.

**Sidelights:** Raised in a German village, Jannings was recruited by the Third Reich. He eagerly complied and moved to Europe in the mid-1930s. With Hitler's backing, motion pictures glorifying Nazi hatred (anti-British, etc.) were made under Janning's guidance. After the fall of the Third Reich, Jannings never worked again. Died: 1950, of cancer; a lonely, penniless man.

## Dolores del Rio    *Actress*      1628 Vine

**Born:** Lolita de Martinez; Aug. 3, 1905, in Mexico.

**Spotlights:** She was a great beauty with big eyes, bow lips, and an oval face: *Joanna* (1925), *No Other Woman* (1928). Her last screen appearance was *The Children of Sanchez* (1978).

**Sidelights:** Discovered at a party by a director struck by her exotic good looks.

## Jeanette MacDonald    *See page 166.*      1628 Vine

## Donald Crisp    [1]   *Actor, director*      1628 Vine

**Born:** July 27, 1880, in Scotland.

**Spotlights:** Learned his craft from D. W. Griffith's *The Birth of a Nation* (1915) and Buster Keaton's *The Navigator* (1924). Wonderfully believable in *Mutiny on the Bounty* (1935).

**Achievements:** 1941, Supporting Actor Academy Award, *How Green Was My Valley*. Died: 1974.

## Tex McCrary    *Performer, newspaper columnist*      1628 Vine

**Born:** John Reagan; in 1910, in Calvert, Tex.

**Spotlights:** Co-host, with his wife Jinx Falkenburg, of talk show "Tex and Jix" (1947–49). The forerunner of the television magazine format.

## Robert Edeson    *Actor*      1628 Vine

**Born:** Jan. 23, 1868, in New Orleans, LA.

**Spotlights:** Silent screen leading man who made a few early talkies. Cecil B. DeMille's *Dynamite* (1929). Died: 1931.

## Barbara Hale  *Actress*

**Born:** April 18, 1921, in DeKalb, Ill.

**Spotlights:** Pretty, brunette secretary Della Street (1957–66) in the law drama "Perry Mason." Capable in films too.

**Achievements:** 1959, Emmy.

## Ted Malone  *Host*

1628 Vine

**Spotlights:** Intellectual Dick Cavett-type host of "Between the Bookends" (CBS, 1935); emcee on "All-American Yankee Doodle Quiz" (ABC, 1943).

## Johnny Mercer  *Composer, lyricist, actor, author*

1628 Vine

**Born:** Nov. 18, 1909, in Savannah, Ga.

**Spotlights:** Started as singer and turned out to be one of the most prolific songwriters America has known. Over 100 songs include: "That Old Black Magic," and "Jeepers Creepers." Singer Billie Holiday gave vibrant life to: "If You Were Mine," "Too Marvelous for Words," and "Sentimental and Melancholy." TV: Panelist on "Musical Chairs" (1955).

**Achievements:** Music Oscars for: "On the Atcheson, Topeka and Santa Fe" (1946); "In the Cool Cool Cool of the Evening" (1951); "Moon River" (1961); "Days of Wine and Roses" (1962). Founder of Capital Records. Recipient of the Grammy-Academy's Trustee Award. Died: 1976.

## Charlton Heston  *Actor*

1626 Vine

**Born:** John C. Carter; Oct. 4, 1923, in Evanston, Ill.

**Spotlights:** Tall, strongly built, sculptured face, blue-eyed dramatic talent. Famous for heroic roles in epic films: Moses in *The Ten Commandments* (1956); Michelangelo in *The Agony and the Ecstasy* (1965). Convincingly played an illiterate middle-aged cowpuncher in *Will Penny* (1968). TV fans see him weekly on "The Colbys" as head of a corporate empire.

**Achievements:** 1959, Best Actor Oscar for *Ben Hur*. 1977, Jean Hersholt Humanitarian Award.

## Arthur Fiedler  *Conductor*

1624 Vine

**Born:** Dec. 17, 1894, in Boston, Mass.

**Spotlights:** Famous for his innovative light readings. Repertoire included classical, light classical, and contemporary works. A musician for 15 years with the Boston Symphony Orchestra, he became conductor of the Boston Pops Orchestra in 1930, until his death. Died: 1979.

## Arlene Dahl  *Actress*

1624 Vine

**Born:** Aug. 11, 1924, in Minneapolis, MN.

**Spotlights:** Luscious, green-eyed redhead whose light comedy graced *A Southern Yankee* (1940), co-starring Red Skelton; on screen 1947–70.

### Alice Lake  *Actress*
1624 Vine

**Born:** Mar. 23, 1897, in Brooklyn, N.Y.

**Spotlights:** *The Infamous Miss Revell* (1921) and *The Price of Success* (1925) were two of the 50 pictures she appeared in; almost all were silents. Career ended in 1934. Died: 1967.

### Lizabeth Scott *Actress*
1624 Vine

**Born:** Emma Matzo; Sept. 29, 1922, in Scranton, Pa.

**Spotlights:** Sexy, husky voice. Hot, blonde "threat" often cast as a cruel, deceiving woman in thrillers; *Too Late for Tears* (1949); *Dark City* (1950) opposite Charlton Heston in his first film.

### Arthur Kennedy *See page 54.*
1624 Vine

### Roy Rogers *See page 134.*
1620 Vine

### Jane Wyman *Actress*
1620 Vine

**Born:** Sarah Fulks; Jan. 4, 1914, in St. Joseph, Mo.

**Spotlights:** Brilliant performance in *The Yearling* (1946); *The Blue Veil* (1951); *Magnificent Obsession* (1954). TV: Angela Channing on "Falcon Crest" (1981–).

**Achievements:** 1948 Best Actress Oscar for *Johnny Belinda*.

**Highlights:** Second husband Ronald Reagan (1940–48). Married and divorced two more husbands.

### Estelle Taylor *Actress*
1620 Vine

**Born:** Estelle Boylan; May 20, 1899, in Wilmington, Del.

**Spotlights:** Fabulous-looking brunette. Female lead in *Manhattan Madness* (1925). The great heavyweight boxer, world champion Jack Dempsey, was her co- star. Taylor's last film was *The Southerner* (1945).

**Sidelights:** Married Dempsey (1925–31). Died: 1958.

| *Charlton Heston* | *Arthur Fiedler* | *Arlene Dahl* |

**Fredric March** 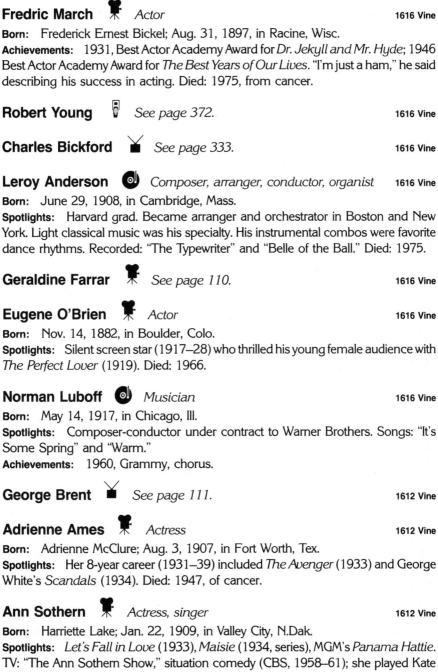 *Actor*　　　　　　　　　　1616 **Vine**
**Born:** Frederick Ernest Bickel; Aug. 31, 1897, in Racine, Wisc.
**Achievements:** 1931, Best Actor Academy Award for *Dr. Jekyll and Mr. Hyde*; 1946 Best Actor Academy Award for *The Best Years of Our Lives.* "I'm just a ham," he said describing his success in acting. Died: 1975, from cancer.

**Robert Young** *See page 372.*　　　　　　　　　1616 **Vine**

**Charles Bickford** *See page 333.*　　　　　　　1616 **Vine**

**Leroy Anderson** *Composer, arranger, conductor, organist*　1616 **Vine**
**Born:** June 29, 1908, in Cambridge, Mass.
**Spotlights:** Harvard grad. Became arranger and orchestrator in Boston and New York. Light classical music was his specialty. His instrumental combos were favorite dance rhythms. Recorded: "The Typewriter" and "Belle of the Ball." Died: 1975.

**Geraldine Farrar** *See page 110.*　　　　　　　1616 **Vine**

**Eugene O'Brien** *Actor*　　　　　　　　　　　1616 **Vine**
**Born:** Nov. 14, 1882, in Boulder, Colo.
**Spotlights:** Silent screen star (1917–28) who thrilled his young female audience with *The Perfect Lover* (1919). Died: 1966.

**Norman Luboff** *Musician*　　　　　　　　　　1616 **Vine**
**Born:** May 14, 1917, in Chicago, Ill.
**Spotlights:** Composer-conductor under contract to Warner Brothers. Songs: "It's Some Spring" and "Warm."
**Achievements:** 1960, Grammy, chorus.

**George Brent** *See page 111.*　　　　　　　　　1612 **Vine**

**Adrienne Ames** *Actress*　　　　　　　　　　　1612 **Vine**
**Born:** Adrienne McClure; Aug. 3, 1907, in Fort Worth, Tex.
**Spotlights:** Her 8-year career (1931–39) included *The Avenger* (1933) and George White's *Scandals* (1934). Died: 1947, of cancer.

**Ann Sothern** *Actress, singer*　　　　　　　　　1612 **Vine**
**Born:** Harriette Lake; Jan. 22, 1909, in Valley City, N.Dak.
**Spotlights:** *Let's Fall in Love* (1933), *Maisie* (1934, series), MGM's *Panama Hattie.* TV: "The Ann Sothern Show," situation comedy (CBS, 1958–61); she played Kate O'Connor.
**Sidelights:** Labeled "Queen of the 'B's."

## Donna Reed   🎥   *Actress*     1612 Vine

**Born:** Donna Mullenger; Jan. 27, 1921, in Denison, Iowa.
**Spotlights:** Fresh-faced, quiet leading lady of wholesome roles. Director Frank Capra cast her opposite James Stewart in *It's a Wonderful Life* (1946), and later said of her, "Just perfect as Mary Bailey, her greatest role."
**Achievements:** 1953, Best Supporting Actress *From Here to Eternity*, the one time she did not play a good girl. Died: 1986.

## Julia Sanderson   🎙   *Actress*     1610 Vine

**Born:** Aug. 20, 1887, in Springfield, Mass.
**Spotlights:** Captain of the female team, "The Battles of the Sexes" (NBC, 1938); "Let's Be Charming" (Mutual, 1943). Died: 1975.

## Cary Grant   🎥   *Actor*     1610 Vine

**Born:** Archibald Leach; Jan. 18, 1904, in England.
**Spotlights:** Classy, elegant, handsome leading man in romantic comedies and thrillers including: *The Awful Truth* (1938), with Irene Dunne; *Bringing Up Baby* (1938), co-starring Katharine Hepburn; Frank Capra's *Arsenic and Old Lace* (1944); *To Catch a Thief* (1955). Much-imitated voice.
**Achievements:** 1969, Special Oscar "for his unique mastery of the art of screen acting."
**Highlights:** Married to two walk-of-famers, first wife Virginia Cherrill (1933–35) and fourth wife (of 5), Dyan Cannon (1965–68), 35 years his junior. Died: 1986; from a stroke.

## Henri Rene   💿   *See page 380.*     1610 Hollywood

## Richard Dix   🎥   *Actor*     1610 Vine

**Born:** Ernest Brimmer; July 8, 1894, in St. Paul, Min.
**Spotlights:** Studied to be a doctor but took off his white lab coat for a local university play and never put it back on. Hollywood screen tests showed his strong potential for silent films, in which he successfully starred before miraculously making it to the talkies. One of his most memorable films was with newcomer Irene Dunne, *Cimarron* (1931). Died: 1949 of heart failure.

## Clark Gable   🎥   *Actor*     1610 Vine

**Born:** William C. Gable, Feb. 1, 1901, in Cadiz, Ohio.
**Spotlights:** Best remembered for his charming, virile, devil-may-care portrayal of Rhett Butler in *Gone with the Wind* (1939). In real life, a thoughtful, humble, friendly, humorous, gentleman. On screen and off, Gable was a man's man *and* a lady's man, in short, admired by all. Films include *A Free Soul* (1932), *Honky Tonk* (1941), and *The Misfits* (1961), his last picture.
**Achievements:** 1934, Best Actor Academy Award for the comedy *It Happened One Night*.

216

**Highlights:**   Married to Carole Lombard (from 1939 to her death in 1942).

**Sidelights:**   Even big studio heads can be wrong about star potential: "What can you do with a guy with ears like that?" Warners asked. MGM said of Gable's screen test, "Awful, take it away." Died: 1960, of a heart attack.

## John Ireland   ■   *Actor*   1610 Vine

**Born:**   Jan. 30, 1914, in Canada.

**Spotlights:**   He played tough-looking Jed Colby (1965–66) on the western "Rawhide." His film career spanned 40 years.

## Mae Marsh   *Actress*   1606 Vine

**Born:**   Mary Marsh; Nov. 9, 1895, in Madrid, N.Mex.

**Spotlights:**   Young beauty whose human spirit was captured in two silent screen classics: *The Birth of a Nation* (1915) and *Intolerance* (1916). Worked sporadically in films for several decades. Died: 1968.

## Jimmy Durante   *Comedian*   1606 Vine

**Born:**   Feb. 10, 1893, in New York.

**Spotlights:**   Nicknamed "Schnozzola" for "the nose." Gravel-voiced singer, fondly remembered shaking his head and saying "It's da condishuns dat prevail!" Film career spanned 3 decades (1930–63), including *The New Adventures of Get-Rich-Quick Wallingford* (1931) and *The Man Who Came to Dinner* (1941). NBC radio: "The Jimmy Durante Show" registered high ratings. The theme song? Why it's "Ink-a-dinka-doo." Died: 1980, from pneumonia.

## Norman Taurog   *Director*   1606 Vine

**Born:**   Feb. 23, 1899, in Chicago, Ill.

**Spotlights:**   Started as a boy actor, then directed comedy shorts. Could move an audience from laughter to tears. Co-directed *If I Had a Million* (1932), with W. C. Fields, *The Adventures of Tom Sawyer* with Tommy Kelly and *Boys' Town*, with

| *Cary Grant* | *Richard Dix* | *Clark Gable* |

Spencer Tracy and Mickey Rooney (both 1938); and *Blue Hawaii* (1961) with Elvis Presley.
**Achievements:** 1931, Academy Award for *Skippy*, in which he directed his nephew, Jackie Cooper. Died: 1981.

### Leopold Stokowski  *Conducter* 1606 Vine

**Born:** April 18, 1882, in England.
**Spotlights:** Played violin, piano, and organ. Brilliant, innovative conductor of the Philadelphia Orchestra (1912–36), New York Philharmonic Symphony Orchestra, then formed Stokowski Symphony Orchestra. Recordings: Tchaikovsky *Symphony No. 5 in E Minor, op. 64*; more.
**Achievements:** 1941 Oscar "for unique achievement in visualized music" in Walt Disney's *Fantasia*. Died: 1977.

### Dick Foran  *Actor* 1600 Vine

**Born:** John Foran; June 18, 1910, in Flemington, N.J.
**Spotlights:** Tall, kind, fair-haired singing cowboy on the Warners lot. As Slim in the situation comedy "O.K. Crackerby" (1965–66), he was an associate of the richest man in the world, who also happened to be extremely uncivilized; more. Died: 1979.

### Webb Pierce  *Singer, musician* 1600 Vine

**Born:** Aug. 8, 1926.
**Spotlights:** Albums: *C & W, In the Jailhouse Now.* Singles: "I Ain't Never," "Good Lord Giveth," "I'm Walkin' the Dog."

*John Ireland*         *Leopold Stokowski*

**Tim McCoy**    *Actor*                    1600 Vine

**Born:**   April 19, 1891, in Saginaw, Mich.

**Spotlights:**   Thirties western star. His third acting role, *Winners of the Wilderness* (1927), was opposite young Joan Crawford. *The Indians are Coming*, a 1930 serial.

**Sidelights:**   Became an expert on Indians by living on a Sioux reservation years before he even thought of be coming an actor. Died: 1978.

**Orson Welles**   *Actor, screenwriter, director, producer*                    1600 Vine

**Born:**   George Orson Welles; May 15, 1915, in Kenosha, Wisc.

**Spotlights:**   The October 30, 1938, radio broadcast of H.G. Wells's "The War of the Worlds" struck panic in the hearts of everyone not aware it was a play. Welles co-wrote, directed, produced and starred in *Citizen Kane* (1941) — all before he was 30 years old.

**Achievements:**   1941, Best Screenplay Oscar; 1970, special Oscar.

**Highlights:**   Married Rita Hayworth (1943–47). Died: 1985, of cardiac arrest.

**Fritz Lang**   *Director*                    1600 Vine

**Born:**   Dec. 5, 1890, in Austria.

**Spotlights:**   Projected a horrifying glimpse into the future in *Metropolis* (1926), a standard for all history of motion picture college classes. *Fury* (1936) and *The Big Heat* (1953) further illustrate his internal struggle with life's confusing inhumanity.

**Sidelights:**   Served in the Austrian Army in World War I. Bravely made an anti-Nazi film, *Das Testament von Dr. Mabuse* (1932) before he fled to America. His wife, however, backed Hitler and remained in Germany. He obtained a divorce in 1934. Died: 1976.

**Kathryn Grayson**   *Actress, singer*                    1600 Vine

**Born:**   Zelma K. Hedrick; Feb. 9, 1922, in Winston-Salem, N.C.

**Spotlights:**   Dark-haired beauty with curvaceous physique; *Show Boat* (1950) and *Kiss Me Kate* (1953), both MGM musicals opposite Howard Keel.

**Tennessee Ernie Ford**   *See page 102.*                    1600 Vine

**Vaughn Monroe**   *Singer, orchestra leader*                    1600 Vine

**Born:**   Oct. 7, 1911, in Akron, Ohio.

**Spotlights:**   Known as "the baritone with muscles." Formed own band in 1940. Radio: Host of "Camel Caravan," musical variety show from 1945 to early 1950s. TV: Fabulous success on "The Vaughn Monroe Show" singing "There I've Said It Again," "Racing with the Moon," "Ghost Riders in the Sky." Died: 1973.

**Madge Kennedy**   *Actress*                    1600 Vine

**Born:**   Aug. 1, 1892, in Chicago, Ill.

**Spotlights:**   Made 25 silent pictures between 1917 and 1926 before retiring, including

*Nearly Married* (1917) and *The Girl with a Jazz Heart* (1921). Made a few sporadic screen appearances from fifties to seventies.

**Frank Sinatra** 🎥 *Singer, actor*                              **1600 Vine**

**Born:** Dec. 12, 1915, in Hoboken, N.J.

**Spotlights:** Sinatra's painfully emotional performance in *The Man with the Golden Arm* (1955), was outstanding in the drama category, but most of his pictures have been light musicals or sophisticated comedies: *Guys and Dolls* (1955); *High Society* (1956). Nicknamed "The Voice," this great singer has recorded a collection of hits including "My Way," "New York, New York," "I've Got a Crush on You," and "She's Funny That Way." TV: "Frank Sinatra: A Man and His Music" (1966).

**Achievements:** 1953, Best Supporting Actor Oscar, *From Here to Eternity*. 1970, Oscar, Jean Hersholt Humanitarian Award. Winner of 7 Grammys.

**Hugo Winterhalter** 💿 *Arranger, conductor.*                  **1600 Vine**

**Born:** Aug. 15, 1909, in Wilkes-Barre, PA.

**Spotlights:** Former school teacher. Arranged for bands such as Count Basie in the early 1940's. Singer Kate Smith adored Winterhalter's creative talents. Composed "How Do I Love Thee?" and "Far Away Blues." Favored large string orchestras. Records include: "Blue Violins/Fandango." Died: 1973.

*Frank Sinatra's star*

# ⋆ 1560 VINE ⋆

### Art Linkletter  *TV Host* 1560 Vine
**Born:** July 17, 1912, in Canada
**Spotlights:** Radio announcer (1939–42); host of "House Party" (NBC, 1943). TV: "People are Funny" (1954–61), "The Art Linkletter Show" (1963).
**Achievements:** 1969, Grammy, for spoken word.

### Ava Gardner  *Actress* 1560 Vine
**Born:** Jan. 24, 1922, in Smithfield, N.C.
**Spotlights:** MGM's stunningly beautiful brunette love goddess with green eyes. Partial film listing: *The Killers* (1946), *Pandora and the Flying Dutchman* (1951), *Show Boat* (1951), *Mogambo* (1953).
**Highlights:** Marriages to Mickey Rooney (1942–43), Artie Shaw (1945–46), Frank Sinatra (1951–57).

### Tommy Sands 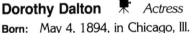 *Singer, actor* 1560 Vine
**Born:** Aug. 27, 1937, in Chicago, Ill.
**Spotlights:** Lively rock 'n roll guitarist on screen in *Sing Boy Sing* (1958), *Babes in Toyland* (1961), and *Ensign Pulver* (1964).

### Dorothy Dalton *Actress* 1560 Vine
**Born:** May 4, 1894, in Chicago, Ill.
**Spotlights:** Gorgeous brunette with delicious dimples who starred in silents from 1915, *The Disciple*, to 1924, *The Moral Sinner*. Died: 1972.

### Mervyn Le Roy *Director, producer, writer, actor* 1560 Vine
**Born:** Oct. 15, 1900, in San Francisco, Calif.
**Spotlights:** A jack-of-all-trades, Le Roy's golden touch made a bundle for Warners in 1931 and catapulted Edward G. Robinson to superstardom in two crime movies; *Little Caesar* and *Five-Star Final*. Le Roy produced *The Wizard of Oz* (MGM, 1939).
**Achievements:** 1945 special Oscar, 1975, special Oscar (Irving Thalberg Memorial Award).

### Billie Holiday *Singer* 1560 Vine
**Born:** Eleanora McKay; April 15, 1915, in Baltimore, Md.
**Spotlights:** Foremost female singer in jazz history. Known as a jazz instrumental soloist: "I don't think I'm singing. I feel like I'm playing a horn. I try to improvise like Lester Young, Louis Armstrong, or someone else I admire. I have to change a tune to my own way of doing it." First recorded with Benny Goodman in 1933, sang with

Count Basie in 1937, and Artie Shaw in 1938. Co-wrote "God Bless the Child." Other songs include "Strange Fruit" (about lynching), "Gloomy Sunday," "Lover Man," "Did I Remember?" and "Fine and Mellow." Film: *New Orleans* (1947).

**Achievements:** Grammy, Lifetime Achievement Award, (presented posthumously).

**Sidelights:** Nicknamed Lady Day when she refused to accept tips without using her hands in an adult club in Harlem. Diana Ross portrayed her in *Lady Sings the Blues* (1972). Holiday was pegged a "Master of the Blues," which ironically she rarely sang, but when she did, it was from the gut. Died: 1959.

## Mischa Elman  Violinist                                               1560 Vine

**Born:** Jan. 20, 1891, in Russia.

**Spotlights:** Made U.S. performance debut in 1908. Virtuoso. Extremely popular following World War I. Records: Mendelssohn's *Concerto in E Minor, op. 64*, Tchaikovsky's *Concerto in D Major, op. 35*; more.

**Sidelights:** Naturalized in 1923. Died: 1967.

## The Three Stooges  Comedy team, slapstick artists              1560 Vine

**Born:** Brothers Moe (1897) and Shemp (1900) Howard of Brooklyn, N.Y., and Larry Fine (1911) of Philadelphia, Pa. Brother Curly (1906) replaced Shemp in 1931. Curly became disabled and was replaced in 1946 by Shemp. Shemp died (1955) and was replaced by Joe Besser. In 1959, Besser was out and Joe DeRita was in.

**Spotlights:** Made over 200 comedy shorts and 14 films. Died: Moe, 1975; Larry Fine, 1974; Curly, 1952; Shemp, 1955; Joe Besser, 1972.

## Chester Conklin  Actor                                              1560 Vine

**Born:** Jules Cowles; Jan. 11, 1888, in Oskaloosa, Iowa.

**Spotlights:** His famous walrus mustache complemented his comic style; with Charlie Chaplin in *Cruel, Cruel Love* (1914) and W. C. Fields in *Tillie's Punctual Romance* (1928). Died: 1971.

## Al Lohman & Roger Barkley                                          1560 Vine

**Born:** Lohman in 1935, in Sioux City, IA; Barkley in 1936, in Odebolt, IA.

**Spotlights:** Teamed together in 1963, this duo became comedy kings of Los Angeles radio for 23 years. Lohman known for his hilarious range of funny voices while Barkley often played the witty straightman. TV and nightclubs, too. They dissolved their professional relationship in 1986. Both have proceeded onto successful careers; Barkley has remained solo, Lohman has teamed with Gary Owens.

**Achievements:** 1969, 1970, Emmys.

## Bobby Driscoll  Actor                                               1560 Vine

**Born:** May 3, 1937, in Cedar Rapids, Iowa.

**Spotlights:** A sparkling gem of a youngster who worked happily for Disney before

reaching his awkward years: *Song of the South* (1946), *Treasure Island* (1950).
**Achievements:** 1949, special Oscar, "outstanding juvenile actor." Died: 1968.

## Mae West  *Actress, writer* 1560 Vine
**Born:** Aug. 17, 1892, in Brooklyn, N.Y.
**Spotlights:** Much imitated "come up and see me some time." Voluptuous, platinum blonde, sex goddess whose own fresh, fast, blatant one-liners on sex saved Paramount from bankruptcy: *She Done Him Wrong* (1933). She was the first to admit, "Goodness has nothing to do with it." *Belle of the Nineties* (1934).
**Achievements:** 1935, top-salaried woman in the U.S. Died: 1980.

## Rick Dees  *Disc jockey, comedian, spokesman, TV host, recording artist* 1560 Vine
**Born:** March 14, in Greensboro, N.C.
**Spotlights:** Funny, quick-witted, knowledgeable entertainer of "The Rick Dees Weekly Top 40," and "American Music Magazine, Starring Rick Dees" heard around the world. A large military following; heard on the Armed Forces radio and television network. His warm, friendly voice has made him one of America's most popular celebrities; more than 30 million people tune in to Gannett Radio's KIIS FM/AM every week. "Comedy is the most important facet of my career," explains Rick. "I love making people laugh and enjoy themselves. It's not the money, it's the amount!"

## Richard Wallace  *Director* 1560 Vine
**Born:** Aug. 26, 1894, in Sacramento, Calif.
**Spotlights:** A "lady's director," he brilliantly guided Tallulah Bankhead, Loretta Young, and others (1925–50) through dramas and romantic comedies; *The Young in Heart* (1938); *Because of Him* (1946). Died: 1954.

## Joan Leslie  *Actress* 1560 Vine
**Born:** Joan Brodel; Jan. 26, 1925, in Detroit, Mich.
**Spotlights:** Reddish-brown hair, warm, beautiful former Warner's *Yankee Doodle Dandy* (1942) star. *Smoke Jumpers* (1956), *The Keegans* (1975). Films frequently shown on TV. Left show biz to become a successful dress designer.

## Isabel Jewell  *Actress* 1560 Vine
**Born:** July 10, 1910, in Shoshone, Wyo.
**Spotlights:** Although her career spanned 2 decades, she was at the pinnacle during the 1930s. Supporting talent in *Lost Horizon* (1937). Died: 1972.

### Hal March  *Actor* 1560 Vine

**Born:** Harold Mendelson; April 22, 1920, in San Francisco, Calif.
**Spotlights:** Radio: Regular on "My Favorite Husband" (CBS, 1948), starring Lucille Ball. On "Too Many Cooks" he was head of the household, Mr. Cook, with 10 children (CBS, 1950). TV: Harry Morton (1950–51) on "The George Burns and Gracie Allen Show." Emcee of "The $64,000 Question" (1955–58). Died: 1970.

### Rod La Rocque ![actor] *Actor* 1560 Vine

**Born:** de la Rour; Nov. 29, 1896, in Chicago, Ill.
**Spotlights:** Handsome lady's man in the twenties: *Stolen Kiss* (1920) and *Jazz Mania* (1923). Superb in *The Hunchback of Notre Dame* (1939), starring Charles Laughton, Cedric Hardwicke, and Maureen O'Hara.
**Highlights:** Married to Hungarian silent star Vilma Bunky (1927 until his death).
**Sidelights:** Retired from show business to become a successful businessman. Died: 1969.

### Jack Carson ![tv] *Actor, comedian* 1560 Vine

**Born:** John Carson; Oct. 27, 1910, in Carmen, Canada.
**Spotlights:** Popular stage, screen, TV, radio and vaudeville actor! Radio; (1943) *The Jack Carson Show* TV: "Live, from New York, it's the U.S. Royal Showcase," hosted by comedian Jack Carson (1952). Also hosted TV's *All Star Revue* (1950–52). Starred with James Cagney and Olivia de Havilland on "The Gulf Screen Guild Theater" (CBS radio, 1939).
**Sidelights:** "A fan club is a group of people who tell an actor he's not alone in the way he feels about himself." Died: 1963, from cancer.

### Esther Williams ![actress] *Actress, champion swimmer* 1560 Vine

**Born:** Aug. 8, 1923, in Los Angeles, Calif.
**Spotlights:** MGM's mermaid made waves in the splashy musical *Bathing Beauty* (1944); in an underwater dream in *Easy to Wed* (1946), with Van Johnson and Lucille Ball. Retired in 1961.
**Highlights:** Wed Fernando Lamas, third husband in 1967.

### Tony Bennett  *Singer* 1560 Vine

**Born:** Antonio Benedetto; Aug. 3, 1926, in New York.
**Spotlights:** Lyric baritone with throaty edge. Recorded hits: "I Left My Heart in San Francisco," "Because of You," "One for My Baby." TV includes "Bennett and Basie Together." Celebrated jazz-oriented stylist with swing bands, and popular orchestras.
**Achievements:** Two 1962 Grammys.

**Sidelights:**   Discovered by Bob Hope in 1949 while Bennett was performing with Pearl Bailey in a New York City nightclub.

**Jeannie Carson**    *Actress*                                        1560 **Vine**
**Born:**   Jean Shufflebottom; May 28, 1929, in England.
**Spotlights:**   Played Jeanie MacLennan, a Scottish lass surviving in New York, in the situation comedy "Hey Jeannie!" (1956–60).

**Corinne Griffith**   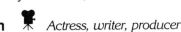 *Actress, writer, producer*                 1560 **Vine**
**Born:**   Nov. 24, 1896, in Texarkana, Tex.
**Spotlights:**   One of the most beautiful women ever to grace the screen, *Miss Ambition* (1916). But in *Lilies of the Field* (1924), in which she starred and was the executive producer, she proved there were brains, too. Only made a few talkies before bowing out gracefully.
**Sidelights:**   Upon retiring from the screen, wrote books and invested wisely in real estate. Died: 1979.

**Helen Vinson**   *Actress*                                                             1560 **Vine**
**Born:**   Sept. 17, 1907, in Beaumont, Tex.
**Spotlights:**   Broadway-trained, this New York socialite's 17-year screen career included wonderful work in *Jewel Robbery* (1932) and *The Thin Man Goes Home* (1945).

**Kurt Kreuger**   *Actor*                                                               1560 **Vine**
**Born:**   July 23, 1916, in Germany.
**Spotlights:**   Frightfully believable as a Nazi officer and soldier: *The Strange Death of Adolf Hitler* (1943), *Hotel Berlin* (1945), *Paris Underground* (1945).
**Sidelights:**   In real life, he pledged his allegiance to the United States.

**Jean Hagen**    *Actress*                                           1560 **Vine**
**Born:**   Jean Verhagen on Aug. 3, 1923, in Chicago, Ill.
**Spotlights:**   Perky, blonde actress who turned in several excellent film roles. As Mrs. Margaret Williams (1953–56), she was the happy, loving mother and wife on "The Danny Thomas Show." Died: 1977, of throat cancer.

**Mary Martin**   *See page 67.*                                                        1560 **Vine**

**Larry Hagman**   *Actor*                                                              1560 **Vine**
**Born:**   Sept. 21, 1931, in Weatherford, Tex.
**Spotlights:**   Starred in a number of TV series. He is best known for his role as Captain (later Major) Tony Nelson on "I Dream of Jeannie" (1965–70), and as John Ross (J.R.) Ewing, Jr., on "Dallas" (1978– ), the ambitious, lying, cheating (and loving every minute of it) eldest son. J.R. is a powerhouse executive of Ewing Oil, manipulator of

every family member of Southfork and all- around bad guy.
**Highlights:** Son of actress Mary Martin.

**Dick Powell** 🎙 *See page 21*                                    1560 Vine

**Evelyn Venable** 🎥 *Actress*                                     1500 Vine
**Born:** Oct. 18, 1913, in Cincinnati, Ohio.
**Spotlights:** Her decade-long career earned her and Kent Taylor the title "The Best Looking Lovers on the Screen." *Mrs. Wright of the Cabbage Patch* (1934). Worked with Katharine Hepburn and Fred MacMurray in *Alice Adams* (1935).

**Yakima Canutt** 🎥 *Stuntman, supporting actor*                   1500 Vine
**Born:** Enos Canut; Nov. 29, 1895, in Colfax, Wash.
**Spotlights:** A world champion rodeo cowboy (twice), who made an easy transition to the screen in the silent era. Later every superstar used him in dangerous scenes. *Stagecoach; Gone with the Wind* (both 1939). Also second- unit director: *Ben Hur* (1959).
**Achievements:** 1966, special Oscar for "achievement as a stuntman and for the

*Larry Hagman*

development of safety devices used by stuntmen everywhere." Died: 1986 (he had been the longest-living stuntman).

### Jinx Falkenburg  *Performer*                                  1500 Vine
**Born:**  Eugenia Falkenburg; Jan. 21, 1919, in Spain.
**Spotlights:**  "Cover girl" on screen and off. Co-starred with her husband on the Tex and Jinx McCrary radio talk show, "Hi Jinx"; same chatty format successful on TV in the late 1940s.

### Xavier Cugat  *Bandleader, actor*                            1500 Vine
**Born:**  Jan. 1, 1900, in Spain.
**Spotlights:**  Violin accompanist to opera great Enrico Caruso. Formed own band to play in nightclubs. Known as "Cugie." On-screen in 1936 in *Go West Young Man*. TV: "The Xavier Cugat Show" (aired in 1957). Formed new band, The Rumba King, at age 87.
**Sidelights:**  Former cartoonist for a Los Angeles newspaper. You can catch a glimpse of the cuban premier Fidel Castro, in one of Cugat's films, *Holiday in Mexico* (1946).

### George Raft  *See page 184.*                                 1500 Vine

### Celeste Holm  *Actress*                                       1500 Vine
**Born:**  April 29, 1919, in New York.
**Spotlights:**  A lovely, blond, blue-eyed actress at home in comedy or drama. TV: Mini series "Backstairs at the White House" (1969); "Trapper John, M.D."; more.
**Achievements:**  1947, Best Supporting Actress Oscar for *Gentleman's Agreement*.

### Jack Conway  *Director*                                       1500 Vine
**Born:**  July 17, 1887, in Graceville, Minn.
**Spotlights:**  Many films before his wild, acerbic comedies: *Libeled Lady* (1936), starring Jean Harlow, Spencer Tracy, and William Powell; *Too Hot to Handle* (1938). Faded in the mid-1940s. Died: 1952.

### Klaus Landsberg  *Executive*                                  1500 Vine
**Born:**  July 7, 1916, in Germany.
**Spotlights:**  Worked as an assistant in one of the earliest TV experimental bureaus in 1934. In 1941 packaged KTLA, a Los Angeles TV station. Produced and directed 3,500 telecasts!

### Louis Hayward  *Actor*                                        1500 Vine
**Born:**  Seafield Grant; March 19, 1909, in South Africa.
**Spotlights:**  Former London stage and Broadway performer. Dark-haired leading and supporting talent in *Absolute Quiet* (1936); *My Son, My Son* (1940). TV: "The Survivors" by Harold Robbins. (1969). Other specials.

**Dorothy Arzner**  *Director* 1500 Vine

**Born:** Jan. 3, 1900, in San Francisco, Calif.

**Spotlights:** Pioneer female editor and screenwriter. Directed Paramount's first talkie, *The Wild Party* (1929); also directed *Christopher Strong* (1933), *First Comes Courage* (1943). Made military training films (WAC) during World War II, then retired from films. Directed TV commercials and produced plays. Died: 1979.

**William K. Howard**  *Director* 1500 Vine

**Born:** June 16, 1899, in St. Mary's, Ohio.

**Spotlights:** *The Power and the Glory* (1933), starring Spencer Tracy and Colleen Moore and written by Preston Sturges; one of Howard's memorable pictures was *The Princess Comes Across* (1936). Died: 1954.

**Michael Landon** ◣ *Actor* 1500 Vine

**Born:** Eugene Orowitz; Oct. 31, 1937, in Forest Hills, N.Y.

**Spotlights:** Landon's rugged good looks and sensitive acting have never lost their appeal to TV viewers; played Little Joe Cartwright on "Bonanza" (1959–73); frequently wrote and directed, as well as produced and starred in "Little House on the Prairie" (1974–82); in 1984 became the angel Jonathan Smith on "Highway to Heaven" and its executive producer and writer.

**Shirley Temple**  *Actress* 1500 Vine

**Born:** April 23, 1928, in Santa Monica, Calif.

**Spotlights:** Shot to stardom in *Stand Up and Cheer* (1934), with her song-and-dance routine, "Baby Take a Bow." By 1938 "Curly Top" was the top U.S. box office attraction and favorite entertainer abroad.

**Achievements:** 1934 special Oscar. 1968 U.S. representative at the U.N. 1974–76, U.S. ambassador to Ghana; promoted to U.S. Chief of Protocol.

**Sidelights:** How popular was she? At age 6: "Mother took me to see Santa Claus in a department store, and he asked me for my autograph."

**Ricardo Cortez**  *Actor* 1500 Vine

**Born:** Jacob Krantz; Sept. 19, 1899, in Austria.

**Spotlights:** Paramount signed this dark-haired, Latin lover-type for *Sixty Cents an Hour* (1923). Cast as the great lover opposite Greta Garbo in her U.S. debut, MGM's *The Torrent* (1926). In 1931 he was the private eye Sam Spade in *The Maltese Falcon* at Warner Brothers. (Ten years later the remake with Humphrey Bogart would become a classic.)

**Sidelights:** Quit show biz in 1940 to pursue other business endeavors. Died: 1977.

**Robert Taylor**  *Actor* 1500 Vine

**Born:** Spangler Brugh; Aug. 5, 1911, in Filley, Nebr.

**Spotlights:** Taylor rivaled screen idol Clark Gable for number of love letters from fans.

He also beat Gable's record of remaining at one studio, MGM, for 24 years! MGM had landed him starting at $35 a week. Tall, dark, and very handsome, Taylor was originally cast in romantic, pretty boy leads. Later, *Yank at Oxford* (1938), *Three Comrades* (1939), *Quo Vadis* (1951), *Ivanhoe* (1953).

**Highlights:** Married to Barbara Stanwyck, co-star of *This is My Affair* (1937), from 1939–52. Died: 1969.

## Clara Bow  *Actress* 1500 Vine

**Born:** Aug. 15, 1905, in Brooklyn, N.Y.

**Spotlights:** Bobbed red hair, red cupid bow lips, beautiful eyes, and hip-thrusting posture helped her to portray the essence of the twenties gal, vivacious, emancipated, sexy. Began her career in 1922, but "The Hottest Jazz Baby" Films didn't become superhot until 1926 with *Mantrap* and *Kid Boots*. Their success led her to the phenomenal box office smash *It* (1927); known as the "It" girl. The number-one favorite actress in 1929. In 1931, with the coming of sound, she suffered a loss of popularity due to her nasal voice and tiresome antics.

**Sidelights:** Had her chow dogs' fur dyed red to match her hair! Died: 1965, of a heart attack.

*Shirley Temple*

## Don Wilson   *Announcer, actor*                    1500 Vine

**Born:** Sept. 1, 1900.

**Spotlights:** Rotund announcer-sidekick. Knew how to warm up the studio audience and keep the folks at home laughing, too, on "The Baby Snooks Show" (NBC, 1939); and hosting "Hollywood Theater" (NBC, 1951). Appeared regularly on radio and later on TV's "The Jack Benny Show" (1950–77). As Benny's foil, Wilson protested: "But Jack..." Died: 1982.

## Frances Langford   *Actress, singer*                    1500 Vine

**Born:** April 6, 1914, in Lakeland, Fla.

**Spotlights:** 5' 3", 108-lb., blond, with brown eyes; "radio's most popular singer in nationwide polls." Began as a lyric soprano, but her voice changed to a deep, smooth contralto after a tonsillectomy at age 16. First hired by Rudy Vallee in 1932, had her own show by 1933. Created "The Bickersons" with Don Ameche (first broadcast in 1947). Made 25 movie musicals including *Yankee Doodle Dandy* (1942) and *The Glenn Miller Story* (1954).

## Norma Talmadge   *Actress*                    1500 Vine

**Born:** May 26, 1893, in Niagara Falls, N.Y.

**Spotlights:** Extremely lovely brunette with brown eyes who usually played courageous, strong-willed, suffering women battling against the odds. Adept at comedy also. *A Tale of Two Cities* (1911), *Panthea* (1917). Made over 300 feature length pictures and shorts before sound forced her retirement.

**Highlights:** Married to producer Joseph Schenck (1917–26). Died: 1957, of a stroke.

## Bob Keeshan – Capt. Kangaroo   *Performer, creator*                    1500 Vine

**Born:** June 27, 1927, in Lynbrook, N.Y.

**Spotlights:** Working as assistant to Howdy Doody's Bob Smith, perfected Clarabelle the Clown. Created special programming for children including "Captain Kangaroo" (1955).

**Achievements:** 1982, two Emmys as star and producer of "Captain Kangaroo."

## Mack Swain   *Comedian*                    1500 Vine

**Born:** Feb. 16, 1876, in Salt Lake City, Utah.

**Spotlights:** Big, burly Keystone Kop with a bushy mustache; an all-around talented funnyman. Delightfully supported Charlie Chaplin as "Big Jim" McKay in *The Gold Rush* (1925). Died: 1935, of an internal hemorrhage.

## Fibber McGee and Molly   *Comedy team*                    1500 Vine

**Born:** Jim Jordan (Fibber) in 1897, in Peoria, Ill. Marian Driscoll (Molly), on April 15, 1897, also in Peoria, Ill.

**Spotlights:** A popular situation comedy radio show. "Fibber McGee and Molly" lived at 79 Wistful Vista. Neighbors and friends always dropped in and became part of the plot. The stars? Husband and wife comedy team Jim and Marian Jordan. NBC aired this long-running show (1935–52). They appeared together in *This Way Please* (1938) and three subsequent films.

## Joan Caulfield  *Actress*  1500 Vine

**Born:** Beatrice J. Caulfield; June 1, 1922, in Orange, N.J.

**Spotlights:** Was the pretty, feebleminded wife, Liz Cooper, in "My Favorite Husband" (1953–55), a suburban situation comedy. Starred as Sally Truesdale on the comedy series "Sally" (1957–58).

## Smokey Robinson  *Singer, composer*  1500 Vine

**Born:** Feb. 19, 1940, in Detroit, Mich.

**Spotlights:** Sensational rhythm-and-blues vocalist. In 1957 formed Smokey Robinson and the Miracles. Recorded hits: "Virgin Mary," "Agony and the Ecstasy," "Sweet Harmony"; more. Dissolved act to go solo. Singles: "Crusin'," "Keep from Crying." Albums: *Being with You, Deep in My Soul*

## Fanny Brice  *See page 86.*  1500 Vine

## The Jacksons  *Musical group*  1500 Vine

**Born:** Michael Joe; Aug. 29, 1958; Sigmund (Jackie), May 4, 1951; Toriano Aldry II (Tito), Oct. 15, 1953; Marlon David, March 12, 1957; and Steven Randall, Oct. 29, 1961.

**Spotlights:** Also known as the Jackson 5. Hit albums led to their own TV show from

*The Jacksons*

1976–77. Singles: "Shake Your Body (Down to the Ground)," "Enjoy Yourself/Show You the Way to Go," "State of Shock/Torture" sold over 100 million records in all.

## Leo McCarey  *Director, screenwriter, producer*  **1500 Vine**

**Born:** Oct. 3, 1898, in Los Angeles, Calif.

**Spotlights:** By the time the sparkle and the wit of the great 1930s comedies were sweeping a delighted nation, McCarey already held credits writing for and/or directing Laurel and Hardy. In 1933, he directed the Marx Brothers' romp, *Duck Soup.*

**Achievements:** 1937, Best Director Oscar for *The Awful Truth* with Cary Grant and Irene Dunne. 1944, Best Director and Screenplay for *Going My Way.* Died: 1969.

## Dick Clark  *TV personality, executive*  **Sunset and Vine**

**Born:** Nov. 30, 1929, in Mt. Vernon, N.Y.

**Spotlights:** Top pop music host of the 1950s, 1960s, 1970s, and 1980s on "American Bandstand." Host of "The $10,000 Pyramid" (in the seventies; now it's worth more money) and other well-received game shows. Head of his own production company. Youthful-looking and one of the richest men in America.

**Sidelights:** To my readers who are Walking the Walk: This corner of Sunset and Vine was the site of Universal Studios back in 1912!

*Dick Clark*

## B.P. Schulberg 🎥 *Producer* Sunset and Vine

**Born:** Jan 19, 1892, in Bridgeport, Conn.

**Spotlights:** Benjamin Percival Schulberg brought "The Hottest Jazz Baby in Films," Clara Bow, to Paramount in 1926 at $50 a week. He churned out a lot of 'B' pictures, but *It* (1927) started a fashion rage in America. Every girl wanted to have "It," plenty of personality, appeal, bobbed hair, and red, bee- stung lips. Died: 1957.

## Beach Boys 💿 *Rock 'n Roll musicians, singers, songwriters* Sunset and Vine

**Born:** Brian, June 20, 1942; Carl, Dec. 21, 1946; and Dennis Wilson, Dec. 4, 1944; Al Jardine, Sept. 3, 1942; and Mike Love, March 15, 1941. The group formed in 1960 with Brian Wilson writing most of their material. Recorded hits "Surfin' USA," "Surfer Girl," and "Good Vibrations." Albums: *Surfin' Safari, All Summer Long, Be True to Your School*, and *California Girls*.

**Sidelights:** Partially deaf Brian Wilson never surfed. Mike Love is the Wilson's first cousin. Paul McCartney of the Beatles was inspired by the Beach Boys' *Pet Sounds* album in 1966; *Sergeant Pepper* was the result! Died: 1983, Dennis Wilson by drowning.

## Spike Jones 💿 *Musical satirist, radio actor, bandleader* Sunset and Vine

**Born:** Lindley Jones; Dec. 14, 1911, in Long Beach, Calif.

**Spotlights:** Strange-looking man, extremely thin, but with a big head (and big talent). Radio: "The Spike Jones Show," comedy variety, also featured Jones's band, The City Slickers, and Dorothy Shay; "The Park Avenue Hillbilly" (first broadcast in 1940). TV: "The Spike Jones Show" featured wife Helen Grayo and his band (NBC, 1954–61). Recorded what many classify as fruitcake music. Still funny: "Dinner Music for People Who Aren't Very Hungry." On-screen debut in *Thank Your Lucky Stars* (1943). Died: 1965 from emphysema.

## Quincy Jones 💿 *Performer (trumpet), composer, conductor, arranger,*
*producer* Sunset and Vine

**Born:** March 14, 1933, in Chicago, Ill.

**Spotlights:** Multitalented, creative, respected arranger for Count Basie, Peggy Lee, others. His diverse talents include producing Michael Jackson's multiplatinum album, *Thriller.*

**Achievements:** More than 10 gold records, a dozen Grammys, and a 1977 Emmy for "Roots."

## Barry Sullivan 📺 *See page 185.* Sunset and Vine

## Neil Sedaka 💿 *Singer, songwriter* Sunset and Vine

**Born:** March 13, 1939, in Brooklyn, N.Y.

**Spotlights:** Double-tracked himself on background vocals for unique sound in early 1960s. Good mixture of writer and performer; still entertains today. Singles: "Calendar

Girl"; "Happy Birthday, Sweet Sixteen." Albums: *Come See About Me*; *Solitaire*. The title "Singer, Songwriter, Melodymaker" aptly describes Sedaka.

**Helene Costello**  *Actress*           **Sunset and Vine**
**Born:** June 21, 1903, in New York.
**Spotlights:** Daughter of Maurice Costello, sister of Dolores Costello; their early screen and dancing performances together were well received. On-screen as an adult in 1925. Beauty was admired in *The Love Toy* (1926). Her popularity diminished with the advent of sound. Died: 1957.

**George Fenneman** *Host, announcer*           **Sunset and Vine**
**Born:** Nov. 10, 1919.
**Spotlights:** "You Bet Your Life" (1950–61) contestants always tried to win the extra $100 by saying that night's secret word, "It's a common word, something you see every day." Listeners always enjoyed this friendly announcer.

**Oliver Hardy** *Comedian, film director*           **Sunset and Vine**
**Born:** Jan. 18, 1892, in Harlen, Ga.
**Spotlights:** This lovable, short-tempered comedian with the funny little mustache (almost nonexistent on his round, chubby face with the trademark double chin) crossed paths with thin, clownish Stan Laurel in *Lucky Dog* (1917). But it wasn't until 1927 when they teamed together for comedy shorts and features that they made their mark on history. Roly-poly Hardy nervously twiddled his tie or looked into the camera in disgust after reprimanding the cry-baby Laurel with "Another fine mess you've gotten me into this time!" Silents: *The Battle of the Century* (1927), *Should Married Men Go Home?* (1928). Talkies: *Unaccustomed as We Are* (1929), *Another Fine Mess* (1930), *Pack Up Your Troubles* (1932), more. Died: 1957, following a stroke.

**David Wolper** *Producer*           **Sunset and Vine**
**Born:** Jan. 11, 1928, in New York.
**Spotlights:** Highly intelligent talent with strong insight. Specialized in documentaries before venturing into entertainment: "Welcome Back, Kotter" (1975–79) and "Roots" (1977). Also feature films.
**Achievements:** 1976–77 Emmy; 1978–79, Emmy.

**Franklin Pangborn:** *Actor*           **Sunset and Vine**
**Born:** Jan. 23, 1893, in Newark, N.J.
**Spotlights:** *Exit Smiling* (1926) was an appropriate title for this very funny character actor with an uppity manner. As a hotel or bank manager, he superciliously raised his eyebrows, sniffed at his employees, and haughtily turned his back on them. Hilarious in Frank Capra's *Mr. Deeds Goes to Town* (1936), with Gary Cooper, and *The Bank Dick* (1940), starring W. C. Fields. Died: 1958.

# · 1501 VINE ·

**Edward Small**   *Producer*　　　　Sunset and Vine

**Born:** Feb. 1, 1891, in Brooklyn, N.Y.
**Spotlights:** A jack-of-all-trades in Hollywood: Went from actor to agent to producer and executive producer. *Witness for the Prosecution* (1958). Died: 1977.

**Anne Jeffreys**  *Actress, singer*　　　　Sunset and Vine

**Born:** Anne Carmichael; Jan. 26, 1923, in Goldsboro, N.C.
**Spotlights:** Very pretty, very classic. Marion Kirby's ghost on "Topper" (1953–56); her husband co-starred with her as George Kirby.

**Johnny Mathis**  *Singer*　　　　Sunset and Vine

**Born:** Sept. 30, 1935, in San Francisco, Calif.
**Spotlights:** Velvety-voiced, extremely smooth performer. Singles: "Certain Smile," "Chances, Are," "Misty," "Too Much, Too Little, Too Late."

*Johnny Mathis*

**Binnie Barnes**  *Actress* Sunset and Vine
**Born:** Gertrude Barnes; March 25, 1905, in England.
**Spotlights:** Sophisticated, wise-cracking, caustic blonde in *Diamond Jim* (1935); *Holiday* (1938).
**Highlights:** Married Columbia Pictures executive producer Mike Frankovich in 1940.
**Sidelights:** Employed as a milkmaid before she broke into two-reel comedies.

**Percy Faith**  *Composer, conductor, pianist* 1501 Vine
**Born:** April 7, 1908, in Toronto, Canada.
**Spotlights:** Percy Faith's Orchestra was featured on "The Carnation Contented Hour" (first aired by NBC, 1931). Listeners tuned in faithfully to that show and to "The Woolworth Hour" and "The Coca-Cola Hour" 1940–50. Songs: "Buy a Bond for Victory," and "My Heart Cries for You." Died: 1976.

**Harold Lloyd** *Actor* 1501 Vine
**Born:** April 20, 1893, in Burchard, Nebr.
**Spotlights:** Lloyd, Chaplin, and Keaton were the three masters of comedy in the twenties. Lloyd in *Safety Last* (1923) shows off the zany craziness which made his characterization of "a regular fellow" with black horn-rimmed glasses so superbly funny. His voice fell flat with the onset of the talkies.
**Achievements:** 1952 Oscar, "Master comedian and good citizen." Audiences loved his clean-cut, wholesome image.
**Sidelights:** Lloyd acted out all of his own stunts; in *Haunted Spooks* (1920) a bomb explosion cost him his right thumb and forefinger and caused extensive nerve damage. Died: 1971, of cancer.

**Rick Nelson** *Singer, actor* 1501 Vine
**Born:** Eric Nelson; May 8, 1940, in Teaneck, N.J.
**Spotlights:** Albums: *All My Best, I Need You.* Singles: "Be Bop Baby/Stood Up," "Dream Lover/Rave On," "Hello, Mary Lou/Sweeter Than You." Died: 1985, in a plane crash.

**Jack Benny** *See page 316.* 1501 Vine

**Clint Walker** *Actor* 1501 Vine
**Born:** Norman Walker; May 30, 1927, in Hartford, Ill.
**Spotlights:** Vital, tall, dark-haired hunk with husky voice. He-man star, Cheyenne Bodie, a western adventurer, on "Cheyenne" (1955–63). Sixteen movies include *The Dirty Dozen* (1967), more.

**Jackie Cooper** *Actor, musician* 1501 Vine
**Born:** John Cooper, Jr.; Sept. 15, 1921, in Los Angeles, Calif.
**Spotlights:** Well-loved child star since age 3. One of the kids in the Our Gang film

series. Excelled in his first starring role, *Skippy* (1931); *The Champ* (1931); and *Treasure Island* (1934). Later films include *Superman* (1978) and *Superman II* (1980). Extremely successful TV director of "Mash," "Hennessey," more.
**Achievements:** 1974, 1979, Emmys.

### Alice White  *Actress*
1501 Vine

**Born:** Alva White; Aug. 28, 1907, in Patterson, N.J.
**Spotlights:** A real-life secretary-turned-silent-screen-star-turned-real-life-secretary, pretty Miss White was at the top in *Naughty Boy* and *Hot Stuff* (both 1929); frequently compared with the "It" girl, Clara Bow. Died: 1983.

### Belle Bennett *Actress*
1501 Vine

**Born:** Oct. 21, 1892, in Milaca, Minn.
**Spotlights:** This leading lady's ethereal looks melted hearts in a number of slients: *Flesh and Spirit* (1922), *Stella Dallas* (1925), *Playing with Souls* (1925). Worked with director John Ford *Mother Machree* (1928). Died: 1932.

### Major Bowes *Actor, composer*
1501 Vine

**Born:** 1874, in San Francisco, Calif.
**Spotlights:** "Major Bowes and His Original Amateur Hour," talent contest. "The Wheel of Fortune goes 'round and 'round and where she stops nobody knows." Long- running show, first broadcast NBC, 1934; CBS, 1936; ABC, 1948. Discovered soprano Beverly Sills when she was 6 years old. In 1937, another hopeful, Frank Sinatra, sang his way to superstardom. Died: 1946.

### Keenan Wynn *Actor*
1501 Vine

**Born:** Francis Wynn; July 27, 1916, in New York.
**Spotlights:** Character actor (with MGM for 13 years), who appeared in countless TV dramatic specials including the production of "Requiem for a Heavyweight." Kodiak on "Troubleshooters" (1959–60), and Willard (Digger) Barnes (1979–80) on "Dallas." In all, Wynn was in 250 TV shows, 220 films, plus stage productions.
**Sidelights:** Started in show biz as Ed Wynn's son. Commented on being a character actor instead of a leading man: "Let the stars take the blame, I had the fun." Died: 1986, from cancer.

### Loretta Lynn *Singer*
1501 Vine

**Born:** Loretta Webb; April 14, 1935, in Butchers Hollow, Ky.
**Spotlights:** Country-and-western singing sensation whose courageous life story was made into the film, *Coal Miner's Daughter* (1979), starring Sissy Spacek. TV, too.
**Achievements:** 1971, Grammy, country vocal.

### Carl Smith *Singer, guitarist*
1501 Vine

**Born:** March 15, 1927, in Maynardsville, Tenn.

**Spotlights:** Dozens of top-rated country and western hits spanning decades. Took off in 1951 with "Let's Live a Little." Songs: "Just Don't Stand There," "Kisses Don't Lie," "Foggy River," more.

**Leo Carillo**    *See page 259.*      **1501 Vine**

**Gale Storm**    *See page 172.*      **1501 Vine**

**Harry Carey**    *Actor*      **1501 Vine**
**Born:** Jan. 16, 1878, in New York.
**Spotlights:** Great, early silent screen western star who made a smooth transition to versatile supporting roles. On-screen from 1909 to 1948 (*Red River* and *So Dear to My Heart* released after his death). Pictures include *Cheyenne's Pal* (1917) and *Mr. Smith Goes to Washington* (1939). Died: 1947, of heart disease.

**Billy Dee Williams**    *Actor*      **1501 Vine**
**Born:** April 6, 1937, in New York.
**Spotlights:** On-screen magnetism and an outstanding smile. Handsome, debonair, leading man in *Lady Sings the Blues* (1972). Supporting role in *The Empire Strikes Back, Star Wars II* (1980). Broadway and TV celebrity too.

**Joan Davis**    *Actress*      **1501 Vine**
**Born:** Madonna Davis; June 29, 1907, in St. Paul, Minn.
**Spotlights:** Top-notch comedienne with a hilariously expressive face and big mouth. *If You Knew Susie* (1948); *Love that Brute* (1950). CBS radio gave her "The Joan Davis Show" (1945). NBC TV starred her in "I Married Joan" (1952–55), with Jim Backus as her husband, Judge Bradley Stevens. Died: 1961, from a heart attack.

**Edith Storey**    *Actress*      **1501 Vine**
**Born:** March 18, 1892.
**Spotlights:** Lovely talent, very popular from 1912 to 1921; *Lincoln's Gettysburg Address* (1912); *The Dust of Egypt* (1915).

**Angela Lansbury**    *See page 64.*      **1501 Vine**

**Jack Pickford**    *Actor*      **1501 Vine**
**Born:** Jack Smith; Aug. 18, 1896, in Canada.
**Spotlights:** His older sister Mary had proved the Pickford name was as good as gold at the box office and he cashed in: *Poor Little Peppina* (1916), *Tom Sawyer* (1917).
**Highlights:** Married to Olive Thomas, "the most beautiful girl in the world," a Ziegfeld Follies star and Alberto Vargas model until her sudden death in 1920. Died: 1933.

## John Ericson  *Actor* 1501 Vine

**Born:** Joseph Meibes; Sept. 25, 1926, in Germany.
**Spotlights:** 6' 2", 180-lb., light brown hair and gray-green eyes. Boyish, good-looking detective Sam Bolt in "Honey West" (1965–66). Numerous TV movies. Before a 1954 contract with MGM, he had three years of stage work. Loved working with Elizabeth Taylor in *Rhapsody* that same year. Brought to U.S. to escape Nazi oppression in 1930.

## Marjorie Reynolds  *Actress, dancer* 1501 Vine

**Born:** Marjorie Goodspeed; Aug. 12, 1921, in Buhl, Idaho.
**Spotlights:** A pretty blonde with blue eyes, she portrayed the tolerant wife, Peg, in the situation comedy, "The Life of Riley" (1953–58). Screen headliner since age 5. Best remembered in *Holiday Inn* (1942), with Bing Crosby and Fred Astaire; more.

## Frances Langford  *Singer, actress* 1501 Vine

**Born:** April 4, 1914, in Lakeland, Fla.
**Spotlights:** Petite, blonde singer with a southern appeal and hourglass figure. Appeared in musicals of the late thirties and forties, *The Hit Parade* (1937), *Yankee Doodle Dandy* (1942). She played herself in *The Glenn Miller Story* (1954). Radio vocalist on "The Bob Hope Show" (NBC, 1934) and later toured with him during World War II. Blanche Bickerson on "The Bickersons" (CBS, 1947).

## Louis Lumiere  *Inventor, producer, director* 1533 Vine

**Born:** Oct. 5, 1864, in France.
**Spotlights:** Called "the father of cinema." With his brother Auguste, invented the camera projector (based on Edison's work) to show *motion* pictures in 1895. By 1900, the Lumieres had produced over 2,000 real-life pictures and had directed 60. These were not standard feature films, but documentary-type newsreels. Died: 1948.

## Lina Basquette  *Dancer, actress* 1533 Vine

**Born:** Lina Baskette; April 19, 1907, in San Mateo, Calif.
**Spotlights:** Dancing, black-haired beauty of the Ziegfeld Follies who basked in her celebrity status *Juvenile Dancer* 1916; *The Godless Girl* (1929), in between court battles over the estate of her late husband, Sam Warner, and over their daughter, of whom she lost custody to the surviving brother, Harry.
**Sidelights:** An animal lover, she moved to Pennsylvania to breed champion Great Danes.

## Perez Prado  *Pianist, bandleader* 1533 Vine

**Born:** 1922, in Matanas, Cuba.
**Spotlights:** Albums: *Grandes Exitos De, This Is the Decade of the 30s, Decade of the 50s*. Singles: "Cherry Pink and Apple Blossom White." Toured America with Latin band in 1951, entertaining audiences with mambo music.

**Pat O'Brien**  *Actor*                               1533 Vine

**Born:**   William J.P. O'Brien; Nov. 11, 1899, in Milwaukee, Wisc.
**Spotlights:**   Extremely popular in both good and evil roles in the 1930s and 1940s.
Especially identifiable as the Irish priest or cop. *Angels with Dirty Faces* (1938). Later
*Some Like it Hot* (1959). One of Hollywood's reliables, with over 100 pictures before
*The End* (1978). Died: 1983.

**Betty Furness**  *See page 55.*                         1533 Vine

**Roger Williams**  *Pianist, composer, arranger*           1533 Vine

**Born:**   Louis Weertz; Oct. 1, 1926, in Omaha, Nebr.
**Spotlights:**   Attended the Juilliard School of Music. Albums: *Music of the 1940s;
Music of the 1950s, Music of the 1970s, To Amadeus with Love, Way We Were.*
Singles: "Almost Paradise," "Born Free," "Impossible Dream."

**Paul Weston**  *Conductor, composer, author*            1533 Vine

**Born:**   P. Wetstein; March 12, 1912, in Springfield, Mass.
**Spotlights:**   Master of mood music. Arranged for Rudy Vallee, Tommy Dorsey, Bing
Crosby, Ella Fitzgerald, Kate Smith, Sarah Vaughan. Albums: *Cinema Cameos, Easy
Jazz.*

**June Allyson**  *Actress*                             1533 Vine

**Born:**   Ella Geisman; Oct. 7, 1917, in Bronx, N.Y.
**Spotlights:**   Allyson's husky voice and toothpaste smile helped her leap from Broadway chorus lines to MGM musicals. Her warm, personable on-screen appearances
endeared her in "the girl next door" roles throughout the 1940s; *Little Women*
(1949). Same qualities enabled her to play "the dutiful wife" throughout the 1950s;
*The McConnell Story* (1955).
**Highlights:**   Her much publicized marriage to Dick Powell (1945–63) ended sadly
when he died of cancer.

**Mel Torme**  *Singer, actor*                          1541 Vine

**Born:**   Sept. 13, 1925, in Chicago, Ill.
**Spotlights:**   His nickname, "The Velvet Fog," says it all. Dynamic jazz spirit who cooks
whenever he performs. Albums: *Lulu's Back in Town, California Suite,* and *Easy to
Remember.* Drums and arranger. On-screen in 1943 in *Higher and Higher.*

**Steve Allen** 🎤 *See page 141.*                                          1541 Vine

**Steve Lawrence and Eydie Gorme**  *Singers, actors*    1541 Vine

**Born:**   Lawrence: Sidney Liebowitz; July 8, 1935; Eydie: Aug. 16, 1931; both in New
York.
**Spotlights:**   Harmonious husband and wife singing team. The duo made their TV

debut on "The Tonight Show," hosted by pal, Steve Allen.
**Achievements:** 1979, Emmys for "Steve and Eydie Celebrate Irving Berlin." 1960, Grammy, vocal group; 1966, Grammy, female.

## John Wayne  *Actor, producer, director* 1541 **Vine**

**Born:** Marion Michael Morrison; May 26, 1907, in Winterset, Iowa. Nicknamed the "Duke."
**Spotlights:** His bigger-than-life characterization of Ringo Kidd in John Ford's 1939 western, *Stagecoach*. But *She Wore a Yellow Ribbon* (1949) was Wayne's favorite. Of his 50-year career, he once said, "I can't remember if I've made 200 or 400 films." He was the highest paid actor in the world (1956). *Time* Magazine said he was "the biggest moneymaker in movie history, nearly $400 million."
**Achievements:** 1969, Best Actor Oscar for *True Grit*. Died: 1979, of complications stemming from cancer treatments.

## Merv Griffin ◢ *TV personality* 1541 **Vine**

**Born:** Mervyn Griffin; June 6, 1925, in San Mateo, Calif.
**Spotlights:** Popular, friendly, syndicated host of "The Merv Griffin Show" (1965–86). Quietly amassed a fortune from his TV production companies, game, quiz, dance shows, including "Wheel of Fortune."
**Achievements:** 1974, Emmy, writing; 1982, Emmy, host.

*John Wayne*

## Ed Wynn  *Actor*                                    1541 Vine

**Born:** Edwin Leopold; Nov. 9, 1886, in Philadelphia, Pa.

**Spotlights:** A former vaudeville clown and Ziegfeld Follies entertainer who became "The Fire Chief" for Texaco on radio on 1932. Strong drama performer too; *The Diary of Anne Frank* (1959). He loves to laugh in *Mary Poppins* (1964).

**Achievements:** 1949, Emmy, best live show "The Ed Wynn Show"; the first Emmy for a TV series!

**Highlights:** Father of actor Keenan Wynn. Died: 1966.

## Shirley Jones  *Singer, actress*                    1541 Vine

**Born:** March 31, 1934, in Smithston, Pa.

**Spotlights:** Theatrical debut in *Lady in the Dark* with the Pittsburgh Civic Light Opera. Wonderful performances on Broadway including the musical *South Pacific*. On-screen in the musical *Oklahoma!* (1955), *The Music Man* (1962). TV: The Partridge Family" co-starring stepson David Cassidy. Commercial spokeswoman.

**Achievements:** 1960, Best Supporting Actress Oscar for *Elmer Gantry*.

## Roy Acuff  *Singer, musician*                       1541 Vine

**Born:** Sept. 15, 1903, in Maynardsville, Tex.

**Spotlights:** Featured on radio's "The Grand Ole Opry" (1925 on) and became a fixture on radio and TV's "Hee Haw." Hit albums include: *Backstage at the Grand Ole Opry, I Wonder If God Likes Country Music, Gospel Glory, Night Train to Memphis*.

*Shirley Jones*                    *Michael Jackson*

## Eleanor Powell  *Actress* 1541 Vine

**Born:** Nov. 21, 1912, in Springfield, Mass.
**Spotlights:** MGM created a string of musicals around "The World's Greatest Tap Dancer." This leggy, vivacious hoofer "put 'em down like a man," according to the king himself, Fred Astaire, in *Broadway Melody of 1940*.
**Highlights:** She realized her inadequacies in acting and only made four pictures after marrying actor Glenn Ford (1943–59).
**Sidelights:** In midlife she was ordained a minister of the Unity Church. Died: 1982.

## Les Paul and Mary Ford  *Singers, musician, inventor* 1541 Vine

**Born:** Lester Polfus; June 9, 1915 in Waukesha, Wisc; Colleen Summers; July 7, 1924, in Pasadena, Calif.
**Spotlights:** Roots in country, then jazz. Husband and wife singing team. He also played guitar. Singles: "How High the Moon" and "Vaya Con Dios" (May God Be With You). Inventor Paul created the solid body electric guitar; 8-track tape recorder; overdubbing and other important musical devices. Died: Mary Ford, 1977.

## Michael Jackson  *Broadcaster* 1541 Vine

**Born:** Apr. 16, 1934, in England.
**Spotlights:** "From age 10 my goal was to work in Hollywood. I grew up in World War II Britain, and every luxury thing was represented in movies from Hollywood. It was a romantic view." He is an intelligent, humorous, informative talk show host with a unique delivery. His lively yet incisive approach to questioning guests and oftentimes biting commentary culminate in the top-rated KABC talk radio program heard nationwide by 3.1 million listeners every weekday.
**Achievements:** Seven Emmys; four Golden Mikes. Regarding the Walk of Fame: "It's a truly unexpected fulfillment of a dream and ambition. Not seeing my star in the pavement, but all that has occurred to me in this city in 25 years that led to that opportunity."
**Highlights:** Married to Alana Ladd, who is daughter of Alan Ladd and Sue Carol (both of whom are recipients of these bronze tributes on the boulevard).
**Sidelights:** His son commented about his star: "That's wonderful Dad, but who will know it's you? (His son was referring to another Michael Jackson, the singer. Actually, the singer is listed with the AFTRA union as Michael J. Jackson. The union rule is if two performers have the exact name and spelling, the newcomer must use his/her middle initial, so fans and credits will not get confused.)

## Richard Rowland  *Pioneer producer.* 1541 Vine

**Born:** 1881, in New York.
**Spotlights:** Became a film distributor at the age of 18; millionaire by age 30. Founded Metro Film Corporation in 1914; he was president and Louis B.Mayer was secretary. Credited with bringing stage celebrities to screen and discovering Rudolph Valentino. In later years he was an executive at Fox. Died: 1947.

## Dick Van Patten  ■  *Actor*                    1541 Vine

**Born:**  Dec. 9, 1928, in Kew Gardens, N.Y.

**Spotlights:**  On Broadway when he was 7 years old in *Tapestry and Gray*. Later, his skills helped to make "Mama" (1949–56) one of TV's earliest family success stories; he played the son, Nels. In "Eight is Enough," (I'll vouch for that, I'm one of eight children), he played the father, Tom Bradford (1977–81).

**Sidelights:**  Van Patten's response to the unveiling of his star on the Walk of Fame: "Please curb your dog."

## Virginia Cherrill  🎥  *Actress*                    1541 Vine

**Born:**  April 12, 1908, in Carthage, Ill.

**Spotlights:**  Cherrill's film debut as the blind flower girl who regains her sight thanks to the love and financial support of "the Tramp" in Charlie Chaplin's sentimental comedy *City Lights* (1931) instantly made her a star. It came as a big surprise to the lovely 23-year-old who had zero desire to be an actress and absolutely no prior experience. A chance meeting with the artistic motion picture genius Chaplin, with his keen eye for talent, altered her life forever. She became an accomplished actress after three years spent under the master's meticulous direction, that included months of painful retakes.

**Highlights:**  Married to actor Cary Grant (1933–35).

## Joe Pasternak  🎥  *Producer*                    1541 Vine

**Born:**  Sept. 19, 1901, in Hungary.

**Spotlights:**  "To me, the writer was always the most important thing." *It Started with Eve* (1941), *Music for Millions* (1945), *The Merry Widow* (1952), *The Courtship of Eddie's Father* (1963). Produced over 85 motion pictures, many of them winning awards in Berlin, Vienna, Budapest, and Hollywood. "A good producer has to be a psychiatrist and a chiseler; you have to know when to tell the truth, and when to lie, when to be kind and when to insist," Pasternak philosophized.

## Frederick Stock  💿  *Musician*                    1541 Vine

**Born:**  Nov. 11, 1872, in Germany.

**Spotlights:**  Master of the baton; brilliantly conducted the Chicago Symphony in 1905 and continued to do so over 3½ decades. Died: 1942.

## Jamie Farr  ■  *Actor.*                    1541 Vine

**Born:**  Jameel Farah on July 1, 1934, in Toledo, OH.

**Spotlights:**  Originally hired for one day's work on "M*A*S*H," the 4077th Mobile Army Surgical Hospital, stationed in Korea. His hilarious characterization of a fake transvestite attempting to get thrown out for a Section Eight (mentally unbalanced discharge) delighted viewers. Fans loved his hairy legs under a skirt, and his chomping cigar antics (1973-83). Film debut as the mentally retarded student Santini in *The Blackboard Jungle* (1955).

**Sidelights:**   While in the U.S. Army, Farr served in Korea (two years); the only cast member of "M*A*S*H" to have actually served there.

### Andrea King    *Actress*                                         1541 **Vine**

**Born:**   Georgette Barry on Feb. 7, 1915, in France.
**Spotlights:**   Extensive stage and film experience before appearing on TV: "Maverick," "Perry Mason," "The Days of Our Lives"; commercials, too.

### Colleen Moore   *Actress*                                         1549 **Vine**

**Born:**   Kathleen Morrison; Aug. 19, 1900, in Port Huron, Mich.
**Spotlights:**   Pretty, vivacious, large-eyed, bow-lipped talent who captured the fun and independent spirit of free-thinking young women in the 1920s: *Flaming Youth* (1923), *The Perfect Flapper* (1924), *Twinkletoes* (1926).

### Brian Donlevy   *Actor*                                         1549 **Vine**

**Born:**   Grosson B. Donlevy; Feb. 9, 1899, in Ireland.
**Spotlights:**   Very handsome, mustached action man whose Steve Mitchell in "Dangerous Assignment" (1951–52) allowed audiences a closer look at his strong physique so often utilized during his bright film career, which included *Beau Geste* (1939). Died: 1972, of throat cancer.

### Ruth Hussey   *Actress*                                         1549 **Vine**

**Born:**   Ruth O'Rourke; Oct. 30, 1914, in Providence, R.I.

*Colleen Moore*

245

**Spotlights:** Hussey did an excellent characterization of a smart, guarded, "rag" photographer in George Cukor's *The Philadelphia Story* (1940), starring Katharine Hepburn, Cary Grant, and journalist James Stewart; 33 more pictures.

### Farley Granger  *Actor* 1549 Vine

**Born:** July 1, 1925, in San Jose, Calif.
**Spotlights:** Dark-haired, handsome, vulnerable type who appeared in numerous plays on "The U. S. Steel Hour" (sporadically, 1953–63). Specials include "The Challenger" (1968), and "The Lives of Jenny Dolan" (1975). In 1976 originated role of Dr. Will Vernon, in the soap opera, "One Life to Live." Film debut in *North Star* (1943); 31 other pictures.

### Warren William 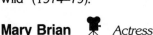 *Actor* 1549 Vine

**Born:** Warren W. Krech; Dec. 2, 1895, in Aitkin, Minn.
**Spotlights:** Dark-haired, mustached leading man since 1920. Celebrated as the intelligent sleuth in the *Lone Wolf* series (1939–43). Cast by Cecil B. DeMille as Julius Caesar to Claudette Colbert's *Cleopatra* (1934). Died: 1948.

### Arthur Godfrey *See page 158.* 1549 Vine

### Lorne Greene *Actor* 1555 Vine

**Born:** Feb. 12, 1915, in Canada.
**Spotlights:** Star of "Bonanza," which takes its place in TV history as the second longest-running western (1959–73). His character, Ben Cartwright, was the widower father of three sons and owner of the 1,000-square mile Ponderosa Ranch. His real love for the outdoors was apparent in his nature show, "Lorne Green's Last of the Wild" (1974–79).

### Mary Brian *Actress* 1555 Vine

**Born:** Louise Dantzler; Feb. 17, 1908, in Coriscana, Tex.
**Spotlights:** The petite brunette's debut as Wendy in *Peter Pan* (1924) typecast her in sweet roles; *The Virginian* (1929).

### Marie Windsor *Actress* 1555 Vine

**Born:** Emily M. Bertelson; Dec. 11, 1922, in Marysvale, Vt.
**Spotlights:** Former beauty contest winner who was very good at being very bad as a leading lady, she made 'B' movies watchable. Convincing in *Force of Evil* (1948), *The Unholy Wife* (1957); more.

### Alec Guinness *Actor* 1555 Vine

**Born:** April 2, 1914, in England.
**Spotlights:** Versatile talent who played eight different roles (one as a woman) in *Kind*

*Hearts and Coronets* (1949). *The Lavender Hill Mob* (1951) and *Doctor Zhivago* (1965) were more evidence of his acting gifts.
**Achievements:** 1957, Best Actor Oscar, *The Bridge on the River Kwai*. Knighted in 1959. 1980, honorary Oscar.

## Max Steiner 🎥 *Composer* 1555 Vine

**Born:** Maximilian Steiner; May 10, 1888, in Austria.
**Spotlights:** "Music by Max Steiner" on "The Most Magnificent Picture Ever," *Gone with the Wind* (1939). Although he was nominated for an Academy Award (and that film won 10), he did not receive one for that work.
**Achievements:** Academy Awards for the following scores: 1935, *The Informer*; 1942, *Now, Voyager*; 1944, *Since You Went Away*. Died: 1971.

## Jules White 🎥 *Director, producer* 1555 Vine

**Born:** 1900, in Budapest, Hungary.
**Spotlights:** Executive in charge of Columbia Pictures' short films unit from 1933–59. Zany hand behind the Three Stooges comedies in 136 comedy shorts! In 1929, created talking dog comedies at MGM called the Barkies. Died: 1985.

## George Carlin 🎤 *Comedian, actor.* 1555 Vine

**Born:** May 12, 1938, in the Bronx, NY.
**Spotlights:** "I grew up in white Harlem." Later, while this 17-year-old was enlisted in the U.S. Air Force, he got a job moonlighting at radio station KJOE, in Shreveport, LA. Arrived in Hollywood in 1962; TV debut in 1965 on "The Merv Griffin Show." He's been a top-rated stand-up comedian ever since. Guest of first "Saturday Night Live" (1975). About his screenwork — *With Six You Get Eggrolls* (1967); *Car Wash* (1978); and *Outrageous Fortune* (1987) — he said, "I try to do a film every ten years."
**Achievements:** A high school drop-out, he makes an average of $10,000 per college performance (has a high school equivalency diploma). 1972 Grammy Award. Wrote book, *Sometimes a Little Brain Damage Can Help*. About his star on the Walk of Fame he said: "At least they've moved me ten feet from the gutter."
**Sidelights:** Arrested in 1972 for saying: "Seven Words You Can Never Use on Television" at the Milwaukee summerfest.

## Robert Shaw 💿 *Conductor.* 1559 Vine

**Born:** Apr. 30, 1916, in Red Bluff, CA.
**Spotlights:** Music pioneer. Established chorale singing as an American tradition. Experts agree that all of his recordings are good and many are absolutely inspired. Director of the choral departments of the Julliard School from 1945-48. Founded the Robert Shaw Chorale, toured internationally through 1966. Albums: *America the Beautiful, Christmas Hymns and Carols, Sea Shanties;* more.
**Sidelights:** Not to be confused with actor Robert Shaw (d. 1978).

# ⋆ 1601 VINE ⋆

## Bob Burns  *Actor*                    1601 Vine

**Born:**  Aug. 2, 1893, in Van Buren, Ark.

**Spotlights:**  He amused audiences with a hillbilly twang and basic down-to-earth concepts. *Quick Millions* (1931) started his career in the thirties. Radio: The Arkansas Traveler on "The Bob Burns Show" (1941). Previously broadcast with Rudy Vallee and Bing Crosby.

**Sidelights:**  The weapon bazooka was named after a musical instrument he played on his show. Died: 1956.

## Frank Crumit  *Host, author, composer, singer*                    1601 Vine

**Born:**  Sept. 26, 1889, in Jackson, Ohio.

**Spotlights:**  Captain of the men's team on the quiz show, "The Battle of the Sexes" (NBC, first broadcast 1938). Quiz show host of "Mr. Adams and Mrs. Eve," again pitting the sexes against each other (NBC, 1942). His song "The Buckeye Battle Cry" became Ohio State University's football tune. Other songs include: "Gay Caballero," and "Abdul Abulbul Amir." Died: 1943.

## Alan Ladd  *Actor*                    1601 Vine

**Born:**  Sept. 3, 1913, in Hot Springs, Ark.

**Spotlights:**  This small (5' 5" or 5' 6") light-haired leading man enjoyed his greatest popularity during the 1940s, thanks to his sharp wife and agent, Sue Carol. He shot to stardom paired with the seductive Veronica Lake (5' 2") in *This Gun for Hire* (1942); the trench coat he wore in the picture became his trademark. The Ladd-Lake team shared that magical screen chemistry, Ladd unsmiling and cool and Lake husky-voiced and blonde, and two more pictures followed that same year: *The Glass Key* and *Star Spangled Rhythm*. Critics claim Ladd gave his best performance in George Steven's *Shane* (1953). Ladd turned down the role of Jett Rink in *Giant* (1956); James Dean, the studio's second choice, was thrilled to accept it.

**Highlights:**  Son Alan Ladd, Jr., is a Hollywood producer and studio executive. Two other children are also successful in the business.

**Sidelights:**  Ladd once said, "I'm the most insecure guy in Hollywood." His lack of stature bothered him tremendously, and it bothered other co-stars such as Sophia Loren who didn't like acting in a ditch to make Ladd appear taller. His pain went beyond the tremendous struggles of any Hollywood actor. Died: 1964.

## Audie Murphy  *Actor*                    1601 Vine

**Born:**  June 20, 1924, in Kingston, Tex.

**Spotlights:**  Murphy was cast most often as a military or western hero. Occasionally he got a break from this routine and played villains, *Kansas Raiders*, as Jesse James.

Over 40 pictures, including *The Red Badge of Courage* (1951) and *To Hell and Back* (1955), based on his autobiography; he played himself.

**Achievements:** The most decorated soldier during World War II; collected 28 medals, including the Congressional Medal of Honor!

**Sidelights:** About his long career in westerns, he said, "The scripts are the same, only the horses have changed." Died: 1971, in a plane crash.

## Preston Sturges   *Director, screenwriter*   1601 Vine

**Born:** Edmond P. Biden on Aug. 29, 1898, in Chicago, Ill.

**Spotlights:** The maestro of screwball comedy, both writing, in the 1930s and directing, in the 1940s; *Easy Living* (1937).

**Achievements:** 1940 Academy Award for script, *The Great McGinty* (Paramount), which he also directed. Died: 1959.

## Paul Whiteman   *See page 166.*   1601 Vine

## Henry Fonda   *Actor*   1601 Vine

**Born:** May 16, 1905, in Grand Island, Nebr.

**Spotlights:** He was quiet, patient, and honest and spoke with a definite midwestern drawl. Surprised himself with his long film career, which he expected would last only two years. Went the distance 1935–81 with 100 films, including, *Young Mr. Lincoln* (1939), *Grapes of Wrath* (1940), and *Mister Roberts* (1955).

**Achievements:** 1980, honorary Oscar; 1981, Best Actor, *On Golden Pond*; 1948 and 1979, Tonys.

**Highlights:** His second wife, Frances Brokaw was the mother of Jane Fonda and Peter Fonda.

**Sidelights:** Marlon Brando's mother, Dorothy, prodded the shy, 20- year-old Fonda on stage at the Omaha Community Playhouse. Baby Marlon watched the rehearsal from his crib. Not bad entertainment for a one-year old! Died: 1982.

## Gisele MacKenzie   *Singer, actress*   1601 Vine

**Born:** Marie Gisele La Fleche; Jan. 10, 1927, in Canada.

**Spotlights:** Vocalist on the music show "Your Hit Parade" (1953–57) before being offered "The Gisele MacKenzie Show" (1957–58). She also danced and acted.

## Lawrence Welk   *See page 66.*   1601 Vine

## Renee Adoree   *Actress*   1601 Vine

**Born:** Jeanne de La Fonte; Sept. 30, 1898, in Lille, France.

**Spotlights:** Kewpie doll-faced daughter of the Big Top. This petite brunette left the circus to join the Parisian Folies Bergere as a chorus girl. Her large, dramatic eyes, like Clara Bow's, were her best asset. *The Big Parade* (1925) boosted her to stardom playing opposite John Gilbert. Died: 1933, from tuberculosis.

## Cyd Charisse  *Actress, dancer* 1601 Vine

**Born:** Tula Finklea; March 8, 1921, in Amarillo, Tex.
**Spotlights:** Glamorous, tall, with a beautiful pair of legs. Films with Fred Astaire, *The Band Wagon* (1953), and Gene Kelly, *Singing in the Rain* (1952), proved she was one of Hollywood's most competent dancers; she was a reliable actress, too.
**Highlights:** Second marriage to singer Tony Martin (since 1948).

## Kay Kyser *Bandleader* 1601 Vine

**Born:** James Kyser; June 18, 1905, in Chapel Hill, N.C.
**Spotlights:** Recorded: "Don't Sit Under the Apple Tree," "On A Slow Boat to China," "Three Little Fishes." Theme song: "Thinking of You." Quiz master of "Kay Kyser's Kollege of Musical Knowledge," first broadcast in 1938. In cap and gown, humorous Kyser talked to his "students" (contestants and studio audience): "That's right, you're wrong!"
**Sidelights:** Left pro showbiz to manage the film and broadcasting departments of Boston Christian Science Church in 1947. Died: 1985.

## Xavier Cugat *See page 227.* 1601 Vine

## Charlotte Greenwood 4 *Actress, dancer* 1605 Vine

**Born:** Frances C. Greenwood; June 25, 1890, in Philadelphia, Pa.
**Spotlights:** A stage and film talent; her own comedy-drama program, "The Charlotte Greenwood Show," aired on NBC in 1944 and further stimulated interest in her movies for Fox. Died: 1978.

## Susan Peters *Actress* 1605 Vine

**Born:** Suzanne Carnahan; July 3, 1921, in Spokane, Wash.
**Spotlights:** Beautiful brunette with classic bone structure and full lips. *Santa Fe Trail* (1940); *Dr. Gillespie's New Assistant* (1942).
**Sidelights:** Groomed for stardom by MGM, but a hunting accident resulted in permanent spinal cord injury; paralyzed from the waist down. Died: 1952, from a chronic kidney infection.

## Ezio Pinza *Opera singer, actor* 1605 Vine

**Born:** Fortunio E. Pinza; May 18, 1892, in Rome, Italy.
**Spotlights:** Rich voice; outstanding basso. *Don Giovanni* at Metropolitan Opera and, on Broadway, *South Pacific*; more. Died: 1957.

## Willard Waterman *Actor* 1605 Vine

**Spotlights:** Busy in comedy and drama productions for over two decades: Dr. Grant Frasier on "The Road to Life" (1937); Throckmorton P. Gildersleeve, bachelor father/uncle on "The Great Gildersleeve" (NBC, 1941); Dad, George Webster, star of "Those Websters" (CBS, 1945).

**George Murphy**  *Dancer, actor* **1605 Vine**

**Born:** July 4, 1902, in New Haven, Conn.

**Spotlights:** Murphy's many years of "putting 'em down" on stage were used in pictures such as Goldwyn's *Kid Millions* (1935), starring Eddie Cantor and Ethel Merman, and MGM's *Broadway Melody of 1938*, co-starring the supreme energetic tap dancer, Eleanor Powell.

**Achievements:** 1950, special Oscar.

**Sidelights:** Left his position of president of the Screen Actors Guild to actor Ronald Reagan (1947). Moved onward to a loftier position as California Republican congressman.

**John B. Kennedy** 4 *Newscaster, commentator* **1615 Vine**

**Spotlights:** *Collier's* magazine brought life to the pre-Depression variety program, "The Collier Hour" (NBC, 1927); RCA sponsored the musical program, "The Magic Key" (1936).

**Victor Schertzinger** 🎥 *Director* **1615 Vine**

**Born:** April 8, 1880, in Mahonoy City, Pa.

**Spotlights:** Directed the very first "road" picture with Hope, Crosby, and Lamour, *Road to Singapore* (1940), in which Hope gained tremendous popularity; and *Road to Zanzibar* (1941). Died: 1941.

**Bud Abbott** 🎥 *Comedian* **1615 Vine**

**Born:** William Abbott; Oct. 2, 1895, in Asbury Park, N.J.

**Spotlights:** His career in show biz started when he was a cashier in a Brooklyn burlesque club. In 1931, headliner Lou Costello was minus his partner at showtime. He asked Abbott to fill in as the straight man; hence the team was formed, with Abbott receiving 40 percent of the take. Kate Smith's radio shows played up their brazen comedy routines and made them stars. In 1940, Universal put the duo in the musical *One Night in the Tropics*. Abbott's slender build towering over roly-poly Costello, combined with their quick cross-talk and slapstick routines, made them hot top-10 box office material for nearly a decade. Baseball's "Who's on first?" was their greatest routine, the only one to stand the test of time. Radio: "The Abbott and Costello Show". Their own syndicated and network daytime TV series ran successfully on bad puns and rowdy slapstick from 1951–53. The team split in 1957.

**Sidelights:** Fought a lifelong battle with epilepsy. Died: 1974, of cancer after suffering two strokes.

**Bing Crosby** 🎥 *Singer, actor* **1615 Vine**

**Born:** Harry Lillis Crosby; May 2, 1901, in Tacoma, Wash.

**Spotlights:** Overnight sensation in radio in 1931; big shows included "Kraft Music Hall" (1934), earning $7,500 a year, plus films and records. "The Bing Crosby Show" (1946). Listeners thought he ad-libbed because of his relaxed style; actually the show

251

was scripted. Earning $175,000+ per picture, *Pennies from Heaven* (1936); *Road to Heaven* (1940), in the first role Fred MacMurray turned down; *Holiday Inn* (1942), with co-star Marjorie Reynolds. Recording: Sold over 350 million records! *White Christmas* sold *over* 30 million copies. By 1938 he made $75,000 a year in recordings alone. *True Love* was his twentieth golden disc (sold a million copies or more).

**Achievements:**   1944, Best Actor Oscar, *Going My Way.*

**Sidelights:**   The title of his autobiography aptly describes what he attributed his enormous success to, *Call Me Lucky* (1953). Died: 1977, of heart failure, on a golf course in Spain.

## Bea Benaderet   *Actress*                    1615 Vine

**Born:**   April 4, 1906, in New York.

**Spotlights:**   She was Blanche Morton, the neighbor, on "The George Burns and Gracie Allen Show" (1950–58)and, when Allen retired from the series, Benaderet stayed on for "The George Burns Show" (1958–59). As Cousin Pearl Bodine (1962–63) she was a colorful addition to "The Beverly Hillbillies." Then the network offered her with her own situation comedy series, "Petticoat Junction" as Kate Bradley (1963–68).

*Bing Crosby*

**Sidelights:** Was the off screen voice of Betty Rubble, from Bedrock, Cobblestone County. She and her husband, Barney, lived in a cave next to their best friends and neighbors, "The Flintstones," (1960–64). It was an innovative adult- oriented cartoon satirized suburbanites. Died: 1968.

### James A. Fitzpatrick  *Producer*     1615 Vine

**Born:** Feb. 26, 1902, in Shelton, Conn.
**Spotlights:** In 1925 combined writing, narrating, directing, producing, and his love of travel into *Fitzpatrick Traveltalks* from his own production company. Distributed through MGM. Also VistaVision shorts for Paramount Pictures. Died: 1980.

### Elissa Landi  *Actress*     1615 Vine

**Born:** Elisabeth Kuehnelt; Dec. 6, 1904, in Italy.
**Spotlights:** Brilliant in Cecil B. DeMille's *The Sign of the Cross* (1932). Thereafter she mixed her passion for writing novels with her acting career.
**Highlights:** Descended from royalty (emperor of Austria), Kuehnelt changed her last name to that of her nobleman stepfather, Count Zanardi-Landi. Died: 1944, of cancer.

### Shirley MacLaine  *Actress, dancer, author*     1615 Vine

**Born:** Shirley MacLean Beaty; April 24, 1934, in Richmond, Va.
**Spotlights:** Brilliant, well-rounded entertainer, with a unique style of performing. Enchanting debut in Hitchcock's *The Trouble with Harry* (1955); *Some Came Running* (1959); *The Apartment* (1960); *Irma La Douce* (1963); *Sweet Charity* (1969).
**Achievements:** 1983, Best Actress Oscar for *Terms of Endearment*. 1976, Emmy.
**Highlights:** Older sister of Warren Beatty, but they've never teamed together on-screen. She's written several best-selling autobiographies.

### Anne Francis  *Actress*     1615 Vine

**Born:** Sept. 16, 1930, in Ossining, N.Y.
**Spotlights:** MGM and 20th Century-Fox miscast her as a sex symbol because of her blonde bombshell-type looks. TV cast her better as the light dramatic lead detective in "Honey West" (1965–66); Terri Dowling (1971–72) in "My Three Sons"; and Arliss Cooper on "Dallas" (1981).

### Theodore Kosloff  *Dancer, actor*     1615 Vine

**Born:** April 5, 1882, in Russia.
**Spotlights:** An extraordinary ballet dancer, he quickly embraced the flapper style in *Children of Jazz* (1923). He had anything but *Feet of Clay* (1924). Died: 1956.

### Ralph Morgan  *Actor*     1615 Vine

**Born:** Raphael Wupperman; July 6, 1882, in New York.

**Spotlights:** Billed beneath the Barrymore trio (John, Ethel, and Lionel) in the cinematic event of the year, MGM's *Rasputin and the Empress* (1932). Worked in leads throughout the 1930s, as well as supporting roles: *Little Men* (1935) and *Wells Fargo* (1937). Died: 1956.

**Charlie Farrell**  *See page 366.*  1615 Vine

**Adolph Zukor** *Executive*  1615 Vine

**Born:** Jan. 7, 1873, in Hungary.

**Spotlights:** Became super rich distributing the film *Queen Elizabeth* (1912), which innovatively brought the theatrical experience of regal history to the average filmgoer and legitimized the art of motion pictures. His production company, Famous Players, later became Paramount. In 1921 alone, the company made over 100 films.

**Achievements:** 1949, special Academy Award.

**Sidelights:** A Horatio Alger story. Arrived in the U.S. penniless and unable to speak English. He once said of his occupation: "Those of us who became film producers hailed from all sorts of occupations — furriers, magicians, butchers, boilermakers — and for this reason highbrows have often poked fun at us. Yet one thing is certain — every man who succeeded was a born showman. And once in the show business he was never happy out of it." Died: 1976.

**Tom Conway** *Actor*  1615 Vine

**Born:** Sept. 15, 1904, in Russia, of British parents.

**Spotlights:** Star of TV's "Inspector Mark Saber" during the 1950s. Guest spots included work on "The Perry Mason Show" (1963); 280 movies; radio star of "The Saint."

**Sidelights:** Made nearly $1 million, but was found destitute in a $2-a-day flophouse in Venice Beach, California in 1965! Died: 1967.

**Dean Martin** *See page 77.*  1615 Vine

**Kim Hunter** *Actress*  1615 Vine

**Born:** Janet Cole; Nov. 12, 1922, in Detroit, Mich.

**Spotlights:** *Planet of the Apes* (1960, serial). TV: "Born Innocent" (1974); "Ellery Queen" (1975); Ellen Wilson in "Backstairs at the White House," (1979 mini-series).

**Achievements:** 1951, Best Supporting Actress Oscar for *A Streetcar Named Desire*.

**Marcus Loew** *Executive*  1615 Vine

**Born:** May 7, 1870, in New York.

**Spotlights:** Loew lived the American dream. Born of penniless, immigrant parents, he worked hard and followed his gut instinct on show biz, owning a chain of 400

theaters by his 40th birthday! Before he was 50, he owned Metro Pictures, and a few years later (1924) corporately controlled Metro-Goldwyn-Mayer (MGM).
**Sidelights:** Self-educated. Only attended a few years of grade school. Died: 1927.

## Ray Milland  🎥 *Actor* 1627 Vine

**Born:** Reginald Truscott-Jones; Jan. 3, 1905, in Wales.
**Spotlights:** Cool, charming, reliable performer: *Charlie Chan in London* (1934); *Lisbon* (1956, also directed). TV: "Ellery Queen: Don't Look Behind You" (1975); "Rich Man, Poor Man" (1976 mini series).
**Achievements:** 1945, Best Actor Oscar for *The Lost Weekend.*

## Vanessa Brown  🎥 *Actress* 1627 Vine

**Born:** Smylla Brind on March 24, 1928, in Austria.
**Spotlights:** Charming at 19 years old when she appeared in *The Ghost and Mrs. Muir* (1947), starring Gene Tierney and Rex Harrison. Panelist on TV's "Leave it to the Girls" (1949–54); more.

## Richard Cromwell  🎥 *Actor* 1627 Vine

**Born:** Roy Radabaugh; Jan. 8, 1910, in Los Angeles, Calif.
**Spotlights:** Supported rotund charlatan W. C. Fields in Paramount's *Poppy* (1936). Excellent in Warner's *Jezebel* (1938), a stylistic pre-Civil War melodrama starring Bette Davis and Henry Fonda. Another period piece, *Young Mr. Lincoln* (1939), starred his friend, Henry Fonda.
**Highlights:** Married to the pretty, porcelain-skinned, 20-year-old Angela Lansbury (for one year).

## Barbara Lamarr  🎥 *Actress* 1627 Vine

**Born:** Rheatha Watson; July 28, 1896, in Richmond, Va.
**Spotlights:** Erotic in *Arabian Love* (1922), sensuous in *Heart of a Siren* (1925). Died: 1926.

## Pete Smith  🎥 *Producer* 1627 Vine

**Born:** Pete Schmidt; Sept. 4, 1892, in New York.
**Achievements:** 1937, Academy Award for *Penny Wisdom*; 1940 for *Quicker 'n a Wink*; shorts. 1955, special Oscar. Died: 1979.

## Rin-Tin-Tin  🎥 *German shepherd* 1627 Vine

**Born:** 1916, in Germany.
**Spotlights:** Man's best friend certainly was to Warner Brothers. "Rinty," as he was affectionately known, was introduced in *Where the North Begins* (1923). This intelligent canine performed every trick imaginable and showed emotions, too! Loved by every child in the world and a hero to everyone else, Rinty became the

globe's most popular dog. In doing so, earned $1,000 a week; his human co-stars earned $150 a week. Rin-Tin-Tin also got top billing! His co-stars, who felt humiliated that a four-legged creature with fleas earned more than they did, was better treated than they were, and received better reviews, had to be careful to conceal their hostility toward the sensitive dog for fear of being attacked. Like many Hollywood stars, this gem was fashion-conscious and sported a large, diamond-studded collar. His daily food: Chateaubriand steak. And, of course, a combo played relaxing music to aid his digestion.

**Achievements:** In making 19 Rin-Tin-Tin features, he became Warner's first super star and saved the studio and a number of theaters from going under!

**Sidelights:** There were 18 trained look-alikes in case of emergency! Owner- trainer Leland Duncan made $5 million on Rin-Tin-Tins's films! Died: 1932.

## Ronald Colman   *See page 36.*
*See page 36.*
1627 Vine

## Gordon Jones   *Actor*
1627 Vine

**Born:** In Alden, Iowa.

**Spotlights:** His slapstick antics as Mike the Cop on "The Abbott and Costello Show" (1951–53) made millions laugh. He was Gordon Jones (1958–60) on "The Adventures of Ozzie and Harriet."

## Dean Jagger   *Actor*
1627 Vine

**Born:** Dean Jeffries; Nov. 7, 1903, in Lima, Ohio.

**Spotlights:** Wonderful character role in Zane Grey's adapted novel, *Western Union* (1941), teaming with Randolph Scott and Robert Young. Enhanced Paramount's production of *White Christmas* (1954), starring Bing Crosby and Danny Kaye.

**Achievements:** 1949, Best Supporting Actor for *12 O'Clock High*.

## Ilona Massey   *Actress, singer*
1627 Vine

**Born:** Ilona Hajmassy; June 16, 1910, in Hungary.

**Spotlights:** Beautiful blond soprano in MGM's *Rosalie* (1938); *Balalaika* (1939); both starred Nelson Eddy.

**Sidelights:** Her beauty mark was real. Died: 1974.

## Melachrino   *Composer, arranger, orchestra leader.*
1627 Vine

**Born:** George Melachrino; May 1, 1909, in England.

**Spotlights:** Organized the Melachrino Strings in 1945. Post-World War II, it was joyous, light, sweet "Music for Relaxation," and "Reverie." Died: 1965.

## Edna May Oliver   *Actress*
1627 Vine

**Born:** E. M. Nutter; Nov. 9, 1883, in Malden, Mass.

**Spotlights:** Delivered perfect characterizations of disapproving relatives, most frequently seen as a spinster or widow; *Little Women* (1933) and *Drums Along the Mohawk* (1939). Died: 1942 (on her birthday), from complications stemming from an intestinal disorder.

**Bobby Sherwood** 📺 *Band leader, trumpeter, actor, comic, host* 1627 Vine
**Born:** Robert Sherwood, Jr., in 1915, in Indianapolis, Ind.
**Spotlights:** Regular (1952–53) on "The Milton Berle Show." Panelist (1954–57) on "Masquerade Party." Died: 1981, from cancer.

**David Niven** 📺 *See page 286.* 1627 Vine

**Jo Stafford** 💿 *Singer* 1627 Vine
**Born:** Nov. 12, 1918, in Coalinga, Calif.
**Spotlights:** Vocalist with the Tommy Dorsey band until going solo in 1943. Recordings: *I'll Never Smile Again*; *Street of Dreams* (with the Pied Pipers); *Tumbling Tumbleweeds*. Radio: "The Jo Stafford Show" (first aired in 1948). TV: Her husband, Paul Weston, and his orchestra played on "The Jo Stafford Show" (1954–55); more.
**Achievements:** 1960, Grammy, comedy. Most popular female singer in America in 1945.
**Sidelights:** Apparently the GIs' favorite singer during World War II; the Japanese played her records on loud-speakers so that American GIs would get homesick and surrender!

**Milton Cross** 🎙 *Narrator, singer, actor* 1627 Vine
**Born:** April 16, 1897, in New York.
**Spotlights:** American commercial broadcasting began in 1920. Cross was an announcer with a clear, strong voice on the "A & P Gypsies," a musical program, that first aired in 1923, thus making him one of the earliest persons to gain radio fame. Also, host of the successful "Metropolitan Opera Broadcasts" from New York (first broadcast NBC, 1931); more. Died: 1975.

**Diana Lynn** 🎥 *Actress, musician* 1627 Vine
**Born:** Dolores Loehr; Oct. 7, 1926, in Los Angeles, Calif.
**Spotlights:** *They Shall Have Music* (1939) showed a very young, gifted Lynn playing piano. Other films include *The Major and the Minor* (1942) and *The Miracle of Morgan's Creek* (1944). TV: "Climax," dramatic anthology (1958). Continued in "live play" performances on "The U.S. Steel Hour." Died: 1971, from a stroke.

**Howard Duff** 📺 *Actor* 1627 Vine
**Born:** Nov. 24, 1917, in Bremerton, Wash.
**Spotlights:** Moved into lead roles from being a studio contract player. Often had a concerned look on his face. Played Detective Sam Stone in "Felony Squad" (1966–69); Sheriff Titus Sample in "Flamingo Road" (1981–82).

## Sidney Blackmer  🎥 *Actor*                                      1627 Vine

**Born:** July 13, 1895, in Salisbury, N.C.

**Spotlights:** Character actor who often played classy criminals, enhanced over 100 pictures with his debonair presence including the swashbuckler, *The Count of Monte Cristo* (1934), and the comedy mystery, *It's a Wonderful World* (1939). Died: 1973, of cancer.

## Horace Heidt  🎙 *Host, orchestra leader*                       1633 Vine

**Born:** May 21, 1901, in Oakland, Calif.

**Spotlights:** Horace Heidt and his Musical Knights were a big band popular on the radio show "Pot o' Gold," where a $1,000 prize drew a large audience. "Hold it, Horace, stop the music," his announcer would call out when a telephone listener won the prize money; first aired 1939. TV: "The Horace Heidt Show," talent contest (1950–51).

**Sidelights:** Discovered Art Carney; he was a singing member of Donna and the Don Juans. Died: 1986 of pneumonia.

## Pat Boone  💿 *Singer, actor*                                    1633 Vine

**Born:** Charles Eugene; June 1, 1934, in Jacksonville, Fla.

**Spotlights:** Recorded such million-selling hits as "Ain't That a Shame," "Tutti Frutti," "April Love," "The Exodus Song," "Love Letters in the Sand," and much more. TV: "The Pat Boone, Chevy Showroom," musical variety (ABC, 1957–60). These tunes run the gamut from country to rhythm and blues to popular, and illustrate good versatility.

**Sidelights:** Well-respected in the Christian community for his good Samaritan efforts.

## Robert Montgomery  📺 *See page 295.*                           1633 Vine

## Floyd Gibbons  🎙 *Newscaster*                                    1635 Vine

**Spotlights:** Host of NBC's "Headline Hunters" (1929); innovative in bringing up-to-the minute news to his faithful audience.

## Samuel Goldwyn  🎥 *Motion picture pioneer, producer*            1635 Vine

**Born:** Samuel Goldfish; Aug. 27, 1882, in Poland.

**Spotlights:** Came to America alone as a poverty-stricken teenager in 1895. By 1913 co-founded the Jesse L. Lasky Feature Play Company with his brother-in-law. With added talent of Cecil B. DeMille (who had never made a film, but said he thought he could), plus $15,000, they made Hollywood's first feature length film, *The Squaw Man* (1914) and grossed over $225,000. In 1916, co-founded the Goldwyn Company (later merged to become Metro-Goldwyn-Mayer — MGM). In 1923, he decided he had had enough with partners — "Include me out" — and formed Samuel Goldwyn Productions. Partial listing of film credits: *Ben Hur* (1925); *The Greeks Had* a *Word for Them* (1932). A tough taskmaster of many award-winning pictures, he once said: "A producer shouldn't get ulcers, he should give them."

**Achievements:** 1946, special Oscar; 1946, Best Picture, *The Best Years of Our Lives.* 1957, Jean Hersholt Humanitarian Award.

**Highlights:** Father of producer-director Samuel Goldwyn, Jr.

**Sidelights:** Coined many phrases, including: "A verbal agreement isn't worth the paper it's written on." Died: 1974.

## Linda Darnell   *Actress*   1635 Vine

**Born:** Monetta Darnell; Oct. 16, 1921, in Dallas, Tex.

**Spotlights:** Brunette dynamo at Fox in the 1940s: *My Darling Clementine* (1946), where her crisp characterization enhanced this western co-starring Henry Fonda. *Forever Amber* (1947). Died: 1965, in a fire at a friend's house.

## Leo Carillo   *Actor*   1635 Vine

**Born:** Aug. 6, 1880, in Los Angeles, Calif.

**Spotlights:** The racketeer in *Love Me Forever* (1935); *The Gay Desperado* (1936). His "put-on" accents (Spanish, southern, etc.) fooled many people, especially when he played TV's Pancho, sidekick of "The Cisco Kid" (1950–56): "Ceesco, the shereef

*Linda Darnell visits convalescing WWII G.I's at VA hospital.*

and hees posse, ees getting closer!" Turned 70 years old before starting the TV series; rode his horse, Loco, like a stuntman during the series' 6-year run. His secret: He didn't believe in old age. Carillo is one of the original California families. Died: 1961.

### Don Fedderson   Executive                                    1635 Vine

**Born:** April 16, in Beresford, S.D.
**Spotlights:** Attended Kansas City School of Law. Produced the "Liberace Show"; "Do You Trust Your Wife?"; "The Betty White Show"; more. Knew how to package deals, and executive produced "My Three Sons"; "Family Affair"; more. Lawrence Welk treasured his relationship with Fedderson, who was his consultant, and later distributed the series.

### Cornel Wilde   *Actor, director*                              1637 Vine

**Born:** Cornelius Wilde; Oct. 13, 1915, in New York.
**Spotlights:** Exquisitely played Chopin in *A Song to Remember* (1945). Started directing in 1955 after 15 years of on-screen experience. Produced, directed and starred in *Lancelot and Guinevere* (1962).

### Frank Sinatra   *See page 220.*                               1637 Vine

### Louis B. Mayer   *Executive, producer*                        1637 Vine

**Born:** Eliezer Meyer; July 4, 1885, in Russia.
**Spotlights:** Went from being a successful junk dealer in 1904 to MGM studio magnate in 1924. Mayer was credited with producing the highest-quality films in the world from that studio including *The Wizard of Oz* (1939). A gifted taskmaker, he bitterly relinquished his executive position at MGM in 1951. MGM's pictures took many Academy Awards over the years, and, in fact, Mayer helped spearhead the formation of the Academy.
**Sidelights:** An astute businessman, he once said: "We are the only company whose assets all walk out the gates at night." Died: 1957.

### George Burns   *Comedian*                                     1637 Vine

**Born:** Nathan Birnbaum; Jan. 20, 1896, in New York.
**Spotlights:** A former vaudeville song-and-dance man. Films include *Here Comes Cookie* (1935), *Oh God!* (1977). On TV and radio, very funny, straight man to wife's scatterbrained antics. Most remembered lines from "The George Burns and Gracie Allen Show" (1950–58) — Burns: "Say goodnight, Gracie." Allen: "Goodnight, Gracie." Always seen with his trademark cigar and horn-rimmed glasses.
**Achievements:** 1975, Best Supporting Actor Oscar, *The Sunshine Boys*.
**Highlights:** Married former vaudeville performer Gracie Allen (1926 until her death in 1964).

### Vera Vague   *See page 141.*                                  1637 Vine

## Sue Carol Ladd   Actress, agent                                    **1637 Vine**

**Born:** Evelyn Lederer; Oct. 30, 1907, in Chicago, Ill.
**Sidelights:** Ingenue in *Slaves of Beauty* (1927) and others, before turning into a powerhouse Hollywood agent (managed husband Alan Ladd's career). She had brains, guts, and charm. Died: 1982.

## Nelson Eddy   *See page 102.*                                     **1637 Vine**

## Harold Peary   Actor                                               **1637 Vine**

**Born:** July 25, 1908, in San Leandro, Calif.
**Spotlights:** According to a publicity release from RKO, "The man who parlayed a sinister laugh into a million dollar asset and became The Great Gildersleeve." That is, Throckmorton P. Gildersleeve. This 5' 9", 210-lb., brown-eyed, black-haired character had a deep, booming voice. Played a pompous windbag, with a kind heart, disguised behind the barrier of a bully. Famous on radio and film for "The Great Gildersleeve" series. Own comedy show in 1950. TV guest spots on "The Girl," "The Ghost and Mrs. Muir," and more. Died: 1985.

*George Burns at his Dedication Ceremony.*

**Dolores Costello**   Actress                              1645 Vine

**Born:**  Sept. 17, 1905, in Pittsburgh, Pa.

**Spotlights:**  Her matinee-idol father, Maurice Costello, placed his large-eyed, angelic, oval-faced, blond, curly-haired daughter in his Vitagraph pictures before she was 6. Popular silent screen ingenue who did only sporadic talkie work. Played the mother in *Little Lord Fauntleroy* (1936).

**Highlights:**  Married co-star (*The Sea Beast*, 1926) John Barrymore (through 1955). Died: 1979, of emphysema.

**Joan Fontaine**  Actress                              1645 Vine

**Born:**  Joan de Havilland; Oct. 22, 1917, in Japan.

**Spotlights:**  Fair-haired, leading actress in *Rebecca* (1940), *The Constant Nymph* (1943), *Jane Eyre* (1944); more.

**Achievements:**  1941 Best Actress Oscar, *Suspicion*.

**Highlights:**  Younger sister of Olivia de Havilland.

**Frankie Laine**  See page 89.                              1645 Vine

**Walter Winchell**  See page 325.                              1645 Vine

**William Steinberg**  Musician                              1645 Vine

**Born:**  Hans Wilhelm Steinberg; Aug. 1, 1899, in Cologne, Germany

**Spotlights:**  Steinberg's remarkable talent for interpreting of musical compositions established him as a "Conductor of Eminence." Recordings: Beethoven's *Symphony No. 6 in F Major, op. 68*, the "Pastoral," with Pittsburgh Symphony; more.

**Jerry Colonna**  Actor                              1645 Vine

**Born:**  Gerald Colonna; Sept. 17, 1904, in Boston, Mass.

**Spotlights:**  Comic guest performer on "The Fred Allen Show" in the early 1930s, recognized by his howling voice. Billed directly beneath the comedy superstar of "The Bob Hope Show," he played the Professor (NBC, first broadcast 1934). With his trademark walrus mustache, he also appeared in several of Hope's movies Died: 1986.

**Jane Froman**  See page 159.                              1645 Vine

**Mary Anderson**  Actress                              1645 Vine

**Born:**  April 3, 1924, in Birmingham, Ala.

**Spotlights:**  Her southern accent was a natural in her first film, *Gone with the Wind* (1939). Her career kept afloat between leading lady and supporting roles in 17 films, including *Lifeboat* (1944).

## Michele Morgan 🎥 *Actress* **1645 Vine**

**Born:** Simone Roussel; Feb. 29, 1920, in France.
**Spotlights:** Ash-blond beauty, with high cheekbones and large eyes, who was an international star. In the U. S., she was her busiest during the 1940s, *Passage to Marseille* (1944) and *The Chase* (1946).

## Sessue Hayakawa 🎥 *Actor* **1645 Vine**

**Born:** Kintaro Hayakawa; June 10, 1889, in Japan.
**Spotlights:** Extremely popular and versatile silent screen star, who brilliantly made the transition to talkies. The Japanese officer Colonel Saito in *The Bridge on the River Kwai* (1957); *The Swiss Family Robinson* (1960).
**Sidelights:** After making over 100 films, he returned to Japan and became a Zen priest. Died: 1973.

## Kent Taylor 🎥 *Actor* **1645 Vine**

**Born:** Louis Weiss; May 11, 1907, in Nashau, Iowa.
**Spotlights:** On-screen from 1931 *Road to Reno* to 1970 *Hell's Bloody Devils*, always turning in a reliable performance, often as the hero. Over 75 pictures include *Death Takes a Holiday* (1934). Star of the TV detective drama, "Boston Blackie" (1951–53); "The Rough Riders" as Captain Jim Flagg (1958–59). Died: 1987.

## Rita Hayworth 🎥 *Actress* **1645 Vine**

**Born:** Margarita Cansino; Oct. 17, 1918, in Brooklyn, N.Y.
**Spotlights:** Voluptuous beauty who made 60 motion pictures: "The Love Goddess" in *You Were Never Lovelier* (1942), with Fred Astaire; and "There never was a woman like" *Gilda* (1946).
**Highlights:** Second marriage to Orson Welles (1943–47), fourth to Richard Haymes (1953–54). Died: 1987.

## Lionel Barrymore 📽 *See page 138.* **1645 Vine**

## Thomas Mitchell 🎥 *Actor* **1645 Vine**

**Born:** July 11, 1892, in Elizabeth, N.J.
**Spotlights:** American-Irish character best remembered in *Mr. Smith Goes to Washington* (1939), *Gone with the Wind* (1939), *High Noon* (1952).
**Achievements:** 1939, Best Supporting Actor Oscar for *Stagecoach*. Died: 1962, of cancer.

## David Powell 🎥 *Actor* **1645 Vine**

**Born:** Around 1870, in England.
**Spotlights:** Handsome, dashing, leading man of the silent era, who played opposite

the most popular actresses, including Mary Pickford in *Less Than the Dust* (1916). One of Paramount's shining attractions in the 1920s; *Glimpse of the Moon* (1923) with Bebe Daniels. Died: 1925.

## Ben Turpin  *Comedian*                                   1645 Vine
**Born:** Sept. 17, 1874, in New Orleans, La.
**Spotlights:** Silent screen talent who was most successful poking fun at superstars such as Valentino; he was cross-eyed with a crumpled face, and audiences went hysterical over his impersonations. *When Love is Blind* (1919). Died: 1940.

## Katrina Paxinou  *Actress*                               1645 Vine
**Born:** Katrinas Constantopoulous; in 1900, in Greece.
**Spotlights:** Exotic, dramatic, international talent who made only 6 American films while she was "visiting."
**Achievements:** 1943, Best Supporting Actress Oscar, *For Whom the Bell Tolls*. Died: 1973.

## Eddie Bracken  *See page 43.*                            1645 Vine

## Francis X. Bushman  *Actor*                               1645 Vine
**Born:** Jan. 12, 1882, in Baltimore, Md.
**Spotlights:** Leads in *Every Inch a King* (1914) and *Romeo and Juliet* (1916) were typical of the roles that this "Greek god of love" was offered. Sporadic work after the arrival of the talkies. Died: 1966.

## William Holden  *Actor*                                   1645 Vine
**Born:** Franklin Beedle, Jr.; April 17, 1918, in O'Fallen, Ill.
**Spotlights:** Handsome, charming leading man. Wonderful performance in *Sunset Boulevard* (1950), directed by Billy Wilder, opposite Gloria Swanson; and *The Bridge on the River Kwai* (1957), with Alec Guinness.

| Rita Hayworth | William Holden | Greer Garson |

**Achievements:**   1953, Best Actor Oscar, *Stalag 17*.
**Highlights:**   Long-time companion of actress Stephanie Powers. Died: 1981, of a head injury after a fall.

## Maurice Chevalier   *Actor, singer*   1645 Vine

**Born:**   Sept. 12, 1888, in France.
**Spotlights:**   He exuded *joie de vivre* in *Love Me Tonight* (1932). Fans recall his roguish smile and twinkling eyes in *Gigi* (1958). Two songs remain uniquely his own: "Every Little Breeze Seems to Whisper Louise" and "Thank Heaven for Little Girls."
**Achievements:**   1958, special Oscar.
**Sidelights:**   Learned English from a fellow P.O.W. during World War I. Died: 1972, from a heart attack.

## Red Buttons   *Actor, comedian*   1645 Vine

**Born:**   Aaron Shwatt; Feb. 5, 1919, in New York.
**Spotlights:**   "The Red Buttons Show" was a comedy variety, which ran from 1952–55.
**Highlights:**   1957, Best Supporting Actor Oscar, *Sayonara*.
**Sidelights:**   His stage name came from the bright uniform he had to wear when he was a singing bellboy. He was first billed as Red Buttons in a burlesque lineup.

## Greer Garson   *Actress*   1645 Vine

**Born:**   Sept. 29, 1908, in Ireland.
**Spotlights:**   Red-haired, refined talent. Discovered by Louis B. Mayer and quickly put under contract to MGM. *Goodbye Mr. Chips* (1939), *Madame Curie* (1942), and *Mrs. Parkington* (1944) were just a few of her many wonderful performances. Often paired in movies with Walter Pidgeon.
**Achievements:**   1942, Best Actress Oscar, *Mrs. Miniver*.

## Bronco Billy Anderson   *Actor, director, producer*   1645 Vine

**Born:**   Max Aronson; March 21, 1882, in Little Rock, Ark.
**Spotlights:**   Prolific star and director of the "Bronco Billy" silent westerns; made over 400 films between 1907 and 1918.
**Achievements:**   1957, special Oscar "for the contributions to the development of motion pictures as entertainment." Died: 1971.

## Alistair Cooke   *Commentator, host*   1645 Vine

**Born:**   Nov. 20, 1908, in England.
**Spotlights:**   Host of "Omnibus" (1953-57), a 1½-hour cultural enjoyment-education program; unique in commercial TV because there were no commercial interruptions! (Ford Foundation financed it.) "America," a documentary history program, was hosted and written by Cooke (1972-73).
**Achievements:**   1973, 1974, Emmys.

### Blanche Thebom  *Opera singer*    Southwest Corner of Hollywood and Vine

**Born:**   Sept. 19, 1918, in Monessen, Pa.

**Spotlights:**   Mezzo-soprano. Metropolitan Opera debut in 1944. Recordings: Igor Stravinsky's *The Rake's Progress* (complete opera in English) with Metropolitan Opera, conducted by the composer (Columbia); Bach's *St. John Passion* (RCA, Victor Symphony Orchestra under Robert Shaw); more.

### Neil A. Armstrong, Edwin E. Aldrin, Jr., Michael Collins 📺

*Astronauts    See page 204.*    Southwest Corner of Hollywood and Vine

### Constance Talmadge  *Actress*    Southwest Corner of Hollywood and Vine

**Born:**   April 19, 1898, in Brooklyn, N.Y.

**Spotlights:**   Hilarious, blonde comedienne in *Buddy's Last Call* (1914). Played the mountain girl in the Babylonian sequence in *Intolerance* (1916); *East is West* (1922). Retired in the late 1920s before sound.

**Highlights:**   Older sister of Norma Talmadge. The two tied for second place as the most popular actress of 1921! Died: 1973.

### Rex Ingram 🎥 *Actor*    Southwest Corner of Hollywood and Vine

**Born:**   Oct. 20, 1895, in Cairo, Ill.

**Spotlights:**   Major role in *The Green Pastures* (1936), but best remembered as the slave Jim in *The Adventures of Huckleberry Finn* (1939) and as the genie who laughed uproariously in *The Thief of Bagdad* (1940). Died: 1969.

### Hank Mann 🎥 *Comedian*    Southwest Corner of Hollywood and Vine

**Born:**   David Liebermann; in 1888, in New York.

**Spotlights:**   Big, walrus-moustached slapstick clown in Mack Sennett's Keystone Kops (1912–14), *City Lights* with Charlie Chaplin; *Abbott and Costello Meet the Keystone Kops* (1955); more. Died: 1971.

# * 6302 HOLLYWOOD *

**Fred Waring** 🎵 *See page 303.*  6302 Hollywood

**Polly Moran** 🎥 *Comedienne*  6302 Hollywood
**Born:** June 28, 1884, in Chicago, Ill.
**Spotlights:** A seasoned performer from vaudeville and silents, this boisterous comedian was extremely popular during the twenties: *The Affair of Anatol* (1921), *Bringing Up Father* (1928). One of her last films was a Tracy-Hepburn vehicle, *Adam's Rib* (1949). Died: 1952.

**Louella O. Parsons** 🎙 *See page 291.*  6302 Hollywood

**Red Foley** 📺 *See page 161.*  6302 Hollywood

**Luise Rainer** 🎥 *Actress*  6302 Hollywood
**Born:** Jan. 12, 1912, in Austria.
**Spotlights:** A Hollywood enigma. Wide-eyed brunette who came to town in 1935, too easily reached the very top, and left 3 years later.
**Achievements:** Oscars for Best Actress in 1936 *The Great Ziegfeld* and 1937, *The Good Earth*. Audiences were shocked that she won over Greta Garbo (Garbo's first nomination and possibly her best work) in *Camille* (1936).

**Marguerite Clark** 🎥 *Actress*  6304 Hollywood
**Born:** Feb. 22, 1884, in Avondale, Ohio.
**Spotlights:** Her very successful 7-year career in the silents made this delicate beauty very rich: *Wildflower* (1914) to *Scrambled Wives* (1921). Died: 1940.

**John Farrow** 🎥 *Director*  6304 Hollywood
**Born:** Feb. 10, 1904, in Australia.
**Spotlights:** The 1940 remake of *A Bill of Divorcement* with Adolph Menjou and Maureen O'Hara; *Wake Island* (1942), World War II drama.
**Highlights:** Married to the dark-haired beauty Maureen O'Sullivan (1936 on). Father of Mia and Tisa Farrow. Died: 1963.

**Charles Boyer** 📺 *See page 268.*  6304 Hollywood

**Frank Borzage** 🎥 *Director*  6306 Hollywood
**Born:** April 23, 1893, in Salt Lake City, Utah.

**Spotlights:** Often labeled "a romantic sentimentalist" because his films, many of them weepies, evolved around themes of love and integrity. *A Farewell to Arms* (1932), *Man's Castle* (1933), and *The Mortal Storm* (1940), sparkle with human triumph and tragedy.

**Achievements:** 1927, Best Director first *ever* presented, for *Seventh Heaven*. 1931 Best Director Academy Award for *Bad Girl*. Died: 1962.

## Ted Mack ☒ *Emcee*                                         6306 Hollywood

**Born:** William Maguiness; Feb. 12, 1904.

**Spotlights:** Host of the all-time most popular talent search, "The Original Amateur Hour" (1948–60 and, sporadically 1960–70). Discoveries include Pat Boone and Gladys Knight.

## James Melton ▯ *Singer, actor*                            6306 Hollywood

**Born:** Jan. 2, 1904, in Moultrie, Ga.

**Spotlights:** Previously sang with the Revelers. Radio: "The James Melton Show" first broadcast in 1943, but he had been performing on the air since 1927. Metropolitan Opera debut in 1942. Films. Star of TV's "Ford Festival," musical variety (1951–52). Died: 1961.

## Charles Boyer 🎥 *Actor*                                    6306 Hollywood

**Born:** Aug. 28, 1899, in France.

**Spotlights:** Tall, dark, and handsome with beautiful bedroom eyes. His accent was sexy or cruel depending on the role. His face often looked as if it had been formed by painful memories. *Conquest* (1938), co-starring Greta Garbo; *Algiers* (1938), co-starring Hedy Lamarr. A much-parodied line, but he never said it, "Comm wiz me to ze Casbah." TV includes: comedy-drama "The Rogues" (NBC, 1964–65) with an all-star cast: Gig Young, David Niven, Gladys Cooper.

**Achievements:** 1942, special Oscar (cultural). Died: 1978; his beloved wife since 1934, British actress Pat Patterson, had died only a few days earlier.

## Jackie Gleason ☒ *Actor, comedian, composer, conductor*  6310 Hollywood

**Born:** Herbert Gleason; Feb. 26, 1916, in Brooklyn, N.Y.

**Spotlights:** "How sweet it is!" "The Jackie Gleason Show" (1952–70) and "The Honeymooners" (1955–56) established the rotund, full-faced, boisterous comedian as one of TV's all-time greats. Nightclubs, Broadway, and films, including *The Hustler* (1961) and *Smokey and the Bandit* (1977), are all media this smart, funny actor uses. Died: 1987.

**Achievements:** 1960, Tony, "Take Me Along."

## Nanette Fabray ☒ *Comedienne, singer, actress*            6310 Hollywood

**Born:** Nanette Fabares; Oct. 27, 1920, in San Diego, CA.

**Spotlights:** A sparkling performer. Vaudeville debut at age 4 as Baby Nanette. A star

268

of *Our Gang* (1927). TV: Variety and guest spots. Specials.
**Achievements:**   1949, Tony, for "Love Life." 1955, two Emmys; 1956, Emmy.

**Joan Bennett**   *Actress*                              6310 Hollywood
**Born:**   Feb. 27, 1910, in Palisades, NJ.
**Spotlights:**   Samuel Goldwyn brought her to the public's attention in *Bulldog Drummond* (1929). The beauty joined Katharine Hepburn in the original *Little Women* (1933) and Edward G. Robinson in the thriller *The Woman in the Window* (1944).
**Highlight/Lowlight:**   Married four times.

**Al Goodman**  ⊚  *Composer, musicologist*                              6310 Hollywood
**Born:**   Alfred Goodman; March 1, 1920, in Germany.
**Spotlights:**   A skilled arranger, emigrated to New York in 1940; arranged music for dance bands and popular theater. In 1961 returned to Munich to found a series of concerts to promote new American music.

**Basil Rathbone**  📽  *See page 71.*                              6312 Hollywood

**Heather Angel**  🎥  *Actress*                              6312 Hollywood
**Born:**   Feb. 9, 1909, in England.
**Spotlights:**   Came to Hollywood in 1932, and one year later made an impression in *Berkeley Square*. Played the heroine in Paramount's *Bulldog Drummond* series (1937–39). Semiretired after *Lifeboat* (1944).

*Jackie Gleason*                              *Joan Bennet*

269

**Helen Mack** 🎥 *Actress*                                6312 Hollywood

**Born:** Helen McDougall; Nov. 13, 1913, in Rock Island, IL.
**Spotlights:** On-screen debut in *Pied Piper Malone* (1930). Retired from the big screen after *Strange Holiday* (1945). Became a radio producer. Died: 1986.

**Patty McCormack** 🎥 *Actress*                          6312 Hollywood

**Born:** Patricia McCormack; Aug. 21, 1945.
**Spotlights:** Played the lying, manipulative 8-year-old murderess in Warner's *The Bad Seed* (1956). Very good at being very bad. More films; TV, too.

**King Baggot** 🎥 *Actor, director*                       6314 Hollywood

**Born:** In 1874, in St. Louis, MO.
**Spotlights:** His stage experience proved useful in both his acting and directing. On-screen debut in *The Scarlet Letter* (1911); then the pioneer *Dr. Jekyll and Mr. Hyde* (1913). In hundreds of profitable silent shorts and films for IMP, Universal, and other studios. Made a few sound movies, mostly as a character actor. Died: 1948.

**Les Baxter**  *Composer, conductor, arranger*          6314 Hollywood

**Born:** March 14, 1922, in Mexia, TX.
**Spotlights:** Albums include *Music Out of the Moon* and *African Jazz*. Over 100 film scores to his credit. TV work, too.

**George Hicks** 🎤 *Announcer*                            6314 Hollywood

**Spotlights:** Announcer with diction well suited for the western "Death Valley Days" (first heard in 1930, the show ran over 15 years). Ronald Reagan, another Walk of Famer, hosted the TV version (1965–66). Introduced the one and only — "because two would cost too much," "The Jack Benny Show" (CBS, 1932; NBC, 1936).

**Rowland Lee** 🎥 *Director*                              6314 Hollywood

**Born:** Sept. 6, 1891, in Findlay, OH.
**Spotlights:** Best remembered for his visually stimulating work in the fantasy-horror genre: *Son of Frankenstein* (1939), starring Basil Rathbone, Boris Karloff, and Bela Lugosi; *Tower of London* (1939), starring Basil Rathbone, Boris Karloff, and Vincent Price; *The Son of Monte Cristo* (1940), starring Louis Hayward and Joan Bennett. Died: 1975.

**Nita Naldi** 🎥 *Actress*                                6314 Hollywood

**Born:** Anita Dooley; April 1, 1899, in New York, NY.
**Spotlights:** Seductress with the Ziegfeld Follies who heated up the screen in *Midsummer Madness* (1920) and *Blood and Sand* (1922), with Rudolph Valentino.
**Sidelights:** Alberto Vargas captured her incredible beauty in a painting in which a Greek god admires her. This work was recently sold for over $500,000!

## Douglas Fairbanks, Jr. 🎥 *Actor*                    **6318 Hollywood**

**Born:** D. Ulman, Jr.; Dec. 9, 1909, in New York, NY.
**Spotlights:** Lived in the shadow of his father's greatness. On-screen when he was 13 years old in *Stephen Steps Out* (1923); then *Having Wonderful Time* (1938), with Ginger Rogers; *Sinbad the Sailor* (1947). TV: "Douglas Fairbanks Presents," filmed in England, (1952–57). Radio guest star on "Silver Theater"; more.
**Achievements:** Knighted in 1949 for promoting Anglo-American relations.
**Highlights:** Married to Joan Crawford (1929–33), first of two. Lieutenant Commander in U.S. Navy; honored numerous times for bravery.

## Margaret Lindsay 🎥 *Actress*                    **6318 Hollywood**

**Born:** Margaret Kies; Sept. 19, 1910, in Dubuque, IA.
**Spotlights:** Mystery fans will recall the pleasant brunette in a number of the Ellery Queen detective series, including *Ellery Queen, Master Detective* (1940), *Ellery Queen and the Murder Ring* (1941), *Ellery Queen's Penthouse Mystery* (1941), *Ellery Queen and the Perfect Crime* (1941). Died: 1981.

## Mae Murray 🎥 *Actress*                    **6318 Hollywood**

**Born:** Marie Koen on May 10, 1889, in Portsmouth, VA.

*Mae Murray*

**Spotlights:** Opening night of the Zeigfeld Follies of 1909 dazzled prestigious theater-goers, including Theodore Roosevelt, with this charming showgirl Cupid. When she arrived on the West Coast, diamond bracelets that had been thrown on stage by her love-struck admirers weighed down her delicate wrists. Powerful executives quickly launched this lovely 31-year-old's career: *Dream Girl* (1916), *Modern Love, Body in Bond*, and *The Delicious Little Devil* (all 1918). Died: 1965.

### August Lumiere  *Inventor, producer, director*                     6320 Hollywood
**Born:** Oct. 19, 1862, in France.
**Spotlights:** See biography of Louis Lumiere for information. The star is misspelled. His name is correctly spelled "Auguste." Died: 1954.

### Tab Hunter  *Singer, actor*                     6320 Hollywood
**Born:** Arthur Kelm (or Gelien); July 11, 1931, in New York, NY.
**Spotlights:** Warner Brothers 1950s teen idol property. Acted and sang beautifully in *Damn Yankees* (1958), "What Lola Wants." Made 24 films, while recording and making TV appearances, but *The Fickle Finger of Fate* (1967) aptly describes the fall of his star from the screen. But busy constantly on stage.

### Johnny Cash  *Singer, actor*                     6320 Hollywood
**Born:** John Ray Cash; Feb. 26, 1932, in King Island, AR.
**Spotlights:** Gutsy, colorful vocalist with rockabilly sound. Successful country-and-western career spanning over a quarter of a century. Many TV specials including "Johnny Cash, Cowboy Heroes." Films include *A Gunfight* (1970), co- starring Kirk Douglas. Achievements: Six Grammys.

### Humphrey Bogart  *Actor*                     6320 Hollywood
**Born:** Dec. 25, 1899, in New York, NY.
**Spotlights:** His break came in *The Petrified Forest* (1936), as gangster Duke Mantee, a role repeated from Broadway. Warners wanted to use Edward G. Robinson, whom

Tab Hunter                     Johnny Cash                     Humphrey Bogart they had under contract and who was a big name, but Leslie Howard (also from the Broadway play) insisted on Bogart and won. Classics include *High Sierra* (1941), *The Maltese Falcon* (1941), *Casablanca* (1942), *To Have and Have Not* (1944), *The Treasure of the Sierra Madre* (1948), *Key Largo* (1948), *The Caine Mutiny* (1954).

**Achievements:** 1951, Best Actor Oscar, *The African Queen*.

**Highlights:** Married to Lauren Bacall (fourth wife) from 1945 until his death; it was a marriage made in heaven.

**Sidelights:** His lisp was the result of a World War I injury. Who nicknamed him Bogie? Spencer Tracy. An independent thinker, Bogart once said: "The only reason to make a million dollars in this business is to tell some fat producer to get lost." Died: 1957, from throat cancer.

## William Frawley  *Actor* 6320 Hollywood

**Born:** Feb. 26, 1887, in Burlington, IA.

**Spotlights:** *Huckleberry Finn* (1939) and *Miracle on 34th Street* (1947) were two of his over 125 films dating from 1915 to 1962! The balding, cigar-chewing actor usually played tough-on-the-outside, soft-on-the-inside roles.

**Sidelights:** TV fans recall him as the cranky Fred Mertz in "I Love Lucy." Died: 1966.

## Nina Foch *Actress* 6324 Hollywood

**Born:** Nina Fock; April 20, 1924, in Holland.

**Spotlights:** A lovely, cool talent whose films range from monster movie, *The Return of the Vampire* (1943), to MGM's Academy Award-winning musical, *An American in Paris* (1951) opposite Gene Kelly. *Executive Suite* (1954); more. Numerous TV specials and movies.

**Sidelights:** Became an independent acting instructor in Los Angeles.

## William Farnum *Actor* 6324 Hollywood

**Born:** July 4, 1876, in Boston, MA.

**Spotlights:** Highly regarded western actor, *Kit Carson* (1940), who previously appeared in a diversified collection of silents: *Samson* (1915), *A Tale of Two Cities* (1917), and *A Man Who Fights Alone* (1925). Character roles until 1952. Died: 1953.

## Sherry Jackson *Actress* 6324 Hollywood

**Born:** Feb. 15, 1942.

**Spotlights:** Played Terry Williams on "The Danny Thomas Show" (1953–58). The show ran in syndication under the title "Make Room for Daddy." Later became leading lady in films.

## Ernest Borgnine *Actor* 6324 Hollywood

**Born:** Ermes Borgnine; Jan. 24, 1917, in Hamden, CT.

**Spotlights:** Versatile, creative artist. Played a despicable heavy in the all-star cast production of *From Here to Eternity* (1953). In *Marty* (1955), he played a compassionate, gentle soul afraid of loneliness. He's always good, even in the TV series, "McHale's Navy."
**Achievements:** 1955, Best Actor Oscar, *Marty*.

## Henry Morgan  *Actor, writer*      6328 Hollywood
**Born:** Henry von Ost; March 31, 1915, in Detroit, MI.
**Spotlights:** Very funny, gutsy comedy writer-performer who held no subject, especially sponsor patronage, too sacred. Guest on "The Fred Allen Show" (early mid-1930's); "Hello, Anybody, Here's Morgan" on "The Henry Morgan Show" (first aired on NBC, 1945).

## Marion Davies *Actress*      6328 Hollywood
**Born:** Marion Douras; Jan. 3, 1897, in Brooklyn, NY.
**Spotlights:** Fun-loving, pretty, stuttering blond comedienne whose career was managed and controlled by newspaper tycoon William Randolph Hearst, who saw her in virgin-type roles, but she was best in comedy. MGM paid her $10,000 a week! *The Patsy* (1928), *Show People* (1928).
**Sidelights:** Davies's name appeared daily in 22 newspapers owned by Hearst. Died: 1961.

## Wendell Corey *Actor*      6328 Hollywood
**Born:** March 20, 1914, in Dracut, MA.
**Spotlights:** Dark-haired, brooding plainclothes officer battling drug smugglers and murderers. Captain Ralph Baxter on "Harbor Command" (1957–58). Co-starred with Nanette Fabray in "Westinghouse Playhouse" (1961). Psychiatrist Dr. Theodore Bassett on "The Eleventh Hour" (1962–63). Died: 1968, of a liver ailment caused by alcoholism.

*William Frawley*      *William Farnum*      *Ernest Borgnine*

**Jayne Mansfield**  🎥  *Actress*                     6328 Hollywood

**Born:**  Vera J. Palmer; April 19, 1933, in Bryn Mawr, PA.
**Spotlights:**  Like bosomy, blond Marilyn Monroe, Mansfield married at 16, had the sense of a publicity hound, and was picked up by 20th Century-Fox. *Will Success Spoil Rock Hunter?* (1957) and *Kiss Them for Me* (1957). Died: 1967, in a tragic automobile accident.

**Henry Rowland**  📺  *See page 380.*                     6328 Hollywood

**Al Pearce**    *Actor, comedian*                     6330 Hollywood

**Born:**  1899, in New York, NY.
**Spotlights:**  Comedy star of "Al Pearce and His Gang" whose cast included the Human Chatterbox, the Laughing Lady, Tizzie Lish (played a a female impersonator), Yahbut, Lord Bilegwater, and Yogi Yorgeson (first NBC broadcast, 1933, but lasted more than 15 years). Most famous character was Elmer Blurt, the shy door-to-door salesman: "Nobody home, I hope, I hope, I hope." TV and films, too. Died: 1961.

**Gene Austin**  🎵  *Actor, singer, composer*                     6332 Hollywood

**Born:**  June 24, 1900, in Gainesville, TX.
**Spotlights:**  "The Whispering Tenor" was a frequent guest on the "Sing It Again" CBS music quiz radio show (1948–51). Also, a vocalist on "The Joe Penner Show," yes, the "Wanna buy a duck?" Penner. Ozzie Nelson was the orchestra leader- vocalist and Harriet Hilliard was the regular vocalist. Appeared in films including *My Little Chickadee* (1940). Died: 1972, from cancer.

**Lillian Roth**  🎥  *Singer, actress*                     6332 Hollywood

**Born:**  Lillian Rutstein; Dec. 13, 1910, in Boston, MA.
**Spotlights:**  Vivacious, singing sensation on Broadway and radio. Films include *Animal Crackers* (1930), with the Marx Brothers and Margaret Dumont; *Paramount on Parade* (1930).
**Sidelights:**  When her best-selling autobiography, *I'll Cry Tomorrow* (1955), was adapted as a film, Roth chose Susan Hayward for the lead. Hayward used her own singing voice, and her portrayal inspired Roth to comment, "It was almost like looking in a mirror." Died: 1980.

**Dorothy Lamour**  🎥  *Actress, singer*                     6332 Hollywood

**Born:**  Mary D. Kaumeyer; Dec. 10, 1914, in New Orleans, LA.
**Spotlights:**  Crowned Miss New Orleans when she was 17. Radio experience with bandleader Herbie Kay (husband, 1935–39) landed her own NBC show. In 1936, Paramount signed her as *The Jungle Princess*. She gained notoriety for wearing sarongs, but gained comic popularity for the "road" pictures starring Bing Crosby and Bob Hope.

### Kim Novak  *Actress* 6336 Hollywood

**Born:** Marilyn Novak; Feb. 13, 1933, in Chicago, IL.

**Spotlights:** Bewitchingly beautiful in Columbia's *Bell, Book, and Candle* (1958), co-starring James Stewart and Jack Lemmon. Also in 1958, she was exceptionally good in Alfred Hitchcock's *Vertigo*, co-starring James Stewart. Credible and strong in *The Mirror Crack'd* (1980), opposite Elizabeth Taylor. 1986, TV work: "Falcon Crest."

### Darryl Zanuck  *Studio executive, producer* 6336 Hollywood

**Born:** Sept. 5, 1902, in Wahoo, NE.

**Spotlights:** Wrote the screenplay, *Find Your Man* (1924), for Warner's biggest star, Rin-Tin-Tin. Promoted to head of production: "For God's sake, don't say yes until I'm finished talking!" In 1933 co-founded 20th Century-Fox; *The Longest Day* (1962) was one of his hits. Retired in 1971. Died: 1979.

### Elizabeth Taylor  *Actress* 6336 Hollywood

**Born:** Feb. 27, 1932, in North London, England.

**Highlights:** Inherited her flair for theatrics from her mother, Sara Southern, although it was her father, Francis Taylor, with the encouragement of a neighbor, who introduced her to MGM. By 10, the violet-eyed, raven-haired angel-faced child was a star. Her classmates at the Little Red School House included co-star Mickey Rooney in *National Velvet* (1944), and Judy Garland.

**Achievements:** Best Actress Oscars, *Butterfield 8* (1960) and *Who's Afraid of Virginia Woolf?* (1966).

| | |
|---|---|
| *Marion Davies* | *Elizabeth Taylor* |

**Sidelights:** The superbeauty's love life has been as spectacular as a Hollywood movie; she has been married 7 times (twice to Richard Burton).

## Marjorie Rambeau  *Actress*     6336 Hollywood
**Born:** July 15, 1889, in San Francisco, CA.
**Spotlights:** Beautiful Broadway star who concentrated on films when she was in her forties through sixties. Versatile: *Torch Song* (1953), *Primrose Path* (1940). Died: 1970.

## Arturo Toscanini  🎙️  *The Maestro*     6336 Hollywood
**Born:** March 25, 1867, in Parma, Italy.
**Spotlights:** Meticulous, spirited conductor true to each composer's music. Both La Scala and the Metropolitan Opera had the fortune to stage his perfect operas. Radio: Broadcast on NBC's General Masters Concerts in 1934. NBC assembled a fine 90-piece orchestra for Toscanini's conductorship in 1936. The NBC Symphony Orchestra enabled everyone in America to hear the most beautiful music in the world and gave many a love of classical music. Died: 1957.

## Laurence Trimble  🎥  *Director*     6338 Hollywood
**Born:** April 1, 1885, in Robbinston, ME.
**Spotlights:** Absolutely the most unusual way to become a director: In 1910 his dog was signed by the studio to become Jean, the Vitagraph Dog. Directed *White Fang* (1925), starring Strongheart — another Walk of Famer. Died: 1954.

## Irene Hervey  🎥  *Actress*     6338 Hollywood
**Born:** Irene Herwick; July 11, 1910, in Los Angeles, CA.
**Spotlights:** She was glorious in Universal's classic western *Destry Rides Again* (1939), starring James Stewart and Marlene Dietrich; *Cactus Flower* (1969).

## Stan Kenton  💿  *Composer, conductor, teacher*     6338 Hollywood
**Born:** Stanley Newcomb Kenton; on Feb. 19, 1912, in Wichita, KS.
**Spotlights:** Formed first band in 1941. Organized the Neophonic Band in 1964. Organizer and arranger of progressive jazz orchestras. Recorded on Creative World, his own label. Songs and instrumental works include "Artistry in Rhythm," "Concerto for Doghouse (a Setting in Motion)," "Jump for Joe," and "007." Died: 1979.

## Robert Wise  🎥  *Director, producer*     6338½ Hollywood
**Born:** Sept. 10, 1914, in Winchester, IN.
**Achievements:** 1961, Best Picture and Best Director Oscars, *West Side Story*; 1965, Best Picture and Best Director Oscars, *The Sound of Music*; 1966, Irving Thalberg Award. President of the Academy of Motion Pictures, Arts and Sciences.

**William Collier**  *Actor, writer*                    6338½ **Hollywood**

**Born:** Nov. 6, 1866, in New York, NY.
**Spotlights:** He was 49 when he made his first film, *Fatty and the Broadway Stars*
(1915). Enjoyed working in *Thanks for the Memory* (1938), starring Bob Hope.
Died: 1944.

**Paul Gilbert** *Comedian, dancer, actor*                    6340 **Hollywood**

**Born:** Paul MacMahon; in 1917.
**Spotlights:** Clowned around as a circus performer, vaudeville celebrity, and film star
(including *The Second Greatest Sex* in 1955), and boxed his way into the lead in TV's
"The Duke" (1954), a situation comedy about a heavyweight fighter who slips into
society life via his love for painting.
**Highlights:** Father of actress Melissa Gilbert and of Jonathan Gilbert. Died: 1976.

**Carlyle Blackwell** *Actor*                    6340 **Hollywood**

**Born:** April 21, 1888, in Troy, PA.
**Spotlights:** Handsome, romantic leading man during silent era only. *Uncle Tom's
Cabin* (1909), *Such a Little Queen* (1914), opposite Mary Pickford. Died: 1955.

**Igor Stravinsky** *Composer, conductor*                    6340 **Hollywood**

**Born:** June 17, 1882, in Russia.
**Spotlights:** A musical genius, this prolific composer gave the world many moving
compositions. His ballet scores, *The Firebird* in 1910, *Petrouchka* in 1911, and *The
Rite of Spring* in 1913, were masterpieces. Decades of music reflecting changes in
his style include *Symphonies of Wind Instruments* in 1920, *Symphony of Psalms*
in 1930, *Symphony in Three Movements* in 1942, 1943, 1944, and 1945, and
*Threni* in 1958. Died: 1971.

**Gale Gordon** *Actor*                    6340 **Hollywood**

**Born:** Charles T. Aldrich, Jr.; Feb. 2, 1906.
**Spotlights:** Regular on "The Burns and Allen Show" (from 1931); Mayor La Trivia on
"Fibber McGee and Molly" (NBC, 1934–52); star of "Granby's Green Acres" (CBS,
1950). Yes, it was the forerunner to TV's "Green Acres." More.

**Eleanor Parker** *Actress*                    6340 **Hollywood**

**Born:** June 26, 1922, in Cedarville, OH.
**Spotlights:** Pretty, strawberry-blonde who co-starred with Agnes Moorehead in
possibly the first women-behind-bars melodrama, *Caged* (1950); *The Sound of
Music* (1965).

**Bela Lugosi** *Actor*                    6340 **Hollywood**

**Born:** B. Blasko on Oct. 20, 1882, in Hungary.
**Spotlights:** "I am — Dra-cu-la." Lugosi played the evil, blood-thirsty, pale-faced,

*Igor Stravinsky*

Transylvanian vampire-count in Universal's first horror film, *Dracula* (1930). The Depression era audience eagerly accepted this terrifying genre, and Lugosi's devilish pose and piercing eyes made him the "Horror King" throughout the thirties and sporadically the forties. Originally Lon Chaney was offered the role of Dracula, but died before the film's shooting. Only then was Lugosi offered the role, which made him a star. *Mark of the Vampire* (1935), with Carol Borland. Later, the atomic bomb stimulated interest in horror/madmen pictures.

**Sidelights:**    Died: 1956, buried in his Dracula cape!

# ⋆ 6350 HOLLYWOOD ⋆

**Bill Haley** 🔘 *Singer, songwriter, guitarist*　　　**6350 Hollywood**
**Born:** William Haley, Jr.; July 6, 1925, in Highland Park, MI.
**Spotlights:** Originally "country," later became first white rhythm-and-blues band with the Comets. Called the "Father of Rock 'n Roll." The term *rock 'n roll* was coined from his song "Rock, Rock, Rock Everybody, Roll, Roll, Roll, Everybody." Became an important part of musical history with dance hits such as "Crazy Man, Crazy" and "Shake, Rattle and Roll." More significant was his 1954 recording "Rock Around the Clock," but it didn't take off until a year later as the high-fi theme song for the movie *Blackboard Jungle.*
**Achievements:** The all-time highest selling rock 'n roll single: "Rock Around the Clock," with over 22 million copies sold.
**Sidelights:** Ironically, he was a very "straight" man who felt he had created "a monster." Died: 1981, from a heart attack.

**Ramon Novarro** 🎥 *Actor*　　　**6350 Hollywood**
**Born:** Ramon Samaniegas; Feb. 6, 1899, in Mexico.
**Spotlights:** The top romantic Chicano star during the silent era. *Ben Hur* (1926) was his biggest hit. Died: 1968.

**Diana Lynn** 📺 *See page 257.*　　　**6350 Hollywood**

**Jane Wyatt** 📺 *Actress*　　　**6352 Hollywood**
**Born:** Aug. 12, 1912, in New York, NY.
**Spotlights:** Millions of American children dreamed that Margaret Anderson was their second mommy. She was pretty, loving, and understanding. When she smiled, her eyes twinkled with a peacefulness that you knew came from her heart. Along with Robert Young on "Father Knows Best" (1954–63), she set family standards, even if they were idealized.
**Achievements:** 1957, 1959, 1969, Emmys.

**Dorothy Phillips** 🎥 *Actress, producer*　　　**6358 Hollywood**
**Born:** Dorothy Strible; Dec. 23, 1892, in Baltimore, MD.
**Spotlights:** Pioneer silent screen star capable of showing great depths of pain and occasionally humor: *The Rosary* (1911), *The Adventures of a Sea-Going Hack* (1915), *A Soul for Sale* (1918). Last film was *The Man Who Shot Liberty Valance* (1962). Died: 1980.

### Dave Willock  *Actor*      **6358 Hollywood**

**Spotlights:** Became a teen idol after his film debut in *Legion of Lost Flyers*, (1939). Regular guest on TV's "Pantomine Quiz" (Wasn't everybody?) from 1953–54. Parlayed his building hobby into a humorous, but informative TV show in 1955, "Do It Yourself." Regular on "The Beautiful Phyllis Diller Show" (1968). More.

### Robert Young  *See page 372.*      **6358 Hollywood**

### Mala Powers  *Actress*      **6360 Hollywood**

**Born:** Mary Powers; Dec. 29, 1931, in San Francisco, CA.
**Spotlights:** Mona Williams (1965–66) on the situation comedy "Hazel." Played secretary Marian Crane to Anthony Quinn's "The Man and the City" (1971–72). Experienced stage and screen celebrity.

### June Lockhart  *Actress*      **6362 Hollywood**

**Born:** June 25, 1925, in New York, NY.
**Spotlights:** Screen debut in *A Christmas Carol* (1938), with her real-life father and mother! *Meet Me in St. Louis* (1944). TV: Played Ruth Martin (1958–64) on "Lassie"; Maureen Robinson on "Lost in Space" (1965–68).
**Sidelights:** Daughter of Gene and Kathleen Lockhart.

### Bill Welsh  *Radio announcer, news sportscaster,*      **6362 Hollywood**
                            *TV personality*

**Born:** William H. Welsh; April 25, in Greeley, CO.

*June Lockhart*                     *Bill Welsh*

281

**Spotlights:** His perfect pronunciation and stylish delivery made him a radio personality in Colorado before he moved to California to cover USC and UCLA football games. His love for sports was clearly heard over his broadcasts, and fans enjoyed his robust play-by-play descriptions almost as much as they would have enjoyed attending the games. Welsh's first television assignment for ice hockey in 1946 occurred when there were only 300 TV sets in Southern California and TV was considered risky business. With KTTV since 1951, Welsh has covered 40 years of the Rose Parade, and along with his other accomplishments, enjoys the distinction of having the longest continuous career in TV history!

## Phil Spitalny  *Orchestra leader, composer, clarinetist*  6364 Hollywood
**Born:** Nov. 7, 1890, in Russia.
**Spotlights:** A child prodigy. Starred on "The Hour of Charm" with his "All-Girl Orchestra" (1929); more. Songs: "Madelaine," and "It's You, No One But You." Died: 1970.

## Jack White  *Actor*  6364 Hollywood
**Born:** J. Irving White; in 1865.
**Spotlights:** Trained on stage, he came to Hollywood for *The Spoilers* and *Girl of the Golden West* (both 1930). Appeared in both the 1932 and 1944 versions of *Sign of the Cross*. Died: 1949.

## Andy Devine  *Actor*  6366 Hollywood
**Born:** Oct. 7, 1905, in Flagstaff, AZ.
**Spotlights:** Roly-poly sidekick, Jingles P. Jones, to "the bravest, strongest, fightingest U.S. Marshal in the whole West!" in "The Adventures of Wild Bill Hickok" (1951–58). Portrayed same character on the radio show (1952). Previously he was a regular on radio's "The Rudy Vallee Show" (1938). Made 150 films, and other TV series.
**Sidelights:** Refused to listen to executives, agents, etc. who told him to quit because no one would like his crackly, high-pitched voice. Died: 1977.

## Paul Henreid  *Actor, director*  6366 Hollywood
**Born:** Jan. 10, 1908, in Austria.
**Spotlights:** 1942 was a grand year for him when Warners developed his European qualities in *Now Voyager*, opposite Bette Davis, and in the classic melodrama *Casablanca*, opposite Ingrid Bergman. Directed 6 'B' films (1951–64). TV: "One Coat of White" (1957); "The Falling of Raymond" (1971).

# · 6370 HOLLYWOOD ·

## Anne Bancroft  *Actress* 6370 Hollywood

**Born:** Anna Maria Luise Italiano; Sept. 17, 1932, in Bronx, NY.
**Spotlights:** Started in show biz at age 4. Her early TV stage name was Anne Marno. A vibrant talent, capable of playing roles of incredible depth, in *The Miracle Worker* (1962) and *The Graduate* (1967). TV: "Jesus of Nazareth" (1976). Always the consummate actress.
**Achievements:** 1962, Best Actress Oscar, *The Miracle Worker*.
**Highlights:** Married to writer-director-producer-actor-comedian, Mel Brooks.

## Lassie 🎥 *Dog* 6370 Hollywood

**Born:** 1941. The original Lassie was a male collie named Pal.
**Spotlights:** *Lassie Come Home* (1943), a sentimental story about a poor family forced to sell their cherished collie, starring Roddy McDowell and Elizabeth Taylor, was a huge commercial success for MGM. Sequels followed including *Son of Lassie* (1945) and *Courage of Lassie* (1946). A radio show (1947–50) and a TV show (1954–71) were extremely popular, too.
**Sidelights:** Trainer Rudd Weatherwax actually handled several male dogs (from Pal's bloodline) who played Lassie. Interestingly, the controversy rages on about that canine's gender. "Dear Abby" has even gotten involved in more than one column! Died: 1959; but his bloodline happily lives on!

*Anne Bancroft*                    *Lassie*

283

**Robert Goulet**  *Singer, actor*          6370 Hollywood

**Born:** Nov. 26, 1933, in Lawrence, MA.

**Spotlights:** Handsome, dark-haired performer. His break on Broadway came when he landed the role of Sir Lancelot in the Lerner-Lowe musical *Camelot* in 1960. Musical star in Rodgers and Hammerstein's *Carousel* and Cole Porter's *Kiss Me Kate*.

**Achievements:** 1962, Grammy, new artist; 1968, Tony, "The Happy Time."

**Robert Z. Leonard** *Director*          6370 Hollywood

**Born:** Oct. 7, 1889, in Chicago, IL.

**Spotlights:** Gloss, beauty, and harmony were his trademarks. *The Great Ziegfeld* (1936); *Maytime* (1937), starring Nelson Eddy and Jeanette MacDonald (her favorite film); *Ziegfeld Girl* (1941), starring James Stewart and Judy Garland. Died: 1968.

**Jack Benny** *See page 316.*          6370 Hollywood

**Rich Little** *Impressionist, comedian, actor*          6372 Hollywood

**Born:** Richard Caruthers Little; Nov. 26, 1938, in Ottawa, Canada.

**Spotlights:** Described as "the most accurate, original, daring, and dependable impressionist this side of Xerox." Popular TV star for over two decades, his special "Liberace in Wonderland" (1965), with Kirk Douglas (as the Cheshire Cat), Jack Lemmon (The March Hare) and Jack Benny (The Queen of Hearts) — with Little playing all of the roles — showed off his hilarious versatility and timing. His Jimmy Stewart, W.C. Fields, Johnny Carson, Richard Nixon, et al., sound like the real thing.

**Achievements:** When David Niven was seriously ill with Lou Gehrig's disease, Little dubbed his voice in the movies, *The Trail of the Pink Panther* and *The Curse of the Pink Panther.*

**Sidelights:** In the late 1970s, when he'd call up room service in a hotel, and the staff informed him it'd be the standard "hour" wait, he'd hang up. He'd call right back, using Cary Grant's voice, and get his food without delay. Little used to walk the Walk of Fame imitating each person as he stepped on his star. He always thought it'd make a great skit! Who can't he imitate? "Bob Hope, because of his unique vocal rhythms the timing is hard to get down."

**Mickey Rooney** *See page 142.*          6372 Hollywood

**George Putnam** *Newscaster*          6372 Hollywood

**Spotlights:** Started as a janitor at WDGY in Minneapolis and pleaded with management to give him a shot at going on the air. For his 20th birthday present they granted his wish and he's been a broadcaster ever since. In 1939 hired by NBC in New York; signed to KTTV in Los Angeles in 1951. On tough assignments, he disrupted City Hall and dug up dirt and corruption where he could find it. By 1972, he was the highest paid newscaster in American TV at $300,000 a year.

## Ronald Reagan ▓ *Actor, politician* 6374 Hollywood

**Born:** Feb. 6, 1911, in Tampico, IL.

**Spotlights:** A Warner Brothers contract player from 1937. Made over 50 motion pictures, including: *Code of the Secret Service* (1939), *Knute Rockne, All-American* (1940), *Bedtime for Bonzo* (1951). TV: Host-star of "General Electric Theater" (1954–62). Host of "Death Valley Days" (1965–66).

**Achievements:** "Well, became the 40th president of the United States in 1980. Governor of California, 1967–75.

**Highlights:** Married actress Jane Wyman (1940–48); married actress Nancy Davis in 1952.

## Mark Goodson ▓ *Producer, writer* 6374 Hollywood

**Born:** Jan. 24, 1915, in Sacramento, CA.

**Spotlights:** Along with associate Bill Todman, Goodson co-produced most of the longest-running quiz shows in TV history, including "Beat the Clock" (1950–58), "To Tell the Truth" (1956–67), "The Price is Right" (1957–64), and "What's My Line?" (1950–67).

*Ronald Reagan*

### Perry Como ■ *Singer, actor* 6376 Hollywood

**Born:** Nick Perido; May 18, 1912, in Canonsburg, PA.
**Spotlights:** "The Perry Como Show," musical variety (1948–63). Frequently sang his latest hit record on the show. Well known for his Christmas specials. Radio: "The Perry Como Show" (1944). Recordings: Song "It's Impossible"; *The Perry Como Christmas Album*.

### Laura La Plante ■ *Actress* 6376 Hollywood

**Born:** Nov. 1, 1904, in St. Louis, MO.
**Spotlights:** Beautiful, blonde leading lady in *Shooting for Love* (1923) and *The Beautiful Cheat* (1926). Delightful in comedies, but best known for *The Cat and the Canary* (1927) — remember those spooky nightmares about a hand reaching out from beneath the bed? In the 1970s retired in Palm Desert, California.

### George Cukor ■ *Director* 6378 Hollywood

**Born:** July 7, 1899, in New York, NY.
**Spotlights:** *A Bill of Divorcement* (1932), starring John Barrymore and introducing Katharine Hepburn; and *Little Women* (1933), again with Hepburn; both were David O. Selznick productions. *The Philadelphia Story* (1940), proved he still had confidence, even after being fired from *Gone with the Wind* one year earlier. Died: 1983.

### Rex Harrison ■ *See page 343.* 6380 Hollywood

### Joseph Cotten ■ *Actor* 6382 Hollywood

**Born:** May 15, 1905, in Petersburg, VA.
**Spotlights:** Struggled for 15 years to break in; his efforts paid off in a big way with his first full-length film, *Citizen Kane* (1941). The dark, wavy-haired, quiet, intelligent actor had a distinctive voice, which Hitchcock cleverly employed in *Shadow of a Doubt* (1943), where Cotten played Uncle Charlie, the merry widow-murderer.

### David Niven ■ *Actor* 6384 Hollywood

**Born:** James Niven; March 1, 1910, in Scotland.
**Spotlights:** Charming, eloquent, mustached leading man in *Thank You Jeeves* (1936), *My Man Godfrey* (1957), *The Pink Panther* (1963), more. TV: Played Alec Fleming on "The Rogues," comedy-drama (1964–65); more.
**Achievements:** 1958, Best Actor Oscar, *Separate Tables*. Died: 1983.

### Dick Whittinghill ■ *Disc jockey, singer* 6384 Hollywood

**Born:** In Helena, MT.
**Spotlights:** Formerly one of the Pied Pipers. Signed on with KGFJ in Hollywood, and KIEV in Glendale, California, before joining KMPC in 1950. His locker-room humor, pranks, skits, and interviews won him millions of daily listeners: "Everyone on the

Hollywood freeway, let's play musical cars. White cars stop. Green cars move a lane right. Japanese cars face the rising sun on the count of 3." Retired in 1979, after 30 years on the air.

**Gene Autry** 🔴  *See page 312.*  **6384 Hollywood**

**Jerry Fairbanks** 🎥  *Producer, director, cameraman*  **6384 Hollywood**

**Born:** Nov. 1, 1904, in San Francisco, CA.

**Spotlights:** Started as a projectionist in 1919; a cameraman by 1924. Famous for his film shorts at Universal and Paramount. Developed numerous techniques and equipment, including the dual plane process by which live animals "were made to talk."

**Achievements:** 1942, Academy Award, *Unusual Occupations*; 1944, *Speaking of Animals.*

**Sidelights:** Became the first showbiz pro to become the president of the Hollywood Chamber of Commerce.

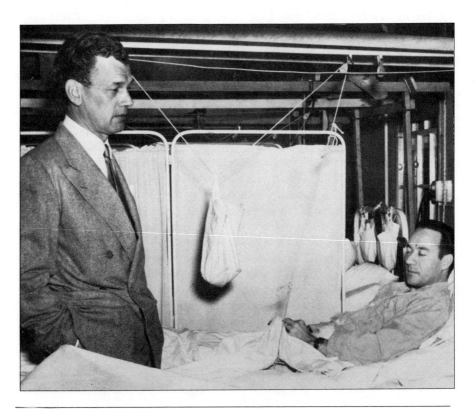

*Joseph Cotton visits convalescing veterans during WWII.*

# ⋆ 6400 HOLLYWOOD ⋆

### Claude Rains  *Actor* 6400 Hollywood

**Born:** William C. Rains; Nov. 10, 1889, in England.

**Spotlights:** An actor's actor. Fair-haired, mustached, clipped accent, arched eyebrow, not terrifically handsome, but superbly skillful in kind or sinister roles: *Mr. Smith Goes to Washington* (1939), *Casablanca* (1942), *Mr. Skeffington* (1944), *Notorious* (1946). He never won an Oscar, but should have. Died: 1967.

### Hank Williams  *Singer, guitarist, songwriter* 6400 Hollywood

**Born:** Hiriam H. Williams; Sept. 17, 1923, in Gero Georgiana, AL.

**Spotlights:** When Williams and the Drifting Cowboys aired on Montgomery, Alabama radio station, WSFA, country and western was largely considered to be hick, hillbilly music. His wide vocal range, straightforward lyrics, and beautiful melodies changed that image. This sensitive, shy, skinny artist could sing honky-tonk to the blues and make any city slicker enjoy it. Brief career spanned only 6 years (1946–52), but left a legacy of goldies: "Move It On Over," Love Sick Blues," "Cold, Cold Heart," "I'm So Lonesome I Could Cry," "Jambalaya (on the Bayou)," more.

**Highlights:** His marriage to Audrey Williams, produced a talented son, Hank Williams, Jr. Died: New Year's Day, 1953.

### Marlene Dietrich 🎥 *Actress* 6400 Hollywood

**Born:** Maria Magdelene Dietrich; Dec. 27, 1901, in Germany.

**Spotlights:** The screen's greatest femme fatale, whose husky rendition of "Falling in Love Again" in *The Blue Angel* (1930), made her an international celebrity. "It took more than one man to change my name to Shanghai Lily," she unashamedly admits in *Shanghai Express* (1932). *The Devil Is a Woman* (1935) was her personal favorite because she felt she was more beautiful "than in any other of my whole career." She co-starred with James Stewart in *Destry Rides Again* (1939).

**Sidelights:** Her gorgeous legs were often covered by slacks — at a time when it simply was not permissible for women to wear slacks — and started a rage that changed American fashion. The Nazis attempted to recruit her for their propaganda war films. She publicly insulted Hitler by refusing. Became an American citizen and made countless anti-Nazi speeches and traveled tirelessly to the front to entertain U.S. troops. A war hero, she was awarded the Medal of Freedom.

### Robert Ripley 🎞 *Actor, author, cartoonist, creator* 6400½ Hollywood

**Born:** Dec. 25, 1893, in Santa Rosa, CA.

**Spotlights:** Ripley created the newspaper column, "Believe It or Not" in 1918. The popularity of these freakish and fantastic true stories led to an NBC radio show, first heard in 1930. "Believe It or Not" moved to NBC-TV in 1949 with Ripley as the host. The series had a successful run again from 1982–86. Died: 1949.

**Charles Walters**  *Director*      6402 Hollywood

**Born:** Nov. 17, 1911, in Brooklyn, NY.
**Spotlights:** An energetic former dancer and choreographer, he naturally complemented the Rogers-Astaire team, Judy Garland, and Leslie Caron. *Easter Parade* (1948), *Lili* (1953), *High Society* (1956). Died: 1982.

**John Reed King**    *Actor, producer, newscaster*      6402½ Hollywood

**Born:** Oct. 25. 1914, in Wilmington, DE.
**Spotlights:** King of game show hosts: "Double or Nothing" (1940); winnings up to $40! "Break the Bank"; (1945); $5 winnings per question! "Go for the House" (ABC, 1948), was one game show I'd like to see brought back. Winnings were household furnishings complete with a small house! Narrated Paramount newsreels. Died: 1979.

**Beatrice Lillie**    *Comedienne*      6404 Hollywood

**Born:** Constance Munston; May 29, 1896, in Canada.
**Spotlights:** Witty, sophisticated personality who graced 7 motion pictures. Adored jetsetter who was loved equally by the British (Winston Churchill, et al.) and the Americans: *Exit Smiling* (1926), *Around the World in 80 Days* (1956), *Thoroughly Modern Millie* (1967).

**Georgia Gibbs**    *Vocalist, actress*      6406 Hollywood

**Born:** Fredda Gibbons (later changed to Gibson); Aug. 17, 1926, in Worcester, MA.
**Spotlights:** "Her singing nibs, Miss Georgia Gibbs." Her hit song was "Tweedle-Dee." Hot singer of the thirties through the sixties. Vocalist on radio's "The Jimmy Durante Show."

**Ginny Simms**    *Hostess, singer*      6408 Hollywood

**Born:** May 25, 1916, in San Antonio, TX.
**Spotlights:** Joined the Kay Kyser band in 1934. "The Ginny Simms Show" musical variety (CBS, 1945); "The Botany Song Shop" (ABC, 1950). Hit songs: "What Is This Thing Called Love?" and "Just One of Those Things." Film celebrity.

**Alma Rubens**    *Actress*      6408½ Hollywood

**Born:** Alma Smith; Feb. 8, 1897, in San Francisco, CA.
**Spotlights:** Immortalized in D.W. Griffith's *Intolerance* (1916). *The Masks of the Devil* (1928). Died: 1931, of pneumonia.

**Cecil Brown**    *Commentator, newscaster*      6410 Hollywood

**Spotlights:** Famous for his news reports during the golden era of the big broadcasts.

**Edwin F. Goldman** *Composer, author*     **6410 Hollywood**

**Born:** Jan. 1, 1878, in Louisville, KY.

**Spotlights:** Joined the Metropolitian Opera orchestra when he was 17 years old. Recorded instrumental works: "Sans Souci," and "The Chimes of Liberty." Frequent guest on radio. Wrote book, *The Foundation to Cornet Playing.* Died: 1956.

**Tex Williams** *Actor, singer, songwriter*     **6412 Hollywood**

**Born:** Sol Williams; Aug. 23, 1917, in Fayette County, IL.

**Spotlights:** Played guitar, banjo, and harmonica. Tex was a country-and-western recording star who was featured prominently on "The Grand Ole Opry" and other popular radio and TV shows (1950–65). His band was the Western Caravan. Hit singles: "The Rose of the Alamo," "California Polka," and "Texas in My Soul."

**Lewis J. Selznick** *Film mogul*     **6412 Hollywood**

**Born:** L. Zeleznik; May 2, 1870, in Russia.

**Spotlights:** Former Universal executive, president and founder of the Selznick Company.

**Highlights:** Father of Myron and David O. Selznick. Myron was a powerhouse agent.

*Former studio of* Gone With The Wind *super talent David O. Selznick (Lewis J. Selznick's son).*

His motto: "Stars should get as much money as they can, while they can. They don't last long."
**Sidelights:** Born dirt poor, one of 18 children. Died: 1933.

## Walter Pidgeon  *Actor, singer* 6412 Hollywood

**Born:** Sept. 23, 1897, in New Brunswick, Canada.
**Spotlights:** Tall (6' 3"), dark (black hair), handsome (blue eyes) baritone. Attended the New England Conservatory of Music. Sang at a friend's party when another guest, Fred Astaire, took notice of him. "Why don't you get on the stage?" Pidgeon responded, "Why don't you put me on the stage?" Astaire provided the first contract. Silent screen debut in *Mannequin* (1926). Wonderful in *How Green Was My Valley* (1941); *Mrs. Miniver* (1942), opposite Greer Garson (he'd play her husband in numerous MGM hits); *Madame Curie*, (1943); 97 other movies.

## Edward R. Murrow ■ *See page 148.* 6412 Hollywood

## Louella O. Parsons  *Columnist* 6418 Hollywood

**Born:** Louella Oettinger on Aug. 6, 1893, in Freeport, IL.
**Spotlights:** Every day over 35 million readers relished every juicy morsel of her tinsel town gossip — while most celebrities were cautious about what they said to her, or both — for the Hearst newspapers. Her arch enemy (competitor) was Hedda Hopper. Radio: Parsons revealed exclusives on "Hollywood Reporters" (1945–51); her listeners treasured her like a star — above all other stars. Died: 1972.

## Andy Griffith ■ *Actor* 6418 Hollywood

**Born:** June 1, 1926, in Mount Airy, NC.
**Spotlights:** He was the patient, kind-hearted small town Sheriff, Andy Taylor, of Mayberry. His down-home wisdom and pleasant southern, twangy-drawl helped to keep "The Andy Griffith Show" in top ratings from 1960–68. Many TV shows.

## Robert Donat ■ *Actor* 6418 Hollywood

**Born:** March 18, 1905, in England.
**Spotlights:** Excellent in Hitchcock's comedy thriller *The Thirty-Nine Steps* (1935).
**Achievements:** 1939, Best Actor Oscar, *Goodbye Mr. Chips.*
**Sidelights:** Efforts to correct his stutter by reading Shakespeare daily turned him into an eloquent speaker. Died: 1958, of a cerebral thrombosis.

## Helen Traubel  *Opera singer, actress* 6420 Hollywood

**Born:** June 20, 1899, in St. Louis, MO.
**Spotlights:** Traubel made her Metropolitan Opera debut in 1937; left in 1953 when she and Rudolf Bing, general manager of the Met, disagreed over her appearing in nightclubs. A fine Wagnerian soprano, she contributed many excellent recordings: Wagner's *Gotterdammerung* (Victor) and *Die Walkure* (Columbia).

**Sidelights:** She has published detective stories, such as *The Ptomaine Canary* and *The Metropolitan Opera Murders*.

**Richard Brooks**  *Screenwriter, director*        6422 Hollywood

**Born:** May 18, 1912, in Philadelphia, PA.

**Spotlights:** Co-wrote *Key Largo* (1948), starring Humphrey Bogart, Lauren Bacall, and Edward G. Robinson; *Cat on a Hot Tin Roof* (1956), starring Paul Newman, Burl Ives, and Elizabeth Taylor.

**Achievements:** 1960, Academy Award, Best Screenplay *Elmer Gantry*.

**Adela St. John** *Journalist, author, screenwriter*        6424 Hollywood

**Born:** May 20, 1894, in Los Angeles, CA.

**Spotlights:** Pioneer for women in sports, news, and films. First woman sportswriter: "Babe Ruth punted it over the fence." Covered the Dempsey-Tunney boxing match. Made movie stars out of actors with her brilliant scripts: *A Free Soul* (1931), starring Clark Gable. Wrote "What Price Hollywood" with David O. Selznick. Selznick's movie *A Star is Born*, (1937) was based partly on this story. Wrote the 1962 best-seller, *Final Verdict*, about her father. Called the "First Lady of American Letters." More.

**Achievements:** Awarded the Medal of Freedom.

**Sidelights:** Awarded Hollywood High School diploma in 1951 (41 years after her class graduated). The principal took into account her many literary accomplishments to make up for the few credits she lacked (she flunked math). Taught journalism at UCLA.

*Andy Griffith*

### Wesley Ruggles  *Director*                                      6424 Hollywood
**Born:** June 11, 1889, in Los Angeles, CA.
**Spotlights:** Mae West got away with her best lines in Ruggles's *I'm No Angel* (1933). It took the devil's debt off Paramount's back, too. Died: 1972.

### Clyde McCoy  *Musician*                                                            6428 Hollywood
**Born:** Dec. 29, 1903, in Ashland, KY.
**Spotlights:** Performed on riverboats as a youth. Formed own band at age 16. Hit recordings: "Sugar Blues" and "Way Down Yonder in New Orleans." Later years (1950's-1970's) audiences loved his dixieland style.

### Ed Wynn  *See page 242.*                                                          6428 Hollywood

### George O'Hanlon  1  *Actor*                                                        6428 Hollywood
**Born:** Nov. 23, 1917, in Brooklyn, NY.
**Spotlights:** Started in the 1930s as a chorus boy in Warner Brothers musicals. Star of 60 comedy shorts. Dozens of film and TV roles. TV writer, too.

### Mitzi Green  *Actress*                                                             6430 Hollywood
**Born:** Elizabeth Keno; Oct. 22, 1920, in Bronx, NY.
**Spotlights:** As a child she played lead roles in Paramount's *Huckleberry Finn* (1931) and *Little Orphan Annie* (1932). Died: 1969, of cancer.

### Arlene Francis  *Actress*                                                          6434 Hollywood
**Born:** Arline Kazanjian; Oct. 20, 1912, in Boston, MA.
**Spotlights:** Radio: Female star of "Betty and Bob" (NBC, 1932); hostess of "Blind Date" (ABC, 1943). TV: Panelist on "What's My Line?" (1950–65). Engaging Broadway celebrity. Character actress on-screen.

### John Hart  *Actor, producer, director*                                            6434 Hollywood
**Born:** Los Angeles, CA.
**Spotlights:** Made his silver screen debut in *Buccaneer* (1937), before cashing in on his silver mine, riding his mount, "Hi-yo Silver, away!" (to the William Tell Overture) and shooting silver ammo to deter the bad guys on TV's "The Lone Ranger" (1952–54). "Hawkeye and the Last of the Mohicans," a starring role as frontier scout Nat Cutler opposite Lon Chaney, Jr. as his sidekick, Chingachgook. Moved behind the scenes to shoot Celebrity International Tours.
**Sidelights:** Took drama at Pasadena High with William Holden. (Don't confuse with Emmy award-winning newscaster John Hart).

### Ernest Gold  *Composer, conductor*                                                 6434 Hollywood
**Born:** July 13, 1921, in Vienna.

**Spotlights:** Film scores include *Judgement at Nuremberg* (1961); *Fun with Dick and Jane* (1976); more.
**Achievements:** 1960, Oscar, *Exodus*; 1960, two Grammys for "It's a Mad Mad Mad Mad World" (song of the year and soundtrack).

## Ben Alexander  🎥 *Actor*                                                          6434 Hollywood
**Born:** Nicholas Alexander; May 26, 1911, in Goldfield, NV.
**Spotlights:** A long and illustrious career began with his adorableness as a child with Lillian Gish in *Hearts of the World* (1918). Excellent in *All Quiet on the Western Front* (1930); *Dragnet* (1954). He also co-starred in the TV series "Dragnet" (1953–59) as the heavy, Officer Frank Smith. "The stories you are about to hear are true...Dum-de-dum-dum." Died: 1969.

## Lucille Ball  🎥 *See page 178*                                                    6438 Hollywood

## Cantinflas  ① *Actor*                                                              6438 Hollywood
**Born:** Mario Reyes; Aug. 12, 1911, in Mexico.
**Spotlights:** He made only two movies in the U.S., *Around the World in 80 Days* (1956), opposite David Niven and an all-star cameo cast of 44; and as star of *Pepe* (1960).

## Tony Martin  🎥 *Singer, actor*                                                    6438 Hollywood
**Born:** Alvin Morris; Dec. 25, 1913, in San Francisco, CA.
**Spotlights:** *Sing Baby Sing* (1936), and boy, could he! *Music in His Heart* (1940), and in his saxophone too. On radio, regular vocalist on "The Burns and Allen Show" (first aired CBS, 1931). Countless radio guest appearances — very popular crooner. Albums: *Tony Martin at the Plaza*, *This Is the Decade of the 30s*. TV: "The Tony Martin Show" (1954–56). Hits include: "There's No Tomorrow," and "I Get Ideas."
**Highlights:** Married to Cyd Charisse since 1948.

## Lou Costello  🎥 *Comedian*                                                        6438 Hollywood
**Born:** Louis Cristillo; March 6, 1906, in Patterson, NJ.
**Spotlights:** Experience as a newsboy, a soda fountain jerk, a prizefighter, a stuntman, and a vaudeville-burlesque performer before Kate Smith's radio show introduced him and Bud Abbott as America's double-talking comedy team, in 1939. Their popularity induced Universal to hire them for a 1940 musical, *One Night in the Tropics*. Specialized in farces: *Keep 'em Flying* and *Pardon My Sarong* put them in the number-one box office position in 1942. The team managed to stay in the top 10 with a succession of formula films for close to a decade with their cross-talk, slapstick routines. The chubby comedian's antics made him the favorite of the team, with his receiving a 60 percent cut. Their baseball routine, "Who's on first?" originally aired on radio and immortalized the pair; considered the best of their work. They had a TV series before splitting, after years of escalating friction, in 1957. Died: 1959, from a heart attack.

## Irene Dunne  *Actress*     6440 Hollywood

**Born:** Dec. 20, 1898, in Louisville, KY.

**Spotlights:** RKO spotted energetic Dunne on stage in *Show Boat*; she later appeared in the film version — 1936. The studio signed the lovely brunette and cast her in their military musical, *Leathernecking* (1930). Spectacularly good in weepies: *Back Street* (1932). Luminous performances in *Life with Father* (1947) and *I Remember Mama* (1948). Her light and airy comedies were superb, too: *My Favorite Wife* (1940), with Cary Grant. Sparkling reputation as the most charming, unaffected, best-rehearsed Hollywood actress. With over 42 films to her credit, she retired.

## Robert Montgomery *Actor*     6440 Hollywood

**Born:** Henry Montgomery, Jr.; May 21, 1904, in Beacon, NY.

**Spotlights:** Suave, handsome, light leading man, but equally convincing in heavy dramas when allowed to do so by his studio, MGM; *Private Lives* (1931), *Night Must Fall* (1937). Directed *The Lady in the Lake* (1949). Also produced. TV: Father and daughter appeared on "Robert Montgomery Presents," dramatic anthology (1950–57); this is where Elizabeth got her TV start.

**Highlights:** Father of actress Elizabeth Montgomery.

**Achievements:** Distinguished military record. Died: 1981.

*Irene Dunne with Charles Coburn*

# · 6500 HOLLYWOOD ·

### Dale Robertson ■ *Actor*                    6500 Hollywood
**Born:** Dayle Robertson; July 14, 1923, in Oklahoma City, OK.
**Spotlights:** As Jim Hardie, he was the faithful employee and adventurer on the "Tales of Wells Fargo" (1957–62). "The Iron Horse" (1966–68) captured the essence of western expansion in the U.S.; he was Ben Calhoun owner of a railroad.

### Jack Lescoulie ■ *Announcer, host*                    6500 Hollywood
**Born:** Nov. 17, 1912, in Sacramento, Calif.
**Spotlights:** Veteran host of TV; was the announcer (1952–59) of "The Jackie Gleason Show," host of "Meet the Champions" (1956–57). Personality on the original "Today Show" (1952).

### Josephine Hull 🎥 *Actress*                    6500 Hollywood
**Born:** Josephine Sherwood; May 30, 1884, in Newton, MA.
**Spotlights:** Only 5 pictures grace her filmography, including *Arsenic and Old Lace* (released 1944). Stage actress for most of her life.
**Achievements:** 1950, Best Supporting Actress, *Harvey*. Died: 1957.

### Edith Head 🎥 *Costume designer*                    6500 Hollywood
**Born:** Oct. 28, 1907, in Los Angeles, CA.
**Spotlights:** Brilliant chief dress designer for Paramount films, 1940s–1960s; later Universal's *Sweet Charity* (1969).
**Achievements:** Academy Awards include: 1949, *The Heiress*; 1950, *Samson and Delilah* and *All About Eve*; 1951, *A Place in the Sun*; 1953, *Roman Holiday*; 1954, *Sabrina*; 1960, *The Facts of Life*; 1973, *The Sting*. Died: 1981.

### James Cagney 🎥 *Actor*                    6502 Hollywood
**Born:** July 17, 1899, in New York, NY.
**Spotlights:** One of America's best-loved actors. He was a hoofer on Broadway before becoming a cocky, fast-talking gangster in Warner's *The Public Enemy* (1931); *Angels with Dirty Faces* (1938); more.
**Achievements:** 1942, Best Actor Oscar for his portrayal of George M. Cohan, a song-and-dance man, in *Yankee Doodle Dandy*. The Medal of Freedom in 1982.
**Highlights:** Married Billie Vernon in 1922.
**Sidelights:** Off-screen he was quiet and charming. Died: 1986, on Easter Sunday. He just closed his eyes and went to sleep.

## Don Alvarado  *Actor* 6504 Hollywood

**Born:** Jose Paige; Nov. 5, 1904, in Albuquerque, NM.
**Spotlights:** Romantic, suave leading man in *Loves of Carmen* (1927). Was excellent as supporting actor in RKO's *The Big Steal* (1949), starring Robert Mitchum. Died: 1967.

## Agnes Ayres *Actress* 6504 Hollywood

**Born:** Agnes Hinkle; Sept. 4, 1896, in Carbondale, IL.
**Spotlights:** Kissing Rudolph Valentino in *The Sheik* (1921), she played one of her more glamorous roles. She must have enjoyed it, for she leaped at the chance to be with him again in *Son of the Sheik*, (1926). It proved to be Valentino's last film; he died that same year of a perforated ulcer. Her career didn't last much longer; her voice was improperly pitched for sound pictures. Died: 1940, of a cerebral hemorrhage.

## Alfred Hitchcock *Director* 6506 Hollywood

**Born:** Aug. 13, 1899, in England.
**Spotlights:** The Master of Suspense. His thrillers produced a magical tension, the likes of which had never been felt before or since. Partial listing of his British and American films: *The Man Who Knew Too Much* (1934), *The Thirty-Nine Steps* (1935), *The Lady Vanishes* (1938), *Rebecca* (1940), *Psycho* (1960), *The Birds* (1963). TV: "Alfred Hitchcock Presents" (1955–65).
**Sidelights:** Portly Sir Alfred always put in a cameo appearance in each of his films. Superstition? Died: 1980.

## Florian Zabach *Composer, violinist* 6508 Hollywood

**Born:** Aug. 15, 1921, in Chicago, IL.
**Spotlights:** Well known for "The Hot Canary" tune, Zabach was a violinist on the musical variety show "Club Embassy" (1952–53). Many records including "This Dream I Have" and "The Funny Fiddle."

*Edith Head (right) on location*   *James Cagney*          *Agnes Ayres*

## Joe Williams 🔘 *Singer* 6508 Hollywood

**Born:** Joseph Goreed; Dec. 12, 1918, in Cordele, GA.
**Spotlights:** The great Count Basie called this jazz vocalist "my son." They worked together in 1950, then again in 1954 — big hit song "Every Day." By 1955, Williams was definitely an inspired contributor to the Count Basie Orchestra's swinging big-band sound. Album recordings include: *Count Basie Swings, Joe Williams Sings.* Associated with his hit song "All Right, Okay, You Win." Named "Top Male Singer of 1955" and "Best Singer with a Band" by musicians' union.

## Gale Robbins 📺 *Actress, singer* 6508 Hollywood

**Born:** May 7, 1924, in Chicago, IL.
**Spotlights:** Ravishing redhead who entered TV after making films, such as *Oh You Beautiful Doll* (1949). TV work included the variety show "Hollywood House" (1949–50). Died: 1980.

## Count Basie 🔘 *Orchestra leader, pianist* 6508 Hollywood

**Born:** William Basie; Aug. 21, 1904, in Red Bank, NJ.
**Spotlights:** Studied piano as a child paying 25 cents per session. In the early 1920s, Basie played Harlem clubs and pianos in silent movie theaters. Joined the Benny Moten band and became bandleader when Moten died suddenly in 1936. Then the Count Basie Orchestra surprised New York with music coined "Jump Rhythm." In 1939, after jazzing Carnegie Hall, "One O'Clock Jump" gained national popularity. "Jumpin' at the Woodside," "April in Paris," and "Every Day" are a few of the Count's smash hits. Count Basie led the band with his refined yet exuberant piano playing; he "built from the rhythm section to the tenors, and then on to the rest." The Count Basie Orchestra had many of the finest musicians and singers assembled, as well as accompanying the best: Ella Fitzgerald, Frank Sinatra, Tony Bennett, et al. Louis Armstrong, Nat "King" Cole, the Dorsey Brothers, Andre Previn, Bill Harris, Dizzy Gillespie, and countless other musicians voted the Count Basie Band *The Greatest Ever.* Died: 1984.

## Phil Harris 🔘 *See page 61.* 6508 Hollywood

## George Burns 📺 *See page 260.* 6510 Hollywood

## Nelson Eddy 🎤 *See page 102.* 6512 Hollywood

## David Rose 🔘 *Composer, conductor, pianist, arranger* 6512 Hollywood

**Born:** June 24, 1910, in England.
**Spotlights:** Formed first orchestra in 1936. Later scored numerous films. Guest conductor symphony orchestras. Songs and instrumentals: "Holiday for Strings," "Our Waltz," "Never Too Late."

**Achievements:** 1959, Emmy; 1971, Emmy, "Bonanza"; 1979 and 1982, Emmys, "Little House on the Prairie."

### Marlin Hurt  *Actor*                                         6512 Hollywood
**Born:** 1906.
**Spotlights:** Dick on "The Affairs of Tom, Dick, and Harry," variety show (1941). Played Beulah, a black maid on the comedy show "Beulah". (No, I'm not kidding. Hurt was a white man who played a black woman!) He also played Beulah's boyfriend, Bill Jackson! (CBS, 1945). Died: 1946.

### Maurice Costello  *Actor*                                   6516 Hollywood
**Born:** Feb. 2, 1877, in Pittsburgh, PA.
**Spotlights:** A Shakespearean silent screen star — *The Merchant of Venice* (1908) and *King Lear* (1909), who traveled the distance to *Hollywood Boulevard* (1936). Died: 1950.

### Lois Weber  *Director, actress, producer*                   6518 Hollywood
**Born:** 1882, in Allegheny, PA.
**Spotlights:** Weber takes a first in many categories: Universal's first ranked woman producer, "the highest-salaried woman director in the world," and seriously dealt with women's issues on film as early as 1916; *The Angel of Broadway* (1927). Died: 1939.

### Gene Autry  *See page 312.*                                 6520 Hollywood

### Walter Lang  *Director*                                     6520 Hollywood
**Born:** Aug. 10, 1898, in Memphis, TN.
**Spotlights:** Ethel Merman said he was her favorite director, *Call Me Madam* (1953) and *There's No Business like Show Business* (1954). Lang's films were delightful entertainment. Directed Yul Brynner's outstanding performance in *The King and I*. Died: 1972.

### Gloria Grahame  *Actress*                                   6522 Hollywood
**Born:** Gloria G. Hallward; Nov. 28, 1925, in Los Angeles, CA.
**Spotlights:** Sultry blonde, with a slight lisp, best cast in tough roles: *The Big Heat* (1953), *Human Desire* (1954).
**Achievements:** 1952, Oscar, Best Supporting Actress, *The Bad and the Beautiful*.

### E. Power Biggs  *Musician*                                  6522 Hollywood
**Born:** March 29, 1906, in England.
**Spotlights:** Esteemed British-born concert organist. His CBS Sunday morning broadcasts (1942–58) had a large audience who favored his bright interpretations of Bach. Recordings: *Toccata; Fugue in D Minor;* more. Died: 1977.

## Hobart Bosworth  *Actor*     6522 Hollywood

**Born:** Aug. 10, 1865, in Marietta, OH.
**Spotlights:** Worked *In the Sultan's Power* (1909), the very first picture made in Los Angeles. Busy leading and character actor in over 100 films. General Lee in *Abraham Lincoln* (1930). Occasionally directed, wrote, and produced. Died: 1943.

## Glenda Farrell *Actress*     6524 Hollywood

**Born:** June 30, 1904,in Enid, OK.
**Spotlights:** Gangsters loved her as a girlfriend, but Hollywood enjoyed her best as a wisecracking blonde. *Lady for a Day* (1933), *Gold Diggers of 1937*, where she played off Joan Blondell. Remembered as the reporter in the Torchy Blane film series.
**Achievements:** 1963, Emmy. Died: 1971, of cancer.

## Lewis Stone *Actor*     6524 Hollywood

**Born:** Nov. 15, 1879, in Worcester, MA.
**Spotlights:** Thin, distinguished, mustached, silent leading man, later character actor; MGM's *Queen Christina* (1933), with the enchanting Greta Garbo. All-American as Judge Hardy in the Andy Hardy series. Died: 1953, from a heart attack.

## Vanessa Brown *See page 255.*     6528 Hollywood

## John Boles *Actor, singer*     6530 Hollywood

**Born:** Oct. 27, 1895, in Greenville, TX.
**Spotlights:** Handsome, reliable, leading man opposite high-powered actresses. Rich voice in early sound picture *The Desert Song* (1929). Worked with Shirley Temple in *Stand Up and Cheer* (1934) and *Curly Top* (1935).
**Sidelights:** Engaged in successful espionage activities against the Germans during World War I. Died: 1969, of a heart attack.

## Alan Hale *Actor, director*     6530 Hollywood

**Born:** Rufus A. McKahan; Feb. 10, 1892, in Washington, DC.
**Spotlights:** Close to 200 films to his credit (1911–59), including his role as Little John in *The Adventures of Robin Hood* (1938), starring Errol Flynn; *Of Human Bondage* (1934); *Stella Dallas* (1937). Directed *Risky Business* (1926).
**Highlights:** Father of actor, Alan Hale, Jr.
**Sidelights:** A renaissance man, Hale wrote, directed, and invented with a marked degree of success. Died: 1950, from a liver ailment.

## Freddy Martin *Band leader, tenor sax, and drums*     6536 Hollywood

**Born:** Dec. 9, 1906, in Cleveland, OH.
**Spotlights:** Formed own band in 1932. Remember vocalist Merv Griffin in 1948 with Martin? Had the hit, "I've Got a Lovely Bunch of Coconuts." A long list of recordings

300

(some under his 5 pseudonyms): "Paris in Spring/Bonjour Mam'selle," "I Should Have Known You Years Ago," "All or Nothing at All," "Everything I've Got." On radio (1934–74), and in films. Theme song came from the 1941 hit, "Tonight We Love." Died: 1983.

**Sidelights:**   Raised in an orphanage.

## Hal March   *See page 224.*                                       6538 Hollywood

## MacDonald Carey   *Actor*                                          6538 Hollywood

**Born:**   March 15, 1913, in Sioux City, IA.

**Spotlights:**   Played a good-guy lawyer, Herbert L. Maris, who defended alleged criminals, on "Lock Up" (1959–61). Most famous for his portrayal of Dr. Tom Horton on the soap opera "Days of Our Lives." His voice can be heard: "Like the sands through the hourglass, so these are the days of our lives." Signed on in 1965 and is still going strong. Carey was the first movie star to become a cast member in a daytime series. It's only fitting, though, his career started in the radio soap, "Stella Davis." He played Dick Grosvenor in the late 1930s.

## Jay Silverheels   *Actor*                                          6540 Hollywood

**Born:**   Harold Smith; May 26, 1919, on Six Nations Indian Reservation, Canada.

**Spotlights:**   "You Kemosabe, it mean trusty scout." Silverheels played Tonto on "The Lone Ranger" (1949–57). He portrayed his real-life people from the Indian Nation as intelligent and kind. Silverheels was the son of a Mohawk chief. Died: 1980.

## Frank Sinatra   *See page 220.*                                    6540 Hollywood

## Louise Dresser   *Actress*                                         6540 Hollywood

**Born:**   Louise Kerlin; Oct. 5, 1878, in Evansville, IN.

**Spotlights:**   Splendid character actress who proved *Mother Knows Best* (1928). She made her sonny boy sing *Mammy* (1930), in an Al Jolson musical. Very funny in the original *State Fair* (1933), starring Will Rogers. Died: 1965.

## Isaac Stern   *Violinist*                                          6540 Hollywood

**Born:**   July 21, 1920, in Russia.

**Spotlights:**   One of the world's top violinists. Virtuoso musician; range from classical to romantic. Albums: *Bach Concertos:* (Columbia), various concertos for violin and orchestra. Motion picture sound tracks include *Fiddler on the Roof.*

**Achievements:**   Grammys, solo, 1961, 1962, 1964, 1981; chamber performances, 1970; classical album of the year, 1977.

**Sidelights:**   Studied at the San Francisco Conservatory.

# ⋆ 6542 HOLLYWOOD ⋆

## Monty Woolley 🎥 *Actor*
6542 Hollywood

**Born:** Edgar M. Woolley; Aug. 17, 1888, in New York, NY.
**Spotlights:** A late bloomer by Hollwood standards, Wooley was 48 when he became a professional actor and 52 when his articulate characterization of Sheridan Whiteside in *The Man Who Came to Dinner* (1941), won him international acclaim. Co-starred with David Niven and Cary Grant in *The Bishop's Wife* (1947).
**Sidelights:** Previously, an English and drama professor at Yale University. Died: 1963, of a heart attack.

## Ralph Bellamy 📺 *Actor*
6542 Hollywood

**Born:** June 17, 1904, in Chicago, IL.
**Spotlights:** In "Man Against Crime," he was steadfast New York private eye, Mike Barnett (1949–54). On "The Eleventh Hour" he was psychiatrist, Dr. L. Richard Starke (1963–64), coping with people on the edge.
**Sidelights:** Movie fans will recall him as Mr. Duke, the older eccentric billionaire in *Trading Places* who uses Dan Ackroyd and Eddie Murphy as guinea pigs in an experiment on heredity versus environment.

## André Kostelanetz 🎙 *Conductor*
6542 Hollywood

**Born:** Dec. 22, 1901, in St. Petersburg, Russia.
**Spotlights:** Orchestra, classical artist. Albums: *Andre Kostelanetz Plays the World's Greatest Love Songs, Oscar Levant playing George Gershwin's Piano Concerto in F with the New York Philharmonic Symphony Orchestra under Kostelanetz,* (Columbia); more. Died: 1980.

## Patric Knowles 📺 *Actor*
6542 Hollywood

**Born:** Reginald Knowles; Nov. 11, 1911, in England.
**Spotlights:** Debonair, light-haired actor, a contemporary of Errol Flynn in movies. Starred in Ibsen's *A Doll's House*, hosted by Ronald Reagan for TV's "General Electric Theater". U.S. film debut in *Give Me Your Heart* (1936) was the beginning of a long and illustrious career.

## John Stahl 🎥 *Director, producer*
6546 Hollywood

**Born:** Jan. 21, 1886, in New York, NY.
**Spotlights:** Work embraced 4 decades and 41 pictures, silents through talkies. Directed and produced *Magnificent Obsession* (1935), a Universal picture starring Irene Dunne and Robert Taylor. Died: 1950.

## Evelyn Brent 🎥 *Actress*

**Born:** Oct. 20, 1899, in Tampa, FL.

**Spotlights:** Started as a teenage extra, developed her talent to play the lead role in Paramount's *Underworld* (1927), directed by Josef Von Sternberg. Died: 1975, of a heart attack.

## Leslie Howard 🎥 *Actor, producer*

**Born:** Leslie H. Stainer; April 24, 1893, in England.

**Spotlights:** Proper English gentleman who brought a unique relaxed style to his roles: *The Scarlet Pimpernel* (1934), *The Petrified Forest* (1936). Immortalized in *Gone with the Wind* (1939), he was Ashley Wilkes, the man Vivien Leigh loved so dearly. Co-produced *Intermezzo* (1939). Died: 1943, in a plane shot down during World War II.

## Orson Welles 🎙 *See page 219.*

## Zasu Pitts 🎥 *Actress, comedienne*

**Born:** Jan. 3, 1898, in Parsons, KS.

**Spotlights:** "Oh dear me!" Thin, dark-haired character actress with big brown eyes and fluttering hands. Close to 400 films to her credit from 1917 to 1963! *Mrs. Wiggs of the Cabbage Patch* (1934), *Ruggles of Red Gap* (1935), *Life with Father* (1947). Died: 1963.

## Ed Gardner 🎙 *Actor*

**Born:** 1901, in Astoria, NY.

**Spotlights:** Both on radio and TV, he played Archie on "Duffy's Tavern," comedy (CBS radio, 1941). Theme: "When Irish Eyes are Smiling." Made one film, *Duffy's Tavern* (1945).

**Sidelights:** Moved to Puerto Rico in 1949 for tax purposes. Died: 1963.

## Fred Waring 🎙 *Composer, conductor, publisher*

**Born:** June 9, 1900, in Tyrone, PA.

**Spotlights:** Radio debut in 1933. "The Fred Waring Show" also featured his band, the Pennsylvanians ("I Hear Music") (NBC, 1938). TV: Christmas music special "The Colgate Comedy Hour" (1955); guest host of "The Chevy Show" (1956). Appeared in Broadway musicals and films. Songs include "Fouled Up in Love."

**Sidelights:** President of Waring Corporation (Waring Blender).

## Tay Garnett 🎥 *Director*

**Born:** William Garnett; June 13, 1894, in Los Angeles, CA.

**Spotlights:** Directed MGM's production of *China Seas* (1935), starring Clark Gable, Wallace Berry, and Jean Harlow. Directed the original *The Postman Always Rings Twice* (1946), for MGM, starring Lana Turner and John Garfield. Died: 1977.

**Franchot Tone** 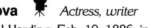 *Actor*    6560 Hollywood

**Born:**   Stanislas F. Tone; Feb. 27, 1906, in Niagara Falls, NY.
**Spotlights:**   Quiet, charming, sometimes callow, brown-haired leading man, frequently depicted as a very successful businessman, but not often seen working; *The Girl from Missouri* (1934). Very masculine and wonderful in *Mutiny on the Bounty* (1935), in the role Robert Montgomery turned down.
**Highlights:**   First actress wife (of 4) was his co-star in *Today We Live* (1933), Joan Crawford (1935–39). Died: 1968.

**Olga Petrova** *Actress, writer*    6562 Hollywood

**Born:**   Muriel Harding; Feb. 19, 1886, in England.
**Spotlights:**   Changed her name to the more exotic Olga Petrova in order to compete with the screen's first vamp, Theda Bara: "Kiss me, my fool!" Never acquired Bara's notoriety, but she did exert some executive control over her projects, and in doing so, helped pave the star-studded boulevard for other women producers, directors, and writers. *Daughters of Destiny* (1917). Died: 1977.

**James Melton**    *See page 268.*    6562 Hollywood

**David Torrence** *Actor*    6562 Hollywood

**Born:**   April 23, 1880, in Scotland.
**Spotlights:**   Former stage performer, busy on screen during twenties and thirties; *Sherlock Holmes* (1922); *Queen Christina* (1933), starring the one-and-only Greta Garbo. Died: 1942.

**Sidney Franklin** *Director, producer*    6562 Hollywood

**Born:**   May 21, 1893, in San Francisco, CA.
**Spotlights:**   Called "a woman's director." Glamor director of Greta Garbo, Norma Shearer, Mary Pickford, more. *The Good Earth* (1937).
**Achievements:**   1942, Best Picture Academy Award, *Mrs. Miniver*; 1942, special Oscar (Irving G. Thalberg Award). Died: 1972.

**H. B. Warner** *Actor*    6602 Hollywood

**Born:**   Henry Bryon Warner; Oct. 26, 1876, in England.
**Spotlights:**   Career spanned over half a century (1914–57) with both leading and supporting roles. His soulful eyes, capable of communicating love, pain, and compassion made him Cecil B. DeMille's choice for Jesus Christ in *The King of Kings* (1927). He was also tall and thin. Amminadab in DeMille's *The Ten Commandments* (1956). Wonderful in Frank Capra's *Lost Horizon* (1937). Died: 1958.

**Van Johnson** *Actor*    6602 Hollywood

**Born:**   Charles V. Johnson; Aug. 25, 1916, in Newport, RI.

**Spotlights:** This blue-eyed performer with reddish-gold-hair rose to stardom at MGM during the war years, after *Murder in the Big House* (1941). *The War Against Mrs. Hadley* (1942), *Thirty Seconds Over Tokyo* (1944); more.
**Sidelights:** World War II military did not consider Johnson fit for service because of a head injury sustained in an automobile accident, after which a metal plate was inserted into his head

### Joseph Szigeti  *Violinist*                                    6602 Hollywood
**Born:** Sept. 5, 1892, in Hungary.
**Spotlights:** Child prodigy. Played in public at age 10. Toured successfully in Europe and America. Noted violinist in the Far East in the thirties. Performed in the Library of Congress in Washington, D.C. in 1940. Died: 1973.

### Ella Raines  *See page 368.*                                    6602 Hollywood

### Sir Cedric Hardwicke  *See page 162.*                           6602 Hollywood

### Burton Holmes  *Actor, producer*                                6602 Hollywood
**Born:** Jan. 8, 1870, in Chicago, IL.
**Spotlights:** Father of travelogues. Loved vacationing and sharing and found a way to channel both into fun and profit. Made films and shorts; the first to show *Italy* (1897) and Hawaii (1898). Died: 1958.

### Peggy Ann Garner  *Actress*                                     6608 Hollywood
**Born:** Feb. 3, 1933, in Canton, OH.
**Spotlights:** Made her screen debut as a child in *Little Miss Thoroughbred* (1938). Endearing in the *Pied Piper* (1942). Sensitive portrayal of young Jane in *Jane Eyre* (1944).
**Achievements:** 1945, special Oscar, "outstanding child performer."
**Sidelights:** A wonderful stage actress, as an adult she's appeared on Broadway in numerous plays. Last film *A Wedding* (1978). TV work.

### Annette Kellerman  *Swimmer, actress*                           6608 Hollywood
**Born:** Dec. 1, 1887, in Australia.
**Spotlights:** Took to films like a duck to water in *Neptune's Daughter* (1914) and *Queen of the Sea* (1918).
**Sidelights:** Arrested when she was 19 years old for wearing a one-piece swim suit! Died: 1975.

### Robert Fuller  *Actor*                                          6608 Hollywood
**Born:** July 29, 1934, in Troy, NY.
**Spotlights:** Cast as the Wyoming drifter, Jess Harper in "Laramie" (1959–63) and as

Cooper Smith in another western, "Wagon Train" (1963–65); in "Emergency," as Dr. Kelly Brackett (1972–77). Fresh talent on the silver screen in *Teenage Thunder* (1957); more.

### Margaret O'Brien  *Actress*  6608 Hollywood

**Born:** Angela O'Brien; Jan. 15, 1937, in Los Angeles, CA.
**Spotlights:** Powerful screen impact had critics calling her a true Hollywood darling at age 4. Ability to cry hysterically or smile hypnotically at the drop of a hat. MGM cast her in *Journey for Margaret* (1942); *Meet Me in St. Louis* (1944). TV: Dramatic anthologies and guest spots.
**Achievements:** 1944, special Academy Award.

### Dyan Cannon  *Actress*  6608 Hollywood

**Born:** Samille Diane Friesen; Jan. 4, 1939, in Tacoma, WA.
**Spotlights:** Sexy, but with a spiritual quality that shines through her eyes, Cannon has excelled in comedies: *Bob and Ted and Carol and Alice* (1969); *Heaven Can Wait* (1978).
**Highlights:** Married to Cary Grant (1965–68); their union produced his only child, a daughter, Jennifer, in 1966.

### Will Rogers  *See page 88.*  6608 Hollywood

### Fleetwood Mac  *Singers, musicians, British blues band*  6608 Hollywood

**Singers:** Stevie Nicks (female, born May 26, 1948) and keyboardist Christine McVie (July 12, 1944); drums, percussion, Mick Fleetwood (June 2, 1942); bassist John McVie (Nov. 26, 1946); and lead guitarist, Lindsey Buckingham (Oct. 3, 1947).
**Spotlights:** Songs: "I Don't Want to Know," "Never Going Back Again," "Songbird," "Stop Messing 'Round/I Need Your Love So Bad."
**Achievements:** 1978, two Grammys.
**Sidelights:** Past members include Peter Green (formed the group in 1967), Jeremy Spencer, Robert Welch, Daniel Kirwan, and Robert Weston.

### Jack Palance  *Actor*  6608 Hollywood

**Born:** Vladmir (changed to Walter) J. Palahnuik, Feb. 18, 1920, in Lattimer, PA.
**Spotlights:** After reconstructive surgery for burn injuries suffered during World War II, Palance successfully auditioned for *Star of Tomorrow* (1950). TV series include "The Greatest Show on Earth" (1963–64) and "Ripley's Believe It or Not" (1982–86); more.
**Achievements:** 1956, Emmy, "Requiem for a Heavyweight."
**Highlights:** Father of actress, Holly Palance.

### Ken Minyard and Bob Arthur  *Radio hosts*  6608 Hollywood

**Born:** Minyard in McAllester, OK; Arthur in Kansas.

**Spotlights:** Minyard broke into radio by hosting "Teenage Platter Party"; Arthur was a reporter for Los Angeles station KNX. Their diversified backgrounds merged to form a special meeting of the minds, currently based in Los Angeles, with Minyard representing listeners on everyday events and Arthur being Mr. News authority. Their present talk radio "Ken and Bob Company Program" (KABC) is humorous, topical news, informational, fun.

**Achievements:** Their numerous awards include Golden Mikes and Press Awards; more.

### Ford Sterling 🎥 *Comedian*                                    6608 Hollywood

**Born:** George F. Stitch; Nov. 3, 1883, in LaCrosse, WI.

**Spotlights:** One of the top slapstick stars with Mabel Normand, of Mack Sennett's Keystone Kops; Chief Teheezal in *Court House Crook* (1915). Very funny in *He Who Gets Slapped* (1924).

**Sidelights:** Unable to resume his career full-time after his leg was amputated as a result of an accident in 1931. Last film *Black Sheep* (1935). Died: 1939.

### Eva Gabor 📺 *Actress*                                         6614 Hollywood

**Born:** Feb. 11, 1924, in Hungary.

**Spotlights:** She played the sexy, scatterbrained socialite, Lisa Douglas, on "Green Acres" (1965–71). Gabor showed her talents as a light comedienne in addition to being beautiful. Films and stage work, too.

**Highlights:** Sister of Zsa Zsa Gabor.

### Frank Capra 🎥 *Director*                                       6614 Hollywood

**Born:** May 18, 1897, in Palermo, Sicily.

**Spotlights:** "There are no rules in filmmaking, only sins. And the cardinal sin is dullness." Usually not a problem for this artistic talent who idealized human beings, and in his films where the good-hearted triumphed over the evil. His films moved gently through comedy or drama, and one of his classic works, *It's a Wonderful Life*, starring Jimmy Stewart, demonstrates his acute sensitivity to human suffering when it's bound to love. It's a wonderful twist of fate that Capra lived to see this film become an all-time favorite. When released, it was less than popular.

**Achievements:** Oscars: 1934, *It Happened One Night*; 1936, *Mr. Deed Goes to Town*; 1938, *You Can't Take It with You*.

### Arthur Godfrey 📀 *See page 158.*                              6616 Hollywood

### Fats Domino  *Singer, musician, songwriter*          6616 Hollywood

**Born:** Antoine Domino; Feb. 26, 1928, in New Orleans, LA.

**Spotlights:** Boogie-woogie rock 'n roller who tickled the ivories with dynamic energy. First hit in 1950: "The Fat Man" recorded with trumpeter-band leader Dave Bartholomew. 1955 rhythm and blues hit: "Ain't that a Shame." Popular singles: "I'm In Love Again," "Blueberry Hill," and "Blue Monday." Album: *Fats on Fire*; more.

## June Havoc 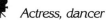 *Actress, writer*     6618 Hollywood

**Born:** June Hovick; Nov. 8, 1916, in Seattle, WA.

**Spotlights:** Baby June's stage mother pushed her to perform as soon as she could place one foot in front of the other. Worked with comedian Harold Lloyd when she was only 2; employed in Hal Roach comedies (1918–24). Later, *Four Jacks and a Jill* (1941). TV: "The Boy Who Stole the Elephants" (1970); more.

**Sidelights:** Her older sister was the stripper, Gypsy Rose Lee.

## Little Jack Little  *Composer, conductor, author,*     6618 Hollywood
*singer, pianist*

**Born:** May 28, 1900, in London, England.

**Spotlights:** Known as "Radio's Cheerful Little Earful" on the music show, "Little Jack Little" (CBS, 1930). Songs: "A Shanty in Old Shanty Town," and "You're a Heavenly Thing." Died: 1956.

## Albert Dekker 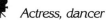 *Actor*     6620 Hollywood

**Born:** Dec. 20, 1904, in New York, NY.

**Spotlights:** Tall, sturdy, mustached character actor cast convincingly in villainous roles: *Dr. Cyclops* (1940); *Gentleman's Agreement* (1947); 79 more pictures, often seen on TV. Died: 1968, from hanging, an apparent suicide ruled as accidental death.

## Gilda Gray  *Actress, dancer*     6620½ Hollywood

**Born:** Marianna Michalska; Oct. 24, 1901, in Poland.

**Spotlights:** Many of the silents she was in were lost or destroyed, but the old MGM library has her shelved in *Rose Marie* (1936) — a Canadian Mountie story shot on location with a cast full of stars: Nelson Eddy, Jeanette MacDonald, James Stewart, David Niven.

**Sidelights:** First to perform the "shimmy" on screen. "When Gilda Gray shakes, San Francisco quakes." Died: 1959.

## Al Jolson  *Singer, actor*     6622 Hollywood

**Born:** Asa Yoelson; May 26, 1886, in Russia.

**Spotlights:** An entertainer bursting with vitality. "Mammy" was recorded in blackface; "Sonny Boy" touched millions of hearts. He's in motion picture history for speaking in the very first talkie: "You ain't heard nothin' yet." The man spoke the truth; Warners *The Jazz Singer* (1927) changed motion pictures forever. He was paid $75,000 for the role, the studio grossed $3.5 million. That was a lot of money then. (Heck, it's not even that bad now.) His next film, *The Singing Boy* (1928), held one of the highest box office records for eleven years. Jolson fared well on the radio, too. Was paid

$5,000 a week for hosting "Kraft Music Hall" (NBC, 1934); "Shell Chateau" (NBC, 1935). Died: 1950.

## Eva Marie Saint 🎥 *Actress* 6624 Hollywood

**Born:** July 4, 1924, in Newark, NJ.
**Spotlights:** Beautiful blonde with delicate features. Got an unusually late start — at 30 years old — but managed to hit a homerun on her first try at bat. Delightful in *The Russians Are Coming, the Russians Are Coming* (1966) with handsome, gifted co-star John Philip Law. TV and Broadway, too.
**Achievements:** 1954, Best Supporting Actress, *On the Waterfront*, her debut role.

## Otto Preminger 🎥 *Director* 6624 Hollywood

**Born:** Dec. 5, 1906, in Austria.
**Spotlights:** 20th Century-Fox enjoyed the prestige from Preminger's unusual murder mystery, *Laura* (1941). *Anatomy of a Murder* (1959) was Columbia's joy. Preminger produced both films, too. More.

## Janis Paige 🎥 *Actress* 6624 Hollywood

**Born:** Donna Mae Jaden; Sept. 16, 1923, in Tacoma, WA.
**Spotlights:** Girlish-looking redhead gifted with a golden throat. Underused in musicals, but extremely good in MGM's *Silk Stockings* (1957), starring Fred Astaire, Cyd Charisse, and Peter Lorre. Proved versatile on stage and TV.

## Walter Huston 🎥 *Actor* 6626 Hollywood

**Born:** Walter Houghston; April 6, 1884, in Toronto, Canada.
**Spotlights:** Huston was Honest Abe in *Abraham Lincoln* (1930) and devilish in *All That Money Can Buy* (1941).
**Achievements:** 1948, Best Supporting Actor, *The Treasure of the Sierra Madre* written and directed by his famous son, John Huston, who also won two awards! Grandfather of Academy Award-winning actress, Angelica Huston. Died: 1950, of an aneurysm.

## Gordon Jenkins 💿 *Pianist, composer, arranger* 6626 Hollywood

**Born:** May 12, 1910, in Webster Groves, MO.
**Spotlights:** Arranger for Benny Goodman, others. Musical director at Paramount in 1938, then established himself at NBC (1939–44). Popular from Las Vegas to New York, he collaborated with Johnny Mercer frequently. Songs: "I Want to Be Loved," "When a Woman Loves A Man," "Bewitched," more.
**Sidelights:** In his youth played the organ at a movie theater. Couldn't keep him away from playing the piano at a St. Louis speakeasy during the Prohibition. Died: 1984.

## Alice Terry 🎥 *Actress* 6628 Hollywood

**Born:** Alice Taafe; July 24, 1899, in Vicennes, IN.

**Spotlights:**   Alluring leading lady (1916–29); *Prisoner of Zenda* (1922), *The Arab* (1924).

**Renata Tebaldi**  *Opera singer*                           6628 Hollywood

**Born:**   Feb 1, 1922, in Pesaro, Italy.
**Spotlights:**   Adored prima donna of Puccini's operas. Toscanini selected this exquisite soprano to perform at the post-World War II reopening ceremony in 1946 of the world-famous Milan opera house, La Scala. U.S. debut in San Francisco in 1950 as Aida. Metropolitan Opera debut in 1954 as Desdemona in *Othello*. Recordings: Puccini's *Madame Butterfly, Manon Lescaut, Tosca*; many others.

**Horace Heidt**    *See page 258.*                           6630 Hollywood

**Charley Chase**   🎥 *Actor, director*                           6630 Hollywood

**Born:**   Charles Parrot; Oct. 20, 1893, in Baltimore, MD.
**Spotlights:**   Had the good fortune to work for the early masters of comedy, Mack Sennett and Charlie Chaplin, in a number of funny silent one-and two-reelers. Later, with his excellent sense of timing, directed numerous comedies including *The Three Stooges*. Also acted successfully in sound pictures. Died: 1940.

**Sonny James** *Singer, guitarist, songwriter*                           6630 Hollywood

**Born:**   James Loden; May 1, 1929, in Hackleberry, Hackleburg, AL.
**Spotlights:**   In the 1950s, he played country-and-western, pop, and rock, but by 1965 he was pure country. Known as the Southern Gentleman because he refused to play in honky tonks. A string of hit singles includes: "Young Love," "Only Love Can Break a Heart." Albums: *You're the Only World I Know, My Love/Don't Keep Me Hangin' On*. Radio, TV, and film celebrity.
**Sidelights:**   Knew what he was going to be at 4, after winning a folk talent contest.

**Roddy McDowall**   📺 *Actor*                           6630 Hollywood

**Born:**   Roderick McDowall; Sept. 17, 1928, in England.
**Spotlights:**   Won American audiences' hearts with his childhood performances in *How Green Was My Valley* (1941), *My Friend Flicka*, and *Lassie Come Home* (both 1943); more. TV: "The Martian Chronicles"; "The Memory of Eva Ryker"; more. Brings a unique and vital presence to each of his roles. Intelligent and attractive.
**Achievements:**   1961, Emmy, "Not Without Honor." 1960, Tony, supporting — "The Fighting Cock."

**Vaughn De Leath**   *Singer, composer, pianist*                           6630 Hollywood

**Born:**   Sept. 26, 1896, in Mt. Pulaski, IL.
**Spotlights:**   Known as "The Original Radio Girl." She was the first woman on the air (as soon as commercial radio production began she pushed her way in). Composer of more than 500 songs; "Hi Yo Silver," and "Madonna's Lullaby." Died: 1943.

## Neil Hamilton 🎥 *Actor*

**Born:** Sept. 9, 1899, in Lynn, MA.

**Spotlights:** Popular silent screen star who got his start in D. W. Griffith's *The White Rose* (1923).

**Sidelights:** TV fans recall him as Police Commissioner Gordon from "Batman" (1966–68).

## Norma Shearer 🎥 *Actress*

**Born:** Edith N. Shearer; Aug. 10, 1900, in Canada.

**Spotlights:** "The First Lady of the Screen" was one of MGM's biggest international box office draws during the early 1930s. She wasn't particularly beautiful by Hollywood standards, but she felt beautiful inside, was always impeccably dressed, and made millions of people think she was gorgeous. *A Lady by Chance* (1928); *A Free Soul* (1931).

**Achievements:** 1930, Best Actress Oscar, *The Divorcee*.

**Highlights:** Married to "The Boy Wonder of Hollywood," Irving Thalberg (from 1927 to his death in 1936), who wisely guided her career.

**Sidelights:** Without her husband's advice, she made two horrendous errors: She

*Roddy McDowall*

turned down the role of Scarlett O'Hara in *Gone with the Wind* and the lead in *Mrs. Miniver*. Died: 1983.

**Dale Evans**  *See page 119.*                6638½ Hollywood

**Billy Eckstine**  *Singer*                6640 Hollywood
**Born:** William Eckstein; July 8, 1914, in Pittsburgh, PA.
**Spotlights:** Known as "Mr. B." Popular vaudeville, nightclub, then recording artist who formed first band in 1944. Keen insight for hiring new talent: Dizzy Gillespie (who went out on his own in 1948), Charlie Parker, and Sarah Vaughan. Assembled and led avant-garde orchestra: "My Foolish Heart," and "My Destiny."

**Schumann-Heink**  *Opera singer*                6640 Hollywood
**Born:** Ernestine Rossler; June 15, 1861, in Lieben, Germany.
**Spotlights:** Gifted contralto at Metropolitan Opera (1899, 1903). Repertoire of 150 roles. Died: 1936.

**Michael Curtiz**  *Director*                6640 Hollywood
**Born:** Mihaly Kertesz; Dec. 24, 1888, in Budapest, Hungary.
**Spotlights:** Perhaps he dipped into the memory of his own refugee status (in World War I) to make the spine-tingling classic melodrama *Casablanca* (1942). A perfect film with the right touch of humor, excitement, romance, and suspense. *Mildred Pierce* (1945), scrutinized money and its effects and stunned middle America. Made 150 films worldwide. Died: 1962.

**Gene Autry**  *Singer, songwriter, guitarist, actor,*                6644 Hollywood
                                   *producer, executive*
**Born:** Sept. 29, 1907, in Tioga, TX.
**Spotlights:** America's favorite singing cowboy. Worked as a telegrapher in Oklahoma. Bought a guitar and taught himself to play it to pass the night. Will Rogers came in to send a telegram, and heard young Autry sing. He responded: "You're wasting your time here, get into radio." By 1927 he was a radio celebrity, by 1929, a recording star. To date, he's recorded over 2,000 songs — 300 of which he wrote or co-wrote — including, "That Silver Haired Daddy of Mine," "The Yellow Rose of Texas." Film debut *In Old Santa Fe* (1934); starred in *Tumblin' Tumbleweeds* (1935); 91 other movies. Top box office western star (1936–42). Radio: "Gene Autry's Melody Ranch" (first aired in 1940). TV: "The Gene Autry Show" (CBS, 1950–56). Extensive rodeo, carnival, arena appearances make Autry the only person on the Walk of Fame to earn one star in each category — Motion Pictures, TV, Radio, Recording, and Live Theater.
**Sidelights:** The song "Here Comes Santa Claus" crystallized while he was riding as Grand Marshal in the Hollywood parade and heard the children excitedly scream, "Here comes Santa Claus!" Owns the California Angels baseball team.

## Arthur Lake   *Actor*

**Born:**   Arthur Silverlake; April 17, 1905, in Corbin, KY.

**Spotlights:**   Born in vaudeville with greasepaint in his veins, he was an experienced comedian by the time he was cast as the rattled Dagwood Bumstead, "B-l-o-o-o-n-d-i-e!", on "Blondie" (CBS, first aired 1939). He had already starred in the first of the film series (1938–50), and later in the TV version (1957).

## Dennis Day   *Singer, actor*

**Born:**   May 21, 1917, in New York, NY.

**Spotlights:**   Cast member (tenor vocalist) on "The Jack Benny Show." Joined the show in 1939, a nervous kid straight out of college. The antithesis of Benny's cranky, stingy show biz character, Day was treated like a favorite son. Moved with the cast to the TV show still playing a lame-brained kid (CBS, 1950–60).

## Cathy Downs   *Actress*

**Born:**   Mar. 3, 1924, in Port Jefferson, NY.

**Spotlights:**   Modeled for *Vogue* and *Mademoiselle* magazines. 5' 6", 122-lb., a 24-inch waist, and "Sweater Girl" top. Blue eyes, brown hair, and a beautiful face encouraged 20th Century-Fox to sign her. Co-starred with Henry Fonda in John

*Gene Autry*

Ford's *My Darling Clementine* (1946); 23 more pictures. Appeared in the "Joe Palooka" TV series. Died: 1976.

### Eddie Cantor   *Actor, singer*      6648 Hollywood

**Born:** Edward Iskowitz; Jan. 31, 1892, in New York, NY.

**Spotlights:** His life started out as anything but a song. Born in the ghetto, he lost both parents early in his childhood. Quit school to work days and perform (amateur) nights in his teens at a burlesque show. By 1917 he was winning audiences' hearts in the Ziegfeld Follies. His first movie, Paramount's *Kid Boots* (1926), co-starred Clara Bow, and was a smash. "Banjo-eyes," as he was affectionately called, earned $5,000 a week from radio fees in addition to recording and motion picture salaries. Eddie Fisher commented, in his autobiography: "Because of his great influence as a singer, every young singer dreamed of being discovered by Cantor." The approval came when Cantor said, "Believe me, ladies and gentlemen, this boy (girl) is really going to be something." TV: Two popular shows "The Colgate Comedy Hour" and "Eddie Cantor Comedy Theater" gave audiences the opportunity to watch this energetic, legendary talent croon "If You Knew Susie," and "Ma!"

**Achievements:** 1956, special Academy Award. Died: 1964, from a heart attack.

### James Caan   *Actor*      6648 Hollywood

**Born:** James Cahn; March 26, 1939, in New York, NY.

**Spotlights:** Outstanding performances in *The Rain People* (1969) and *The Godfather* (1972). Caan's talent extends beyond drama; his charismatic cheerfulness can light up a screen. *Chapter Two* (1979).

### George Arliss   *Actor*      6648 Hollywood

**Born:** George Andrews; on April 10, 1868, in England.

**Spotlights:** An upper-crust Englishman who made his American stage debut when he was 33. Made the transition to films, 19 years later, in the silent movie, *The Devil* (1921).

**Achievements:** 1929, Best Actor Academy Award, *Disraeli*.

**Sidelights:** Known as "The Gentleman of the Screen." This was largely attributed to his aristocratic presence in portraying famous historical characters. Retired after *Dr. Syn* (1937) to care for his ailing wife. Died: 1946, from a bronchial infection.

# ⋆ 6650 HOLLYWOOD ⋆

## Red Skelton   Actor

6650 Hollywood

**Born:** Richard Skelton; July 18, 1913, in Vicennes, IN.

**Spotlights:** Radio: The star of the long-running "The Red Skelton Show" played a variety of hilarious roles including Junior, the Mean Widdle Kid, "I dood it!" Clem Kadiddlehopper, and Willie Lump Lump, "bwess his widdle heart" (NBC, first broadcast in 1941). Clowned around on TV's "The Red Skelton Show" (1952–71), adding Freddie the Freeloader to this already established repertoire of radio characters.

**Achievements:** 1951, Emmy, Best Comedy Show; 1960–61, Emmy, Outstanding Writing Achievement in comedies.

**Sidelights:** His beloved father was a circus clown. Closed each show with a loving, "God Bless."

## Norm Crosby  Comedian

6650 Hollywood

**Born:** Sept. 15, 1927, in Boston, MA.

**Spotlights:** A regular on "The Beautiful Phyllis Diller Show" (1968); a comic panelist (1976–78) on "Liar's Club"; host of "The Comedy Shop" (1978).

*Jack Benny and Marilyn Monroe*

### Jack Benny 🎥 *Comedian* 6650 Hollywood

**Born:** Benjamin Kubelsky; Feb. 14, 1894, in Waukegan, IL.

**Spotlights:** Motion pictures: *Charley's Aunt* (1941), *To Be or Not to Be* (1942). Radio: "Wait a minute. Wait a minute. Wait a minute." Benny's self-portrait of a man so tight he squeaked when he walked, a vain eternally 39-year-old who drove an antique Maxwell automobile (and owned a polar bear named Carmichael who ate the utilities man), became as important to America as apple pie. First aired on CBS in 1932. TV: "Now cut that out." Loyal to his radio co-workers, Benny brought the entire cast with him to network TV (1950–60). Audiences continued to roar at the running gag about his vault in the basement guarded by a security man who hasn't seen the light of day for years. His violin playing inspired much laughter.

**Sidelights:** In later years he once said, "With Bob Hope imitating my walk, and Rich Little doing my voice, I can do nothing and be a star." Died: 1974.

### Smilin' Ed McConnell 🎤 *Singer, actor* 6650 Hollywood

**Born:** James Ed McConnell; in 1892.

**Spotlights:** Featured as Old Smiling Ed on "The Buster Brown Gang" children's show (NBC, 1943). For those of you old enough to remember Buster Brown's dog, but can't recall his name, it was Tige. Died: 1954.

### Bessie Barriscale 🎥 *Actress* 6652 Hollywood

**Born:** 1884, in New York, NY.

**Spotlights:** Former vaudeville actress. Dark-haired, lovely star of silents: *A Painted Soul* (1915), *Wooden Shoes* (1917); 23 others. Died: 1965.

### Errol Flynn 🎥 *Actor* 6654 Hollywood

**Born:** June 20, 1909, in Tasmania.

**Spotlights:** Best in action pictures. The screen's magnificent swashbuckler got his break when Robert Donat didn't show up for *Captain Blood* (1935). It co-starred beautiful Olivia de Havilland, who appeared with handsome, charming Flynn in 9 more films including *The Adventures of Robin Hood* (1938). *Virginia City* (1940) was one of his westerns. TV: "Goodyear TV Playhouse" (1958); TV theater. Sadly, by 1957 he was reduced to minor roles. Died: 1959, from a heart attack.

### Debbie Reynolds 🎥 *Actress* 6654 Hollywood

**Born:** April 1, 1932, in El Paso, TX.

**Spotlights:** America's sweetheart during the 1950s. Bundle of energy both singing and dancing. *Tammy and the Bachelor* (1957); *The Unsinkable Molly Brown* (1964); more. Enhances every movie she appears in. Frequent TV guest.

**Highlights:** Married to Eddie Fisher (1955–59). The union produced actress Carrie Fisher *Star Wars*.

### Raymond Burr 📺 *Actor* 6656 Hollywood

**Born:** May 21, 1917, in Canada.

**Spotlights:** "Perry Mason" was the most successful defense attorney in TV history, losing only one criminal case from 1957–66. On "Ironside" (1967–75) he was a paralyzed detective who didn't let his handicap prevent him from tracking dangerous felons.

## Eartha Kitt  *Singer, actress, dancer*      6656 Hollywood

**Born:** Jan. 26, 1928, in Columbia, SC.

**Spotlights:** Sweet 16 really was for this poor teenager when she won a scholarship to study dance with Katherine Dunham. Her sensuous voice and sultry looks later played well to full houses in Europe; she won hearts with her multilingual repertoire, including "C'est Si Bon." Adored darling of Broadway, movies, and TV. Albums include *Fabulous Eartha Kitt, That Bad Eartha, New Faces of 1952*.

**Sidelights:** This daughter of a sharecropper knows no personal limitations. Her two autobiographies, *Thursday's Child* (1956), and decades later, *Alone with Me* have impressed critics.

## Paul Robeson    *Actor, singer*      6658 Hollywood

**Born:** April 9, 1898, in Princeton, NJ.

**Spotlights:** His powerful, moving rendition of "Ol' Man River" in James Whale's supermusical *Showboat* (1936) remains a classic. Intelligent, handsome, and athletic. Spent a good portion of his career on stage and on screen in Great Britain. Died: 1976.

## Marsha Hunt    *Actress*      6658 Hollywood

**Born:** Oct. 17, 1917, in Chicago, IL.

*Errol Flynn*      *Debbie Reynolds*

**Spotlights:** Former film actress (on-screen from 1935), active on TV since the 1950s. Jennifer Peck on the situation comedy, "Peck's Bad Girl" (CBS, 1959–60). "Playhouse Theater"; frequent guest spots on shows such as "Barnaby Jones"; numerous made for TV movies.

### Rhonda Fleming  🎥 *Actress*  6660 Hollywood

**Born:** Marilyn Louis; Aug. 10, 1923, in Los Angeles, CA.
**Spotlights:** A striking redhead with large green eyes who appeared in over 50 films, including *A Connecticut Yankee in King Arthur's Court* (1949), co-starring Bing Crosby; *Pony Express* (1953); more.
**Sidelights:** Graduated from Beverly Hills High School.

### James Wallington  📻 *Announcer*  6660 Hollywood

**Born:** 1907.
**Spotlights:** One of the highest-paid comedy announcers, with great talent for ad-libbing. "The Eddie Cantor Show" (NBC, 1931); "The Burns and Allen Show" (CBS, 1931); and "The Allan Young Show" (ABC, 1944). These shows made him almost as famous as the personalities who starred in them. Died: 1972.

### Hans Conreid  📺 *Actor*  6664 Hollywood

**Born:** April 15, 1917, in Baltimore, MD.
**Spotlights:** Often looked like a mad professor. Character comedian talent in films (1938–80) and on TV: Uncle Tonoose (1958–71) on "The Danny Thomas Show"; "American Dream"; (voice) "Scruffy"; more. Died: 1982.

### Boris Karloff  📺 *See page 120.*  6664 Hollywood

### Esther Ralston  🎥 *Actress*  6664 Hollywood

**Born:** Sept. 17, 1902, in Bar Harbor, ME.
**Spotlights:** Highly paid silent screen star: *The Little French Girl* (1925); later, supporting role in *Tin Pan Alley* (1940), starring Alice Faye and Betty Grable.

### Michael Ansara  📺 *Actor*  6666 Hollywood

**Born:** April 15, 1922, in Lowell, MA.
**Spotlights:** Of Lebanese descent, he was cast in the Indian role of Apache Chief Cochise in "Broken Arrow" (1956–60); Lame Beaver in the historical drama "Centennial" (1978–80); more.
**Highlights:** Married to actress Barbara Eden (1958–73).

### Kenny Rogers  🎵 *Singer, songwriter, guitarist*  6666 Hollywood

**Born:** Aug. 21, 1938, in Crockett, TX.
**Spotlights:** After two decades of work pursuing the golden disc, "Lucille" in 1977 brought him international recognition. His unique voice and intimate style of perform-

ing made "Lady" his number-one hit on pop, country, and soul charts in 1980. Overworked at 200 concerts annually, he cut back, but his loyal fans are kept happy with wonderful TV specials. Albums include: *The Gambler*; more.

**Achievements:** 1977, 1980 Grammys. His 1987 photography book illustrating America.

**Highlights:** "Don't Fall in Love with a Dreamer" couldn't have convinced his beautiful actress wife, Marianne Gordon, to look elsewhere.

**Sidelights:** Born with a tin spoon in his mouth, he was one of 8 children (welfare recipients). Rogers — a very rich man — is a generous supporter of worthy causes.

## Marty Robbins  *Singer, songwriter, guitarist, pianist*　6666 Hollywood

**Born:** Sept. 26, 1925, in Glendale, AZ.

**Spotlights:** Cowboy's cowboy. Popular Nashville singer of C & W music, but with a strong following in rockabilly and pop. Prominent figure on radio's Grand Ole Opry from 1953 to his death. International concert celebrity. Hit songs include "Singing the Blues," "Stairway of Love," "El Paso," "Beggin' to You," "My Woman, My Woman, My Wife."

**Achievements:** 1960, 1970, Grammys. Recorded 60 albums.

**Sidelights:** Learned to play the guitar (Hawaiian tunes) while in the Navy stationed in the Pacific. Chose the hobby of stock car racing (NASCAR) and learned how unforgiving walls are at 150 m.p.h. in a near fatal collision. Died: 1982.

## Crosby, Stills & Nash  *Recording artists*　6666 Hollywood

**Born:** David Crosby (guitar), Aug. 14, 1941 in Los Angeles, CA); Stephen Stills, (guitar/bass) Jan. 3, 1945, in Dallas, TX; Graham Nash (guitar), Feb. 2, 1942, in England.

**Spotlights:** Group formed in 1969. Songs include "Marrakesh Express," "Judy Blue Eyes," "Wooden Ships," and "Long Time Gone." In 1970, with guitarist Neil Young, recorded the gigantic selling album *Deja Vu*. Songs: "Our House," "Teach Your Children," and "Woodstock," among others.

**Sidelights:** Members formerly associated with The Byrds, Buffalo Springfield, and The Hollies (Young's birthday: Nov. 12, 1945, in Toronto, Ontario, Canada).

## Guy Lombardo  *See page 54.*　6666 Hollywood

## Jean Parker  *Actress*　6670 Hollywood

**Born:** Luisa-Stephanie Zelinska; Aug. 11, 1912, in Butte, MT.

**Spotlights:** She was Beth in David O. Selznick's wonderful original production of *Little Women* (1933), starring Katharine Hepburn; *The Gunfighter* (1950), starring Gregory Peck; more.

## William Lundigan  *Actor*　6670 Hollywood

**Born:** June 12, 1914, in Syracuse, NY.

**Spotlights:** Veteran of radio and films who became host of two Chrysler Corporation shows (1954–58): "Climax" (dramatic anthology) and "Shower of Stars" (musical variety). Was the only regular on "Men into Space" (1959–60) as Colonel Edward McCauley. Died: 1975, of heart and lung congestion.

## George Burns  *See page 260.*

6670 Hollywood

## Gracie Allen  *Actress*

6672 Hollywood

**Born:** July 26, 1902, in San Francisco, CA.
**Spotlights:** Practically born on stage; both her parents were vaudevillians. She met future husband George Burns when she was 20, and to their mutual delight, they discovered a comic electricity running between them. Burns and Allen comedy team was formed, and it was the beginning of a happy relationship — both in business (theater, radio, films and TV) and marriage (1926). Played a very funny scatterbrained wife on their long-running hit TV program, "The George Burns and Gracie Allen Show" (1950–58). Died: 1964.

## Ruth Roman  *Actress*

6672 Hollywood

**Born:** Dec. 22, 1924, in Boston, MA.
**Spotlights:** Dark-haired, sultry, cool mistress Minnie Littlejohn of Boss Will Varner on "The Long, Hot Summer" (1965–66); "Marcus Welby"; more. 40 motion pictures.

## Ed Gardner  *See page 303.*

6674 Hollywood

## Laraine Day  *Actress, writer*

6674 Hollywood

**Born:** Laraine Johnson; Oct. 13, 1917, in Roosevelt, UT.
**Spotlights:** She portrayed the kindly, antiseptic Nurse Mary Lamont in her crisp, white uniform in the *Dr. Kildare* series. She made seven *Dr. Kildare* films between 1939–42; more. TV work.

## Charles Vidor  *Director*

6674 Hollywood

**Born:** July 27, 1900, in Budapest, Hungary.
**Spotlights:** A Wagnerian opera singer who turned to making movies at the advent of sound. Among them, *Blind Alley* (1939), *Cover Girl* (1944) and *Gilda* (1946); both starred Rita Hayworth; *Hans Christian Anderson* (1952). Died: 1959.

## Vincente Minnelli  *Director*

6674 Hollywood

**Born:** Feb. 28, 1910, in Chicago, IL.
**Spotlights:** Part of the Minnelli brothers' family act at 3 years old, performing in the circus and on stage. MGM signed him in 1940, but it wasn't until 1943 that he got the chance to direct an entire movie. Partial listing: *Meet Me in St. Louis* (1944), *The Band Wagon* (1953), *The Long, Long Trailer* (1953). Visually stimulating films with superb acting were characteristics of this talented man's work.
**Achievements:** 1958, Oscar *Gigi*.
**Highlights:** Married to Judy Garland (1945–50). Father of Liza Minnelli. Died: 1986.

# * 6700 HOLLYWOOD *

### Thomas A. Edison   *Inventor*     6700 Hollywood

**Born:** ("A" stands for Alva). Feb. 11, 1847, in Milan, OH.
**Spotlights:** The world's all-time greatest inventor. His carbon filament lightbulb (1879) lit up the world — just one of his more than 1,000 patents. After inventing the phonograph, he decided its enjoyment would be enhanced by visual effects. Thus, the birth of the motion picture camera (1889 — the Kinetograph camera and Kinetoscope viewer). A caring man, he spoke of his latest invention: "I consider the greatest mission of the motion picture is first to make people happy...to bring more joy and cheer and wholesome good will into this world of ours. And God knows we need it." Died: 1931.

### Frank Morgan   *See page 145.*     6700 Hollywood

### Eugene Pallette   *Actor*     6702 Hollywood

**Born:** July 8, 1889, in Winfield, KS.
**Spotlights:** Rotund, well-groomed, dark-haired supporting actor with over 150 films to his credit; capable of exuding great gentleness or cruelty. *The Adventures of Huckleberry Finn* (1931), *My Man Godfrey* (1936), *Topper* (1937), *The Adventures of Robin Hood* (1938). Died: 1954.

### Morris Stoloff   *Music director, conductor*     6702 Hollywood

**Born:** 1893, in Philadelphia, PA.
**Spotlights:** Morris Stoloff and Stars Orchestra. Albums: *Soundtracks, Voices and Themes.* Played violin on concert tours at 16, then became youngest member of Los Angeles Philharmonic. Became music director for Columbia in 1936. *From Here to Eternity* (1953).
**Achievements:** Academy Awards: 1944, *Cover Girl*; 1946, *The Jolson Story*; 1960, *Song Without End.* Died: 1980.

### Zino Francescatti   *Violinist*     6704 Hollywood

**Born:** Aug. 9, 1905, in France.
**Spotlights:** Virtuoso Francescatti exemplified the ultra-refined French style of violin playing. U.S. debut in 1939 with the New York Philharmonic. Performed encores of fiddle repertoire with precision and esprit. Many recordings, including Paganini *Concerto No. 1 in D Major* (Columbia).

### Ford Bond   *Announcer*     6706 Hollywood

**Born:** David Bond; in 1905.

**Spotlights:** "Backstage Wife" — a dramatic serial — first broadcast 1935; "Stella Dallas" a serial drama which Bond would solemnly introduce as the true-to-life story of mother love and sacrifice in which Stella saw her own beloved daughter Laurel marry into wealth and society and, realizing the differences in their tastes and worlds, went out of Laurel's life (first broadcast NBC, 1937, lasted almost two decades). "Highway in Melody," musical variety (NBC, 1944), more. Died: 1962.

## Ken Carpenter 🎙 *Announcer, sportscaster*   6706 Hollywood

**Born:** Aug. 21, 1900, in Avon, IL.
**Spotlights:** Ace announcer on "The Edgar Bergen and Charlie McCarthy Show" (first broadcast in 1936); "Kraft Music Hall" hosted by Bing Crosby (on the West Coast) (1936–46). During the golden years of radio, announcers such as Carpenter were celebrities. Became sportscaster for Santa Anita Handicaps, the Rose Bowl football games, (he broadcast the first one between Stanford and Columbia in 1934), other sports events.

## Bernadette Peters 🎤 *Singer, actress, comedienne*   6706 Hollywood

**Born:** Bernadette Lazzara; Feb. 28, in Ozone Park, Queens, New York, NY.
**Spotlights:** Once asked what she would do if she wasn't an actress, she replied: "I don't know how to do anything else." Professionally employed (paid) since age 5 on TV's "Horn and Hardart Children's Hour." Broadway debut at age 18 in "Johnny No Trump." Biggest Broadway breakthrough in "Dames at Sea" in 1969; it was called the "New-thirties' musical." Peters, who looks like a Kewpie doll from the 1920s or 1930s, was outstanding in her role. Some artists say she resembles a beautiful 19th century painting come to glorious life, and with her porcelain skin and pursed lips she was ideal for the 1984 award-winning Broadway hit, "Sunday in the Park with George." Used to be in love with *The Jerk* (1979) — Steve Martin — on-screen and off.
**Sidelights:** Joins the list of Walk of Fame lovelies to be exquisitely painted by Vargas for her 1980 album cover.

## Raymond Massey 📺 *See page 115.*   6706 Hollywood

## Dolly Parton 💿 *Singer, songwriter, guitarist, banjoist, actress* 6712 Hollywood

**Born:** Jan. 19, 1946, in Locust Ridge, Sevier County, TN.
**Spotlights:** Gifted fourth child of 12 children. Composed at age 5 before she could write. Sang in the Church of God in the foothills of the Smoky Mountains before moving to Nashville. Her album, *Hello, I'm Dolly* and her featured spot on Porter Wagoner's syndicated TV series (1967–74) brought her national attention. Numerous hit singles: "Coat of Many Colors" (which she wrote about the poverty of her youth), "Jolene," "I'll Always Love You," "Here You Come Again," and "9 to 5" (she excelled as a light comic actress in the movie of the same title in 1980). Signed to her own TV show in 1987. Has her own theme park called Dollywood, in Tennessee.
**Sidelights:** Bright eyes, big smile, delightfully unique voice complement her

voluptuous figure. Her trademark big hairdo has attracted much attention. Keeps her sense of humor though; she once told a Las Vegas audience, "You'd be amazed how expensive it is to make a wig look this cheap." Her Walk of Fame dedication ceremony was a dual event with her opposite of opposites, Sylvester Stallone!

**Douglas Fairbanks, Jr.**   *See page 271.*                          6712 Hollywood

**Scatman Crothers**   *Actor, comedian, singer, musician*   6712 Hollywood
**Born:**   Benjamin Crothers; May 23, 1910, in Terre Haute, IN.
**Spotlights:**   Self-taught musician who started playing drums, guitar, and singing at a speakeasy when he was 14 years old. "I entertained for all the gangsters." Radio and films including *One Flew Over the Cuckoo's Nest* (released 1975) led to his TV roles as Louie the garbageman on "Chico and the Man" (1974–78) and Mingo on the mini-series "Roots" (1977). Died: 1986.

**Cass Daley**   *See page 105.*                          6712 Hollywood

**Diana Ross**   *Singer, actress*                          6712 Hollywood
**Born:**   March 26, 1944, in Detroit, MI.
**Spotlights:**   Former member of the Supremes. Solo artist now. Collaborated with Marvin Gaye, Lionel Ritchie, and others. Female lead in films: *Lady Sings the Blues* (1972). TV and concert appearances. Albums: *Where Did Our Love Go?* (with Supremes); *Eaten Alive, Swept Away, Why Do Fools Fall in Love?*
**Sidelights:**   For insight into history's best selling female musical act, pick up a copy of *My Life as a Supreme* by Mary Wilson, published in 1985 by St. Martin's Press.

**Mack Sennett**   *Director, producer, actor*                          6712 Hollywood
**Born:**   Michael Sinnott; Jan. 17, 1884, in Canada.
**Spotlights:**   Head of Keystone Company in 1912, nicknamed the "fun factory," where virtually every significant comedy star performed under his comic bossiness, among

*Bernadette Peters*          *Dolly Parton*          *Scatman Crothers*

323

them Mabel Normand, Charlie Chaplin, Louise Fazenda. His creation of the Keystone Kops was madcap genius. In 1917 head of Mack Sennett Comedies Company. More.
**Achievements:** 1937, special Oscar. Died: 1960.

## Sylvester Stallone  *Actor, screenwriter, director*  6712 Hollywood

**Born:** July 6, 1946, in New York, NY.
**Spotlights:** His life story reads like *Rocky* (1976). He's a champ at the box office, too, with *No Place to Hide* (1977) on earth where he isn't a household name. Not afraid to give a rival his *F.I.S.T.* (1978), if he complains about *Paradise Alley* (1978). Muscular, dark-haired Stallone is all macho man in *Rambo* (1985) and the Rocky series. A hero to audiences far and wide, a "superman" to young boys, this man's a movie star.
**Achievements:** Number-one box office star in 1985. One of the top box office attractions since 1976.
**Sidelights:** Not fond of his first name; his pals call him Sly.

## Yehudi Menuhin  *Violinist*  6712 Hollywood

**Born:** April 22, 1916, in New York, NY.
**Spotlights:** Child prodigy whose early concerts presaged his growing status as an eminent violinist. Master instructor. Many recordings.
**Sidelights:** His charity efforts for World War II victims helped thousands.

## Bob Barker  *Emcee, host*  6714 Hollywood

**Born:** Robert Barker; Dec. 12, in Darrington, WA.
**Spotlights:** Likable, youthful, all-American quiz show host of popular games and

*Diana Ross*                    *Sylvester Stallone*

variety shows "Truth or Consequences" (1956–65; 1966–74); "The New Price is Right" (1972–75); Emcee for Miss U.S.A. Pageant and Miss Universe since 1967.

**Eve Arden**  *Actress*                                      6714 Hollywood
**Born:** Eunice Quedens; April 12, 1912, in Mill Valley, CA.
**Spotlights:** Wisecracking blonde beauty. Dozens of films including *Mildred Pierce* (1945). Situation comedy "The Mothers-in-Law" (1967–69); more. Radio: Star of "Our Miss Brooks"; played Connie Brooks, English teacher (CBS, 1948).
**Achievements:** 1953, Emmy for TV's "Our Miss Brooks."
**Sidelights:** Career began as a Ziegfeld Follies showgirl!

**Walter Winchell**  *Journalist, commentator*                6714 Hollywood
**Born:** April 7, 1897, in New York, NY.
**Spotlights:** "Good evening Mr. and Mrs. North America, and all the ships at sea. Let's go to press!" was the familiar opening to Sunday evenings Walter Winchell news and commentary. This long-running show, first aired in 1930, was listened to faithfully by millions of Americans. "Flash! This is hot off the wires!" exclaimed Winchell for "Hollywood Reporters" (1945–51). His rapid-fire delivery was punctuated by a telegraph key which he used aggressively to dramatize gossip items. TV: Narrator of "The Untouchables" (1959–63). Died: 1972.

**Sam Wood** 🎥 *Director*                                                       6718 Hollywood
**Born:** July 18, 1883, in Philadelphia, PA.
**Spotlights:** A superb director at MGM who gave us among the best of the Marx Brothers in *A Night at the Opera* (1935); also *Goodbye Mr. Chips* (1939), starring Robert Donat. Donat won the Best Actor Oscar over Clark Gable in *Gone with the Wind* (1939). Ironically Sam Wood had directed scenes of that, too! Died: 1949.

**Kate Smith**  *See page 167.*                               6720 Hollywood

**Cliff Arquette** 📻 *Entertainer*                                               6720 Hollywood
**Born:** Dec. 28, 1905.
**Spotlights:** Also known as Charley Weaver, he was The Old Timer at 79 Wistful Vista, home of "Fibber McGee and Molly" (1935–52). Played Mrs. Wilson and Captain Billy on the variety show *Glamour Manor* (1944). TV buffs remember his regular appearances on Hollywood Squares (1968).
**Highlights:** Granddaughter is actress Rosanna Arquette (of *Desperately Seeking Susan* (1985) fame). Died: 1974.

**Mabel Taliaferro** 🎥 *Actress*                                                 6720 Hollywood
**Born:** In 1887, in New York, NY.
**Spotlights:** Her engaging smile took her from *Cinderella* (1911) to *The Rich Slave* (1921). Died: 1979.

325

# · 6724 HOLLYWOOD ·

**Norman Kerry**  *Actor*                    6724 Hollywood
**Born:** Arnold Kaiser on June 16, 1889, in Rochester, NY.
**Spotlights:** Debonair Kerry was *The Love Thief* (1926) and *The Irresistible Lover* (1927) — leading man of silents. Died: 1956.

**Eddy Howard**  *Orchestra conductor, composer, guitarist*   6724 Hollywood
**Born:** Sept. 12, 1914, in Woodland, CA.
**Spotlights:** Attended Stanford University Medical School, then formed own band in 1941. Bandleader of NBC's radio show, "Carton of Smiles" (1944). Songs: "Something Old — Something New," "Lonesome Tonight." Albums: *Eddy Howard and His Orchestra Play 22 Original Big Band Recordings, Happy Birthday/ Anniversary Waltz.* Died: 1963.

**Anita Stewart**  *Actress*                    6724 Hollywood
**Born:** Anna Stewart on Feb. 7, 1895, in Brooklyn, NY.
**Spotlights:** Silent screen star only, who got up into the top 5 boxoffice draw in the early 20s: film debut *The Wood Violet* (1912), *Her Mad Bargain* (1921); *A Question of Honor* (1922). Made over 90 films. Died: 1961.

**Nelson Riddle**  *Conductor, composer, arranger,*   6724 Hollywood
                                *trombone player*
**Born:** June 1, 1921, in Oradell, NJ.
**Spotlights:** Arranged for big bands like Tommy Dorsey in the 1940s; arranger and conductor for Judy Garland, Frank Sinatra, other superstars. Singer Linda Ronstadt worked with the legend on her 1983 album, *What's New*. Scores include *Paint Your Wagon* and TV's "Cagney and Lacey"; more.
**Achievements:** 1975 Oscar for *The Great Gatsby*. 1958 Grammy. In charge of inauguration ceremonies: Pres. J. F. Kennedy in 1961; Pres. Reagan in 1985. Died: 1985.

**Oscar Levant**  *Musician, pianist, composer, actor, author*   6724 Hollywood
**Born:** Dec. 27, 1906, in Pittsburgh, PA.
**Spotlights:** Incomparable pianist. Devotee to George Gershwin, Levant became the foremost performer of his music. Witty, cynical personality appeared in films, television, and on radio. Recordings: Gershwin's Concerto in F with the New York Philharmonic under Andre Kostelanetz. Died: 1972 of a heart attack.

**Gilbert Roland** 🎥 *Actor*                                       6724 Hollywood

**Born:** Luis Alanso on Dec. 11, 1905, in Mexico.
**Spotlights:** Handsome, aristocratic-looking man. Mixture of glamour and swash-buckler. Played exotic, romantic types or hot-tempered Latin toughies: opposite pretty Norma Talmadge in *Camille* (1927); played the Cisco Kid in six films — among them, *The Gay Cavalier* (1946); *Bullfighter and the Lady* (1951) — in real life his father was a bullfighter.
**Sidelights:** He was destined to follow in his father's footsteps until Pancho Villa attacked the city of Juarez, Mexico, and forced the family to flee to the U.S. (Texas).

**Eva Marie Saint** 🎥 *See page 309.*                              6724 Hollywood

**Ruby Keeler** 🎥 *Actress, dancer*                                6724 Hollywood

**Born:** Ethel Keeler on Aug. 25, 1909, in Canada.
**Spotlights:** "I couldn't act. I had that terrible sining voice, and now I can see I wasn't the greatest tap dancer in the world either," Keeler once admitted to nostalgic fans. Regardless, she was wonderful paired with Dick Powell in such Busby Berkeley beauties as *42nd Street* (1933) and *Gold Diggers of 1933*, both extravagant musicals.
**Highlights:** Married supertalent Al Jolson (1928-39).

**George M. Cohan** 🎥 *Actor, singer, dancer, writer,*             6724 Hollywood
*composer, producer*

**Born:** George Michael Cohan on July 4, 1878, in Providence, RI.
**Spotlights:** In 1942, Warner's made the musical biography of one of America's greatest writer/performers, *Yankee Doodle Dandy*. This four-star patriotic profile of Cohan, played in an Oscar-winning performance by James Cagney, was just what the country needed to boost spirits in the first year of World War II. Supertalent Cohan also excelled in songwriting: "Give My Regards to Broadway," "Mary's A Grand Old Name," "Over There"; more. Died: 1942.

**Broderick Crawford** ▪ *Actor*                                   6724 Hollywood

**Born:** Dec. 9, 1911, in Philadelphia, PA.
**Spotlights:** An accomplished stage, screen, and television star, he made East Coast theater audiences teary-eyed by his portrayal of the slightly retarded Lennie in John Steinbeck's *Of Mice and Men* (1937). His large body and gruff voice fit Hollywood's image of tough guys, and he was cast repeatedly in both westerns and gangster movies. For the first time since the Battle of the Bulge in World War II, he was called sergeant Dan Matthews on the popular TV series "Highway Patrol." America tuned in to hear this tough-talking cop say: "Ten-four, ten-four" (1957-67). Died: 1986 from heart failure.

**Ella Fitzgerald**  *Singer*  6740 Hollywood

**Born:** Apr. 25, 1918, in Newport News, VA.

**Spotlights:** Great jazz and blues singer, who kicked off her career as a band vocalist in the 30s. Especially noted for her scat singing. Albums: *Best is Yet to Come, Billie, Ella, Lena, Sarah, Dream Dancing, Fine and Mellow, Jazz Heritage, Ella Swings the Band* (1936-39); more. TV and films attempt to capture her big, beautiful, powerful voice.

**Achievements:** Winner of 10 Grammys.

**Jack Douglas** *Producer, narrator, host*  6740 Hollywood

**Spotlights:** Host of the high quality travelog show, "Golden Voyage" (1954-66).

**Sidelights:** Don't confuse with Emmy award winner, Jack Douglas, known as a great gag writer for radio and TV for over two decades (since 1937), and author of two books.

**Bud Abbott** *See page 251.*  6740 Hollywood

**Al Jolson** *See page 308.*  6752 Hollywood

**Rev. James Cleveland** *Gospel singer, composer, pianist*  6752 Hollywood

**Born:** Dec. 5, 1932, in Chicago, IL.

**Spotlights:** Made his solo debut at age 8 at a Baptist Church in Chicago. Composed first hit by 16, "Grace is Sufficient." Known as the "King of Gospel." Has performed all over the world spreading the word of God to enthusiastic crowds. Hit songs include: "Walk on by Faith," "Lord, Help Me to Hold Out," "Ain't That Good News," "As Long as There's God," "It's My Lord." Albums: *Angelic Choir, Cleveland Singers, Down Memory Lane, Everything Will Be All Right, God's Promises, I Walk with God, Songs of Dedication.*

**Achievements:** Grammy awards (two); gold records (six). Organized the Gospel Music Workshop of America in 1968. Pastor of the Cornerstone Institutional Baptist Church, in Los Angeles, since 1971.

**Gloria Swanson** *Actress*  6752 Hollywood

**Born:** Mar. 27, 1897, in Chicago, IL.

**Spotlights:** Silent screen queen whose debut in 1914, *The End of a Perfect Day*, set her up for a perfect career. In Cecil B. DeMille's *Don't Change Your Husband* (1919) and *The Affairs of Anatol* (1921). Paramount's *Sadie Thompson* (1928) peaked her international popularity. She played an aging silent movie queen in Billy Wilder's *Sunset Boulevard* (1950). Died: 1983.

**Harold Russell** *Actor, hero, ex-paratrooper*  6752 Hollywood

**Born:** 1914, in Canada.

**Spotlights:** Sergeant Russell's hands were blown off by a grenade explosion during

World War II. His heroic efforts on the path to recovery led to an important role in Goldwyn's provocative story of three soldiers who return home after the war to a small town in America's heartland, *The Best Years of Our Lives* (1946), superbly directed by William Wyler.

**Achievements:** 1946 Best Supporting Actor, 1946 special Oscar ("bringing hope and courage to fellow veterans" for his portrayal of Homer Parrish). Russell is the only performer ever to win two Academy Awards for the same role.

**Sidelights:** 1964 chair of the President's Committee on Hiring the Handicapped.

## Jack Oakie  *Actor*          6752 Hollywood

**Born:** Lewis Offield on Nov. 12, 1903, in Sedalia, MO.

**Spotlights:** Portly, dark-haired comedian whose greatest role was supporting Charlie Chaplin in *The Great Dictator* (1940), although he was busiest during the 30s. Played Tweedledum in *Alice in Wonderland* (1933). Died: 1978.

## Frank Albertson   *Actor*          6752 Hollywood

**Born:** Feb. 2, 1909, in Fergus Falls, MN.

**Spotlights:** Worked behind the scenes in prop departments for six years before getting a shot in front of the cameras in the 1928 production of *The Farmer's Daughter*. For 35 years his character roles enhanced such films as *It's a Wonderful Life* (1946), *Psycho* (1960), and *Bye-Bye Birdie* (1963). Died: 1964.

## Fred Astaire   *Actor, dancer, singer, choreographer*      6756 Hollywood

**Born:** Frederick Austerlitz on May 10, 1899, in Omaha, NE.

**Spotlights:** "Can't act. Can't sing. Balding. Can dance a little," wrote an MGM executive upon viewing Astaire's screen test in 1928. (Really? Well, he sure fooled all of us.) His second film, *Flying Down to Rio* (1933), teamed him with Ginger Rogers. In 1934, *The Gay Divorcee* established them as the screen's hottest dancing properties. Eight pictures followed. Paired with Judy Garland in *Easter Parade* (1946). Died: 1987.

**Achievements:** 1949 special Oscar.

**Sidelights:** His sister Adele nicknamed her perfectionist brother "Moaning Minnie." They began dancing together professionally as children and went from vaudeville to Broadway superstardom.

## Bob Hope   *See page 72.*          6756 Hollywood

## Andy Clyde   *Actor*          6758 Hollywood

**Born:** Mar. 23, 1891, in Scotland.

**Spotlights:** *It's a Wonderful World* (1939) and *Abe Lincoln in Illinois* (1940) were two of the choice films he made. Had a knack for getting cast in consistently good vehicles. Died: 1967.

## Patti Page   *Singer, actress*                    6760 Hollywood

**Born:** Clara Ann Fowler on Nov. 8, 1927, in Claremore, OK.

**Spotlights:** Radio celebrity. Country/pop recording artist; her exquisite rendition of the "Tennessee Waltz" was so popular it became the official state song. "How Much Is That Doggie in the Window" remains an American favorite. Other songs: "Mocking Bird Hill" and "Old Cape Cod." Album: *Say Wonderful Things*. Her appearance on "The Ed Sullivan Show" encouraged producers to give her "The Patti Page Olds Show" (1958-59). Supporting actress in *Elmer Gantry* (1960); leading role in *Dondi* (1960).

**Sidelights:** From a large family; she has seven sisters and three brothers.

## Henry Koster  *Director*                    6760½ Hollywood

**Born:** Hermann Kosterlitz on May 1, 1905, in Berlin, Germany.

**Spotlights:** Popular for fantasy-type films: *Spring Parade* (1940), where a lowly baker's assistant falls in love with a member of Austrian royal family; *The Bishop's Wife* (1947), where an angel takes human form (Cary Grant) to help a bishop (David Niven) get back in touch with his wife (Loretta Young) and parishioners; and *Harvey* (1950), where a drunk's imaginary pal turns out to be a "magical," very tall, white rabbit named Harvey, who causes a well-meaning family member to try to have him institutionalized.

## Olivia de Havilland  *Actress*                    6764 Hollywood

**Born:** July 1, 1916, in Japan.

**Spotlights:** Signed for *A Midsummer's Night Dream* at 19, after being spotted in a college production of the same. At Warners she became the pretty, leading lady opposite such greats as James Cagney, Errol Flynn, and Leslie Howard. One of her toughest and best roles was as Melanie in *Gone with the Wind* (1939). Worked with her best friend Bette Davis in *Hush Hush, Sweet Charlotte* (1964). Her sister is actress Joan Fontaine.

## Judy Garland  *See page 112.*                    6764 Hollywood

## Kay Francis  *Actress*                    6764 Hollywood

**Born:** Katherine Gibbs on Jan. 13, 1903, in Oklahoma City, OK.

**Spotlights:** A lovely, graceful brunette whose face belonged to the 30s: *Strangers in Love* (1932); *I Found Stella Parrish* (1935). Died: 1968 from cancer.

## Ray Bolger  *Actor, singer, dancer, comedian*                    6764 Hollywood

**Born:** Raymond Bolger on Jan. 10, 1904, in Dorchester, MA.

**Spotlights:** "I belong to an American classic." He won hearts worldwide playing the floppy, rubbery-legged, lovable scarecrow in *The Wizard of Oz* (MGM, 1939) and was immortalized on the path down the Yellow Brick Road. Excellent lead in Warners *Where's Charley?* (1952). TV: "The Ray Bolger Show" (1953-55) was a situation comedy. A flunkie in vaudeville, the 5' 10", 135-pound dancer was featured on stage in "George White's Scandals of 1931." Achieved Broadway stardom in "On Your Toes" in 1936. Died: 1987.

### Elsie Janis   *Actress*

6776 Hollywood

**Born:**  Elsie Bierbauer on Mar. 16, 1889, in Columbus, OH.

**Spotlights:**  Not lacking in talent, she was a stage, screen, and vaudeville celebrity, as well as a busy composer, author and screenwriter. Faced the cameras in *The Caprices of Kitty* (1915); *Betty in Search of a Thrill* (1919); more. Admired a young man, Walter Pidgeon, she saw auditioning for a Hammerstein musical, and guided his career, often casting him in her revues in 1924 and 1925. Romantically linked offstage too. A wonderful impersonator (she could do a great John Barrymore), her career faltered after vaudeville died: simultaneously the advent of sound destroyed her silent screen career. Died: 1956.

### Feodor Chaliapin   *Opera singer*

6776 Hollywood

**Born:**  Feb. 11, 1873, in Kazan, Russia.

**Spotlights:**  Russian basso Chaliapin was notorious for his grandiose manner and bossy temperament; Metropolitan Opera debut in 1907 (until 1929). To hear him in a special performance of Mussorgsky's *Boris Godunov* (as did the British Royal family in 1912) was next to heavenly. Unrivaled as a singing actor. Died: 1938.

### Ginger Rogers   *Actress, dancer*

6776 Hollywood

**Born:**  Virginia McMath on July 16, 1911, in Independence, MO.

*Fred Astaire*                    *Ginger Rogers*

331

**Spotlights:**   Stage mother guided her career from a wisecracking blonde flapper *42nd Street* (1933) to teaming with Fred Astaire in a succession of popular 30s musicals, including *The Gay Divorcee* (1934).

**Achievements:**   1940 Best Actress *Kitty Foyle*.

**Sidelights:**   Her mother was Lucille Ball's drama coach. Behind the scenes gossip: Rogers' beautiful gowns were often made with hundreds and hundreds of decorative bugle beads. When she was swirling, they would lift up and smack Astaire in the face!

## Marilyn Monroe   🎥   *Actress*                              6776 Hollywood

**Born:**   Norma Jean Mortensen on June 1, 1926, in Los Angeles, CA.

**Spotlights:**   The world's most famous sex symbol. Her soft, husky voice, pout, bottom-wiggle, and aura of vulnerability made her 20th Century-Fox's biggest boxoffice attraction. Probably more has been written about her than any other movie star. The myth, or the legend, remains a powerful fixture in movie buffs' imaginations. Played a femme fatale in *Niagara*, before exuding innocence as the fatuous seductress Lorelei in *Gentlemen Prefer Blondes* (1953) co-starring with Jane Russell. Brilliant in light comedy *The Seven Year Itch* (1955) and *Some Like It Hot* (1959). Last film co-starred her idol, Clark Gable, in *The Misfits* (1961).

**Highlights:**   Married to Joe DiMaggio (1954-55), Arthur Miller (1956-61). Died: 1962 from an overdose.

*Marilyn Monroe*

## Edward Arnold 🎥 *Actor* 6776 Hollywood

**Born:** Gunther E. A. Schneider on Feb. 18, 1890, in New York, NY.
**Spotlights:** Incredibly versatile character actor. Frequently cast as a statesman, judge, and other powerful positions in over 100 roles from 1932-1956. Portrayed the political administrator Jim Taylor in *Mr. Smith Goes to Washington* (1939); "Diamond" Jim Brady in *Lillian Russell* (1935). Died: 1956.

## Victor Mature 🎥 *Actor* 6780 Hollywood

**Born:** Jan. 29, 1915, in Louisville, KY.
**Spotlights:** Handsome, dark-haired wonderful talent. Sensitive but powerful in a variety of characterizations. Specialized in action films because of his strength and size: *My Darling Clementine* (1946), *Stella* (1950), *Every Little Crook and Nanny* (1975); more.

## Dorothy Kilgallen 🎙 *Columnist, panelist* 6780 Hollywood

**Born:** July 3, 1913, in Chicago, IL.
**Spotlights:** Her job (1950-65) on "What's My Line?" was to try and find out the occupation of the contestant or identify the mystery guest by asking questions which could be answered with yes or no. She was clever and amusing. Died: 1965 from an overdose of medication.

## Charles Bickford 🎥 *Actor* 6780 Hollywood

**Born:** Jan. 1, 1889, in Cambridge, MA.
**Spotlights:** Hardy, curly-haired actor; capable in romance, drama, or comedy: *Anna Christie* (1930), *The Song of Bernadette* (1944), *The Farmer's Daughter* (1947), and *Johnny Belinda* (1948). TV work since 1956; played John Grainger (1966-67) on "The Virginian."
**Achievements:** 1944, 1947, 1948 Academy nominations. Died: 1967 of emphysema.

## Joseph Schildkraut 🎥 *Actor* 6780 Hollywood

**Born:** Mar. 22, 1895, in Austria.
**Spotlights:** Dark-haired, mustached character actor frequently cast as evil criminals. Strong performance in *The Diary of Anne Frank* (1959).
**Achievements:** 1937 Best Supporting Actor *The Life of Emile Zola*. Died: 1964 of a heart attack.

## Lou Costello 🎙 *See page 294.* 6780 Hollywood

# ⋆ 6800 HOLLYWOOD ⋆

**Art Laboe**　*Radio and music personality*　6800 Hollywood
**Born:** Aug. 7, 1925, in Salt Lake City, UT.
**Spotlights:** The classic 1950s d.j. First to play rock 'n roll on the West Coast, broadcast live from Scrivner's drive-in restaurant on Sunset and Cahuenga. Rick Nelson and other kids from Hollywood High came by faithfully to place their song requests. Requests for "Earth Angel" and a variety of other songs inspired Laboe to assemble the first *Oldies but Goodies* album, combining a variety of artists. Owns the Original Sound Entertainment (Record) Company in Hollywood.

**Evelyn Rudie**　*Actress*　6800 Hollywood
**Born:** Evelyn R. Bernauer; March 28, in Hollywood, CA.
**Spotlights:** Multitalented child star of the 1950s, won critical acclaim and audience hearts with her portrayal of "Eloise." Other TV appearances include "Wagon Train" and "77 Sunset Strip." Presently producer-artistic director at Santa Monica Playhouse, California.

**Richard Widmark**　*Actor*　6800 Hollywood
**Born:** Dec. 26, 1914, in Sunrise, MN.
**Spotlights:** Handsome, light-haired, former drama instructor. Mainly cast in villainous roles; perfect performance in his debut film, *Kiss of Death* (1947); starred in the World War II flick, *Halls of Montezuma* (1950); *Coma* (1978); more.

**Buddy Clark**　*Pop vocalist*　6800 Hollywood
**Born:** Samuel Goldberg; July 26, 1912, in Dorchester, MA.
**Spotlights:** Vocalist on "Ben Bernie," the "Old Maestro," music radio show during the 1930s; "Let's Dance" radio show (1934–36) with Benny Goodman. Records: *Isn't It a Shame? I Married an Angel, Linda, It Had to Be You, Let's Do It* (with Dinah Shore). Died: 1949, when he was thrown from a small plane which crashed landed.

**Elia Kazan**　*Director*　6800 Hollywood
**Born:** Elia Kazanjoglous; Sept. 7, 1909, in Turkey.
**Spotlights:** His first Hollywood film for Fox, *A Tree Grows in Brooklyn* (1945) secured his career. A dozen near-perfect films include *East of Eden* (1954) and *Baby Doll* (1956).
**Achievements:** Best Director Oscars: 1947, *Gentleman's Agreement*; 1954, *On the Waterfront*.

### Spade Cooley  🎙  *Singer, fiddler, band leader*  6800 Hollywood

**Born:**  Donnell Clyde Cooley; Dec. 17, 1910, in Pack Saddle Creek, OK.
**Spotlights:**  Born dirt poor — literally — in a storm cellar under a shack. Break in showbiz came because he was a dead ringer for Roy Rogers, and doubled for him. Early 1940s hit became his theme song, "Shame, Shame on You." Appeared in films and got his own Saturday night TV show, "The Hoffman Hayride" in 1947, where he was labeled "King of Western Swing."
**Sidelights:**  Nickname "Spade" came from his terrific poker playing. Died: 1969.

### Don De Fore  📺  *Actor*  6800 Hollywood

**Born:**  Aug. 25, 1917, in Cedar Rapids, IA.
**Spotlights:**  Screen celebrity who became Thorney Thornberry (1952–58), the "knowledgeable" neighbor in "The Adventures of Ozzie and Harriet." "Hazel" never thought employer George Baxter (De Fore) was king of his castle (1961–65).
**Achievements:**  1981, President Reagan's "goodwill ambassador" to Swaziland.

### Woody Herman  💿  *Musician, singer*  6806 Hollywood

**Born:**  Woodrow Herman; May 16, 1913, in Milwaukee, WI.
**Spotlights:**  Jazz big bandleader from 1936–1970s. Played clarinet and saxophone. Theme song: "Blue Flame." Hot jazz numbers include "Bijou," "Northwest Passage," and "Happiness Is Just a Thing Called Joe," Records: *The Three Herds*; *Jazz, the Utmost*; more. Appeared in films.
**Achievements:**  1963, 1973, 1974, Grammys.

### Bill Goodwin  🎙  *Announcer, entertainer*  6808 Hollywood

**Born:**  1914.
**Spotlights:**  "The George Burns and Gracie Allen Show" (first broadcast CBS, 1931) "The Bob Hope Show" (NBC, 1934); "Blondie," "Uh-uh-uh don't touch that dial!" (CBS, 1939). Died: 1958.

### Claudette Colbert  🎥  *Actress*  6810 Hollywood

**Born:**  Lily Chauchoin; Sept. 13, 1905, in France.
**Spotlights:**  Came to America in 1911. Broadway career before Paramount signed her. Outstanding in sophisticated comedies. *It's a Wonderful World* (1939) and *Boom Town* (1940) sparkle with her talent. Enhances every work she appears in, including TV, films and Broadway into the 1980s.
**Achievements:**  1934, Best Actress Academy Award, *It Happened One Night*, opposite Clark Gable.

### Joni James  💿  *Singer*  6814 Hollywood

**Born:**  Joan Babbo; Sept. 22, 1930, in Chicago, IL.
**Spotlights:**  Popular vocalist during the 1950s: "Your Cheatin' Heart," "Why Don't You Believe Me?" "Is it Any Wonder?" and "My Love, My Love" were her hits.

## Spencer Tracy  *Actor*                 6814 Hollywood

**Born:** April 5, 1900, in Milwaukee, WI.

**Spotlights:** "Spence," as his co-workers called him, had a penchant for drinking and fighting. But he was also a natural, powerful actor–widely admired by colleagues, except those he didn't like. In *Mannequin* (1938), he didn't like his co-star, Joan Crawford, and chewed garlic before kissing her. *Father of the Bride* (1950); *Guess Who's Coming to Dinner* (1967).

**Achievements:** Best Actor Oscars: (1937) *Captains Courageous* — the statuette was incorrectly engraved to "Dick Tracy"; (1938) *Boys Town*.

**Highlights:** Katharine Hepburn was his companion for over 25 years.

**Sidelights:** The film he had the most fun making? John Ford's *Up the River* (1930). During the shooting, he nicknamed pal and supporting actor Humphrey Bogart, "Bogey." Died: 1967, from heart failure.

## Irving Cummings  *Director*                 6816 Hollywood

**Born:** Oct. 9, 1888, in New York, NY.

**Spotlights:** Although his prior experience included acting in *Uncle Tom's Cabin* (1914) and he occasionally wrote and produced, his skill at guiding talent was

*Claudette Colbert*

strongest: *Curly Top* (1935) and three others, with Shirley Temple; *Down Argentine Way* (1940), with Betty Grable and Don Ameche. Died: 1959.

## Kent Taylor   *Actor*   6818 Hollywood

**Born:** Louis Weiss; May 11, 1907, in Nashau, LA.
**Spotlights:** Films since 1931 proved him reliable as both leading and supporting actor. TV star of "Boston Blackie" (1951–53); "The Rough Rider" (1958–59).

## Jane Powell   *Singer, actress*   6818 Hollywood

**Born:** Suzanne Burce; April 1, 1929, in Portland, OR.
**Spotlights:** Signed to MGM as a teenage soprano under Joe Pasternak's tutelage: *Holiday in Mexico* (1946), starring Walter Pidgeon. Demonstrated potential box office material for MGM to bank on — to fill the anticipated void of another MGM great musical star, Judy Garland. MGM also hoped Powell would be as popular as another teenage star they rejected and Universal gratefully signed, Deanna Durbin. In fact, when Garland failed to show up for rehearsal for *Royal Wedding* (1951), starring Fred Astaire, MGM put the lively blonde-haired, blue-eyed Powell in her place! Powell's large eyes, exquisite voice, and winsome girlishness enhanced many commercially successful light musicals. Her best work was as Milly in the beautifully scored *Seven Brides for Seven Brothers* (1954), opposite Howard Keel.

## Spike Jones   *See page 233.*   6818 Hollywood

## Erich Von Stroheim   *Director, actor*   6820 Hollywood

**Born:** Sept. 22, 1885, in Austria.
**Spotlights:** Mastermind of *The Merry Widow* (1925); *The Wedding March* (1927). Extravagant, psychological themes and opulent spending of the studio's money were his trademarks, along with his usual military costume attire (black boots, sword, et al.). Made the fatal mistake of trying to push around another Walk of Famer, Irving Thalberg. "The Boy Wonder" simply breathed and Von Stroheim was out. Died: 1957.

## Adolphe Menjou   *Actor*   6822 Hollywood

**Born:** Feb. 18, 1890, in Pittsburgh, PA.
**Spotlights:** Waxed mustache, dark-haired, worldly, winsome lady's man; both leading and later character roles: *A Parisian Romance* (1916), *A Star is Born* (1937), *A Bill of Divorcement* (1940), *Pollyanna* (1960). Died: 1963.

## Bill Hay   *Announcer*   6822 Hollywood

**Born:** William G. Hay; in 1887, in Scotland.
**Spotlights:** Key announcer with a stylish flair. Started in the late 1920s on the long-running comedy program, "the all-time favorite," "The Amos 'n Andy Show." Died: 1978.

**Louise Glaum** 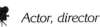 *Actress*                    6834 Hollywood

**Born:** In 1900, in Baltimore, MD.

**Spotlights:** With a fetching face for silents, Glaum appeared in Mack Sennett comedies. Also, *Hell's Hinges* (1916), *I Am Guilty* (1921). Died: 1970.

**Buck Jones**  *Actor, director*                    6834 Hollywood

**Born:** Charles Gebhart; Dec. 4, 1889, in Vincennes, IN.

**Spotlights:** A happy, easy-going, real-life cowboy whose screen appearances emulated what the world thought a cowboy stood for: a man of action, ethics, and justice. *The Fighting Buckaroo* (1926); *Black Jack* (1927); starred in and directed *Law for Tombstone* (1937). Died: 1942 — a hero's death — rescuing victims during a fire in Boston.

**Ann Rutherford**  *Actress*                    6834 Hollywood

**Born:** Nov. 2, 1917, in Canada.

**Spotlights:** In over 15 pictures as Mickey Rooney's sweetheart, Polly Benedict, in MGM's *Andy Hardy* series. Introduced in *You're Only Young Once* (1938). TV: Panelist on "Leave It to the Girls" (1949), *Love American Style* (1969); more.

**Jose Iturbi**  *Pianist, conductor, actor*                    6834 Hollywood

**Born:** Nov. 28, 1895, in Valencia, Spain.

**Spotlights:** To comprehend how popular this eminent pianist was, one would have to see *Holiday in Mexico* (1946), where the plot evolved around the American ambassador's daughter (Jane Powell) falling in love with Jose Iturbi. Also featured is a young

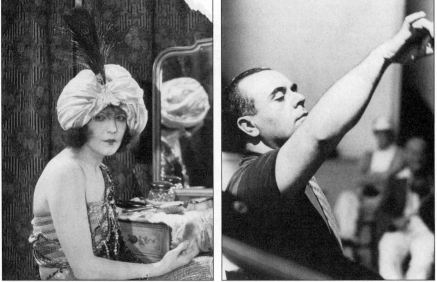

*Louise Glaum*                    *Jose Iturbi*

Roddy McDowell and Iturbi's pianist sister, Amparo. Previously, in MGM's *Thousands Cheer* (1943), Judy Garland sang "The Joint is Really Jumpin' Down at Carnegie Hall," accompanied by Iturbi. Guest radio appearances grace his Hollywood profile.
**Sidelights:** A musical prodigy. He *taught* piano when he was 7 years old! Educated at the Paris Conservatory. Toured internationally. Died: 1980.

**Sarah Vaughan**  *See page 139.*  **6834 Hollywood**

**Danny Kaye** *See page 69.*  **6834 Hollywood**

**Steve McQueen** *Actor*  **6834 Hollywood**
**Born:** Terrence S. McQueen; March 24, 1930, in Indianapolis, IN.
**Spotlights:** A rugged man, McQueen was a deckhand on a Greek oil tanker, a California lumberjack, an oil rigger in Texas, and a barker in a traveling carnival before his TV success in the western series, "Wanted, Dead or Alive." In 1958 he also made the classic 'B' picture, *The Blob*. His rebellious, macho personality enhanced films such as *The Magnificent Seven* (1960), *The Great Escape* (1963), and more.
**Sidelights:** Deserted by his father when he was a baby, McQueen spent most of his youth in a California reform school, the Boys Republic. Died: 1980, from cancer.

**Ray Bolger** *See page 330.*  **6834 Hollywood**

**Victor Moore** *Actor*  **6838 Hollywood**
**Born:** Feb. 24, 1876, in Hammonton, NJ.
**Spotlights:** Comic character actor whose acknowledgement in films came when he was in his sixties: *Star-Spangled Rhythm* (1942) and *Ziegfeld Follies* (1946). *The Seven Year Itch* (1955), starring Tom Ewell and Marilyn Monroe was his last work. Died: 1962.

**Garry Marshall** *Writer, director, producer*  **6838 Hollywood**
**Born:** Nov. 13, 1934, in New York, NY.
**Spotlights:** Comedy writer, creator, and producer of the outstanding American series "Happy Days" (1974–83); "Laverne and Shirley" (1976–82), a spinoff from an episode of "Happy Days."
**Highlights:** Marshall's sister, Penny played Laverne. His father, Tony, and sister, Ronny, worked as producers on his shows.

\* \* \* \* \*

*Note to my readers walking the Walk: I recommend that you visit the* On Location *shop/restaurant. And make sure to see the* Hollywood Minatures *on display. It's well worth it for this outstanding exhibit.*

**Pee Wee Hunt**  *Vocalist, jazz trombonist*    6838 Hollywood

**Born:** Walter Hunt; May 10, 1907, in Mt. Healthy, OH.

**Spotlights:** Big band trombone player, bandleader. Orchestra. *On the Sunny Side of the Street*. Single: "Twelfth Street Rag" sold over 3 million copies — the biggest selling ragtime record ever; "Oh!" Died: 1979.

**Burt Reynolds**  *Actor, director*    6838 Hollywood

**Born:** Feb. 11, 1936, in Waycross, GA.

**Spotlights:** Raised in Palm Beach, Florida, where "money is everything. If you're not rich, you're nothing. We were very poor." Originally planned a career in sports, and won a football scholarship to Florida State University. A knee injury put an end to his athletic aspirations, instead he channeled his energy into dramatics. Eagerly jumped at doing stunts in early period of entertainment career, before his good looks helped him land bigger roles on TV series: Ben Frazer on "Riverboat" (1959-60); Quint Asper on "Gunsmoke" (1962- 65); Deputy Lt. August on "Dan August" (1970-71; rerun through 1975); more. Made his movie debut in *Angel Baby* (1960), but it wasn't until his perfect dramatic performance in *Deliverance* (1972) that he became an internationally recognized movie star. Other films include: *Smokey and the Bandit* (1977); *Starting Over* (1979); *Best Friends* (1982); more. Directed *Gator* (1976) and *The End* (1978), showing his skills went behind the camera as well.

**Achievements:** Is the only person in motion picture history to hold his Number One position at the box office for five years (1978-82).

**Highlights:** Lovely actress Loni Anderson is his longtime companion.

**Sidelights:** Has yet to win an Oscar, but with his versatile talents in both comedy and drama one should be on the horizon. Ironically he turned down the role Jack Nicholson took in *Terms of Endearment* (1983) which won Nicholson an Oscar! (A note to my readers: If you have ever wondered what Burt Reynolds is *really* like, I can tell you in all honesty that he is 100 percent true gentlemen. He is witty, funny, kind, personable, and a talent through and through. It was a great pleasure to work with him.)

**Jan Sterling** *Actress*    6838 Hollywood

**Born:** Jane S. Adriance on April 3, 1923, NY.

**Spotlights:** Thin, blonde dramatic supporting actress in Warner's *Johnny Belinda* (1948) starring Jane Wyman. *Caged* (1950); *The High and the Mighty* (1954). Her comic side, rarely seen on the silver screen, occasionally surfaces on TV.

**Ron Howard** *Actor, director*    6838 Hollywood

**Born:** March 1, 1954, in Duncan, OK.

**Spotlights:** Grew up as Opie Taylor in Mayberry, North Carolina on "The Andy Griffith Show" (1960–68) and as Richie Cunningham (1974–80) on "Happy Days." This bright, charismatic actor started on the stage with his parents as soon as he could walk. Films followed, including his delightful roles in *The Music Man* (1962) and *The*

*Courtship of Eddie's Father* (1963). Sensitive and intelligent with a keen eye for what works on screen, he has to date directed two commercial successes, *Splash* (1984) and *Cocoon* (1985). We can look forward to many more wonderful films from Ron Howard.

**Sidelights:** Howard has a reputation in Hollywood for being honest, kind, understanding, and productive.

### Pearl White  *Actress*
6838 Hollywood

**Born:** March 4, 1889, in Green Ridge, MO.

**Spotlights:** Immortalized in *The Perils of Pauline* (1914–19) serial, known as cliff-hangers.

**Sidelights:** Performed most of her own stunts, even though she had a previous spinal injury from a horseback riding accident. Died: 1938, from liver disease.

### Chuck Connors *Actor*
6840 Hollywood

**Born:** Kevin Connors; April 10, 1921, in Brooklyn, NY.

**Spotlights:** His best-known work was as Lucas McCain on "The Rifleman." His personalized trick Winchester rifle kept him alive from 1958–63. Played Tom Moore on the "Roots" mini series (1977).

**Sidelights:** Former professional baseball player.

### George Gobel *Comedian, actor*
6840 Hollywood

**Born:** May 20, 1919, in Chicago, IL.

**Spotlights:** Host of the comedy variety "The George Gobel Show," "Well, I'll be a dirty bird!" (1954–60). Guest star.

**Achievements:** 1954, Emmy, "The George Gobel Show."

### Ann Harding *See page 163.*
6840 Hollywood

### Shirley Booth *Actress*
6840 Hollywood

**Born:** Thelma Booth Ford; Aug. 30, 1907, in New York, NY.

**Spotlights:** Left her successful stage career on Broadway when she was widowed in 1951. Outstanding performance in first film *Come Back, Little Sheba* (1952). She made only 6 films but gained fame in TV's "Hazel" series.

**Achievements:** 1952, Academy Award.

### Clifton Webb *Actor*
6840 Hollywood

**Born:** Webb Hollenbeck; Nov. 19, 1893, in Grossville, TN.

**Spotlights:** Thin, fair-haired, mustached, persnickety. *Laura* (1944), *The Razor's Edge* (1946), *Sitting Pretty* (1948) — first of the Mr. Belvedere series. Died: 1966.

### Harold Lloyd *See page 236*
6840 Hollywood

## Jane Russell  *Actress* 6840 Hollywood

**Born:** Ernestine J. Russell; June 21, 1921, in Bemidji, MN.
**Spotlights:** Big, beautiful brunette whose voluptuous hourglass figure held back her career at the onset, but whose humor finally won over critics. In *Paleface* (1948), Russell played Calamity Jane to Bob Hope's Painless Potter, D.D.S.; the fun sets in when Bob is mistaken for Wild Bill Hickok. *Gentlemen Prefer Blondes* (1953), where she held her own against co-star Marilyn Monroe.

## Paul Anka  *Singer, songwriter* 6840 Hollywood

**Born:** July 30, 1941, in Ottawa, Canada.
**Spotlights:** When most 16-year-olds have "Diana" on their minds, it's just "Puppy Love." This gifted teen wrote about her and rose to stardom. Early rock 'n roll stylist with incredible writing talent. Highly prolific, he's written over 400 songs (many of them winning awards), including, "My Way," and "You are My Destiny." TV: The theme song for "The Tonight Show" starring Johnny Carson, and film work too. Albums include: *She's a Lady* and *Anka's 21 Golden Hits*.

## Fred Thomson 6840 Hollywood *Actor*

**Born:** Feb. 26, 1890. in Pasadena, CA.
**Spotlights:** Cowboy star who rode his horse Silver King throughout the 1920s: *Galloping Gallagher* (1924), *The Wild Bull's Lair* (1925); more.
**Sidelights:** Broke his leg while serving in World War I. As a chaplain, he probably didn't think the injury was a blessing from God, but he met Mary Pickford and his future wife, screenwriter Frances Marion, while they were making hospital rounds. Postwar, the women convinced him to move to Hollywood. A top-notch horseback rider, and good looking to the hilt, he became an instant hit in westerns! Died: 1928, on Christmas day, from pneumonia.

## Morey Amsterdam ▮ *Comedian* 6840 Hollywood

**Born:** Dec. 14, 1914, in Chicago, IL.

| *Shirley Booth* | *Paul Anka* | *Bruno Walter* |

**Spotlights:** Host of "The Laugh and Swing Club" (1946), a variety show-music, songs and sketches. Comedy panelist on Milton Berle's "Stop Me If You've Heard This One" (NBC, 1939; Mutual 1947).

**Sidelights:** Famous on TV as Buddy Sorrell on "The Dick Van Dyke Show" (1961-66).

### Francis Lederer  *Actor* 6904 Hollywood

**Born:** Nov. 6, 1906, in Czechoslovakia.

**Spotlights:** Dark, handsome, square-jawed heartthrob in *A Man of Two Worlds* (1934); *The Gay Deception* (1935); *My American Wife* (1936); *Confessions of a Nazi Spy* (1939). Speaks 4 languages.

### Marguerite De La Motte  *Actress* 6904 Hollywood

**Born:** June 22, 1902, in Duluth, MN.

**Spotlights:** Appeared with Douglas Fairbanks in *Arizona* (1918), *The Mark of Zorro* (1920), and *The Three Musketeers* (1921). Died: 1950.

### Bruno Walter  *Conductor* 6904 Hollywood

**Born:** Bruno Schlesinger; Sept. 15, 1876, in Berlin, Germany.

**Spotlights:** Forced to flee Europe because of the Nazis. Best known in the U.S. for his remarkable renderings of Viennese symphonic music. Many recordings. Died: 1962.

### Rex Harrison  *Actor* 6904 Hollywood

**Born:** Reginald Harrison; March 5, 1908, in England.

**Spotlights:** Handsome, elegant gentleman of both stage and screen: *The Ghost and Mrs. Muir* (1947); *Unfaithfully Yours* (1948); TV playhouse theaters.

**Achievements:** 1964, Best Actor Oscar *My Fair Lady*. Three Tony Awards.

**Sidelights:** Married to Lili Palmer (1943–57).

### Dane Clark ▮ *Actor* 6908 Hollywood

**Born:** Bernard Zanville; Feb. 18, 1913, in Brooklyn, NY.

**Spotlights:** A real-life attorney who couldn't find work after the crash of 1929; ironically, he played Lieutenant Arthur Tragg on the law drama "Perry Mason" (1973–74). Appeared in numerous plays, which were telecast live.

### Gregory La Cava  *Director* 6908 Hollywood

**Born:** March 10, 1892, in Towanda, PA.

**Spotlights:** Directed Claudette Colbert and Melvyn Douglas in the light romantic comedy, *She Married Her Boss* (1935); Carole Lombard and William Powell in the comedy, *My Man Godfrey* (1936); and Katharine Hepburn and Ginger Rogers in the comic melodrama, *Stage Door* (1937). Died: 1952.

**Phillips Holmes**  *Actor*                    6910 Hollywood

**Born:** July 22, 1907, in Grand Rapids, MI.
**Spotlights:** His starring role as the ambitious, treacherous lover in *An American Tragedy* (1931), directed by Josef Von Sternberg for Paramount, made national headlines. Died: 1942, in a military midair collision plane crash during World War II.

**Snow White**  *Cartoon character*                    6910 Hollywood

**Created:** 1937 by Walt Disney.
**Spotlights:** "Mirror, mirror on the wall, who's the fairest of us all?" 50 years after that question was posed by the wicked queen, the darling princess with "hair as dark as night, her skin like snow, her name — Snow White!" continues to reign in the imaginations of millions of youngsters around the world. *Snow White and the Seven Dwarfs* (1937) was Walt Disney's first feature length film. It brought animation to the highest technical level, produced a beautifully detailed background, perfect character development, and, for the first time, made a cartoon character seem human.
**Achievements:** In 1938 Shirley Temple presented Disney with his Oscar and seven dwarf-sized Oscars (for Doc, Bashful, Dopey, Sleepy, Happy, Grumpy and Sneezy). Also became highest grossing film until 1939, when *Gone with the Wind* knocked it out of its place.
**Spotlights:** Model was another Walk of Famer, Marge Champion (she'd act out the scenes for reference). Voice was a young singer with an opera background, Adriana Caselotti.

**Jean Harlow**  *Actress*                    6912 Hollywood

**Born:** Harlean Carpentier; March 3, 1911, in Kansas City, MO.
**Spotlights:** MGM's *Platinum Blonde* was a wisecracking, sexy gal who excelled in comedy; *Dinner at Eight* (1933); *Libeled Lady* (1936).
**Highlights/Lowlights:** Engaged to the witty William Powell at the time of her death. Died: 1937, of uremic poisoning.

*Rex Harrison*                    *Snow White*                    *Jean Harlow*

## Tom Cruise  *Actor* 6912 Hollywood

**Born:** July 3, 1962, in Syracuse, NY.

**Spotlights:** Two hit movies of 1986, *Top Gun* and *The Color of Money*, make it less than *Risky Business* (1983) to hire this relative newcomer on big-budget films. Screen debut in *Endless Love* (1981); then supporting role as the psychotic cadet, David Shawn, *Taps* (1981). Natural actor with a relaxed style. Dark-haired handsome leading man.

**Sidelights:** To establish longevity in show biz, a person has to survive 5 years, one of the requirements Cruise met to be the 1,835th star on the Walk of Fame. Suffers from dyslexia; as a child was heavily involved with sports.

## Phillips Lord  *Actor, producer* 6914 Hollywood

**Born:** Oct. 1, 1897, in Chicago, IL.

**Spotlights:** Narrator on "Gangbusters" drama based on true crime stories (CBS, 1935); Frazier Mitchell on "The Story of Mary Marlin," a political drama (NBC, 1935). Produced "We the People" (NBC, 1936). Died: 1968.

## Roy Clark  *Singer, musician, songwriter,* 6914 Hollywood
*guitarist, banjoist, fiddler*

*Tom Cruise*

**Born:** April 15, 1933, in Meherrin, VA.

**Spotlights:** Gained national recognition as the star of "Hee Haw," a TV variety comedy series. Warm, comic actor. Albums: *Greatest Gospel Songs, Last Word in Jesus is Us*. Hit singles: "Tips of My Fingers," "Yesterday When I Was Young," "Thank God and Greyhound," "Come Live with Me"; more. A Las Vegas entertainer, Clark is an all-around excellent performer.

**Achievements:** 1949, 1950 winner of national Country Music Banjo Championship.

## Irving Reis  *Director* 6914 Hollywood

**Born:** May 7, 1906, in New York, NY.

**Spotlights:** Pictures include *The Bachelor and the Bobbysoxer* (1947); *Enchantment* (1948), about a house that tells a story about the family who has occupied it for several generations. Died: 1953.

## Ann Miller  *Actress, dancer* 6914 Hollywood

**Born:** Lucille A. Collier; April 12, 1919, in Chireno, TX.

**Spotlights:** Dark-hair, high cheekboned, big smile, beautiful legs, energetic tap dancer: *Stage Door* (1937), *Hit Parade of 1941, Easter Parade* (1948). Worked in Hollywood 1936–56; many years with MGM. Still doing TV guest spots in 1987.

## Charles Fries  *Producer, executive* 6916 Hollywood

**Born:** Sept. 30, 1928, in Cincinnati, OH.

**Spotlights:** Attended Ohio State University. Began TV career in 1952; vice president of production at Screen Gems (1959-68); v. p. prod. Columbia Pictures (1968-70). Former head of production for Metromedia (1970-74): "The Martian Chronicles." Formed own company and has become a busy and successful independent. Numerous shows include: "Leave 'em Laughing," and "Rosie — The Rosemary Clooney Story."

**Sidelights:** His own building is located on Hollywood Blvd., and his star has been relocated in front of it.

## Dinah Shore  *Singer, hostess* 6916 Hollywood

**Born:** Frances Shore; March 1, 1917, in Winchester, TN.

**Spotlights:** Elegant southern belle. Introduced as star quality vocalist on radio's "The Eddie Cantor Show" (late 1930s). Debut recording with Xavier Cugat. TV: "The Dinah Shore Show," musical variety (1956–63); more.

**Achievements:** Emmys: 1954, 1955, 1957, 1959, singer; 1956, personality; 1973 and 1974, Emmys "Dinah's Place"; 1976, "Dinah!"

## Bobby Vinton  *Singer* 6916 Hollywood

**Born:** April 16, 1935, in Canonsburg, PA.

**Spotlights:** Super hot, handsome talent, who has sold millions of records. Organized four-piece band, the Bachelors in 1962. Female fans swooned over his romantic, entertaining style. Songs include "Take Good Care of My Baby," "Roses Are Red (My Love)," "No Arms Can Ever Hold You."

## Veronica Lake  🎥 *Actress*    6916 Hollywood
**Born:** Constance Ocklem; Nov. 14, 1919, in Brooklyn, NY.
**Spotlights:** Arrived in Los Angeles via the beauty contest circuit. Performed in local plays, then in bit parts for RKO, MGM, and Paramount. Paramount signed the petite, husky-voiced blonde for a 7-year contract. Her breakthrough role was in *I Wanted Wings* (1941), with Ray Milland and William Holden. Paired with Alan Ladd in *This Gun for Hire* and *The Glass Key* (both, 1942).
**Sidelights:** Her peek-a-boo hair style was quickly copied by women across America, which caused unsightly accidents for machinists in defense factories; the U.S. government asked her studio to alter Lake's coiffure. In *So Proudly We Hail* (1943) the hair was in a tight bun. She was never really popular after that. Died: 1973, from acute hepatitis.

## Richard & Robert Sherman  🎥 *Composers, lyricists*    6916 Hollywood
**Born:** Richard M.; June 12, 1928; Robert B.; Dec. 19, 1925, both in New York, NY.
**Spotlights:** Richard and Robert formed a dynamic song-writing team that produced the music and lyrics for Disney's *Jungle Book* (1967). Worked in over 20 pictures each. Songs: "Things I Might Have Been," "You're 16," and "Maggie's Theme."
**Achievements:** 1964, Oscar for the song, "Chim Chim Cher-ee" in Disney's *Mary Poppins*. Upon receiving their Oscar they said: "There are no words. All we can say is supercalifragelisticexpialidocious."

## Jeffrey Hunter  📺 *Actor*    6916 Hollywood
**Born:** Henry McKinnies, Jr.; Nov. 25, 1925, in New Orleans, LA.
**Spotlights:** Played the handsome lead in the western "Temple Houston" (1963–64). Feature films (Jesus Christ in *King of Kings*, 1961) and TV films. Died: 1969, of complications stemming from brain surgery following an accident.

## Gary Collins  📺 *Actor, host*    6916 Hollywood
**Born:** April 30, 1938, in Los Angeles, CA.
**Spotlights:** Tall, fair-haired, blue-eyed, rugged, handsome leading man in films. On TV Collins played World War II Lieutenant Richard (Rip) Riddle on "The Wackiest Ship in the Army" (1965–66). "The Iron Horse" had him back in the wild west of the 1880s as Dave Tarrant (1966–68). Specials include his role as Grill on "Roots" (1977). An intelligent, personable man, Collins hosts his own show, "Hour Magazine."
**Highlights:** Married to former Miss America, Mary Ann Mobley.
**Achievements:** An accomplished lyric baritone.

## Sonny Burke  💿 *Bandleader, composer*    6916 Hollywood
**Born:** March 22, 1914, in Scranton, PA.

**Spotlights:**   Played piano and violin from age 5. Arranger for Buddy Rogers, Xavier Cugat, Jimmy Dorsey. Album: *Let's Mambo*. Most popular tune "Mambo Jambo."

**Ray Rennahan**    *Cinematographer*                    6916 Hollywood

**Born:**   May 1, 1896, in Las Vegas, NV.
**Achievements:**   1939, Academy Award *Gone with the Wind*; 1941, *Blood and Sand* (shared), brilliant composition. Died: 1980.

**Peter Lawford**   *Actor*                    6916 Hollywood

**Born:**   Sept. 7, 1923, in England.
**Spotlights:**   A busy contract player with bobbysox appeal at MGM (1942–52), he joined the ranks of other screen actors on the tube impersonating "female" columnist in "Dear Phoebe" (1954–56). "The Thin Man" (1957-59).
**Highlights:**   Married Patricia Kennedy, sister of President J.F.K. (1954–66). Son of Lady May Somerville Lawford. Died: 1984.

**Dionne Warwick**   *Singer*                    6920 Hollywood

**Born:**   Dec. 12, 1941, in East Orange, NJ.
**Spotlights:**   "I Say a Little Prayer for You," might have been inspired by her upbringing in a gospel-singing family. Teamed with composer Burt Bacharach and lyricist Hal David. Starting in 1962, the trio had a string of hits: "Don't Make Me Over," "Anyone Who Had a Heart," "Walk On By," and "You'll Never Get to Heaven."
**Achievements:**   1969, Grammy, "Do You Know the Way to San Jose?"; 1979, "I'll Never Love This Way Again," and "Deja Vu"; the first woman to win awards simultaneously in both pop and R & B.

**Tennessee Ernie Ford**   *See page 102.*                    6920 Hollywood

**Aretha Franklin**   *Singer*                    6920 Hollywood

**Born:**   March 25, 1942, in Memphis, TN.
**Spotlights:**   Queen of soul. Golden-voiced rhythm-and-blues and gospel singer whose longevity in the business has suprisingly won her new, younger audiences while not diminishing her popularity among seasoned listeners. Songs include: "Respect," and "Pink Cadillac"; more.
**Achievements:**   A dozen Grammys.
**Highlights:**   Her father was a Baptist minister.

**James Cruze**    *Director, producer*                    6922 Hollywood

**Born:**   March 27, 1884, in Ogden, UT.
**Spotlights:**   Cruze's background included acting experience in comedy silents in the early 1900s. Some of his directorial work with Fatty Arbuckle has never been seen. Public outrage over the "Fatty Scandal" made it box office poison. Strong in westerns: *The Pony Express* (1925). Died: 1942.

## The Harlem Globetrotters   *Basketball team*                  6922 Hollywood

**Spotlights:** Known as the "Clown Princes" of basketball — although the team does have a female member — their TV break came on "The Ed Sullivan Show" in 1954. "Live" appearances in over 100 countries, seen by over 100 million spectators. As in any sport, the team members change.

## Eugene Ormandy   *Conductor*                  6922 Hollywood

**Born:** Eugene Blau; Nov. 18, 1899, in Budapest, Hungary.
**Spotlights:** At age 3, Ormandy was already an accomplished violinist. Conductor of Philadelphia Orchestra for 50 years.
**Achievements:** 1967 Grammy, classic performance, choral.

## Max Factor   *Makeup artist*                  6922 Hollywood

**Born:** Max Faktor; Aug. 5, 1877, in Poland.
**Spotlights:** Brilliant pioneer in beauty industry. Coined the word *makeup*. Early Hollywood film stars flocked to Factor's store for special makeup techniques and improved cosmetics. Factor created for the first time, *thin* greasepaint in 12 different shades, followed by "sanitary" greasepaint in a tube (not a jar). He also created color harmony, a principle that established for the first time that certain combinations of a woman's complexion, hair, and eye coloring were most effectively complemented by specific makeup shades. Other products include "pancake makeup" for color motion pictures, which worked so well it quickly became the standard. Created the only standard makeup acceptable for black and white and later color TV. Factor also personally made up the most beautiful faces in Hollywood. Name any great beauty; Factor did her makeup! The company carries on the tradition of excellence in beauty products.
**Achievements:** 1928, special Academy Award for creating new formulas in a wide range of shades for the sensitive new Panachromatic film.
**Sidelights:** When you're in Hollywood, be sure to visit the Max Factor Museum in their beautiful art deco building on Highland and Hollywood. It's free, and quite a treat. Died: 1938.

Dionne Warwick                    Eugene Ormandy                    Max Factor

## Eleanor Boardman ♥ *Actress*     6922 Hollywood

**Born:** Aug. 19, 1898, in Philadelphia, PA.

**Spotlights:** Starred in one of the first realistic screen dramas, MGM's *The Crowd* (1928). It was co-written and directed by future husband King Vidor. One of MGM's top leading women in their early days.

## Billy Barty ♥ *Actor*     6922 Hollywood

**Born:** Oct. 25, 1919, in Millsboro, PA.

**Spotlights:** Stage and screen talent. Barty has appeared regularly on a number of TV variety shows as well as in guest spots. He was Little Tom, the midget, on "Circus Boy" (1956–58) and Inch, owner of the shanty bar on "Ace Crawford, Private Eye" (1983).

## Alice Faye ♥ *Actress, singer*     6922 Hollywood

**Born:** Ann Leppert; May 5, 1912, in Hell's Kitchen, NY.

**Spotlights:** Discovered by crooner Rudy Vallee while she was singing at a party. He launched her film career by demanding she get the lead in George White's *Scandals* (1934). Got along famously with Shirley Temple in *Stowaway* (1936).

**Highlights:** Married to entertainer Phil Harris in 1941.

## Bill Cosby ♥ *Actor, comedian*     6922 Hollywood

**Born:** July 12, 1938, in Philadelphia, PA.

**Spotlights:** Broke new ground when he was the first black man to star in a dramatic series "I Spy" (1965–68) as Alexander Scott. Bill Cosby has had three incarnations: first, as Chet Kincaid (1967–71), second, on "The New Bill Cosby Show" (1972–73); third, as the wildly popular Dr. Cliff Huxtable.

**Sidelights:** When it was time for the unveiling of Cosby's star — a gleaming bronze monument which would remain there for many, many years — all eyes and cameras were upon him. As it was slowly uncovered, Cosby smiled wider and wider, his eyes sparkling. Everyone pleaded with him for more. They began chanting, "Speech, speech!" Cosby flashed that long-awaited trademark grin, then took a wad of chewing gum out of his mouth, dropped it on his star, stepped on it, and remarked, "I wanted to be the first one to do that."

**Achievements:** 1965–66, 1966–67, 1967–68, Emmys.

## Carole Lombard ♥ *Actress*     6922 Hollywood

**Born:** Jane Peters; Oct. 6, 1908, in Fort Wayne, IN.

**Spotlights:** Screwball blonde comedienne in *Twentieth Century* (1934), co-starring John Barrymore as a moody Broadway producer. Intelligent, witty sparkplug in the comedy-drama *Hands Across the Table* (1935), with Fred MacMurray. Sensational in the zany *My Man Godfrey* (1936), opposite her ex-husband, William Powell. Many critics say her best work was *To Be or Not to Be* (1942)-it was also her last.

**Highlights:** Married to actor William Powell (1931–33) and Clark Gable (1939 until her death).

**Sidelights:** Fox dropped her $75-a-week contract in 1926 after she was in an automobile accident. Her subsequent plastic surgery, however, was 100 percent successful, and she looked as lovely as ever. In 1930 Paramount signed her for a 7-year contract starting at $350 a week. Died: 1942, in a plane crash while returning from a U.S. bond-selling tour of the Midwest.

**Bette Midler** 🔘 *Singer, actress* 6930 Hollywood

**Born:** Dec. 1, 1945, in Honolulu, HI.

**Spotlights:** Broadway and nightclub performer who gained national recognition first as a campy entertainer. Albums include: *Bette Midler, The Divine Miss M,* and *The Rose.* Established acting skills in both drama and comedy. Films include *Down and Out in Beverly Hills* (1986); *Ruthless People* (1986); and *Outrageous Fortune* (1987).

**Achievements:** 1972, Grammy, Best New Artist; 1980, Best Female Vocalist. Two best-selling books.

**George E. Stone** 🎥 *Actor* 6930 Hollywood

**Born:** George Stein; May 23, 1903, in Poland.

**Spotlights:** Tough-looking character actor who often played big-time criminals; *Guys and Dolls* (1955); *Some Like it Hot* (1959). Died: 1967.

**Mickey Gilley** 🔘 *Singer, songwriter, pianist* 6930 Hollywood

**Born:** March 9, 1937, in Natchez, LA.

**Spotlights:** Country songs include "Room Full of Roses," "She's Pulling Me Back

*Bill Cosby*                    *Bette Midler*

351

Again," "Don't the Girls All Get Prettier at Closing Time," "Talk to Me."
**Sidelights:** First cousin of singer Jerry Lee Lewis. Cousin also of TV evangelist Jimmy Swaggart. Owns the world's largest honky-tonk, Gilley's, in Pasadena, Texas. It provided the setting for *Urban Cowboy* (1980).

### Richard Denning      *Actor*                              6932 Hollywood
**Born:** Louis A. Denninger; March 27, 1914, in Poughkeepsie, NY.
**Spotlights:** Publisher-turned-detective in comedy-mystery "Mr. and Mrs. North" (1952–54), as Mr. North. More prestigious as Governor Philip Grey on police drama "Hawaii Five-O" (1968-80).

### Dennis Weaver   *Actor*                              6930 Hollywood
**Born:** June 4, 1924, in Joplin, MO.
**Spotlights:** Tall, lanky, attractive cowboy-type with a southwestern twang. Over 25 years in TV and 6 series, including "Gunsmoke," "Kentucky Jones," "Gentle Ben," "Stone," and "Emerald Point, N.A.S.," have established Weaver as a Hollywood reliable.
**Achievements:** 1959, Emmy, for his role as Chester on "Gunsmoke."

### Ethel Clayton   *Actress*                              6930 Hollywood
**Born:** In 1884, in Illinois.
**Spotlights:** This lovely lady starred or was the supporting actress in a number of "women's" films: *A Woman's Way* (1916) and *Women and Money* (1919). Died: 1966.

### Stan Chambers   *Newscaster, special events coverage*   6930 Hollywood
**Born:** Aug. 11, 1923, in Los Angeles, CA.
**Spotlights:** Signed on with Los Angeles station, KTLA, two months after its inception (March, 1947). Covered the 1952 atom bomb blast in Nevada; Watts riots in 1965; and continually tackles challenging stories and special events. Highly acclaimed and respected.
**Achievements:** 1987, Los Angeles Press Club Award; numerous Emmys.
**Sidelights:** To young, aspiring broadcasters, he advises: "It's one of the most rewarding fields, but there are many hurdles to overcome; be persistent."

### Chad Everett   *Actor*                              6930 Hollywood
**Born:** Ray Cramton; June 11, 1936, in South Bend, IN.
**Spotlights:** Bright, beautiful aquamarine eyes and good looks make him a romantic leading man type. Started on-screen in 1961 in *Claudelle Inglish*. Starred in four TV series including "The Dakotas," (1963) and "Medical Center" (1969–76).

*Stan Chambers*

**Elton Britt** 🔘 *Singer, guitarist*                    **6930 Hollywood**

**Born:**  July 7, 1917, in Marshall, AR.

**Spotlights:**  Talent scouts discovered the half-Cherokee, half-Irish 15-year-old plowing a field. Country-and-western hits include: "Candy Kisses," "I Hung My Head and Cried," "There's a Star Spangled Banner Waving Somewhere." Recorded 56 albums; appeared in films and on TV.

# ⋆ 7000 HOLLYWOOD ⋆

### The Mills Brothers  💿  *Singers*                    7000 Hollywood

**Born:**  Harry, Aug. 19, 1913, Donald, April 29, 1915, Herbert, April 2, 1912, and John, Jr., date unknown; all in Piqua, OH. Their father, John, Sr., Feb. 11, 1882, in Bellafonte, PA.

**Spotlights:**  Mellow harmony was this family's vocal trademark. Career spanned decades, transcending the big band era, early rock 'n roll, and pop. Guitarist Norman Brown played with the group from 1936–69. Hit songs: "Lazy River," "Paper Doll," "Glow Worm." Many film appearances.

**Achievements:**  First black group heard on national radio — hired by CBS — in 1929.

**Sidelights:**  John, Sr. joined the group when Jr. died. Then Sr. retired in 1957 after a leg amputation. Died: John, Jr., 1935; John, Sr., 1967; Harry, 1982.

### Guy Mitchell  💿  *Singer, actor*                    7000 Hollywood

**Born:**  Al Cernik; Feb. 27, 1925, in Detroit, MI.

**Spotlights:**  Former child actor with Warner Brothers. Big career for this handsome baritone during the 1950s. Hits: "My Heart Cries for You," "The Roving Kind" and "My Truly Truly Fair" (last two with Mitch Miller and his orchestra).

### Pauline Frederick  🎥  *Actress*                    7000 Hollywood

**Born:**  Beatrice Libbey; Aug. 12, 1883, in Boston, MA.

**Spotlights:**  *Slave Island* (1917), *A Slave of Vanity* (1920), *Devil's Island* (1926). Died: 1938, from respiratory problems.

### Julie London  💿  *Singer, actress*                    7000 Hollywood

**Born:**  Julie Peck; Sept. 26, 1926, in Santa Clara, CA.

**Spotlights:**  Sensuous blues singer who started out in nightclubs and later made her debut in movies in 1944; later TV.

### Stephen J. Cannell  📺  *Writer, producer*                    7000 Hollywood

**Born:**  Feb. 5, 1942, in Pasadena, CA.

**Spotlights:**  Attended the University of Oregon. Career took off selling script ideas and then as story editor for "Adam 12" (1968–75). Writer at Universal, creating series: "The Rockford Files" (1974–80), "Baretta" (1975–78), "Baa Baa Black Sheep" (1976–78). Formed own production company in 1980 and has created, produced, and written numerous successful series, including "The Greatest American Hero" (1980–83), "The A-Team" (1983–86), "Hardcastle and McCormick" (1983–86); more.

**Achievements:** 1978, Emmy, "The Rockford Files." 1979, Mystery Writers of America Award; 1980, Writers Guild Award; more.

**Sidelights:** Has set an extraordinary example in overcoming the reading disorder, dyslexia. Supporter of special schools.

### Maureen O'Hara   *Actress*                                    7000 Hollywood

**Born:** Maureen Fitzsimmons; Aug. 17, 1920, in Ireland.

**Spotlights:** Open-faced, red-haired, high-spirited, naturally talented beauty of John Ford's tearjerker *How Green Was My Valley* (1940). Admired annually in the Christmas classic *Miracle on 34th Street* (1947). Very good in John Ford's *The Long Gray Line* (1955); *Big Jake* (1971) co-starred John Wayne.

### Ed McMahon   *Actor, host, spokesman*                        7000 Hollywood

**Born:** March 6, 1923, in Detroit, MI.

**Spotlights:** Tall, robust, affable McMahon appeared as a clown on the circus show "Big Top" (first aired in 1950). He hooked up with pal Johnny Carson on daytime show called "Who Do You Trust?" (1957–62). Carson was the emcee and McMahon the on-screen announcer. It was a version of the evening quiz show "Do You Trust Your Wife?" (I guess Carson could have fun with that one.) McMahon has enjoyed a

*Ed McMahon*

25-year run as co-host on "The Tonight Show Starring Johnny Carson" (since 1962). Other shows include "Star Search," "TV's Bloopers and Practical Jokes" and more.

## W. C. Fields  *Actor, screenwriter*  7000 Hollywood

**Born:** William Claude Dukenfield; Feb. 10, 1879, in Philadelphia, PA.

**Spotlights:** "Any man who hates small dogs and children can't be all bad," he joked. Fields was an international juggling celebrity before becoming the first talkies comedy hero. A raspy-voiced, bulbous red-nosed anarchist, he was always "thirsty for a martini" and wrote many of his scripts under the pen name of Mahatma Kane Jeeves (and others just as off-base). Funny, funny films. Partial listing include: *Six of a Kind*, *It's a Gift* (both 1934), *The Man on the Flying Trapeze* (1935), Universal's *You Can't Cheat an Honest Man* (1939), *The Bank Dick* (1940). Radio guest star on "The Edgar Bergen and Charlie McCarthy Show."

**Sidelights:** Left on his own in early childhood, young Fields got in many street scrapes. His cauliflower nose attests to the fact he was punched numerous times. Died: 1946, of liver and heart disease on Christmas Day — a day he said he detested.

## Hugh M. Hefner  *Publishing, executive*  7000 Hollywood

**Born:** Apr. 9, 1926, in Chicago, IL.

**Spotlights:** Changed the way America looked at women. As editor and publisher of the popular but controversial *Playboy* magazine, Hefner's thrust combined intellect with pictures au naturel; supported feminist organizations and even persuaded the top artist of his former employer, *Esquire*, Alberto Varga to join his growing publication. Vargas (The "s" added to his name upon leaving *Esquire*) thrived in this relationship. Early black and white TV sported a crewcut Hefner hosting "Playboy's Penthouse" (syndicated 1960). Later, Hefner lounged around on "Playboy After Dark" — syndicated 1969 — entertaining a room full of celebrities and beauties while millions of American men watched with envy.

**Sidelights:** His Walk of Fame star was reproduced for the grounds of his mansion in the Beverly Hills area.

## John Drew Barrymore  *Actor*  7000 Hollywood

**Born:** John Blythe Barrymore, Jr.; June 4, 1932, in Beverly Hills, CA.

**Spotlights:** On the big silver screen in 1950, Barrymore made the transition to the small screen in "Pantomime Quiz" (1953–54). Later TV work included guest spots on "Kung Fu" (with pal David Carradine in 1974).

**Highlights:** Descendent of "the Fabulous Barrymores." Theatrics still run in the Barrymore bloodline, with the latest offspring, Drew Barrymore (child star of *E.T.*), showing great promise.

## Julio Iglesias  *Singer*  7000 Hollywood

**Born:** Sept. 23, 1943, in Spain.

**Spotlights:** Attractive, Latin lover with international following. Took top award at the acclaimed Benidorn Song Festival in Spain in 1968 and then took the world by surprise. Every minute of every day Iglesias is played on a radio station somewhere on the globe. Albums: *Julio* and *1100 Bel Air Place*.

**Achievements:**   Worldwide 965 gold and 365 platinum records have made him the only recipient of *The Guinness Book of World Records'* "Diamond Disc" award. Records in Spanish, Portuguese, French, German, Japanese, and English.

**Sidelights:**   Former goalie for the pro-soccer team, Real Madrid.

## Irving Thalberg   *Producer*                              7000 Hollywood

**Born:**   May 30, 1899, in Brooklyn, NY.

**Highlights:**   The "Boy Wonder of Hollywood" became the head of production at Universal in 1919 — at the tender age of 20. His record for spotting and developing stars and cleverly repairing scripts quickly led him into partnership with Louis B. Mayer. Made a string of hits at MGM including *Ben Hur* (1925), *Mutiny on the Bounty* (1935), and *A Night at the Opera* (1935).

**Achievements:**   In 1937 the Academy instituted the Irving G. Thalberg Memorial Award.

**Highlights:**   Wed screen darling Norma Shearer in 1927. Died: 1936, of pneumonia.

## John Chambers   *Makeup artist*                           7000 Hollywood

**Spotlights:**   Film and TV master of special makeup.

**Achievements:**   1969, special Oscar for makeup *Planet of the Apes* (presented by Walter Matthau and a rep from apeland, a tuxedoed monkey). 1974, Emmy for the "Struggle for Survival" segment of David Wolper's "Primal Man" series.

**Sidelights:**   Trekkies will appreciate this: Chambers fitted Leonard Nimoy, Mr. Spock, with his famous ears. Generously donates his time and skill to making prosthetics for cancer victims.

## Lily Pons   *Opera singer*                                7000 Hollywood

**Born:**   Alice Josephine Pons; April 12, 1904, in Cannes, France.

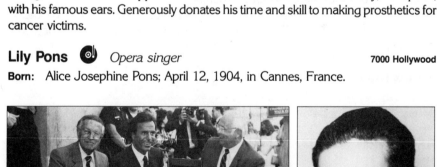

| Julio Iglesias | Irving Thalberg |

**Spotlights:** Soprano; Metropolitan Opera debut in 1931. Played young romantic leading ladies in a few musicals, which are memorable for her exquisite trills; RKO's *I Dream Too Much* (1935), co-starring Henry Fonda (and a supporting role by Lucille Ball).
**Highlights:** Married to conductor Andre Kostelanetz (1938–58). Died: 1976, of cancer.

## Walter Lantz  *Cartoon producer*　　　　　7000 Hollywood

**Born:** April 27, 1900, in New Rochelle, NY.
**Spotlights:** A gifted newspaper cartoonist who drew the Katzenjammer Kids and Krazy Kat cartons in 1916. In 1941 created Woody Woodpecker, Chilly Willy, others. Woody Woodpecker TV show followed in 1957.
**Achievements:** 1978, honorary Oscar for "bringing joy and laughter to every part of the world through his unique animated motion pictures."
**Highlights:** Wife, Gracie, provides the voice for Woody Woodpecker.

## Errol Flynn  *See page 316.*　　　　　7000 Hollywood

## Natalie Wood  *Actress*　　　　　7000 Hollywood

**Born:** Natasha Gurdin; July 20, 1938, in San Francisco, CA.
**Spotlights:** Her first bit part at age 5 was in *Happy Land* (1943), and by 1947 she had made her first classic, *Miracle on 34th Street*. She was a lovely teenager, but a *Rebel Without a Cause* (1955), along with James Dean and Sal Mineo, before enjoying *Splendor in the Grass* (1961), with Warren Beatty. She had *Love with the Proper Stranger* (1964) with Steve McQueen; more.
**Highlights:** Married to Robert Wagner twice, 1957—63 and 1972 until her death.
**Achievements:** Her Walk of Fame star was dedicated posthumously on the 100th birthday celebration of Hollywood. Died: 1981, of drowning.

## James Dunn  *Actor*　　　　　7000 Hollywood

**Born:** Nov. 2, 1901, in New York, NY.
**Spotlights:** On stage before appearing in *Bad Girl* (1931); *Baby Take a Bow* (1934). Played Uncle Earl on TV's situation comedy "It's a Great Life" (1954–56).
**Achievements:** 1945, Best Supporting Oscar, *A Tree Grows in Brooklyn*. Died: 1967.

## The Everly Brothers   *Singers*　　　　　7000 Hollywood

**Born:** Don, Feb. 1, 1937; Phil, Jan. 19, 1939; both in Brownie, TX.
**Spotlights:** Legendary early rockabilly music recording artists. First hit in 1957 with "Bye Bye Love." Vocal range versatility into pop, country, and rhythm-and-blues. Unique and instantly recognizable harmony branded them one of the most popular duos in music history. Other hits include "Cathy's Clown" and the album *Born Yesterday*.

## Jo Van Fleet  *Actress*

**7000 Hollywood**

**Born:** Dec. 30, 1919, in Oakland, CA.
**Spotlights:** *Gunfight at the O.K. Corral* (1957), *I Love You, Alice B. Toklas!* (1968).
**Achievements:** 1955, Oscar, Best Supporting Actress *East of Eden*, her very first screen role!

## Gene Autry 🎭 *See page 312.*

**7000 Hollywood**

## William Haines 🎥 *Actor*

**7000 Hollywood**

**Born:** Federico Nobile; Jan. 1, 1900, in Staunton, VA.
**Spotlights:** Silent screen star often seen in wisecrack character roles: *A Fool and His Money* (1925). Died: 1973.

## Fred Niblo 🎥 *Director*

**7000 Hollywood**

**Born:** Jan. 6, 1874, in York, NE.
**Spotlights:** *The Three Musketeers* (1921), starring that swashbuckling heartthrob, Douglas Fairbanks; *Blood and Sand* (1922), starring the most exciting Italian lover ever to appear on screen, Rudolph Valentino; *The Mysterious Lady* (1928), starring the most beautiful Swedish star who ever graced the American screen, Greta Garbo. Died: 1948.

## Sid Caesar 📺 *Comedian*

**7000 Hollywood**

**Born:** Sept. 8, 1922, in Yonkers, NY.
**Spotlights:** This master of comedy was matched with Imogene Coca on the truly

*Natalie Wood's Star*          *Everly Brothers*

359

funny "Your Show of Shows" (1950–54). "Caesar's Hour" (1954–57), "Sid Caesar Invites You" (1958), and "The Sid Caesar Show" (1963–64) made him one of TV's most recognizable comedians.

**Achievements:** 1951, Best Actor, also 1951, for "Your Show of Shows," Best Variety Show. 1956, Best Continuing Performance by a comedian in a series, "Caesar's Hour."

### Lionel Hampton  *Musician, bandleader* 7000 Hollywood

**Born:** April 12, 1913, in Birmingham, AL.

**Spotlights:** Played vibraharp, piano, drums. Started off with a chance meeting with Benny Goodman and his orchestra and became his vibrophonist. Played with them on and off for two decades. Formed his own band in 1940. Recorded *Flyin' Horn*; *Just Jazz*; more. Hampton was the first musician to use the "vibes."

### Louis Armstrong  *Trumpeter, singer, actor* 7000 Hollywood

**Born:** Daniel L. Armstrong; July 4, 1900, in New Orleans, LA.

**Spotlights:** Grew up dirt poor with no adult supervision. Sent to the Home for Colored Waifs for juvenile deliquency and was given his first musical instrument, a cornet, and a reason for living. Music influenced by early years in New Orleans quarter; leader of the "Hot Five," "Hot Sevens" recordings. Broke ground with his scat singing on *Heebie Jeebies*. It was true he *Ain't Misbehavin'* anymore, and proved it with his full-fledged star status in 1937. Moved into big band music with great success. His virtuoso jazz trumpet playing, big smile and raspy voice were his trademarks. Songs include: "Hello, Dolly!" "Got a Lot of Livin' to Do," "A Kiss to Build a Dream On," "When the Saints Come Marching In," more. Appeared in 20 films.

**Achievements:** Sponsored by the U.S. Dept. of State on numerous international tours, he earned the title of "America's Ambassador of Goodwill" or, for those in-the-know, "Ambassador Satch." (Other affectionate nicknames were Satchelmouth, Satchmo, Pops, and Dippermouth). Died: 1971.

### Mary Margaret McBride  *Broadcaster, author* 7000 Hollywood

**Born:** Nov. 16, 1899, in Catskill, NY.

**Spotlights:** Achieved the greatest recognition and the largest audience of any female "conversation" personality as interviewer of Presidents and other famous people during golden years of radio. Her own radio show from 1935 to 1954. Like those of Barbara Walters, her celebrity interviews were very popular. Called "Female Arthur Godfrey." Sincerity and homespun chitchat were her trademarks: "Is everybody comfy?" Died: 1976.

### Anne Shirley  *Actress* 7000 Hollywood

**Born:** Dawn Paris; April 17, 1918, in New York, NY.

**Spotlights:** Billed as Dawn O'Day when she was a 5-year-old child talent, she borrowed the name Anne Shirley from the lead character she played in *Anne of Green Gables* (1934). Retired in 1945 after *Murder, My Sweet*.

## Joyce Compton 🎥 *Actress* 7000 Hollywood

**Born:** Eleanor Hunt; Jan. 27, 1907, in Lexington, KY.

**Spotlights:** Specialized in dim-witted blondes at the beginning of her career: *Dangerous Curves* (1929). Worked with screen giants Cary Grant and Irene Dunne in the box office smash *The Awful Truth* (1937).

## Douglas Fairbanks 🎥 *Actor* 7000 Hollywood

**Born:** Douglas Ulman; May 23, 1883, in Denver, CO.

**Spotlights:** Former Broadway sensation whose charm, vitality, and athletic prowess made him one of the most famous stars; worth the $2,000-a-week salary in 1914. The motion picture industry's greatest swashbuckler: *The Mark of Zorro* (1920), *The Three Musketeers* (1921), *Robin Hood* (1922), more. By 1931 he was making over $5,000 a day.

**Achievements:** 1919, co-founded United Artists with Mark Pickford, Charlie Chaplin, and D. W. Griffith.

**Highlights:** His marriage to Beth Sully (1907–18) produced son Douglas Fairbanks, Jr. Married to the "Queen of Hollywood," Mary Pickford (1920–35), he was the "King." Married Sylvia, Lady Ashley (1936 until his death); she later married Clark Gable (1949–52). Died: 1939.

*Douglas Fairbanks*

## Ann Sheridan  *Actress*                              7000 Hollywood

**Born:** Clara Lou Sheridan; Feb. 21, 1915, in Denton, TX.
**Spotlights:** Known as the red-haired "oomph girl"; *Angels with Dirty Faces* (1938), *King's Row* (1941), *Shine on Harvest Moon* (1944). TV soap opera queen. Died: 1967.

## Charles Butterworth  *Actor*                         7000 Hollywood

**Born:** July 25, 1895, in South Bend, IN.
**Spotlights:** Character actor whose face was familiar in comedies of the thirties and early forties: *Bulldog Drummond Strikes Back* (1934), *Thanks for the Memory* (1938). Died: 1946.

## James Gleason  *Actor, screenwriter*                7038 Hollywood

**Born:** May 23, 1886, in New York, NY.
**Spotlights:** Co-wrote *Broadway Melody* (1929) — the *first* screen musical! Acted mainly in blue-or white-collar character roles, occasionally was the lead: *Forty Naughty Girls* (1937), *Arsenic and Old Lace* (1944). Died: 1959.

## Kathleen Williams  *Actress*                          7038 Hollywood

**Born:** In 1888, in Butte, MN.
**Spotlights:** Star of the silent screen: *Lost in the Jungle* (1911), *The Adventures of Kathleen* (1913, a serial), *The Spanish Dancer* (1923). A fine dramatic talent. Busy until 1947. Lost a leg in a car crash in 1949; spent her remaining years in a wheelchair.

## Jack Webb  *See page 197.*                            7040 Hollywood

## Dick Jones  *Actor*                                   7040 Hollywood

**Born:** Feb. 25, 1927, in Snyder, TX.
**Spotlights:** "Dickie" provided the voice and model for Disney's *Pinnochio* (1940) before he was Dick West pondering "Home on the Range" in his buckskins on "The Range Rider" (1951–52). Star of "Buffalo Bill, Jr." (mid-to-late 1950s). Made 150 pictures, usually rugged westerns. Retired to a Northern California ranch.

## Ernst Lubitsch  *Director*                            7040 Hollywood

**Born:** Jan. 28, 1892, in Germany.
**Spotlights:** Handled light, witty comedies with a subtle touch. Films include *Eyes of the Mummy Ma* (1918), starring Pola Negri and Emil Jannings; *One Hour with You* (1932), starring Maurice Chevalier and Jeanette MacDonald; *Trouble in Paradise*, with Herbert Marshall, Miriam Hopkins, and Kay Francis. More. Died: 1947, of a heart attack.

## Elmo Lincoln  *Actor*                                 7044 Hollywood

**Born:** Otto Linkenhelter; June 14, 1899, in Rochester, NY.

**Spotlights:** His first two dramatic appearances were in motion pictures' most significant historical works, D. W. Griffith's *The Birth of a Nation* (1915) and *Intolerance* (1916). Successful as the lead in the film newly adapted from the novel *Tarzan of the Apes* (1918)-a silent. Died: 1952.

## Ethel Merman   *See page 380.*
1749 Vine

## Lon Chaney   *Actor*
7046 Hollywood

**Born:** Alonso Chaney; April 1, 1883, in Colorado Springs, CO.
**Spotlights:** "The man of a thousand faces" was the silent era's most versatile dramatic star. Creating menacing yet expressive characters such as Fagin in Charles Dickens' *Oliver Twist* (1922), Quasimodo in Victor Hugo's *The Hunchback of Notre Dame* (1923), and the disfigured musician in *The Phantom of the Opera* (1925), he set the industry's standard for horror in films. Very few actors since have been able to hold a candle to the terror or empathy he evoked in audiences worldwide. His popularity extended beyond one-legged, one-armed, or one-eyed costumes. Underneath the masks — which were often painful to wear — Chaney proved himself a true acting talent.
**Sidelights:** Skills to communicate ideas nonverbally (through facial expressions and body movements) were learned when he was a boy; both parents were deaf. James Cagney starred in the movie about his life, *Man of a Thousand Faces* (1957). Died: 1930, from throat cancer.

## Adele Jergens   *Actress*
7046 Hollywood

**Born:** Nov. 28, 1922, in Brooklyn, NY.
**Spotlights:** Model height, platinum blonde, buxom beauty. 1939 "Miss World's Fairest," she was a regular on TV's "Pantomime Quiz" (1950–52); more. Successful screen debut in the *Black Arrow* serial (1944), followed by dozens of flicks at Columbia Pictures. Often cast as the wisecracking tootsie.

## George Marshall   *Director*
7046 Hollywood

**Born:** Dec. 29, 1891, in Chicago, IL.
**Spotlights:** *Their First Mistake* (1932), starred Laurel and Hardy; *You Can't Cheat an Honest Man* (1939), starred W. C. Fields, Edgar Bergen, and dummies; *The Ghost Breakers* (1940), starred Bob Hope and Paulette Goddard; *Murder He Says* (1945), starred Fred MacMurray; more. Died: 1975.

## Dennis Day   *See page 313.*
7046 Hollywood

## Ann B. Davis   *Actress*
7046 Hollywood

**Born:** May 5, 1926, in Schenectady, NY.
**Spotlights:** Likable comedienne in family-oriented shows, including Shultzy on "The Bob Cummings Show" (1955–59), Alice on "The Brady Bunch" (1969-74). Character in films, too.
**Achievements:** 1958–59 Best Supporting Actress Emmy.

# · 7047 HOLLYWOOD ·

## Jimmie Dodd  *Actor, songwriter* 7047 Hollywood

**Born:** Mar. 29, 1910, in Cincinnati, OH.
**Spotlights:** The Walt Disney children's show, "The Mickey Mouse Club" was televised each weekday afternoon, 1955–59. "Jimmie" (as he was known to oodles of kids) was the adult host of the young group of "Mouseketeers." Composed the "Mickey Mouse March." "Who's the leader of the club that's made for you and me? M-i-c, k-e-y, M-o-u-s-e." Wrote over 50 songs for the show. He proudly wore his Disney "mouseketeer" ears in his salute to youthfulness.
**Sidelights:** His composition "Washington" became the official song of Washington, D.C. in 1951. Died: 1964.

## Richard Boleslawski  *Director* 7047 Hollywood

**Born:** Ryszard Boleslawsky; Feb. 4, 1889, in Poland.
**Spotlights:** He was taught method acting by Stanislavsky himself at the Moscow Arts Theater in 1905. Directed MGM's *Rasputin and the Empress* (1932) and *Les Miserables* (1935). Died: 1937.

## Walt Disney  *Animator, writer, producer, executive* 7047 Hollywood

**Born:** Dec. 5, 1901, in Chicago, IL.
**Spotlights:** Genius talent who made a remarkable dent in the world's happiness. Started his career in a Kansas City commercial art studio at age 18. There he met Ub Iwerks, who would become a longtime friend and associate. After the two successfully created and sold animated cartoons locally, Disney's initial entrepreneurial effort — his company, Laugh-O-Gram — went bankrupt. With confidence, talent and perseverance, he forged ahead to Hollywood. At 22, Disney and his brother (and new partner), Roy and Iwerks teamed up to produce a live-action series "Alice in Cartoonland" from their new location in the entertainment capital. In 1928, Mickey Mouse was "born." *Snow White and the Seven Dwarfs* (1938) was the first full-length animated motion picture, the beginning of a glorious string of films for family entertainment.
**TV:** "Walt Disney" (since 1954) is the longest-running TV series in history.
**Achievements:** 29 Academy Awards. Opening Disneyland in Anaheim, CA in 1955. Conceptualization of Disney World and EPCOT Center. Died: 1966. Millions worldwide mourned his death.

## Vilma Banky  *Actress* 7047 Hollywood

**Born:** Vilma Lonchit; Jan. 9, 1898, in Hungary.
**Spotlights:** It was every actor's dream to be in a movie where the credits rolled: "Samuel Goldwyn Presents." Banky was even luckier; she was discovered by Gold-

wyn himself. Starred in *The Dark Angel*, with Ronald Colman; *The Eagle*, with Rudolph Valentino (both 1925).

**Noah Berry, Jr.** ⚊ *Actor*                    7047 Hollywood

**Born:**   Aug. 10, 1915, in New York, NY.

**Spotlights:**   He was James Garner's father, Joseph (Rocky) Rockford, on "The Rockford Files" (1974–80).

**Sidelights:**   Greasepaint ran in his veins. He made his first film, a silent titled *The Mark of Zorro* (1920), starring Douglas Fairbanks, when he was only 5! His dad was Noah Berry, his uncle Wallace Berry.

**Jimmy Boyd** 🎵 *Singer, actor*                    7047 Hollywood

**Born:**   Jan. 9, 1940; McComb, MS.

**Spotlights:**   Western singing talent who recorded the gigantic hit Christmas song, "I Saw Mommy Kissin' Santa Claus." When he sold over 2,200,000 copies in less than three months and earned $100,000 in royalties at age 12, the press labeled him "The Early Boyd." The freckled face, red headed kid always wore denims, a plaid shirt and cowboy hat. TV: Played Howard Meechim on "Bachelor Father" (1958-61).

*Walt Disney*

## Alan Curtis  *Actor*                7047 Hollywood

**Born:** Harold Neberroth; July 24, 1909, in Chicago, IL.
**Spotlights:** Strong and attractive in the action melodrama *High Sierra* (1941), starring Humphrey Bogart. His career spanned one decade. Died: 1953, of complications from kidney surgery.

## Kitty Kallen  *Singer, actress*                7047 Hollywood

**Born:** May 25, 1926, in Philadelphia, PA.
**Spotlights:** Hit song was "Little Things Mean a Lot." Regular radio vocalist on "Harry James and His Orchestra" (1945); hostess on "Holiday for Music" (1946). Appeared in films, too. Retired after marrying TV producer Budd Granoff.

## Charles Farrell  *Actor*                7047 Hollywood

**Born:** Aug. 9, 1901, in Onset Bay, MA.
**Spotlights:** Romantically paired with Janet Gaynor on-screen in Frank Horzage's *Seventh Heaven* (1927). They were coupled in a 7-year successful series. TV: Played Vernon Albright on "My Little Margie" (1952–55).
**Sidelights:** Founded The Palm Springs Racquet Club; later became the mayor of that city. Died: 1962.

## Mae Busch  *Actress*                7047 Hollywood

**Born:** Jan. 20, 1897, in Australia.
**Spotlights:** Rose to stardom in a million-dollar production, back in 1922, of Erich Von Stroheim's love triangle *Foolish Wives*. Comedy buffs will remember her in Laurel and Hardy films. Died: 1946.

## Fred Allen  *See page 51.*                7021 Hollywood

## Fay Bainter  *Actress*                7021 Hollywood

**Born:** Dec. 7, 1892, in Los Angeles, CA.
**Spotlights:** Film debut in 1934, *This Side of Heaven*, came after 22 years on Broadway. A strong character actress, often cast in matronly roles. *The Children's Hour* (1962) was the antithesis of her kindly, mature ladies.
**Achievements:** 1938, Best Supporting Academy Award *Jezebel*. Also nominated for Best Actress that same year for *White Banners*. This combination forced the Academy to change their rules. Died: 1968.

## Bill Thompson  *Actor*                7021 Hollywood

**Born:** July 8, 1913, in Terre Haute, IN.
**Spotlights:** Regular on "The Breakfast Club," variety (NBC, 1933). Played Wally Wimple, the hen-pecked husband, on the incredibly popular "Fibber McGee and Molly" (NBC, 1939–57). He did not go on to the TV show in 1959. Died: 1971.

## Nancy Kelly 🎥 *Actress*

**Born:** March 25, 1921, in Lowell, MA.

**Spotlights:** Brunette talent of *Stanley and Livingston* (1939), with Spencer Tracy and Cedric Hardwicke; star of the melodrama *Scotland Yard* (1941). Talent improved over the years; in *The Bad Seed* (1956), she was the sorrowful, worried, strong mother of a manipulative 8-year-old.

## Ricardo Montalban 📺 *Actor*

**Born:** Nov. 25, 1920, in Mexico.

**Spotlights:** Suave, handsome, romantic talent who signed with MGM in 1947. Proved versatile in films. TV: Cast as the magical Mr. Roarke on "Fantasy Island" (1978–84).

**Achievements:** 1977–78, Emmy for "How The West Was Won, Part II."

## Donald O'Connor 📺 *See page 203.*

## Claire Windsor 🎥 *Actress*

**Born:** Clara Cronk; April 14, 1897, in Cawker City, KS.

**Spotlights:** Classic blonde beauty who was favored by all the studios during the glamor era of the 1920s: *Rich Men's Wives* (1922), *Souls for Sables* (1925). Only made a few talkie pictures. Died: 1972.

## David Brian 📺 *Actor*

**Born:** Aug. 5, 1914, in New York, NY.

**Spotlights:** His features, tall, light-haired, slightly round face, with pale, penetrating eyes, worked well in TV drama-adventures. In 1954 he was "Mr. District Attorney," and in "The Immortal" (1970–71) he was the rich, pitiless Arthur Maitland.

## Lewis Milestone  *Director*

**Born:** Sept. 30, 1895, in Russia.

**Spotlights:** He spent 40 years in Hollywood; his work went from excellent to good. Directed and produced *Of Mice and Men* (1940) and a remake of *Les Miserables* (1952); it was good, but not outstanding like the 1935 original; also the 1962 remake of *Mutiny on the Bounty*.

**Achievements:** 1927–28, Best Director, for *The Arabian Nights*, at the first ever Academy Awards presentation. 1929–30, Best Director, *All Quiet on the Western Front*. Died: 1980.

## Regis Toomey 🎬 *Actor*

**Born:** Aug. 13, 1902, in Pittsburgh, PA.

**Spotlights:** Fast talking, fair-haired, minor leading, then popular, character talent in over 200 films from 1925–77. Enthusiastic and gentle-faced, he mainly played good guys — the average American Joe. *The Big Sleep* (1947), *Show Boat* (1951), *Guys and Dolls* (1955).

**Nina Foch**  📺  *See page 273.*                    7021 Hollywood

**Stan Laurel**  🎥  *Actor*                    7021 Hollywood
**Born:**  Arthur S. Jefferson; June 16, 1890, in England.
**Spotlights:**  Thin, baby-faced, ear-wiggling funnyman. Was the creative genius behind the famous comedy team of Laurel and Hardy. When confronted by pompous, frustrated Hardy (fat man), befuddled Laurel would remove his characteristic derby hat and, with a blank look on his face, scratch his head. When all hope was lost, he got teary-eyed, choked up, then began whimpering. Always trying to improve their lot in life, they referred to each other as "Mr. Laurel" and "Mr. Hardy." Pictures — shorts and features: *From Soup to Nuts* (1928), *Angora Love* (1929). Their first all-talkie, *The Laurel and Hardy Murder Case* (1930); *The Music Box* (1930).
**Achievements:**  1960, special Oscar.
**Sidelights:**  What color was Stan Laurel's hair? Red! What did plump "Ollie" Hardy want to become when he grew up? A lawyer! When Oliver Hardy died in 1957, Stan Laurel was so heartbroken, he pledged never to perform again. Died: 1965, from a heart attack.

**Ella Raines**  🎥  *Actress*                    7021 Hollywood
**Born:**  Ella Raubes; Aug. 6, 1921, in Snoqualmie Falls, WA.
**Spotlights:**  Lovely brunette who enjoyed a 10-year run in pictures starting with *Corvette K-225* (1943). Made 22 pictures. Starred on the TV series "Janet Dean, Registered Nurse."
**Highlights:**  Wed Brigadier General Robin Olds in 1947.

**Mitch Miller**  💿  *Musician, conductor*                    7013 Hollywood
**Born:**  July 4, 1911, in Rochester, NY.
**Spotlights:**  His "Sing Along with Mitch" albums introduced the joy of singing to many Americans during the 1960s. Well-respected classical oboe player.

**Alfred Hitchcock**  📺  *See page 297.*                    7013 Hollywood

**Lilli Palmer**  📺  *Actress*                    7011 Hollywood
**Born:**  Lilli Peiser; May 24, 1914, in Germany.
**Spotlights:**  In Hollywood in the 1940s, she made several films before working on dramatic TV specials.
**Highlights:**  Married to Rex Harrison (1943–57). They appeared together in "The Man in Possession" and "The U. S. Steel Hour."
**Sidelights:**  Fled her native land when Hitler's Nazi dreams became horribly apparent in 1932.

**Lloyd Bacon**  🎥  *Director, actor*                    7011 Hollywood
**Born:**  Jan. 16, 1890, in San Jose, CA.

**Spotlights:** Directed the first all-talkie, *The Singing Fool* (1928), starring Al Jolson. Perfect timing directing musical comedies such as *42nd Street* (1933) and *Gold Diggers of 1937*. Earlier acting jobs include *The Tramp* (1915) and the *Vagabond* (1916). Died: 1955.

**Lurene Tuttle** *Actress*                                    7007 Hollywood

**Born:** Aug. 20, 1906, near Phoenix, AZ.
**Spotlights:** Phenomenal character actress. Known as the "First Lady of Radio." Radio: Played Harriet's mother on the long-running show, "The Adventures of Ozzie and Harriet" (first aired in 1944); more. TV: Doris Dunston on "Father of the Bride" (1961–62); Hannah Yarby (1968–70) on "Julia"; more. Dozens of films. Died: 1986.

**Bugs Bunny** *Cartoon character*                            7007 Hollywood

**Created:** 1930, in Hollywood, CA.
**Spotlights:** Hopped into Warner Brothers as "Bugs Rabbit." Star of *Knighty Knight Bugs, Looney, Looney, Looney Bugs Bunny Movie, 1001 Rabbit Tales*. His TV show co-stars include Daffy Duck, Yosemite Sam, and Sylvester. "What's up Doc?" Warner Brothers' chief production executive Steven Greene, reveals that the "wascally wabbit" was created by Ben Hardaway, art by Charlie Thorson, character treatment by Tex Avery, voice by Mel Blanc.

**Rory Calhoun** *Actor*                                       7007 Hollywood

**Born:** Francis Durgin; Aug. 8, 1922, in Los Angeles, CA.
**Spotlights:** Sturdy, black-haired, often leading man in actions and westerns. Talent crystalized in *The Red Horse* (1947), starring Edward G. Robinson. TV series: Played the good-looking Bill Longley in the post-Civil War western, "The Texan" (1958–60).

**George Sanders** *See page 210.*                            7005 Hollywood

**Robert Stack** *Actor*                                       7005 Hollywood

**Born:** Robert Modini; Jan. 13, 1919, in Los Angeles, CA.
**Spotlights:** Handsome, 6' 1", strong leading man, gifted in both light comedy and drama. Very funny in Ernst Lubitsch's classic *To Be or Not to Be* (1942); Academy Award nomination for *Written on the Wind* (1956). His zany characterization in *Airplane* (1980) proved he was still flying high with fans. 1987 guest star of TV's "Falcon Crest."
**Achievements:** 1960, Emmy for his portrayal of Eliot Ness, "The Untouchables" (The TV show ran from 1959–63).
**Highlights:** Married since 1956 to the extremely beautiful Rosemarie Bowe — fashion and beauty editor of *Movieline* magazine.

**Gene Raymond** *Actor*                                       7003 Hollywood

**Born:** Raymond Guion; April. 13, 1908, in New York, NY.

369

**Spotlights:** Debut in *Personal Maid* (1931). His good looks were desirable and kept him busy throughout the thirties; *The Woman in Red* (1935). Sporadic film appearances throughout forties, fifties, and sixties. TV: Host of "Fireside Theater" (1953–55); more.

**Highlights:** Married to singer, actress Jeanette MacDonald (1937, until her death in 1965).

### Phyllis Diller  *Comedienne* 7003 Hollywood

**Born:** July 17, 1917, in Lima, OH.

**Spotlights:** She became famous for her outlandish costumes, outrageous hairstyles, and zany humor. Played the wacky, scheming Mrs. Poindexter Pruitt on "The Pruitts of Southhampton" (1966–67) and had her own comedy variety "The Beautiful Phyllis Diller Show" (1968). Guest spots.

**Sidelights:** No relation to the highly intelligent, powerhouse head of 20th Century-Fox, Barry Diller.

### Roger Wagner  *Musician* 7003 Hollywood

**Spotlights:** Successful West Coast choirmaster. Wagner's remarkable ability to interpret music written for chorus brought him an identity in choral emsembles, the Wagner Chorale. Recordings: Bach's *Cantata No. 65* and *Cantata No. 106*; *Roger Wagner Chorale in Lyrichord*; Monteverdi's *Madrigals*; *Lyrichord*.

### Barry Fitzgerald  *See page 191.* 7001 Hollywood

*Bugs Bunny*                    *Robert Stack*

## Mike Douglas  ▄  *Talk show host, singer*                 7001 Hollywood

**Born:** Michael Delaney Dowd, Jr.; Aug. 11, 1925.

**Spotlights:** Amiable host of long-running syndicated light interview program "The Mike Douglas Show." Relaxed, easy-going, friendly style.

**Achievements:** 1967, Emmy.


## Wallace Beery  🎥  *Actor*                 7001 Hollywood

**Born:** April 1, 1885, in Kansas City, MO.

**Spotlights:** Known for his comic impersonation of Sweedie, a stupid Swedish maid (the proverbial bull in a china shop), in a series at Essanay in 1913. During most of the silent era he played big, bad guys in comedies. Smooth transition to talkies with better roles: *Grand Hotel* (1932) and *Dinner at Eight* (1933).

**Achievements:** 1931, Best Actor Oscar, *The Champ*.

**Highlights:** Wed Gloria Swanson, "a darn sweet kid" (1916–18).

**Sidelights:** Dropped out of school after third grade — at age 14. Died: 1949.


## Houdini  🎥  *Magician*                 7001 Hollywood

**Born:** Ehrich Weiss; March 24, 1874, in Hungary.

**Spotlights:** Harry Houdini's breath-taking, death-defying acts were often amazingly scary to watch, but people could not resist. He made only a handful of silents, including *The Grim Game* (1919) and *The Man from Beyond* (1922). Died: 1926.


## Ethel Barrymore  🎥  *Actress*                 7001 Hollywood

**Born:** Aug. 15, 1897, in Philadelphia, PA.

**Spotlights:** The "Fabulous Barrymores" teamed on the silver screen in *Rasputin and the Empress* (1933); she played the czarina brilliantly. *None but the Lonely Heart* (1944), proved she still had it 11 years later.

**Achievements:** 1944, Best Supporting Actress Oscar, *None but the Lonely Heart*. Died: 1959, of a heart attack.

# · 6935 HOLLYWOOD ·

### Pola Negri  *Actress*

**Born:** Appolonia Chalupec on Dec. 31, 1894, in Poland.
**Spotlights:** She arrived in Hollywood early in the glorious twenties, when the champagne poured freely and the stars' fantasies and eccentricities were wholeheartedly encouraged. Imagine a black-haired beauty with a wide face and dark red lips, resplendent in a lynx fur coat and black high heels taking her tiger for an afternoon stroll down Sunset Boulevard! Her friendship with Rudolph Valentino was the envy of millions of women worldwide. *Forbidden Paradise* (1924), *Good and Naughty* (1926). Died: 1987.

### Lee Majors *Actor*

**Born:** April 23, 1942, in Wyandotte, MI.
**Spotlights:** "The Big Valley" (1965–69), as Heath Barkley; in a million-to-one odds, Majors landed this role on his very first dramatic audition; "Owen Marshall, Counselor at Law" as Jess Brandon (1971–74); "The Six Million Dollar Man" (1974–78) as Colonel Steve Austin; "The Fall Guy" (1981–) as Colt Seavers.
**Highlights:** Married and divorced actress Farrah Fawcett, his second wife.
**Sidelights:** Orphaned when he was an infant (later adopted).

### Robert Young *Actor*

**Born:** Feb. 22, 1907, in Chicago, IL.
**Spotlights:** Brown eyes and hair and 6 feet of warmth; *The Bride Comes Home* (1935), with Fred MacMurray; *Florian* (1940), with Helen Gilbert. Radio: "Father Knows Best," as Jim Anderson (NBC, 1949); went to TV format (1954–63). Was "Marcus Welby, M.D." (1969–76).
**Achievements:** 1956 and 1957, Emmys, "Father Knows Best"; 1970, Emmy, for "Marcus Welby, M.D."
**Highlights:** Happily married since 1932: "We're still in love."

### Lou Rawls *Singer*

**Born:** Dec. 1, 1936, in Chicago, IL.
**Spotlights:** Rhythm-and-blues vocalist with sensational style. His roots are in gospel music with the group, The Pilgrim Travelers. Albums: *All Things in Time, In Harmony 2, Let Lou Be Good to You.* TV and films, too.
**Achievements:** 1961, 1971, 1977, Grammys.

### Larry Semon *Actor, producer, director, screenwriter*

**Born:** July 16, 1889, in West Point, MI.

**Spotlights:** A casualty of fame, Semon's meteoric rise to stardom included world-wide popularity that rivaled top silent screen comedians, more money than he ever dreamed existed, and marriage to two beautiful actresses. Pictures include *Spooks and Spasms* (1917) and *Babes and Boobs* (1918).

**Spotlights:** His cocky disregard for production costs and penchant for womanizing cost him everything. A "has-been," bankrupt, and lonely. Died: 1928, of pneumonia.

## Paul Williams  💿  *Singer, songwriter, composer, actor*        6933 Hollywood

**Born:** Sept. 19, 1940, in Omaha, NE.

**Spotlights:** Multitalented entertainer with a string of hits: "Just an Old Fashioned Love Song," "Rainy Days and Mondays," "We've Only Just Begin." Has scored numerous films including *A Star is Born*; title song for *Grease*. Albums: *Classics; Phantom of the Paradise.*

**Achievements:** 1976, Oscar for song, "Evergreen." 1976 Grammy.

## Jon Hall  📺  *See page 139.*        6933 Hollywood

## The Carpenters  💿  *Singers, musicians*        6933 Hollywood

**Born:** Richard, Oct. 15, 1945; Karen, March 2, 1950; both in New Haven, CT.

**Spotlights:** Sister and brother singing team. Karen's unique, throaty delivery propelled them to stardom with "We've Only Just Begun," "Solitaire," "Rainy Days and Mondays." Albums: *Close to You; Now and Then.*

**Sidelights:** Made a tape cassette recording in their garage, sent it off to record companies, and landed a contract. Died: Karen, in 1982.

## Glenn Ford  🎥  *Actor*        6933 Hollywood

**Born:** Gwyllyn Newton; May 1, 1916, in Canada.

**Spotlights:** His big break came playing opposite sex goddess Rita Hayworth in *Gilda* (1946), although this determined-looking man was on-screen as early as 1937.

| | | |
|---|---|---|
| *Lee Majors* | *Robert Young* | *Glenn Ford* |

Reached hero status as an actor for a variety of roles in dramas, comedies, westerns, etc. *Superman* (1978).
**Highlights:** Married to Eleanor Powell (1943–59), first of 3.

## Jerry Weintraub  *Producer, manager, promoter, executive* 6933 Hollywood
**Born:** Jerome Weintraub; Sept. 26, 1937, in New York, NY.
**Spotlights:** Managed top talents: Beach Boys, Neil Diamond, Bob Dylan, and Waylon Jennings. Produced: *Oh God!* (1977), starring George Burns; his *Karate Kid* (1984), has knocked blocks off the competition; more.
**Achievements:** 1974, Emmy, "John Denver's Rocky Mountain Christmas."
**Sidelights:** Resides at "Blue Heaven" in Malibu, California, an estate that would put the Dallas Ewings to shame.

## Gloria De Haven  *Actress* 6933 Hollywood
**Born:** July 23, 1924, in Los Angeles, CA.
**Spotlights:** She got off to a good start by appearing in Charlie Chaplin films: *Modern Times* (1936) and *The Great Dictator* (1940).
**Sidelights:** In the big band era she sang with Bob Crosby (Bing's brother). Lovely, high-cheekboned, sexy starlet who appeared with Donald O'Connor in *Yes, Sir, That's My Baby* (1949).

## Gail Russell  *Actress* 6933 Hollywood
**Born:** Sept. 21, 1924, in Chicago, IL.
**Spotlights:** Russell had it all: a beautiful oval face; large eyes, full lips, and dark, thick, curly hair. She also had signed with Paramount, making *Henry Aldrich Gets Glamor* (1943) when she was only 19 years old!
**Sidelights:** What she didn't have was a personal sense of security. Unable to cope with the pressures of stardom, she drowned her worries in alcoholism. Died: 1961.

## Guy Madison  *See page 96.* 6933 Hollywood

## Ward Bond  *Actor* 6933 Hollywood
**Born:** April 9, 1903, in Denver, CO.
**Spotlights:** He was the California-bound wagonmaster Major Seth Adams (1957–61) on the series "Wagon Train."
**Sidelights:** Former Univeristy of Southern California Trojan football player and teammate of John Wayne. Director John Ford recruited both of these big, hunky guys to the film business. Died: 1960, of a heart attack.

## Herb Alpert  *Musician* 6933 Hollywood
**Born:** March 31, 1936, in Los Angeles, CA.
**Spotlights:** Talented, stylized trumpeter and leader of the instrumental group, Ti-

juana Brass, whose distinct "Ameriachi" style music (Americanization of the mariachi) has earned an enormous following. Started with hit "The Lonely Bull" in 1962.

**Achievements:** 1962, formed A & M Records with Jerry Moss; each man had to scrape together $100 to form the company. 1965, three Grammys for "A Taste of Honey"; 1966 two Grammys, for "My Love"; 1979, Grammy, "Rise."

## Claire Trevor  *Actress*                                    6933 Hollywood

**Born:** Claire Wemlinger; March 8, 1909, in New York, NY.
**Achievements:** Oscar: Best Supporting Actress for *Key Largo* (1948); nominated for *Dead End* (1937), *The High and Mighty* (1954).
**Sidelights:** Retired wealthy after investing in real estate.

## Lois Wilson  *Actress*                                    6933 Hollywood

**Born:** June 28, 1896, in Pittsburgh, PA.
**Spotlights:** She covered stage, more than 200 motion pictures, and TV in 6 decades. Films include *Ruggles of Red Gap* (1923), *The Great Gatsby* (1926). Retired from the big screen in 1949. Died: 1983.

*Casey Kasem and wife at his dedication ceremony.*

## Casey Kasem   *Disc jockey, TV host, actor*     6933 Hollywood

**Born:** Detroit, MI.

**Spotlights:** Smooth-voiced, easy-going style, articulate creator and host of the popular radio program "American Top 40," which is heard around the world. Host of TV's "America's Top Ten." Countless voiceover jobs. TV and film acting, too.

**Sidelights:** During military service Kasen performed in radio drama on the Armed Forces Network in Korea.

## John Charles Thomas   *Opera singer*     6933 Hollywood

**Born:** Sept. 6, 1891, in Meyersdale, PA.

**Spotlights:** Baritone with warm, rich, powerful voice. 1925 operatic debut singing Verdi's *Aida* (his favorite opera) in Washington, D.C. Sang with the Los Angeles Civic Light Opera House (1930-34); Metropolitan Opera (1934-44). Vocalist on radio's "Bell Telephone Hour" (1942-47). As American as apple pie, but he once commented on the culturally advanced musical environment of Italy: "The adult Italian was singing arias when he was a child; Americans were singing 'Yes, We Have No Bananas.'"

**Sidelights:** Known for his sense of humor, he'd often show up in his bare feet for a concert rehearsal. Died: 1960.

## Dorothy McGuire   *Actress*     6933 Hollywood

**Born:** June 14, 1918, in Omaha, NE.

**Spotlights:** Under David O. Selznick's wing, she starred in her first film *Claudia* (1943). Pretty, light-haired, leading lady with an open face and kind eyes. Moved into wholesome character roles. Worked in Disney films *Old Yeller* (1957), *The Swiss Family Robinson* (1960).

## Glen Campbell   *Singer, guitarist, host*     6927 Hollywood

**Born:** April 22, in Delight, AR.

**Spotlights:** Two hits in 1967 — "Gentle on My Mind," and "By the Time I Get to Phoenix" — shot him to stardom. "The Glen Campbell Goodtime Hour" (1969–72) was a musical variety program that featured country singers and comedy sketches; more.

**Achievements:** Grammys: 1967 (four); 1968, Album of the Year.

**Sidelights:** He is the seventh son of a seventh son.

## Hattie McDaniel   *See page 114.*     6927 Hollywood

## Army Archerd   *Columnist*     6927 Hollywood

**Born:** Armand Archerd; Jan. 13, in New York, NY.

**Spotlights:** Everyone who's anyone, or hopes to be, reads Archerd's "Just for Variety" column in the *Daily Variety*. Trusty reports on international social activities, movie and TV deals, agents and clients, fundraisers, celebrity illnesses, etc. In short, he's the inside track to the goings-on of Hollywood people. TV commentator and guest appearances.

**Achievements:**   Founder, president of the Hollywood Press Club. Numerous "Newsman" awards.

**Sidelights:**   Joined Associated Press Hollywood Bureau in 1945.

### Lefty Frizzel 🔴 *Country-and-western performer*      6927 Hollywood

**Born:**   William Frizzel; March 31, 1928, in Corsicana, TX.

**Spotlights:**   Hit singles: "If You've Got the Money (Honey), I've Got the Time," "Everything Keeps Coming Back (But You)," "Watermelon Time in Georgia."

**Sidelights:**   Nicknamed "Lefty" from boxing days.

### Michael Jackson 🔴 *Singer, actor*      6927 Hollywood

**Born:**   Aug. 29, 1958, in Gary, IN.

**Spotlights:**   Enjoys one of the most successful careers of any contemporary performer. Formerly with family members, The Jacksons, he is now a sole recording artist: "Off the Wall" and "Thriller," crossing pop, rhythm and blues, jazz, and rock. Unprecedented number of singles on the chart: "Don't Stop 'Til You Get Enough," "Billie Jean," "Beat It," and others.

**Achievements:**   Handful of Grammys; Black Gold Awards; more.

**Sidelights:**   Star of a very expensive 3-D George Lucas production, *Captain E-0*, at Disneyland.

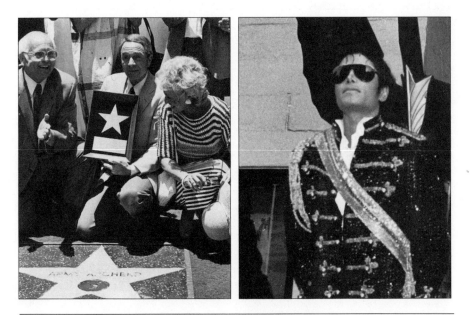

| Army Archerd | Michael Jackson |

## Lupe Velez   🎥   *Actress*       6927 Hollywood

**Born:** Maria Velez de Vallalobos; July 18, 1908, in Mexico.
**Spotlights:** RKO fashioned the *Mexican Spitfire* (1940) comedy series around the dark-haired, dark-eyed, spirited, temper-tantrum throwing artist.
**Highlights:** Married to Johnny Weissmuller (1933-38). Died: 1944.

## Mickey Mouse   🎥   *Cartoon character*       6925 Hollywood

**Created:** 1928, in Hollywood, CA.
**Spotlights:** Walt Disney created Mickey Mouse on a train to Hollywood. He originally named him "Mortimer," but Mrs. Disney thought it sounded too haughty, and suggested Mickey. Disney's artist associate, Ub Iwerks, drew him. In 1928 the animated creature which seemed to think for itself, made his film debut with Minnie in *Steamboat Willie* — in sound. Mickey's theme song: "Minnie's Yoo Hoo." Oddly enough, Disney had a tough time persuading distributors to handle this unique new personality. Refusing to be discouraged, the 26-year old persevered, and in time was able to get Manhattan's Colony Theater to screen it. The rest is history. Mickey Mouse has starred in many pictures, among them, *Fantasia* (1940) and is well-loved by children and adults alike.
**Achievements:** 1931-32 special Oscar to Disney "for the creation of Mickey Mouse." On June 6, 1944, D-Day, the Allied Forces used "Mickey Mouse" for their password. Walt Disney commented on his TV show, while the cameras were scanning Disneyland: "I hope we never lose sight of one fact...that this was all started by a Mouse." Today Mickey Mouse is is the world's most recognizable identity.
**Sidelights:** Disney used his own voice for Mickey's squeaky falsetto for nearly two

Mickey Mouse and Pluto                 Donald Duck

decades. Mickey passed his half-century mark but is as youthful and popular as ever. Robert Develle, vice president of Walt Disney Imagineering, commented on the conspicuous absence of one star on the Walk. "Our friend Donald Duck just gets left out of everything."

## Alan Young   *Actor*     6925 Hollywood

**Born:** Angus Young; Nov. 19, 1919, in England.
**Spotlights:** This talented comedian had his own 30 minute comedy series when he was only 25 years old, "The Alan Young Show" (ABC, 1944; NBC, 1946). Delightfully faced the camera in *Margie* (1946). Very interested in children's programming, he enjoyed working in the fairy tale, *Tom Thumb* (1958). Called the "Charlie Chaplin of TV" when his own show aired (1950-53).
**Sidelights:** Formerly a cartoonist.

## James Garner   *Actor*     6925 Hollywood

**Born:** J. Baumgarner; April 7, 1928, in Norman, OK.
**Spotlights:** Played easy-going, twinkling-eyed Bret Maverick (1957-60) on the hit western "Maverick." As private eye, ex-con Jim Rockford in "The Rockford Files" (1974-80), the tall, dark, handsome actor was constantly confronting danger from modern thugs.
**Achievements:** Emmy 1976-77, Outstanding Lead Actor in a drama series "The Rockford Files" (NBC). Awarded Purple Heart (Korean War).

## Charles McGraw   *Actor*     6925 Hollywood

**Born:** May 10, 1914, in New York.
**Spotlights:** Played Rick James in TV's "Casablanca" (1955). Captain Hughes in "The Smith Family" (1971-72) starring Henry Fonda. Died: 1980.

## Barbra Streisand   *Singer, actress*     6925 Hollywood

**Born:** Barbara Streisand; April 24, 1942, in Brooklyn, NY.
**Spotlights:** Celebrated on Broadway, then brilliant film debut as Fanny Brice in *Funny Girl* (1968); effervescent performance in *Hello Dolly* (1969); co-starred with Robert Redford in *The Way We Were* (1973); starred in, sang, co-wrote, directed and produced *Yentl* (1983). One of the greatest female vocalists of this century; the top-paid singer in the world.
**Achievements:** 1968, Best Actress Oscar for her first film, *Funny Girl* (in a tie with Katharine Hepburn). 1977, Oscar for music "Evergreen," 1970, Tony, 1965, Emmy, 8 Grammys.
**Highlights:** Younger half-sister, Roslyn Kind, is an extremely gifted vocalist.
**Sidelights:** Powerhoused her way from an impoverished Jewish childhood, raised by her grandmother, to a personal worth of $100 million.

## Ethel Merman  *Actress*

**Born:** Ethel Zimmerman, Jan. 16, 1909, in Astoria, Queens, NY.

**Spotlights:** Her dynamic stage presence and voice won the hearts of showbiz insiders and audiences alike. Stage: Irving Berlin said, "You better not write a bad lyric for Merman, because people will hear it in the second balcony." In Hollywood, she loved working with Director Walter Lang in *Call Me Madam* (1953). She said, "Walter won my foolish heart. He told me, 'Get out there and be as brassy and as full of bounce and gusto as you want.' "

**Highlights:** Married briefly to Ernest Borgnine in 1964 (fourth of four husbands). Died: 1984.

## Henry Rene  *Arranger, conductor.*

**Born:** Dec. 29, 1906, New York, NY.

**Spotlights:** Called an "A & R man (Artist and Repertoire)" whose extensive work in records and motion pictures from 1925 to 1975 brought him acclaim. Stars he worked with ranged from Dinah Shore to Artur Rubenstein to Spike Jones.

## Henry Rowland  *Actor*

**Spotlights:** TV Playhouse work includes "Johnny Guitar," CBS Production 1969.

**Hollywood Star Monthly:** If you would like to receive regular monthly updates on the stars added to the Walk of Fame, please send $4.95 + $2.00 shipping and handling for a full year — six issues — of exciting information, gossip, and stars' biographies to:

*Acme Publishing, Post Office Box 1486, LCF, California 91011*

# ⋆ INDEX ⋆

Page numbers in *italic* denote pages where a star for that individual appears without a biography.
Page numbers in **bold** denote pages where a photograph of that star appears.

# ⋆ PHOTO CREDITS ⋆

★ DANNY THOMAS

★ HUGH O'BRIAN

★ GARY COLLINS

★ PAT BOONE

★ SCATMAN CROTHERS

★ CHUCK CONNORS

★ NORM CROSBY

★ GREER GARSON

★ EYDIE GORME

★ GEORGE PEPPARD

★ JERRY DUNPHY

★ ROY ROGERS

★ DALE EVANS

★ HELEN REDDY

★ DENNIS DAY

★ ANNE MURRAY

★ ROBERT GOULET

★ JOHNNY MATHIS

JUL 1988

★ MONTY HALL

★ ROBERT YOUNG

★ LARRY HAGMAN

★ PAUL WILLIAMS

★ DOUGLAS FAIRBANKS, JR.

★ BUDDY EBSEN

★ DAVID WOLPER

★ DALE ROBERTSON

★ ERNEST BORGNINE

★ JAMIE FARR

★ LEE MAJORS

★ RED SKELTON

★ RODDY McDOWALL

★ JIM BACKUS

★ SHARI LEWIS

★ TENNESSEE ERNIE FORD

★ ROSEMARY CLOONEY